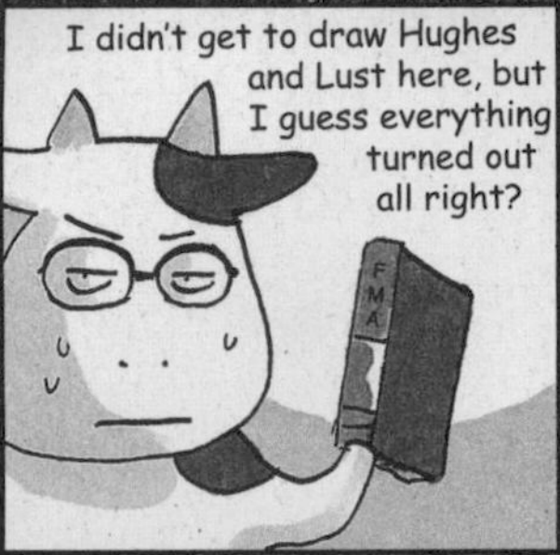
I didn't get to draw Hughes and Lust here, but I guess everything turned out all right?
FMA

Recently, I realized that the characters I've been so casually drawing on the spine of the cover only consist of the ones that made it to the final arc of the story.

—Hiromu Arakawa, 2009

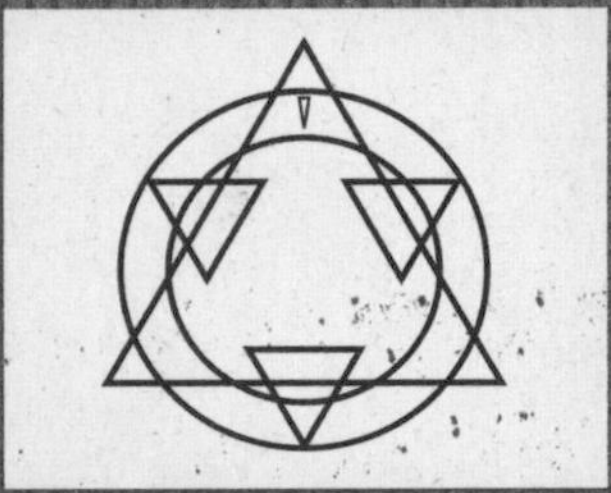

Born in Hokkaido (northern Japan), Hiromu Arakawa first attracted national attention in 1999 with her award-winning manga *Stray Dog*. Her series *Fullmetal Alchemist* debuted in 2001 in Square Enix's monthly manga anthology *Shonen Gangan*.

FULLMETAL ALCHEMIST
VOL. 22

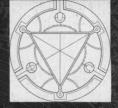

VIZ Media Edition

Story and Art by Hiromu Arakawa

Translation/Akira Watanabe
English Adaptation/Jake Forbes
Touch-up Art & Lettering/Wayne Truman
Design/Julie Behn
Editor/Alexis Kirsch

VP, Production/Alvin Lu
VP, Publishing Licensing/Rika Inouye
VP, Sales & Product Marketing/Gonzalo Ferreyra
VP, Creative/Linda Espinosa
Publisher/Hyoe Narita

Hagane no RenkinJutsushi vol. 22 © 2009 Hiromu Arakawa/SQUARE ENIX. First published in Japan in 2009 by SQUARE ENIX CO., LTD. English translation rights arranged with SQUARE ENIX CO., LTD. and VIZ Media, LLC.

Printed in the U.S.A.

Published by VIZ Media, LLC
P.O. Box 77010
San Francisco, CA 94107

10 9 8 7 6 5 4 3 2 1
First printing, January 2010

www.viz.com

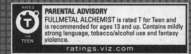

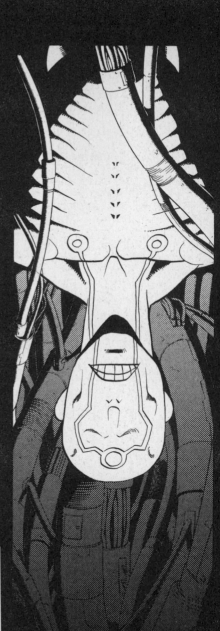

鋼の錬金術師

FULLMETAL ALCHEMIST

HIROMU ARAKAWA

荒川弘

22

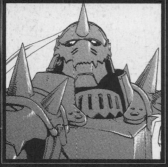

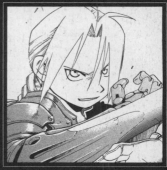

■ アルフォンス・エルリック

Alphonse Elric

■ エドワード・エルリック

Edward Elric

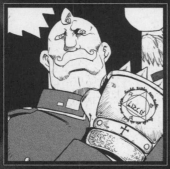

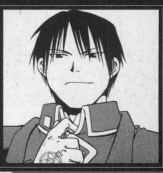

■ アレックス・ルイ・アームストロング

Alex Louis Armstrong

■ ロイ・マスタング

Roy Mustang

OUTLINE
FULLMETAL ALCHEMIST

Using a forbidden alchemical ritual, the Elric brothers attempted to bring their dead mother back to life. But the ritual went wrong, consuming Edward Elric's leg and Alphonse Elric's entire body. At the cost of his arm, Edward was able to graft his brother's soul into a suit of armor. Equipped with mechanical "auto-mail" to replace his missing limbs, Edward becomes a state alchemist in hopes of finding a way to restore their bodies. Their search embroils them in a deadly conspiracy that threatens to take the innocence, if not the lives, of everyone involved.

As the "Day of Reckoning" approaches, an intricate chess game has emerged in Amestris. On one side stand the Elrics, Mustang's crew, Olivier Armstrong and a ragtag bunch of chimeras; on the other, Military Command, Kimblee, the Homunculi and their mysterious "Father." As our scattered heroes converge upon Central City, a dormant enemy steps up to stop them. To casual observers, Selim Bradley, the president's son, is the face of innocence. But behind that facade, he is the deadliest of the Homunculi—Pride—an amorphous mass of teeth and destruction.

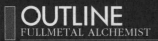

鋼の錬金術師
FULLMETAL ALCHEMIST

CHARACTERS
FULLMETAL ALCHEMIST

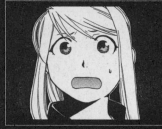

☐ ウィンリィ・ロックベル

Winry Rockbell

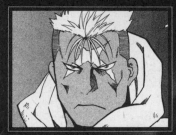

☐ スカー

Scar

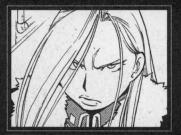

☐ オリヴィエ・ミラ・アームストロング

Olivier Mira Armstrong

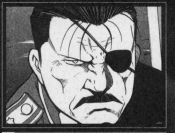

☐ キング・ブラッドレイ

King Bradley

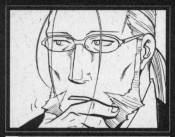

☐ ヴァン・ホーエンハイム

Van Hohenheim

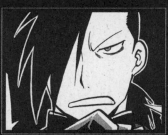

☐ リン・ヤオ（グリード）

Lin Yao (Greed)

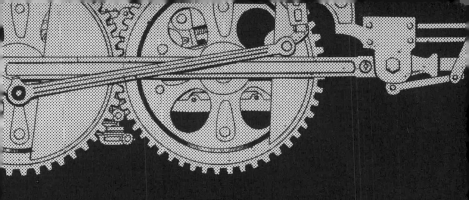

CONTENTS

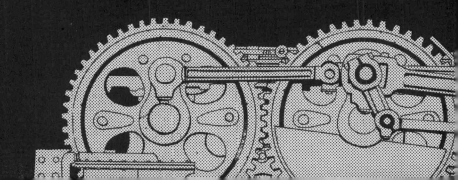

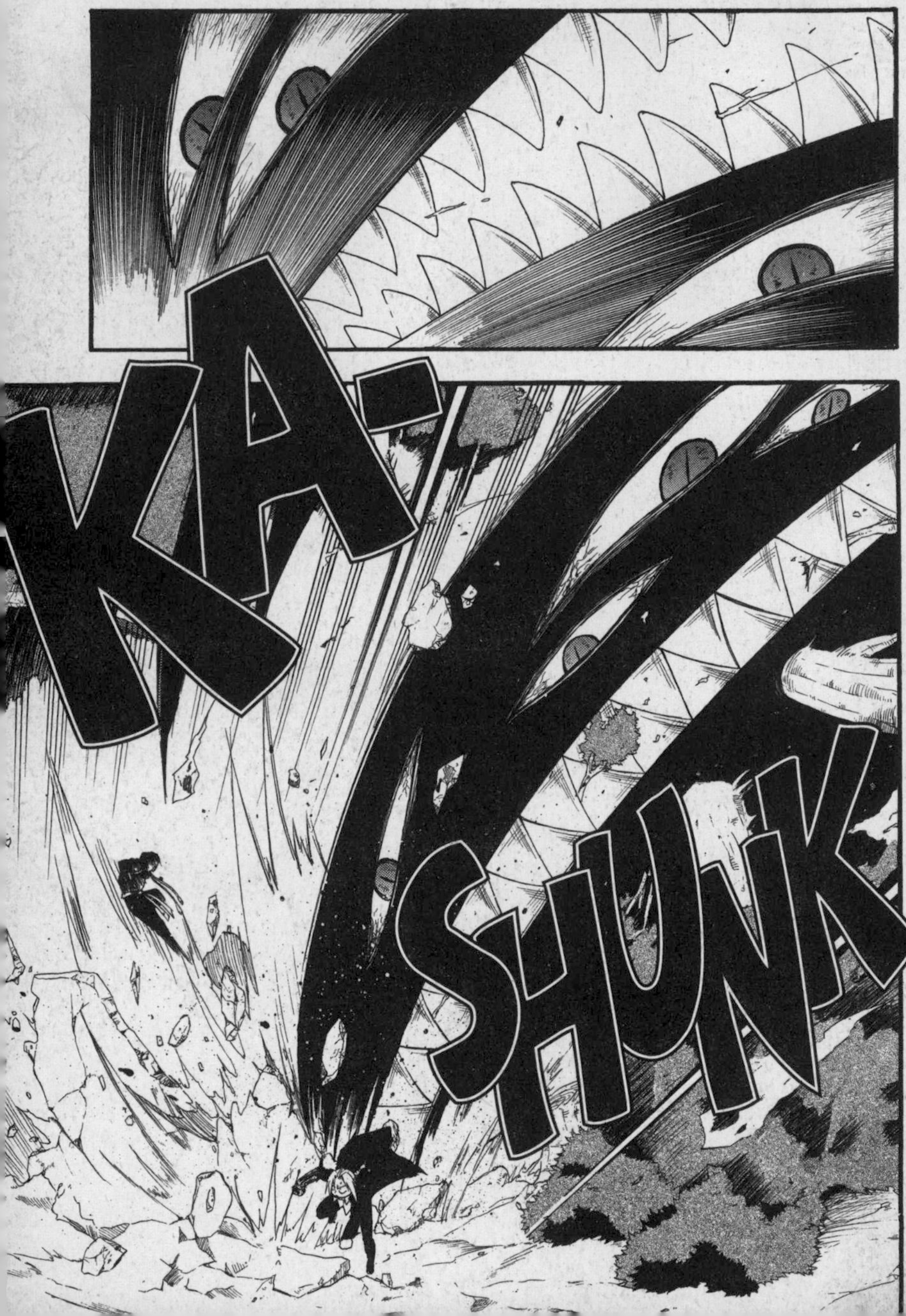
KA-
SHUNK

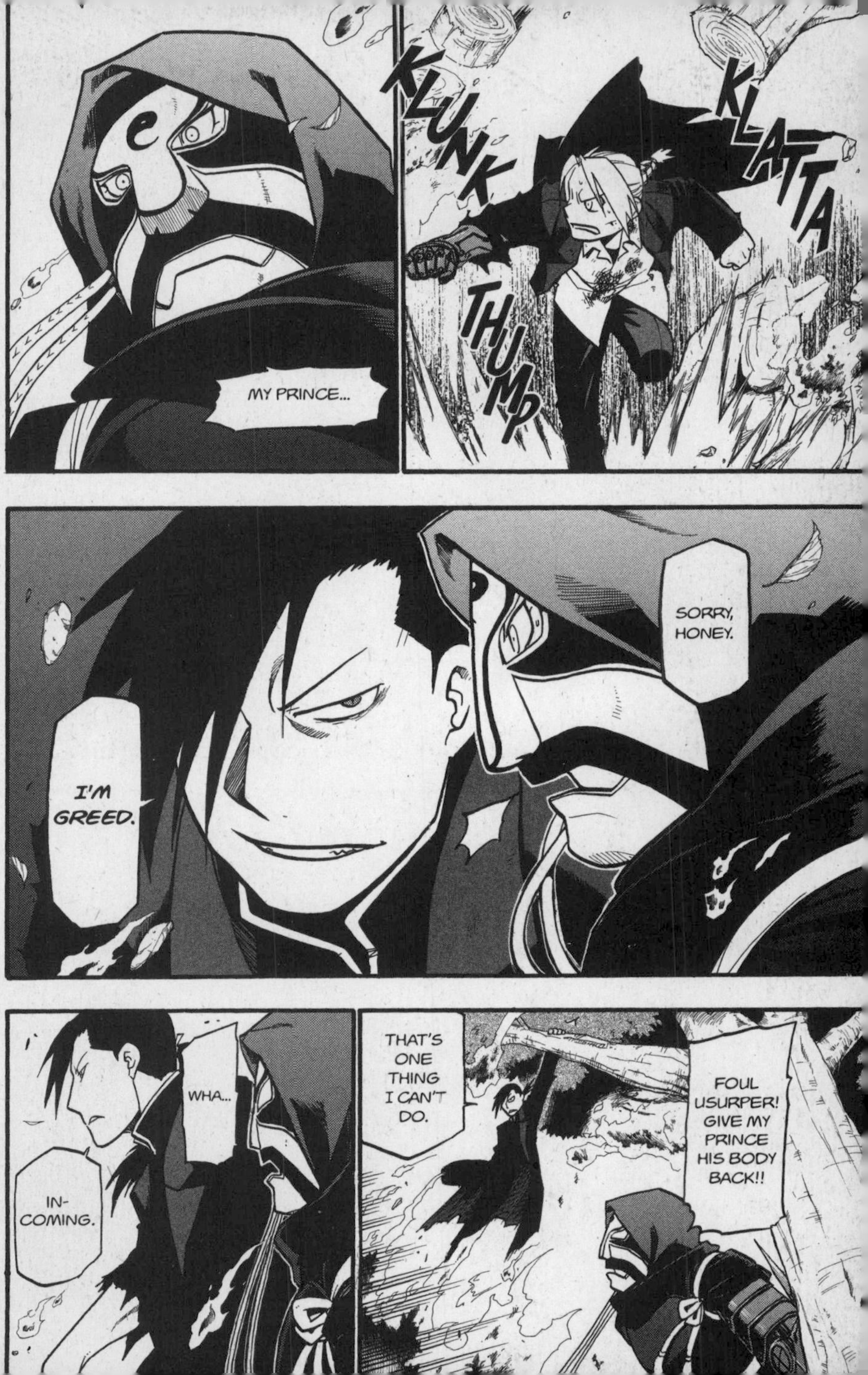
KLUNK
KLATTA
THUMP
MY PRINCE...
SORRY, HONEY.
I'M GREED.
THAT'S ONE THING I CAN'T DO.
FOUL USURPER! GIVE MY PRINCE HIS BODY BACK!!
WHA...
IN-COMING.

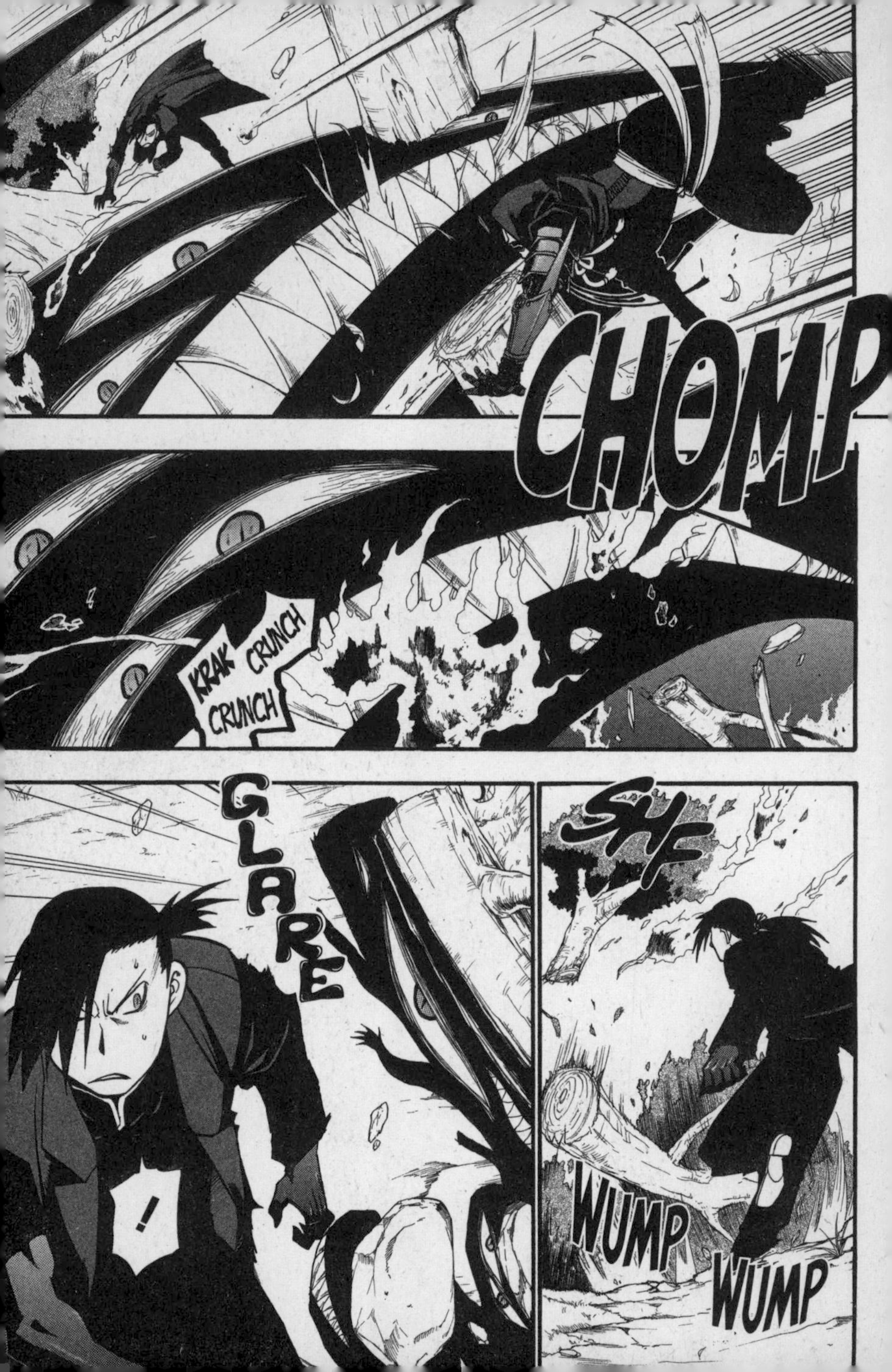
CHOMP
KRAK CRUNCH CRUNCH
SHF
WUMP
WUMP
GLARE
!

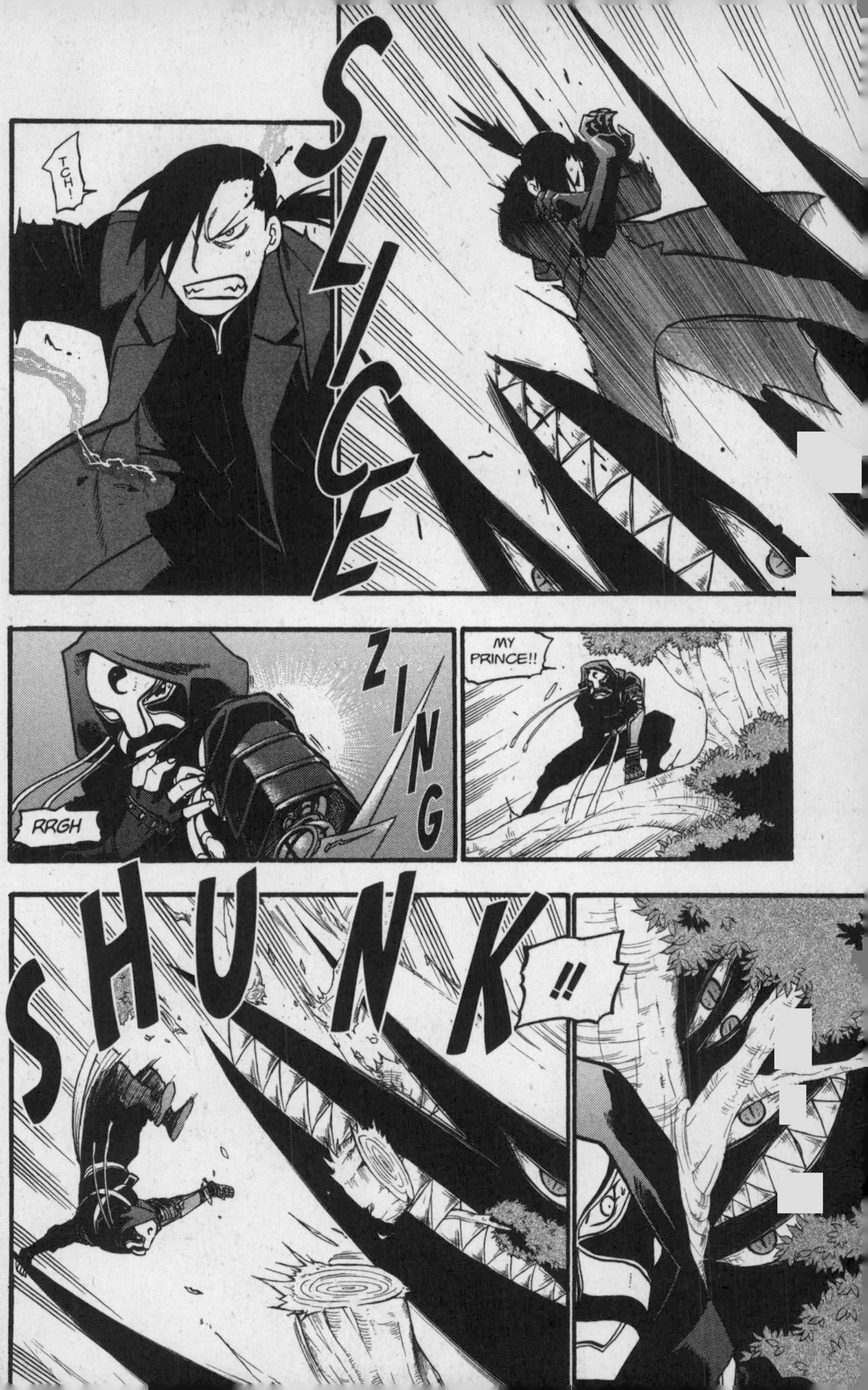
SLICE
TCH!
MY PRINCE!!
ZING
RRGH
SHUNK
!!

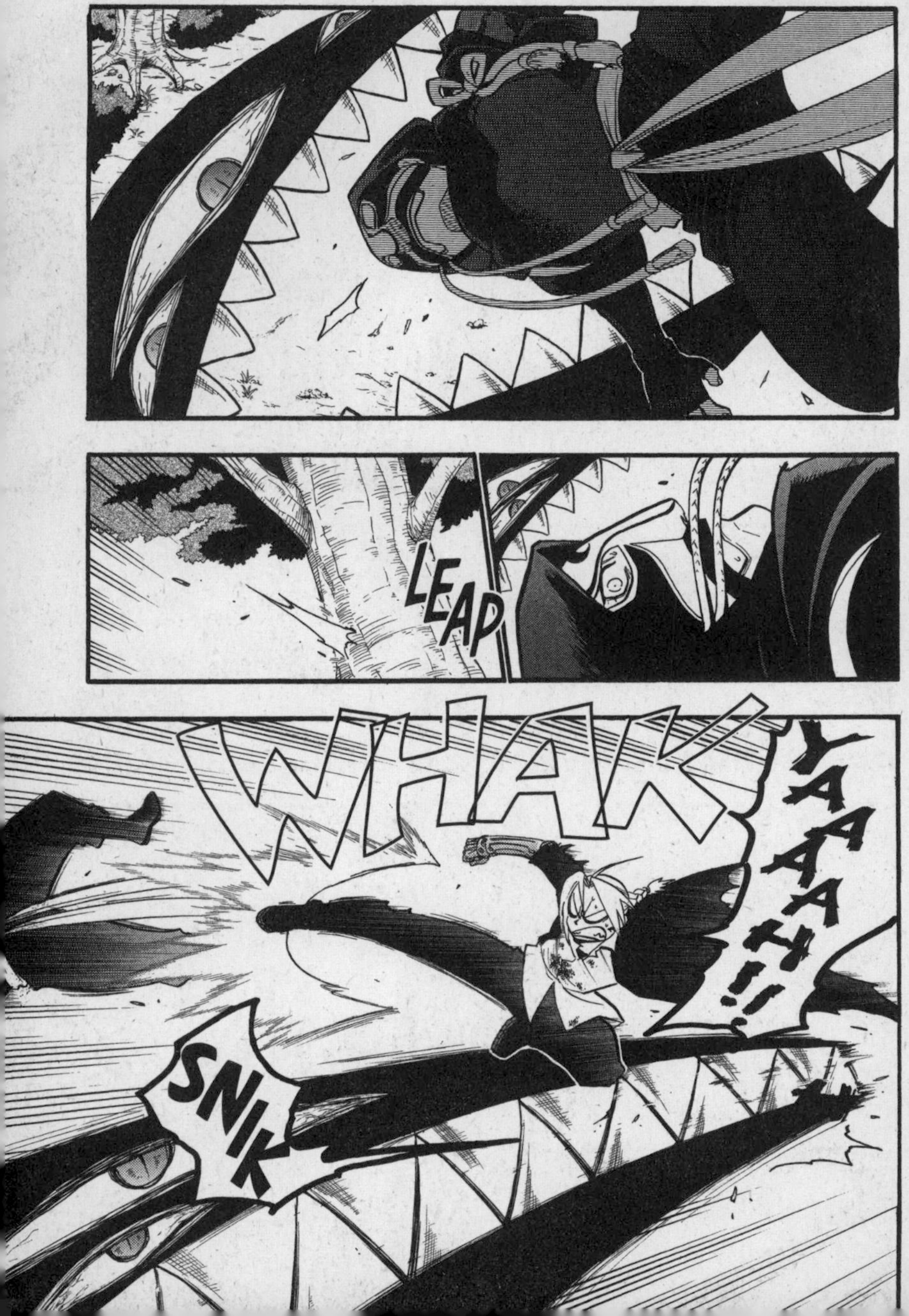
LEAP
YAAAAH!!!
WHAK
SNIK

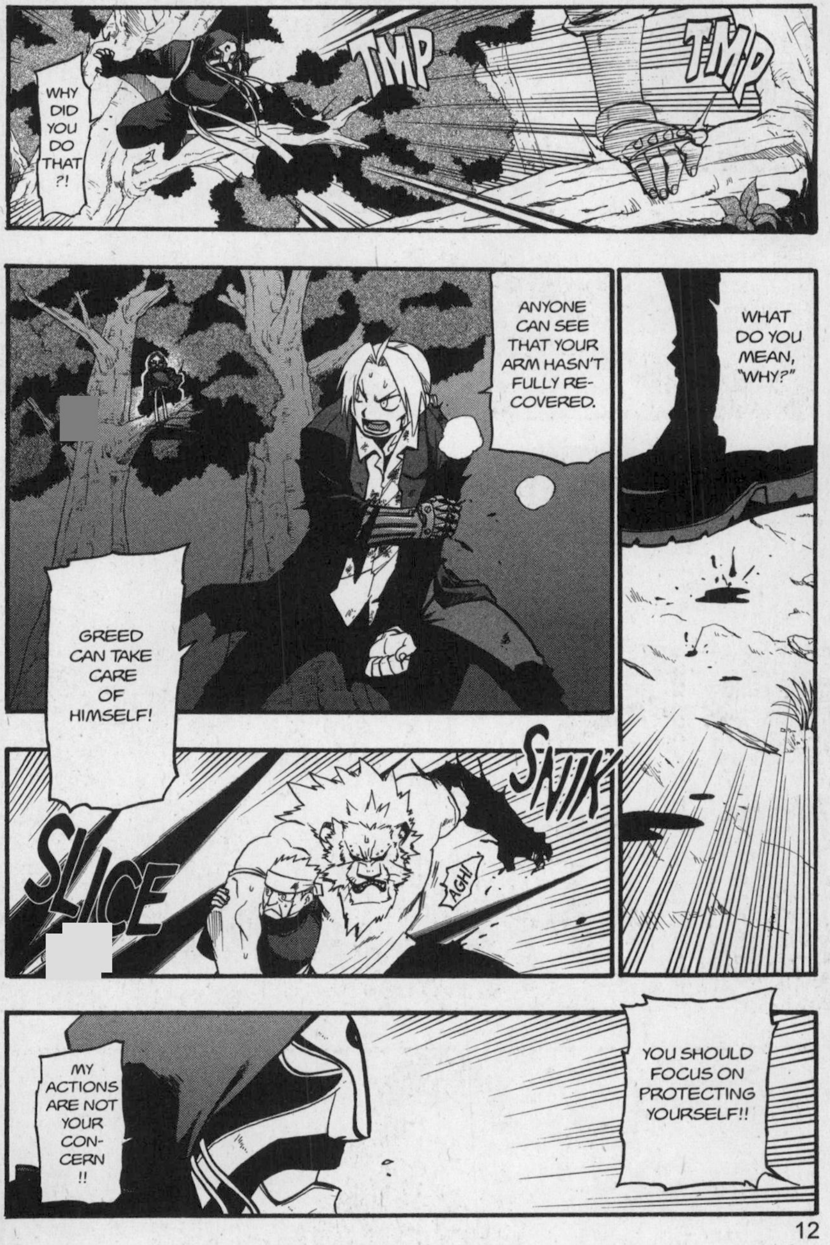
TMP
TMP
WHY DID YOU DO THAT?!
WHAT DO YOU MEAN, "WHY?"
ANYONE CAN SEE THAT YOUR ARM HASN'T FULLY RE-COVERED.
GREED CAN TAKE CARE OF HIMSELF!
SNIK
AGH!
SLICE
YOU SHOULD FOCUS ON PROTECTING YOURSELF!!
MY ACTIONS ARE NOT YOUR CON-CERN!!

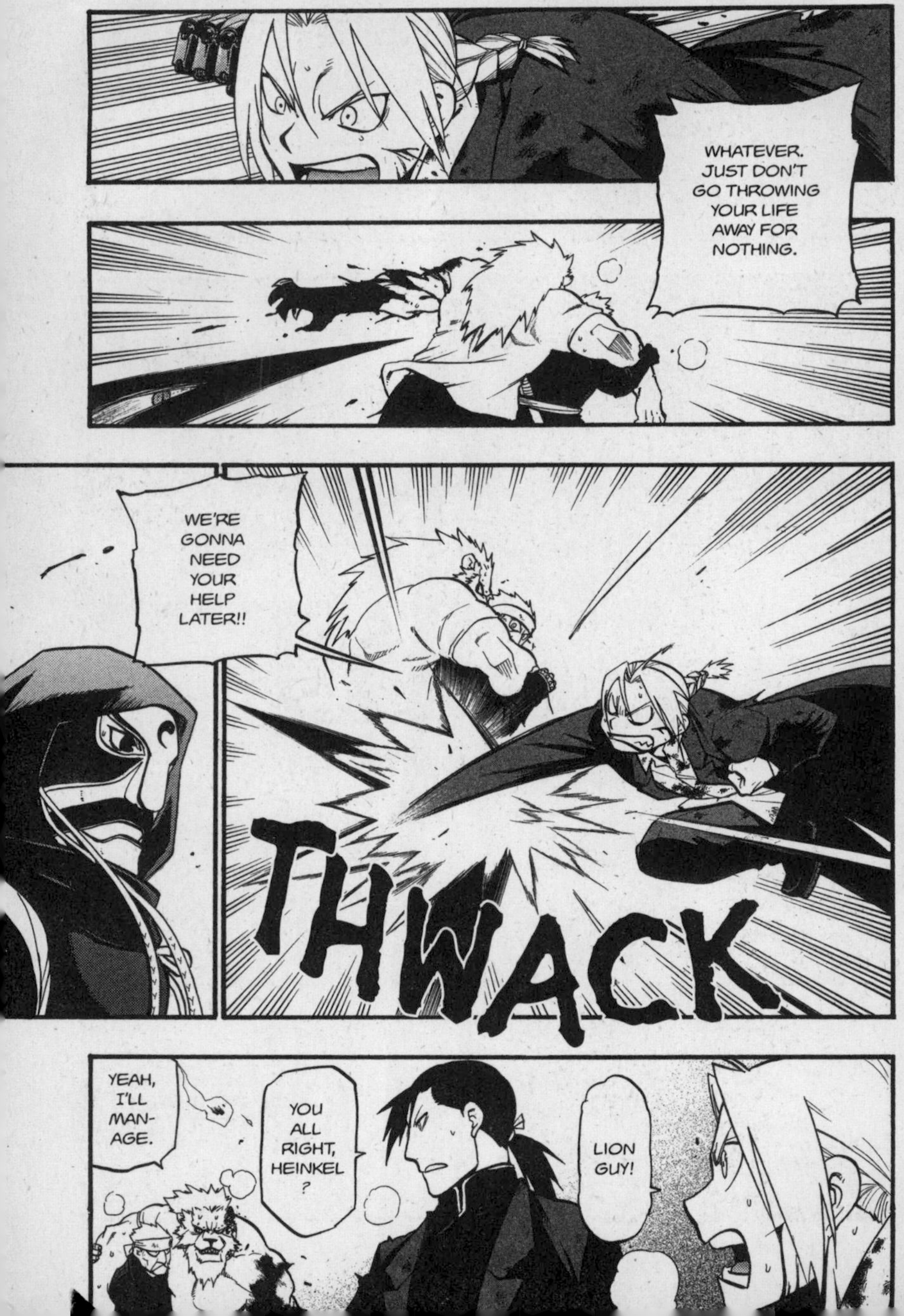
WHATEVER. JUST DON'T GO THROWING YOUR LIFE AWAY FOR NOTHING.
WE'RE GONNA NEED YOUR HELP LATER!!
THWACK
LION GUY!
YOU ALL RIGHT, HEINKEL?
YEAH, I'LL MAN-AGE.

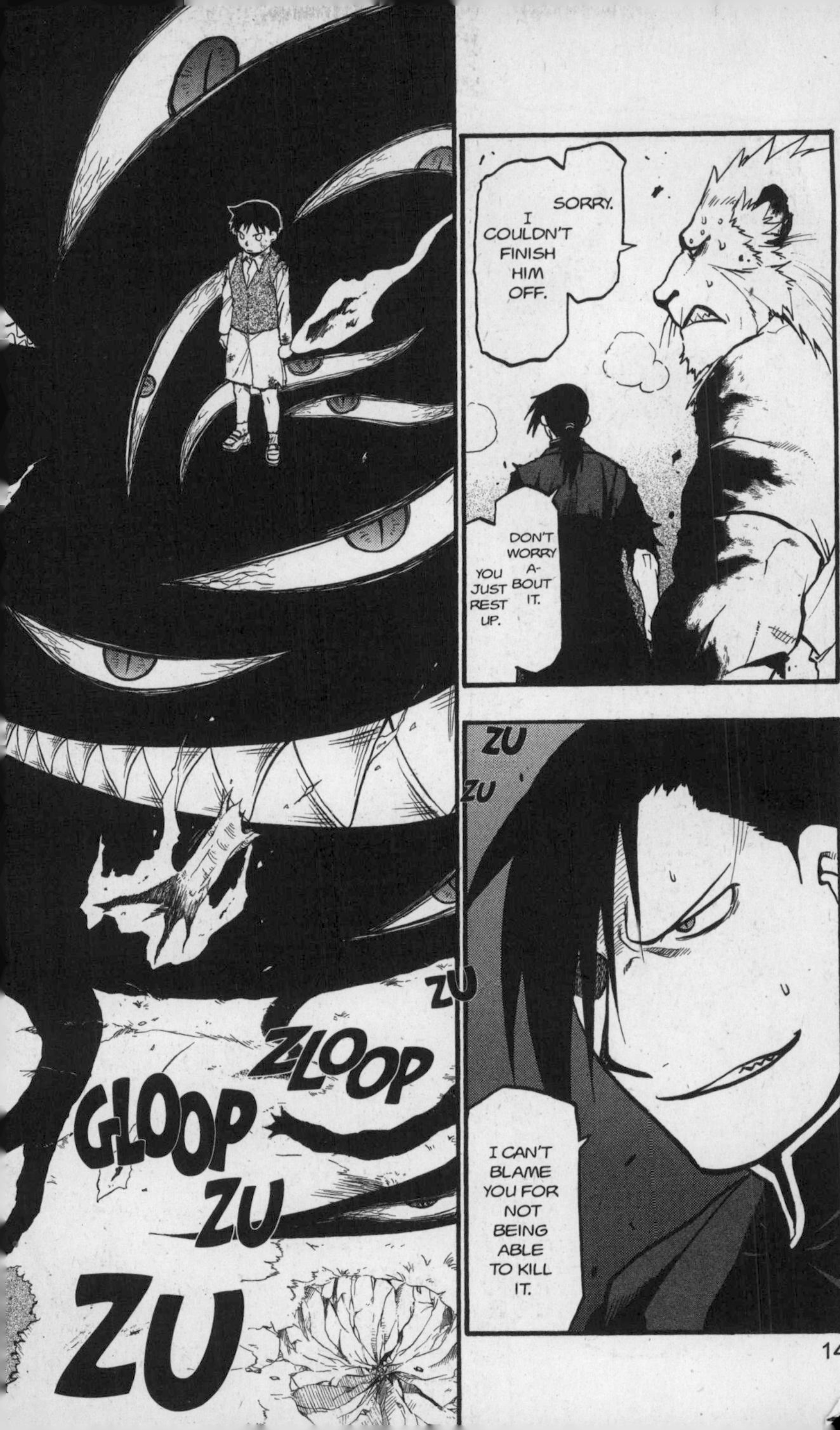

SORRY. I COULDN'T FINISH HIM OFF.
DON'T WORRY ABOUT IT.
YOU JUST REST UP.
ZU
ZU
I CAN'T BLAME YOU FOR NOT BEING ABLE TO KILL IT.
ZU
ZLOOP
GLOOP
ZU
ZU

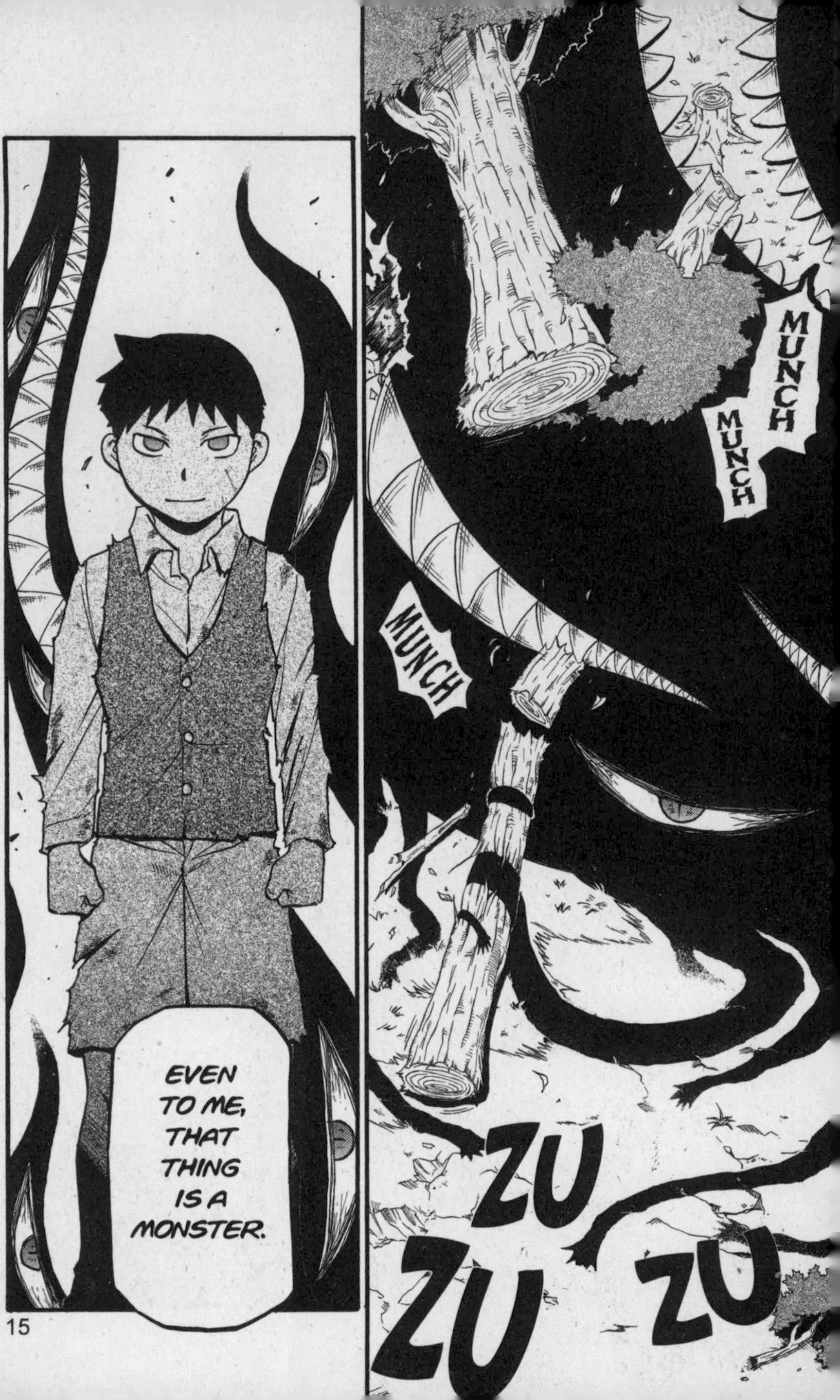
MUNCH
MUNCH
MUNCH
ZU
ZU ZU
ZU
EVEN TO ME, THAT THING IS A MONSTER.

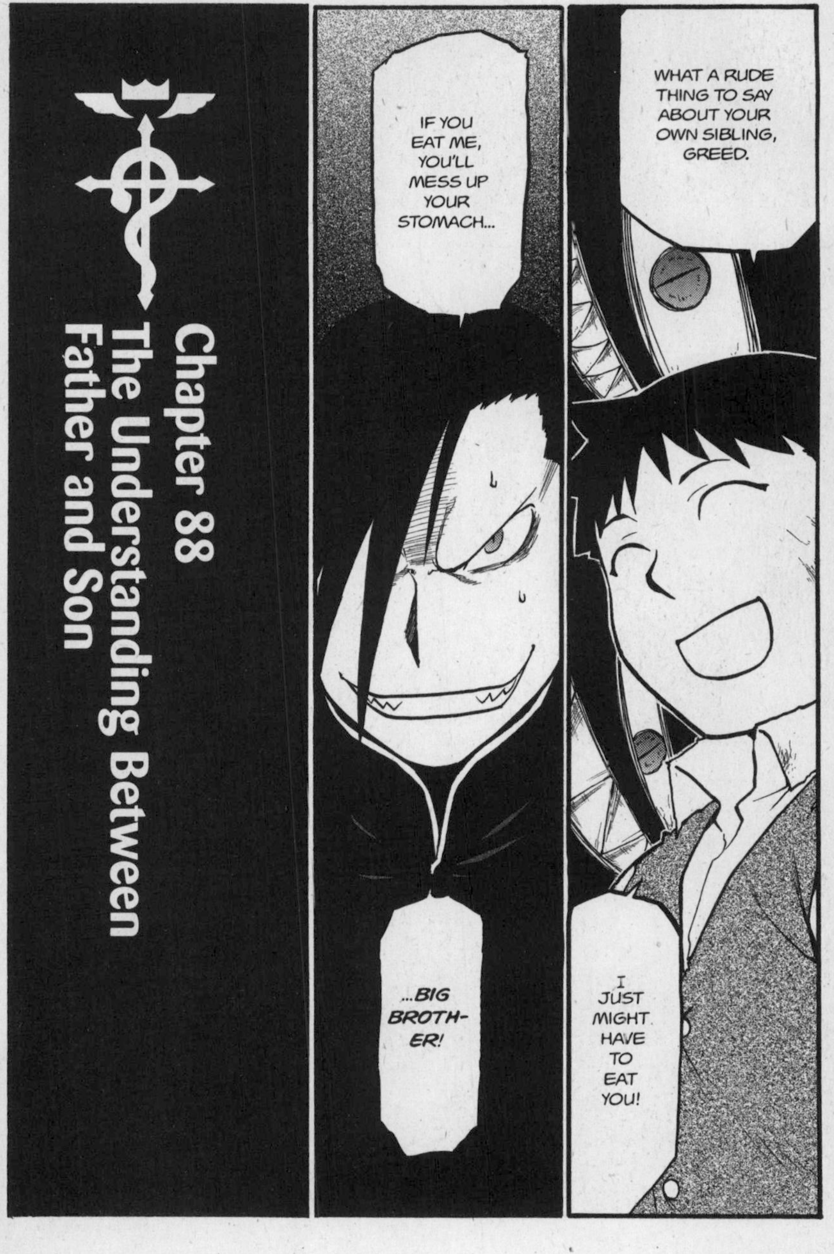
WHAT A RUDE THING TO SAY ABOUT YOUR OWN SIBLING, GREED.
I JUST MIGHT HAVE TO EAT YOU!
IF YOU EAT ME, YOU'LL MESS UP YOUR STOMACH...
...BIG BROTHER!

Chapter 88 The Understanding Between Father and Son

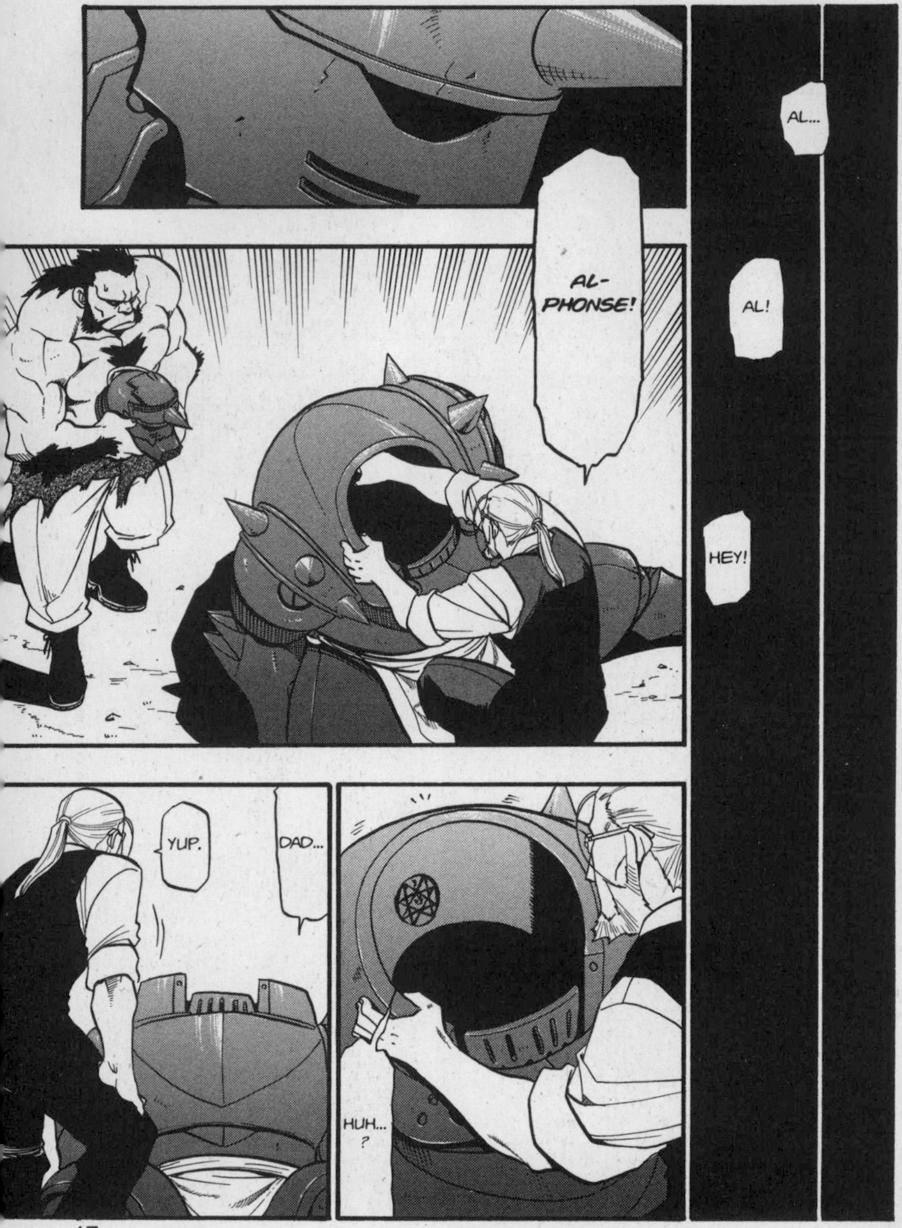
AL...
AL!
HEY!
AL-PHONSE!
HUH...?
DAD...
YUP.

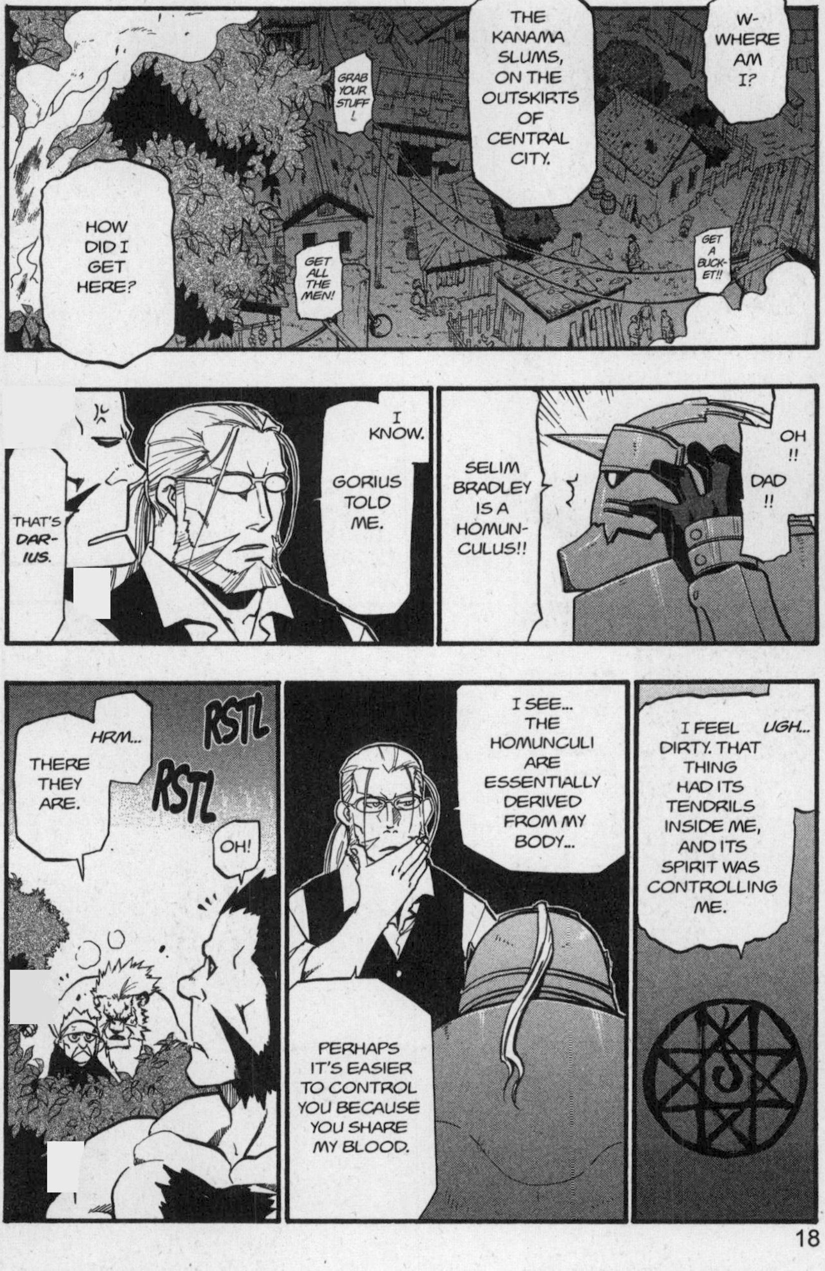
W-WHERE AM I?
THE KANAMA SLUMS, ON THE OUTSKIRTS OF CENTRAL CITY.
GRAB YOUR STUFF!
GET A BUCK-ET!!
GET ALL THE MEN!
HOW DID I GET HERE?
OH!! DAD!!
SELIM BRADLEY IS A HOMUN-CULUS!!
I KNOW.
GORIUS TOLD ME.
THAT'S DAR-IUS.
UGH...
I FEEL DIRTY. THAT THING HAD ITS TENDRILS INSIDE ME, AND ITS SPIRIT WAS CONTROLLING ME.
I SEE... THE HOMUNCULI ARE ESSENTIALLY DERIVED FROM MY BODY...
PERHAPS IT'S EASIER TO CONTROL YOU BECAUSE YOU SHARE MY BLOOD.
RSTL
RSTL
HRM... THERE THEY ARE.
OH!

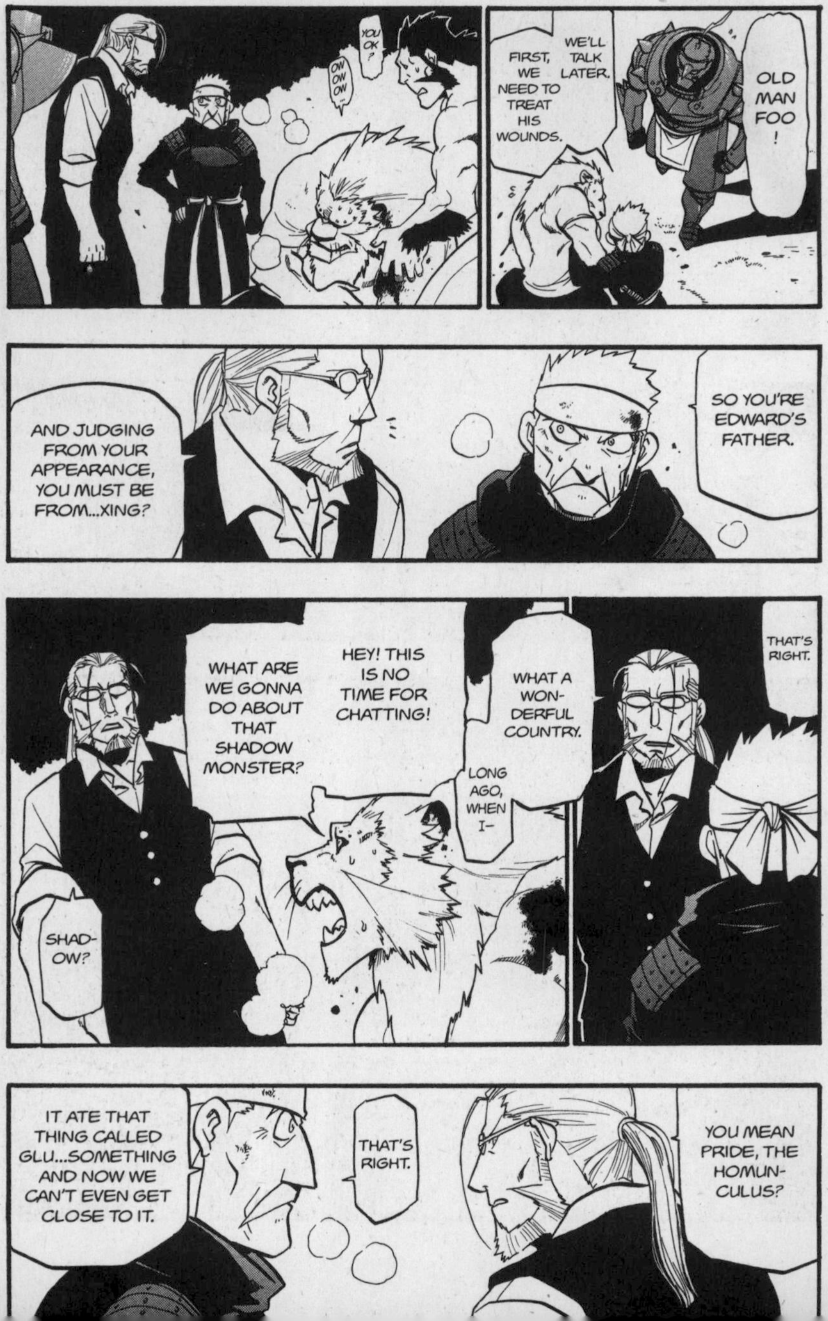
OLD MAN FOO!
WE'LL TALK LATER.
FIRST, WE NEED TO TREAT HIS WOUNDS.
YOU OK?
OW OW OW
SO YOU'RE EDWARD'S FATHER.
AND JUDGING FROM YOUR APPEARANCE, YOU MUST BE FROM...XING?
THAT'S RIGHT.
WHAT A WON-DERFUL COUNTRY.
LONG AGO, WHEN I-
HEY! THIS IS NO TIME FOR CHATTING!
WHAT ARE WE GONNA DO ABOUT THAT SHADOW MONSTER?
SHAD-OW?
YOU MEAN PRIDE, THE HOMUN-CULUS?
THAT'S RIGHT.
IT ATE THAT THING CALLED GLU...SOMETHING AND NOW WE CAN'T EVEN GET CLOSE TO IT.

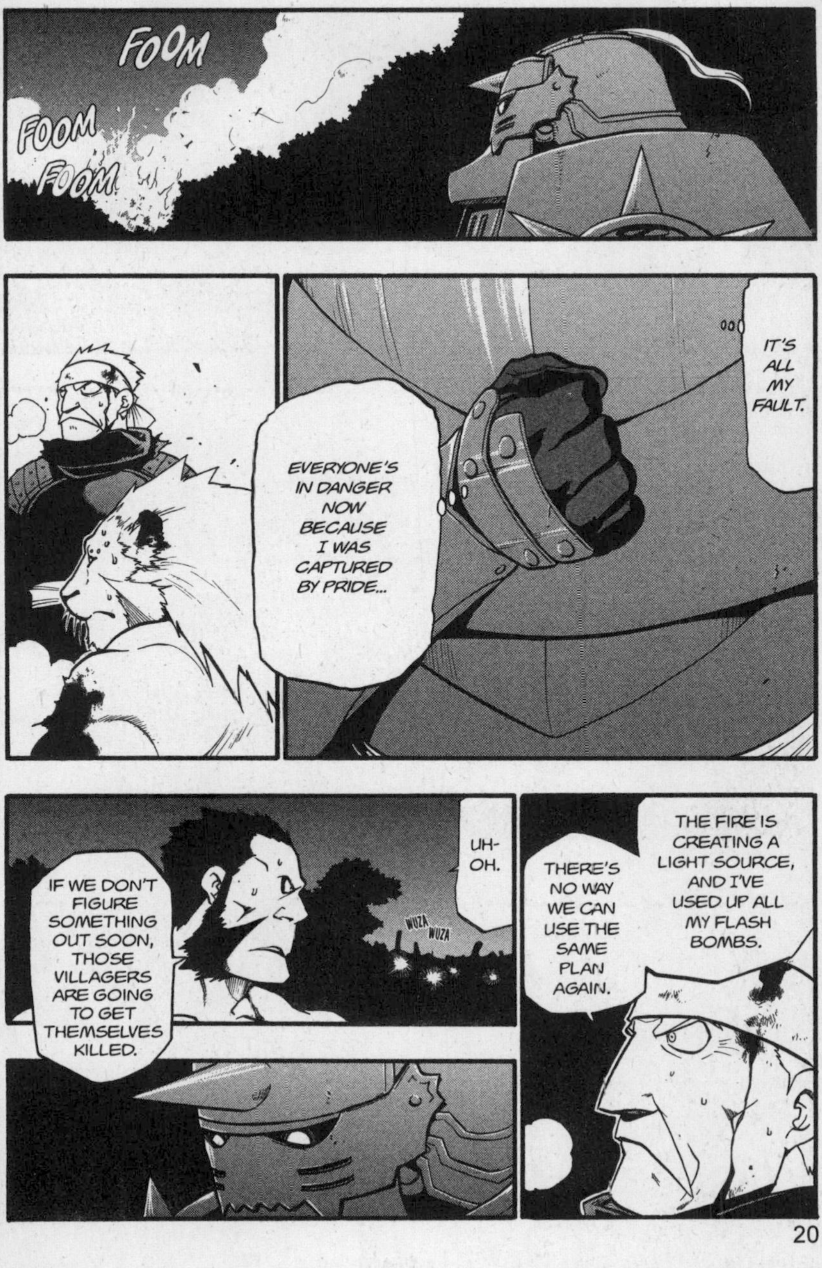
FOOM
FOOM
FOOM
IT'S ALL MY FAULT.
EVERYONE'S IN DANGER NOW BECAUSE I WAS CAPTURED BY PRIDE...
THE FIRE IS CREATING A LIGHT SOURCE, AND I'VE USED UP ALL MY FLASH BOMBS.
THERE'S NO WAY WE CAN USE THE SAME PLAN AGAIN.
UH-OH.
IF WE DON'T FIGURE SOMETHING OUT SOON, THOSE VILLAGERS ARE GOING TO GET THEMSELVES KILLED.
WUZA
WUZA

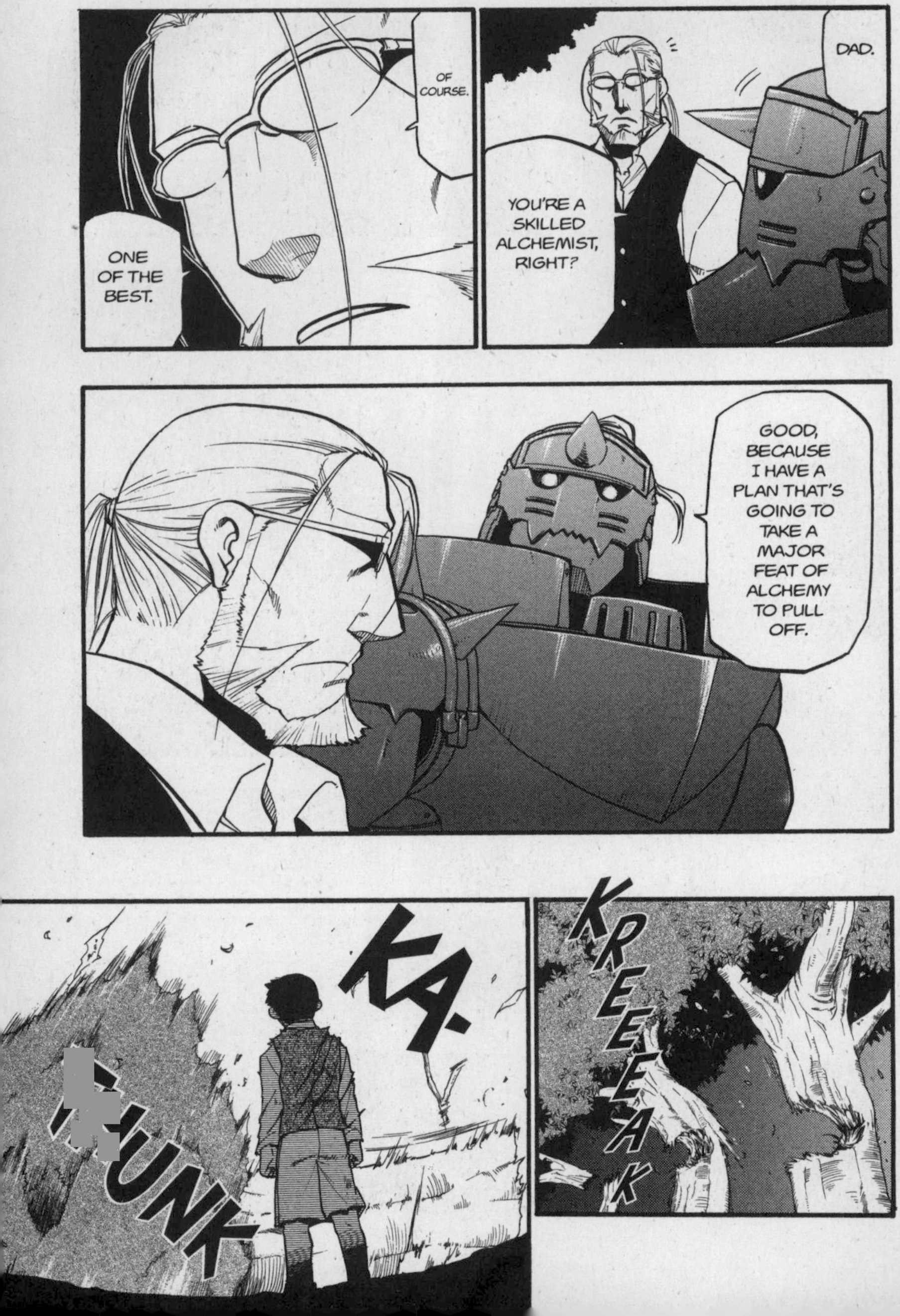
DAD.
YOU'RE A SKILLED ALCHEMIST, RIGHT?
OF COURSE.
ONE OF THE BEST.
GOOD, BECAUSE I HAVE A PLAN THAT'S GOING TO TAKE A MAJOR FEAT OF ALCHEMY TO PULL OFF.
KREEEEAK
KA-
HUNK

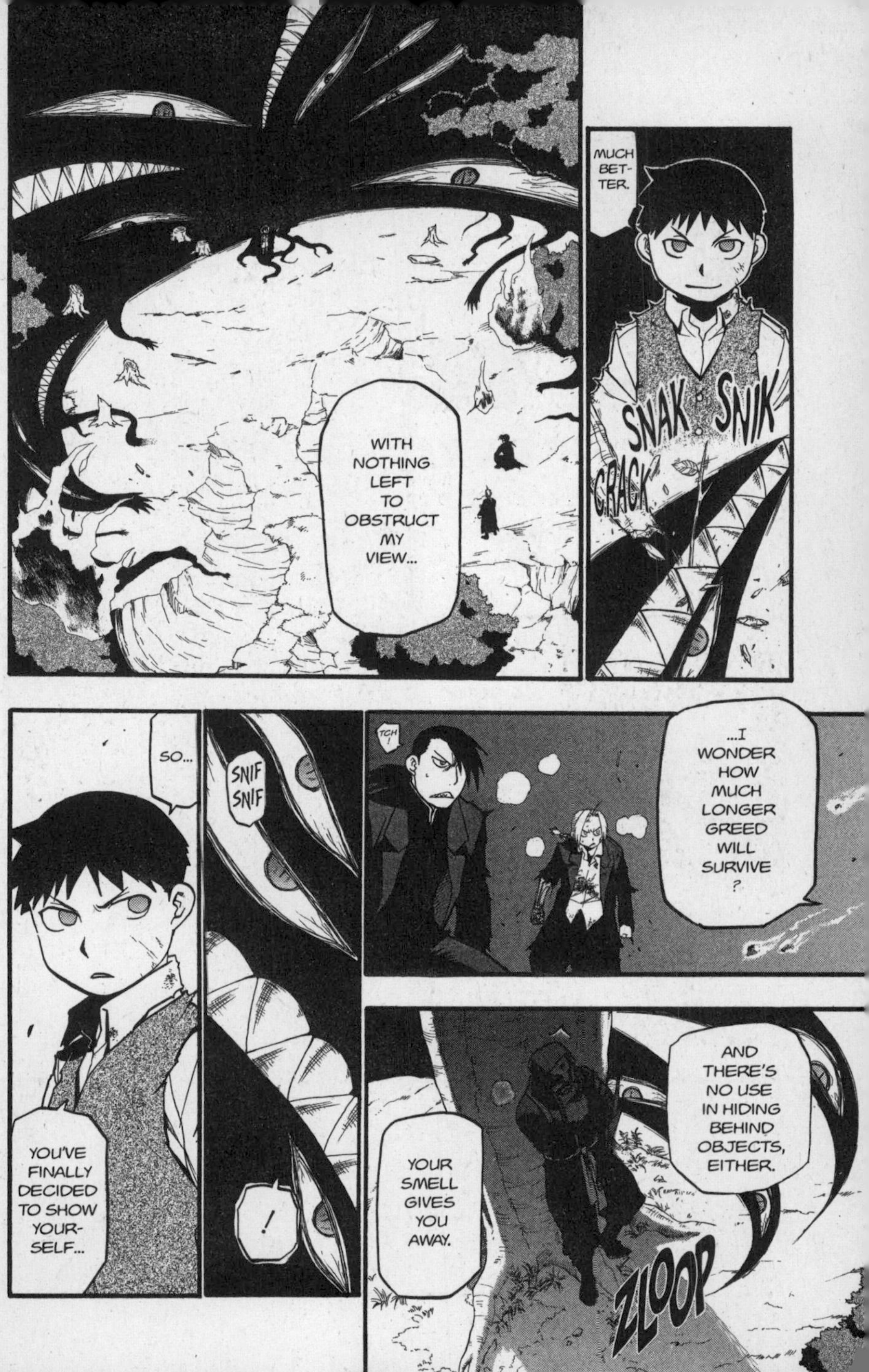
MUCH BETTER.
SNAK SNIK
CRACK
WITH NOTHING LEFT TO OBSTRUCT MY VIEW...
TCH!
...I WONDER HOW MUCH LONGER GREED WILL SURVIVE?
AND THERE'S NO USE IN HIDING BEHIND OBJECTS, EITHER.
YOUR SMELL GIVES YOU AWAY.
ZLOOP
SNIF SNIF
!
SO...
YOU'VE FINALLY DECIDED TO SHOW YOURSELF...

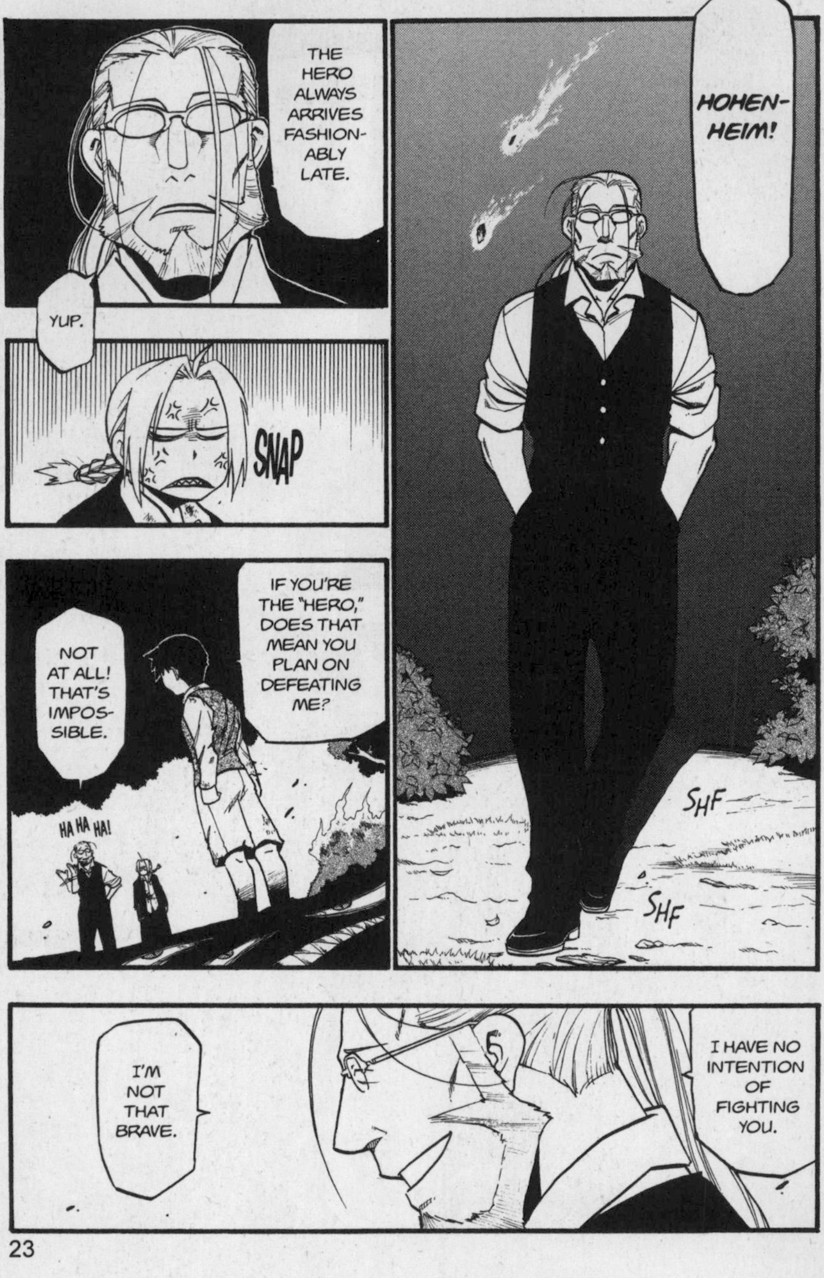
HOHEN-HEIM!
SHF
SHF
THE HERO ALWAYS ARRIVES FASHION-ABLY LATE.
YUP.
SNAP
IF YOU'RE THE "HERO," DOES THAT MEAN YOU PLAN ON DEFEATING ME?
NOT AT ALL! THAT'S IMPOS-SIBLE.
HA HA HA!
I HAVE NO INTENTION OF FIGHTING YOU.
I'M NOT THAT BRAVE.

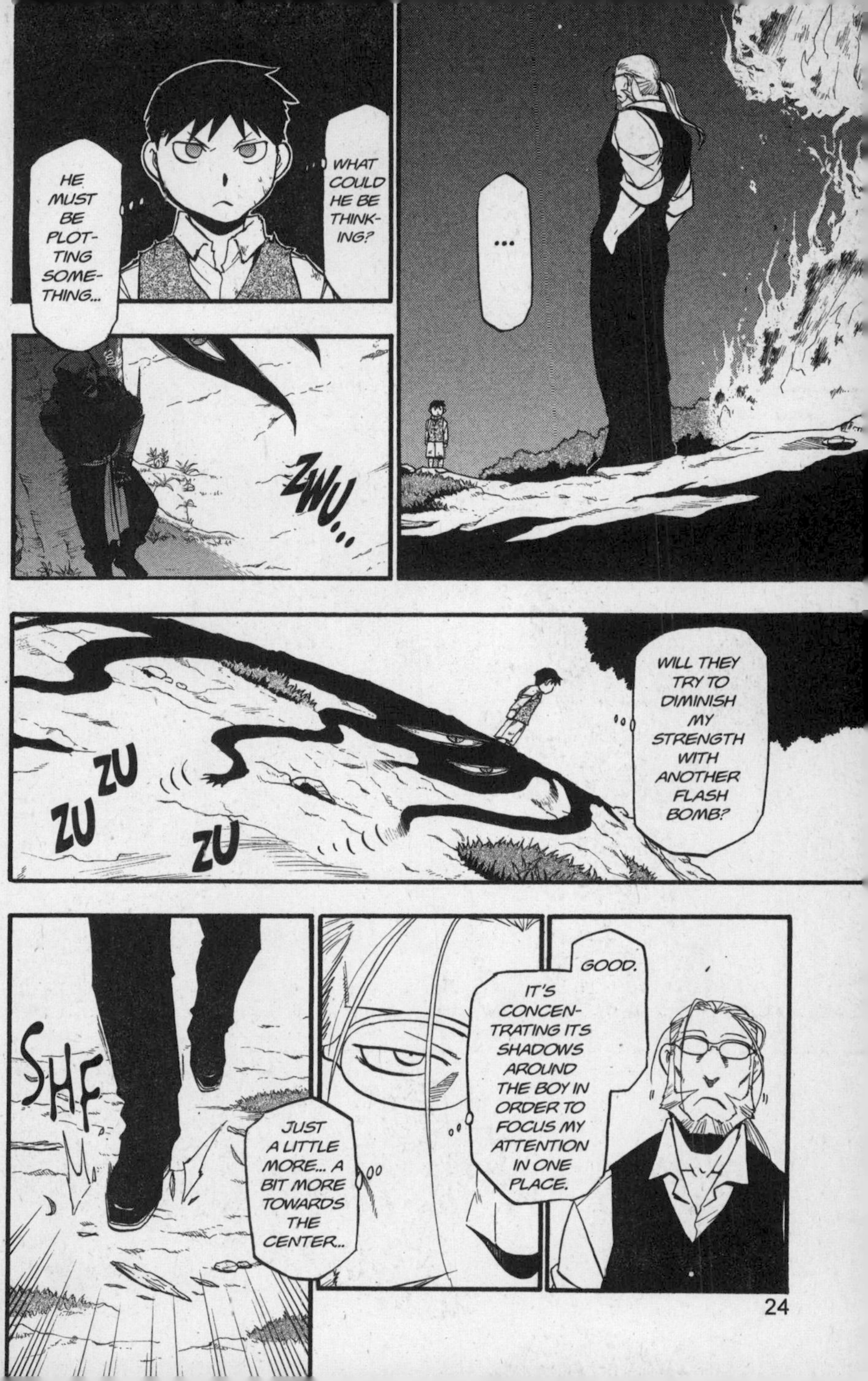
...
WHAT COULD HE BE THINKING?
HE MUST BE PLOTTING SOMETHING...
ZWU...
WILL THEY TRY TO DIMINISH MY STRENGTH WITH ANOTHER FLASH BOMB?
ZU
ZU
ZU
ZU
GOOD.
IT'S CONCENTRATING ITS SHADOWS AROUND THE BOY IN ORDER TO FOCUS MY ATTENTION IN ONE PLACE.
JUST A LITTLE MORE... A BIT MORE TOWARDS THE CENTER...
SHF

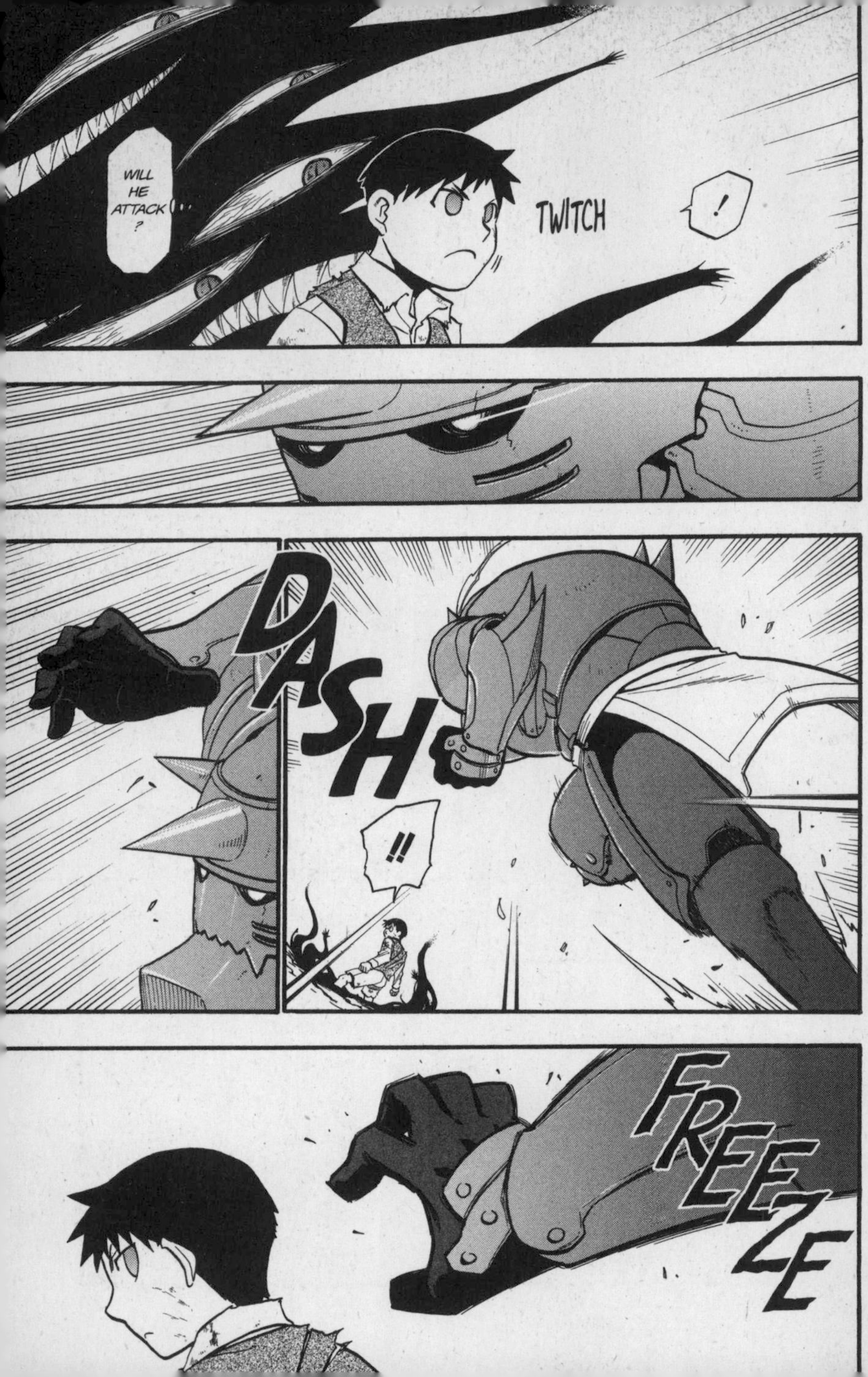
!
TWITCH
WILL HE ATTACK...?
DASH
!!
FREEZE

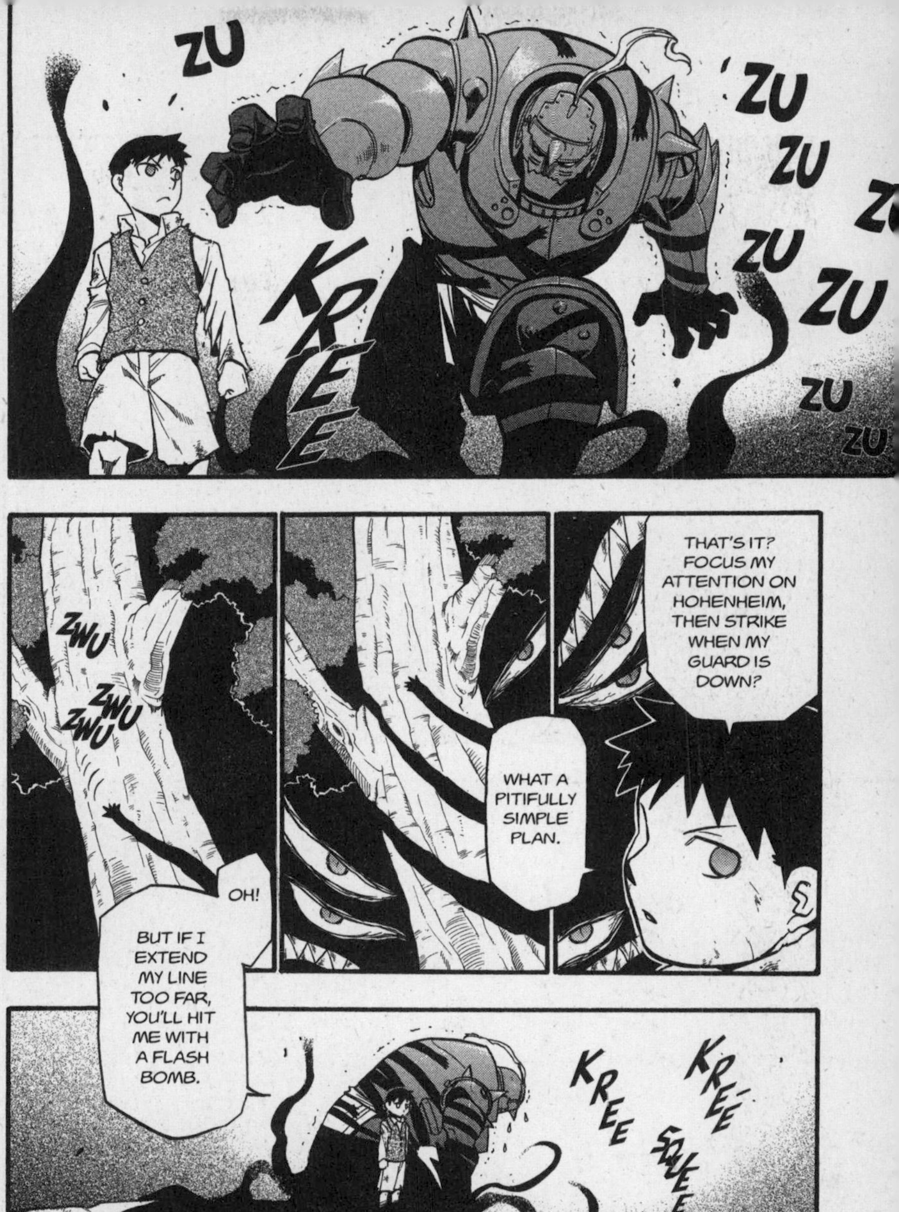
ZU
ZU
ZU
ZU
ZU
ZU
ZU
ZU
KREEE
THAT'S IT? FOCUS MY ATTENTION ON HOHENHEIM, THEN STRIKE WHEN MY GUARD IS DOWN?
WHAT A PITIFULLY SIMPLE PLAN.
ZWU
ZWU
ZWU
OH!
BUT IF I EXTEND MY LINE TOO FAR, YOU'LL HIT ME WITH A FLASH BOMB.
KREÉ
KREE
SQUEE
ZWU
ZWOO
ZWOOP

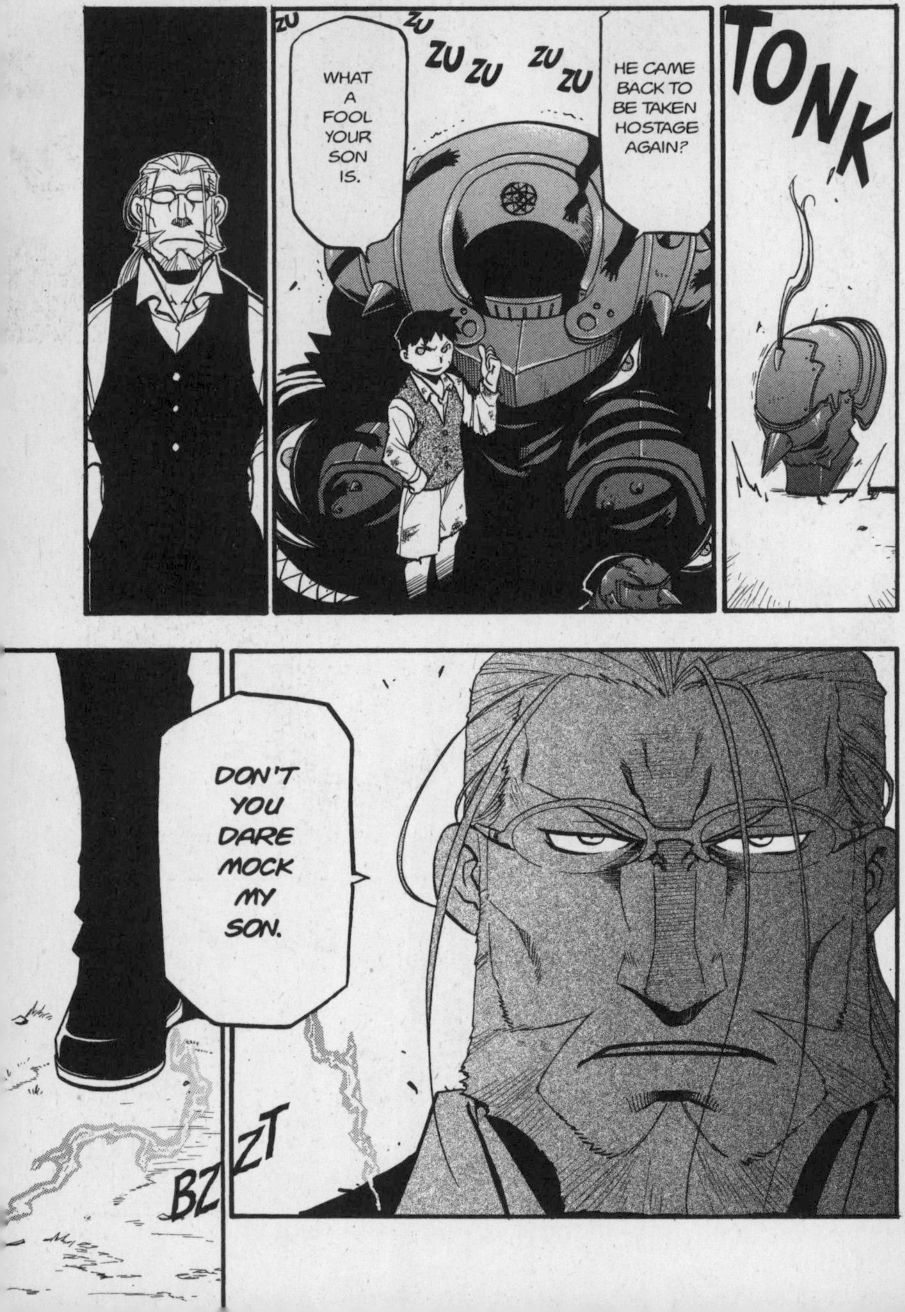
TONK
ZU ZU ZU ZU ZU ZU ZU
HE CAME BACK TO BE TAKEN HOSTAGE AGAIN?
WHAT A FOOL YOUR SON IS.
DON'T YOU DARE MOCK MY SON.
BZZT

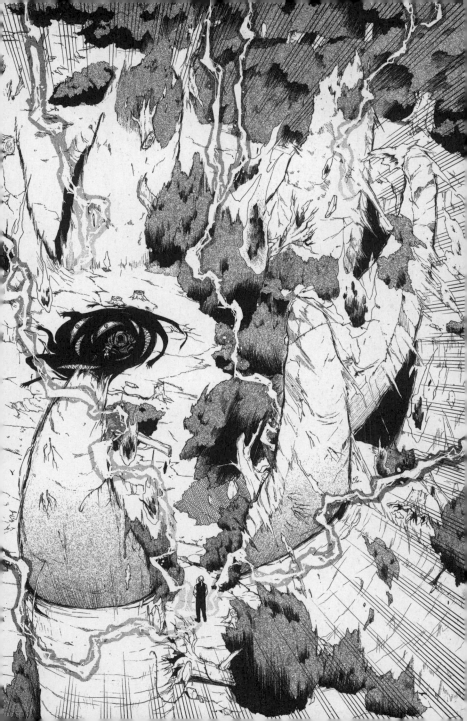

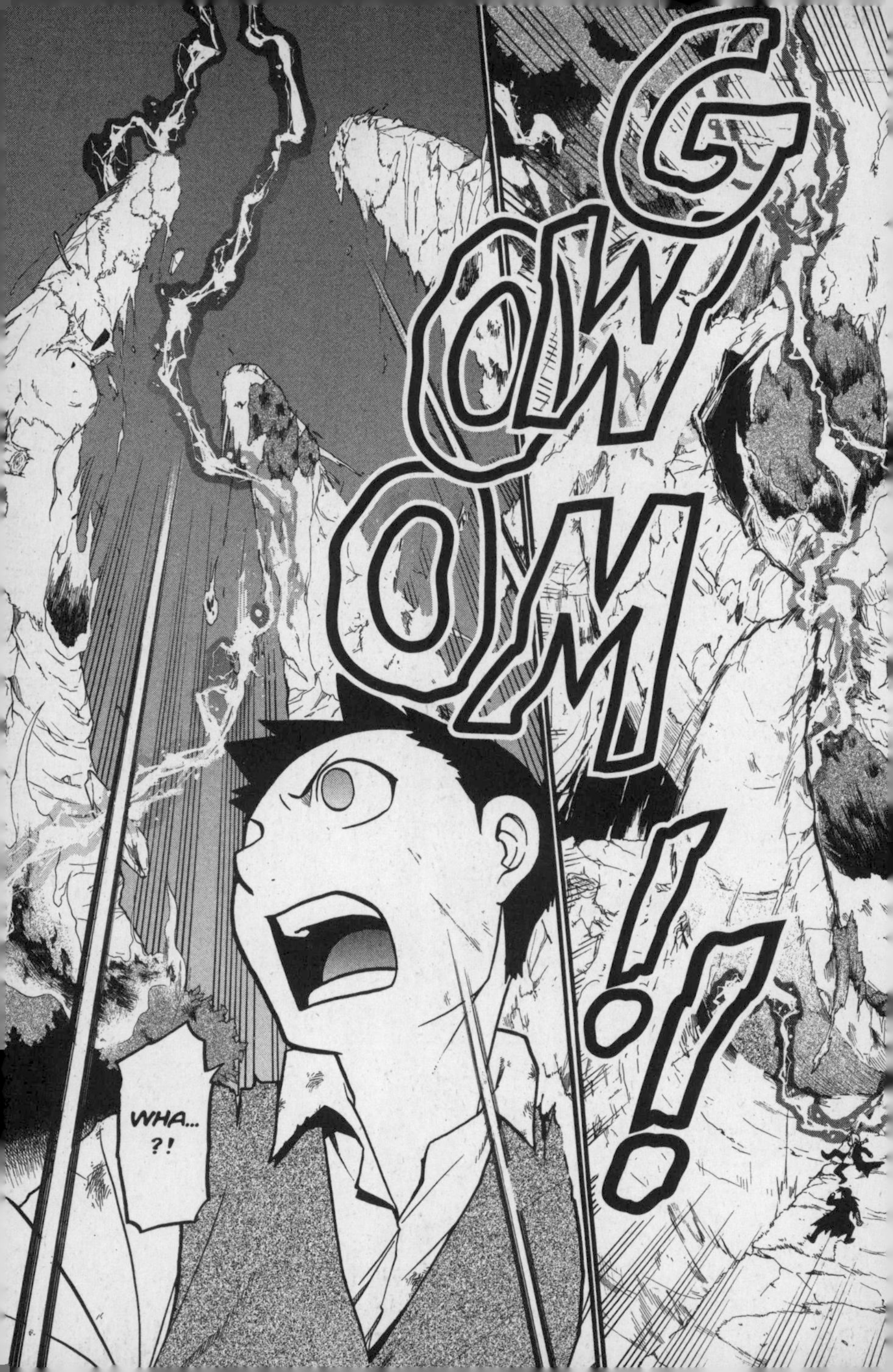
GOWOOM!!
WHA... ?!

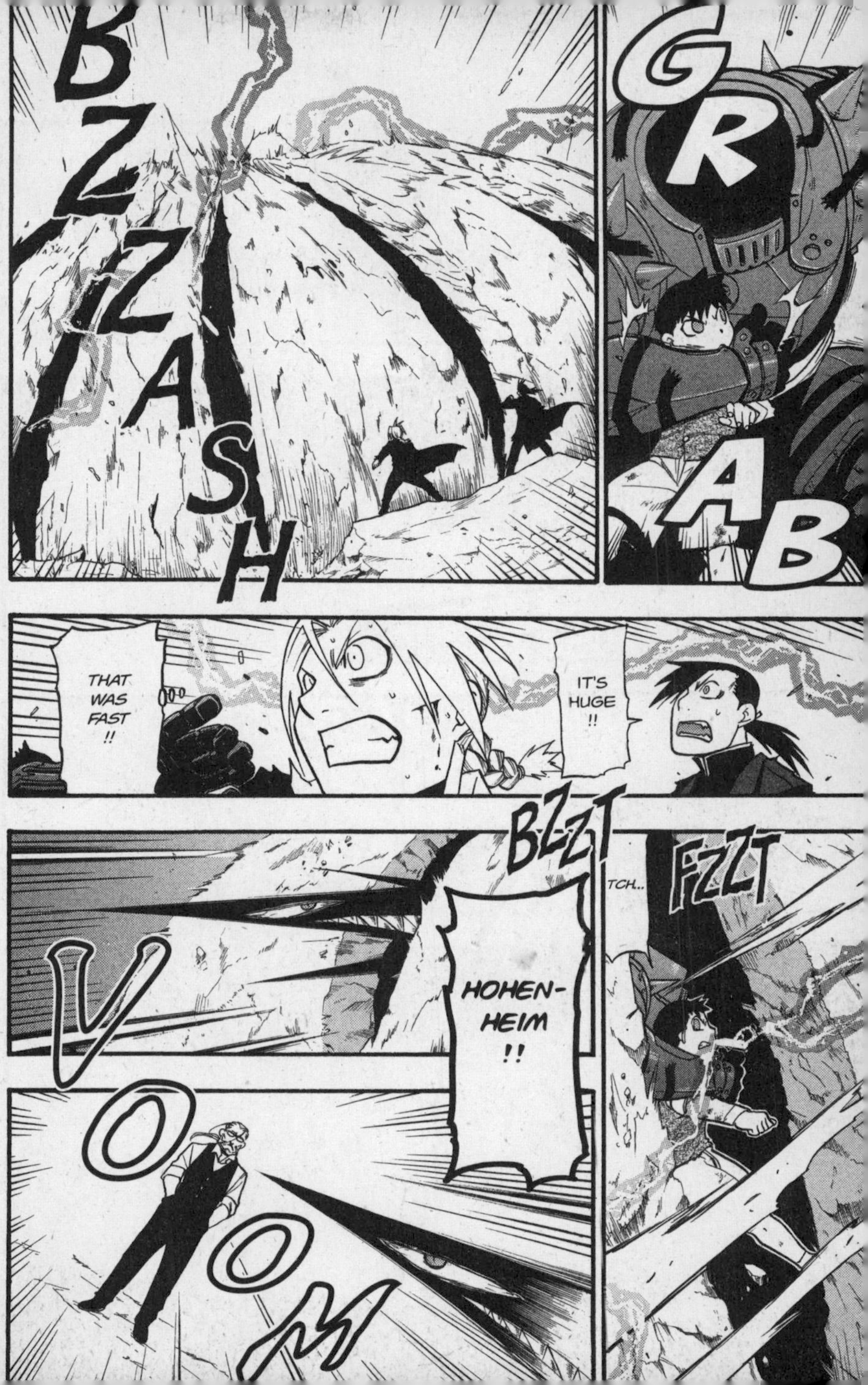
GRAB
BZZASH
IT'S HUGE!!
THAT WAS FAST!!
BZZT
TCH...
FZZT
HOHEN-HEIM!!
VOOM

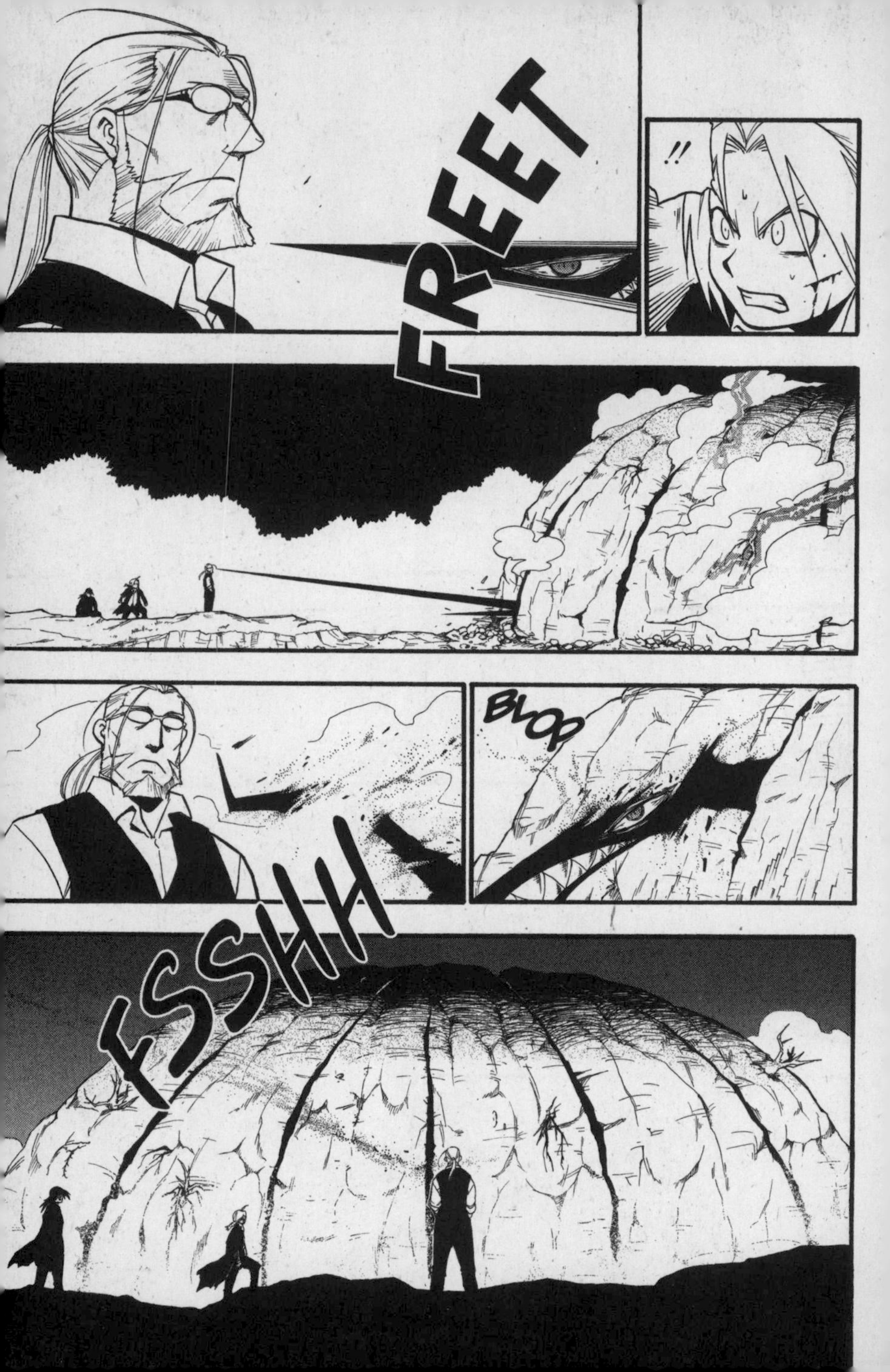
!!
FREET
BLOP
FSSHH

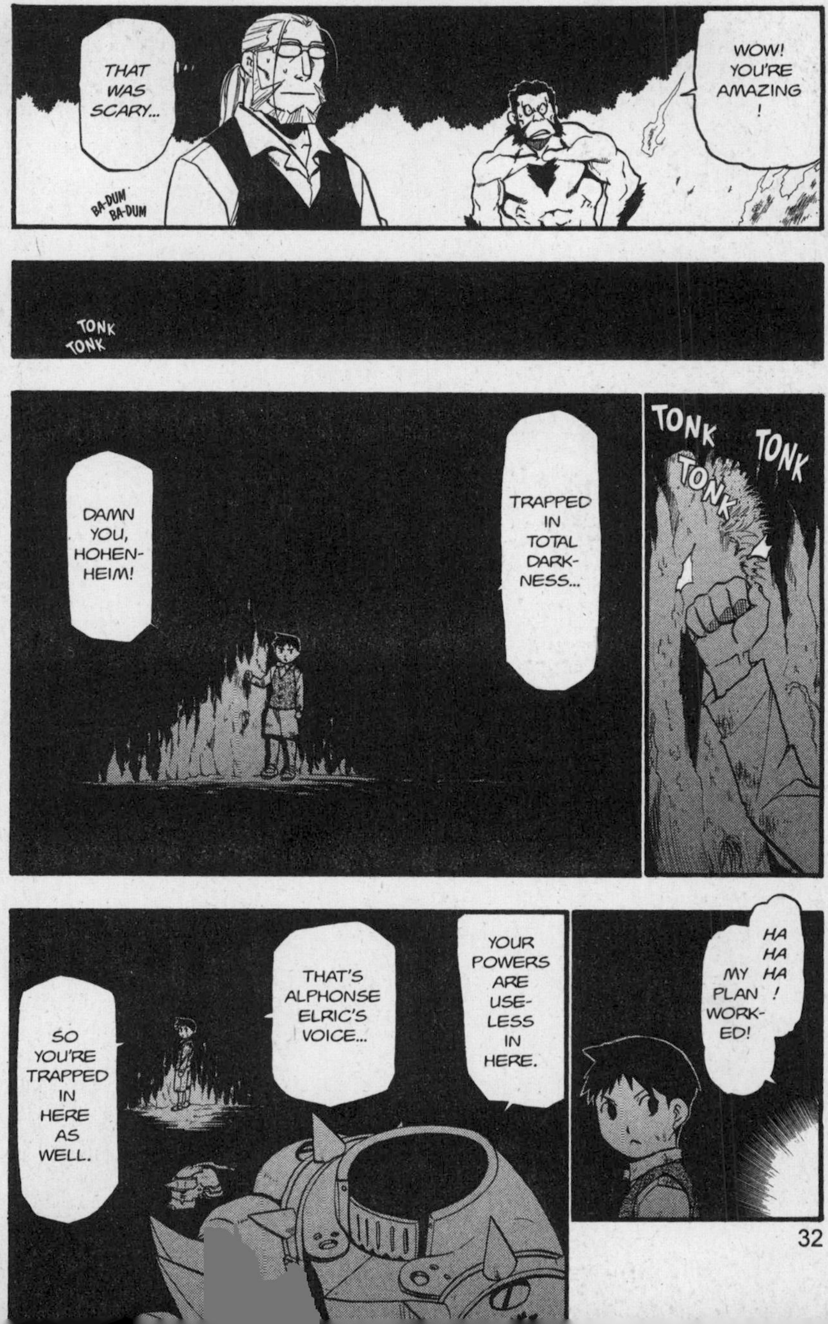
WOW! YOU'RE AMAZING!
THAT WAS SCARY...
BA-DUM BA-DUM
TONK TONK
TONK TONK TONK
TRAPPED IN TOTAL DARKNESS...
DAMN YOU, HOHENHEIM!
HA HA HA! MY PLAN WORKED!
YOUR POWERS ARE USELESS IN HERE.
THAT'S ALPHONSE ELRIC'S VOICE...
SO YOU'RE TRAPPED IN HERE AS WELL.

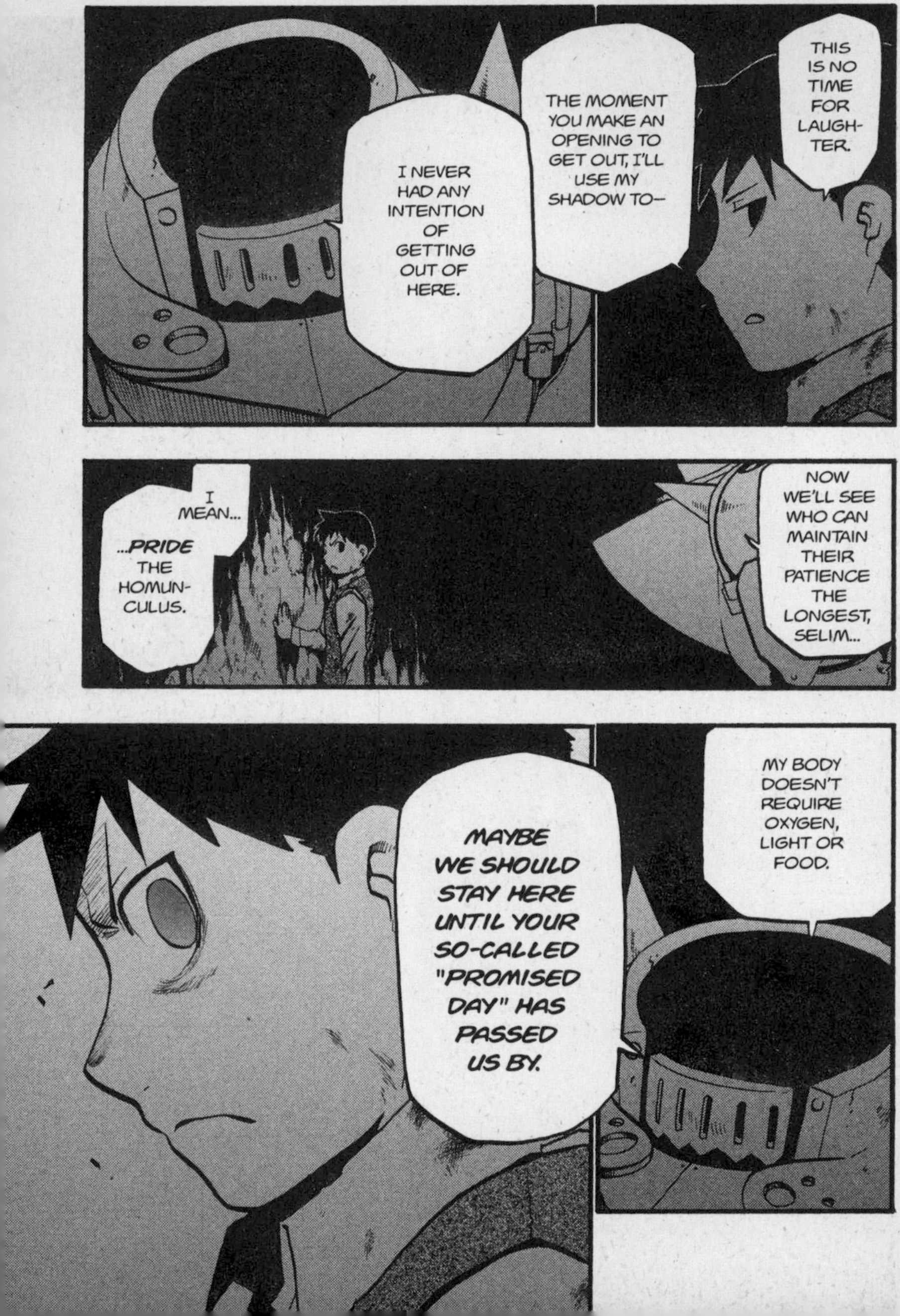
THIS IS NO TIME FOR LAUGH-TER.
THE MOMENT YOU MAKE AN OPENING TO GET OUT, I'LL USE MY SHADOW TO—
I NEVER HAD ANY INTENTION OF GETTING OUT OF HERE.
NOW WE'LL SEE WHO CAN MAINTAIN THEIR PATIENCE THE LONGEST, SELIM...
I MEAN... ...PRIDE THE HOMUN-CULUS.
MY BODY DOESN'T REQUIRE OXYGEN, LIGHT OR FOOD.
MAYBE WE SHOULD STAY HERE UNTIL YOUR SO-CALLED "PROMISED DAY" HAS PASSED US BY.

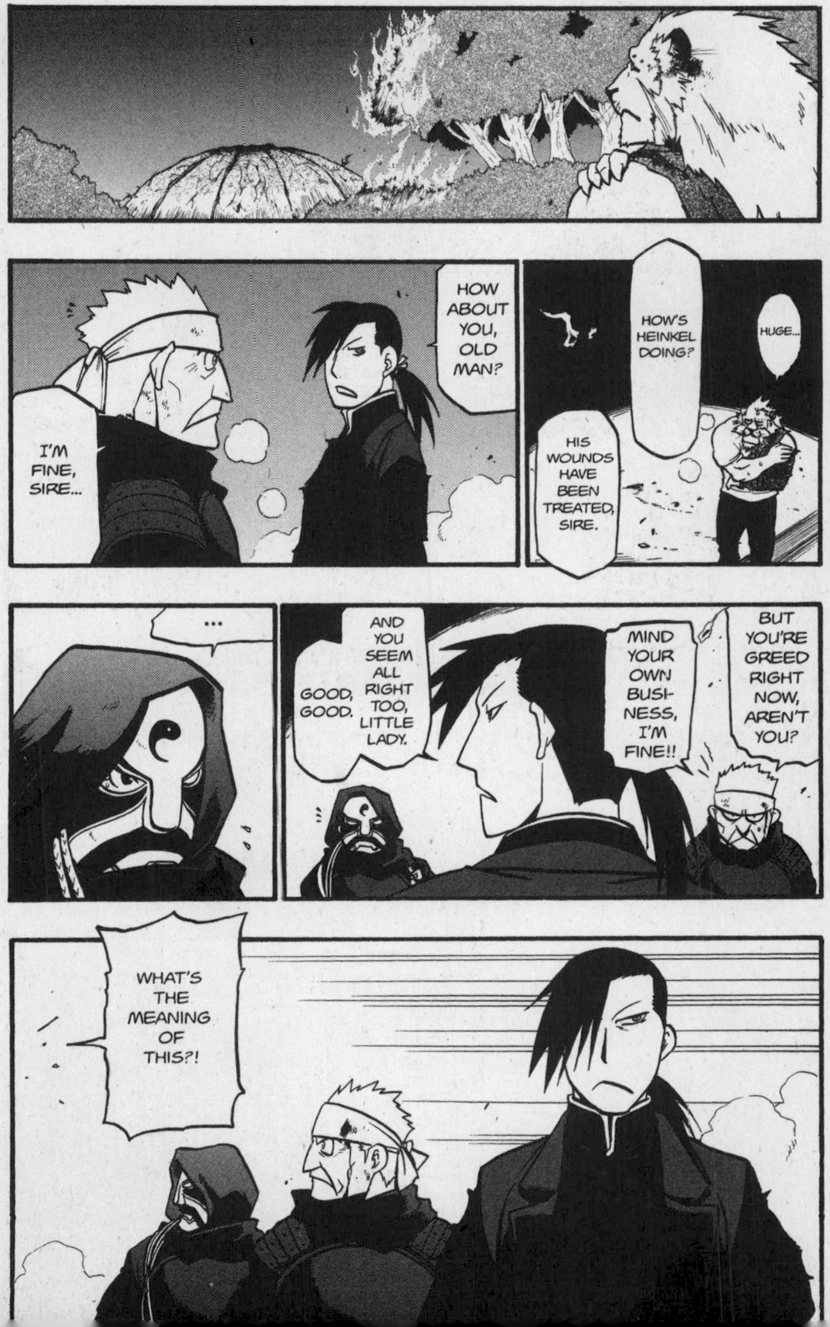

HOW'S HEINKEL DOING?
HUGE...
HIS WOUNDS HAVE BEEN TREATED, SIRE.
HOW ABOUT YOU, OLD MAN?
I'M FINE, SIRE...
BUT YOU'RE GREED RIGHT NOW, AREN'T YOU?
MIND YOUR OWN BUSINESS, I'M FINE!!
AND YOU SEEM ALL RIGHT TOO, LITTLE LADY.
GOOD, GOOD.
...
WHAT'S THE MEANING OF THIS?!

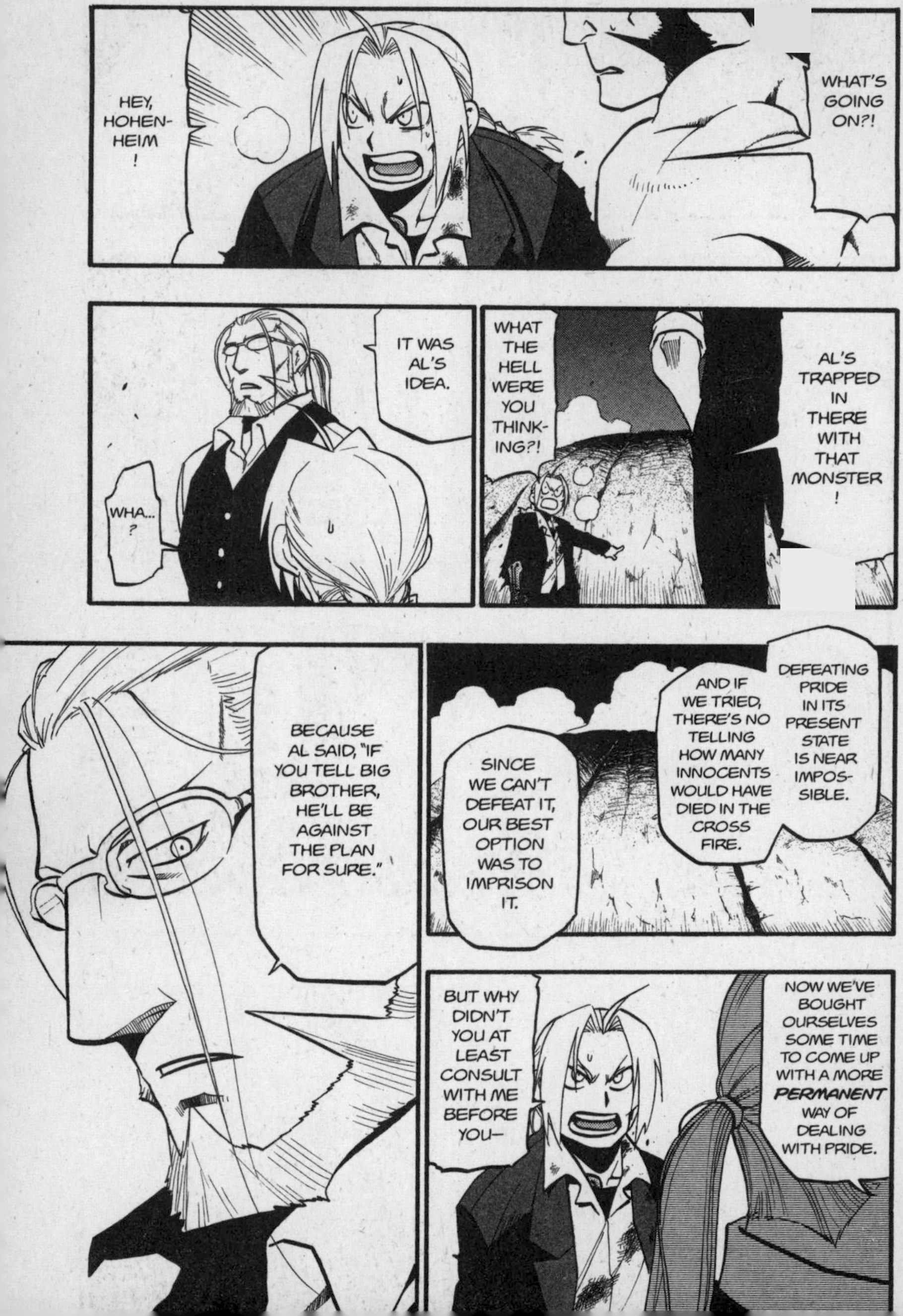

WHAT'S GOING ON?!
HEY, HOHENHEIM!
AL'S TRAPPED IN THERE WITH THAT MONSTER!
WHAT THE HELL WERE YOU THINKING?!
IT WAS AL'S IDEA.
WHA...?
DEFEATING PRIDE IN ITS PRESENT STATE IS NEAR IMPOSSIBLE.
AND IF WE TRIED, THERE'S NO TELLING HOW MANY INNOCENTS WOULD HAVE DIED IN THE CROSS FIRE.
SINCE WE CAN'T DEFEAT IT, OUR BEST OPTION WAS TO IMPRISON IT.
NOW WE'VE BOUGHT OURSELVES SOME TIME TO COME UP WITH A MORE ***PERMANENT*** WAY OF DEALING WITH PRIDE.
BUT WHY DIDN'T YOU AT LEAST CONSULT WITH ME BEFORE YOU–
BECAUSE AL SAID, "IF YOU TELL BIG BROTHER, HE'LL BE AGAINST THE PLAN FOR SURE."

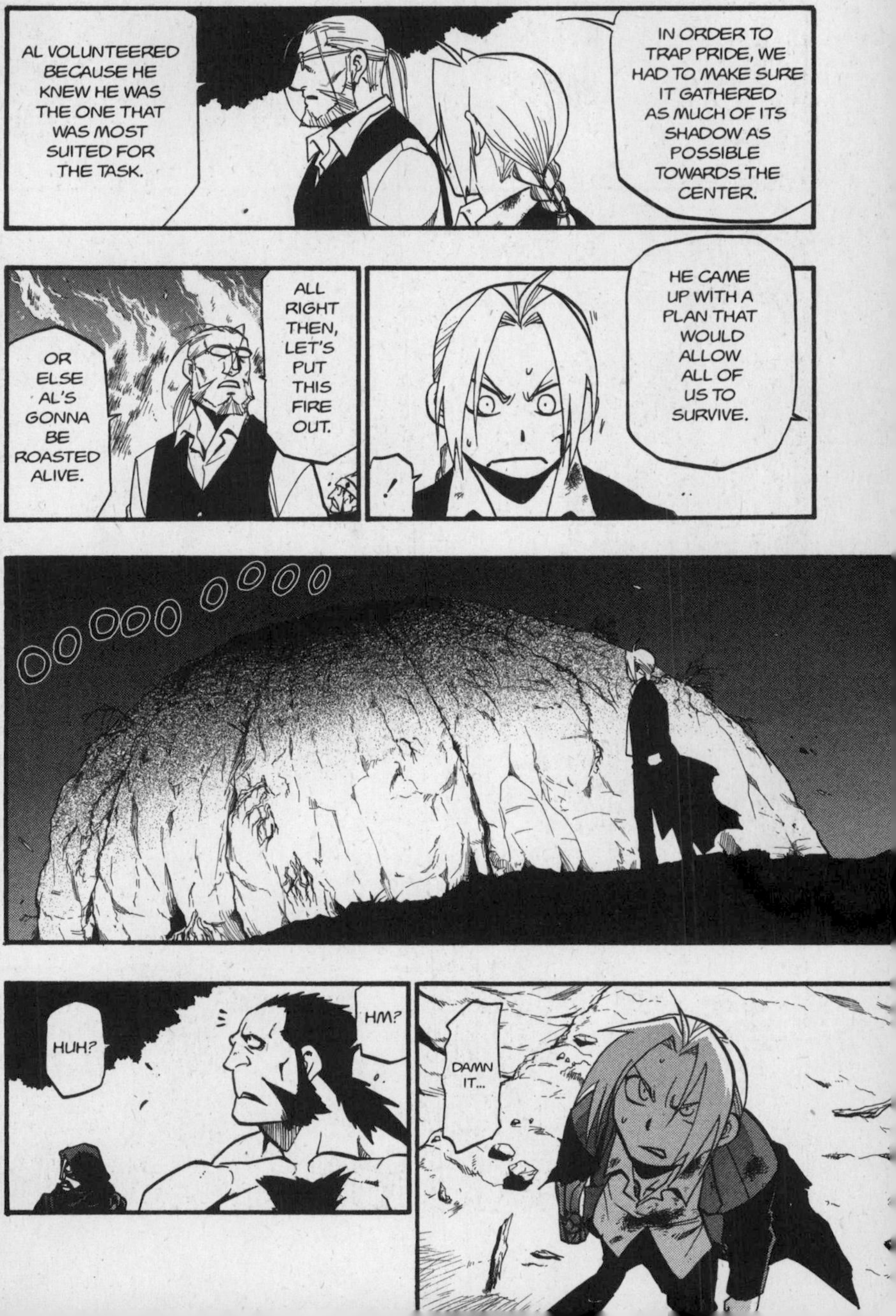
IN ORDER TO TRAP PRIDE, WE HAD TO MAKE SURE IT GATHERED AS MUCH OF ITS SHADOW AS POSSIBLE TOWARDS THE CENTER.
AL VOLUNTEERED BECAUSE HE KNEW HE WAS THE ONE THAT WAS MOST SUITED FOR THE TASK.
HE CAME UP WITH A PLAN THAT WOULD ALLOW ALL OF US TO SURVIVE.
!
ALL RIGHT THEN, LET'S PUT THIS FIRE OUT.
OR ELSE AL'S GONNA BE ROASTED ALIVE.
OOOOOOOOOO
DAMN IT...
HM?
HUH?

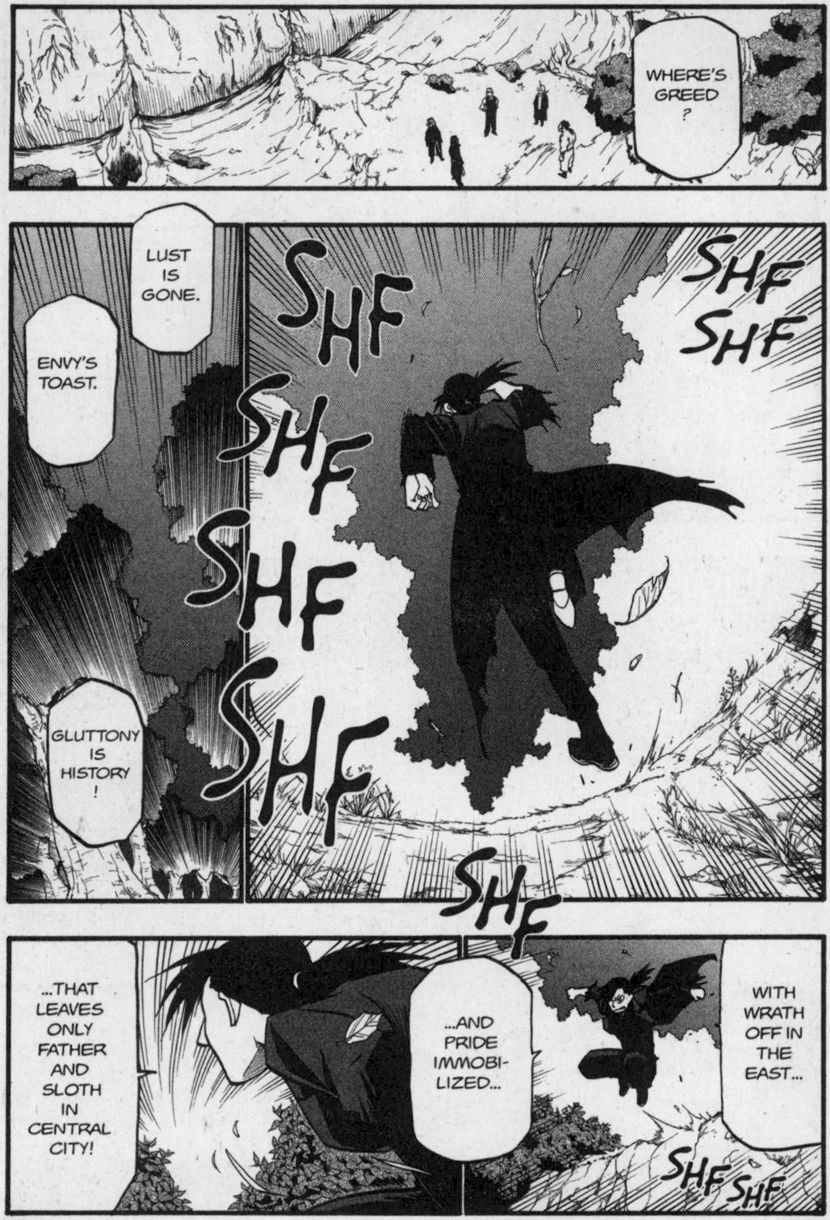
WHERE'S GREED ?
SHF SHF SHF
SHF
SHF
SHF
SHF
LUST IS GONE.
ENVY'S TOAST.
GLUTTONY IS HISTORY !
SHF
WITH WRATH OFF IN THE EAST...
SHF SHF
...AND PRIDE IMMOBI-LIZED...
...THAT LEAVES ONLY FATHER AND SLOTH IN CENTRAL CITY!

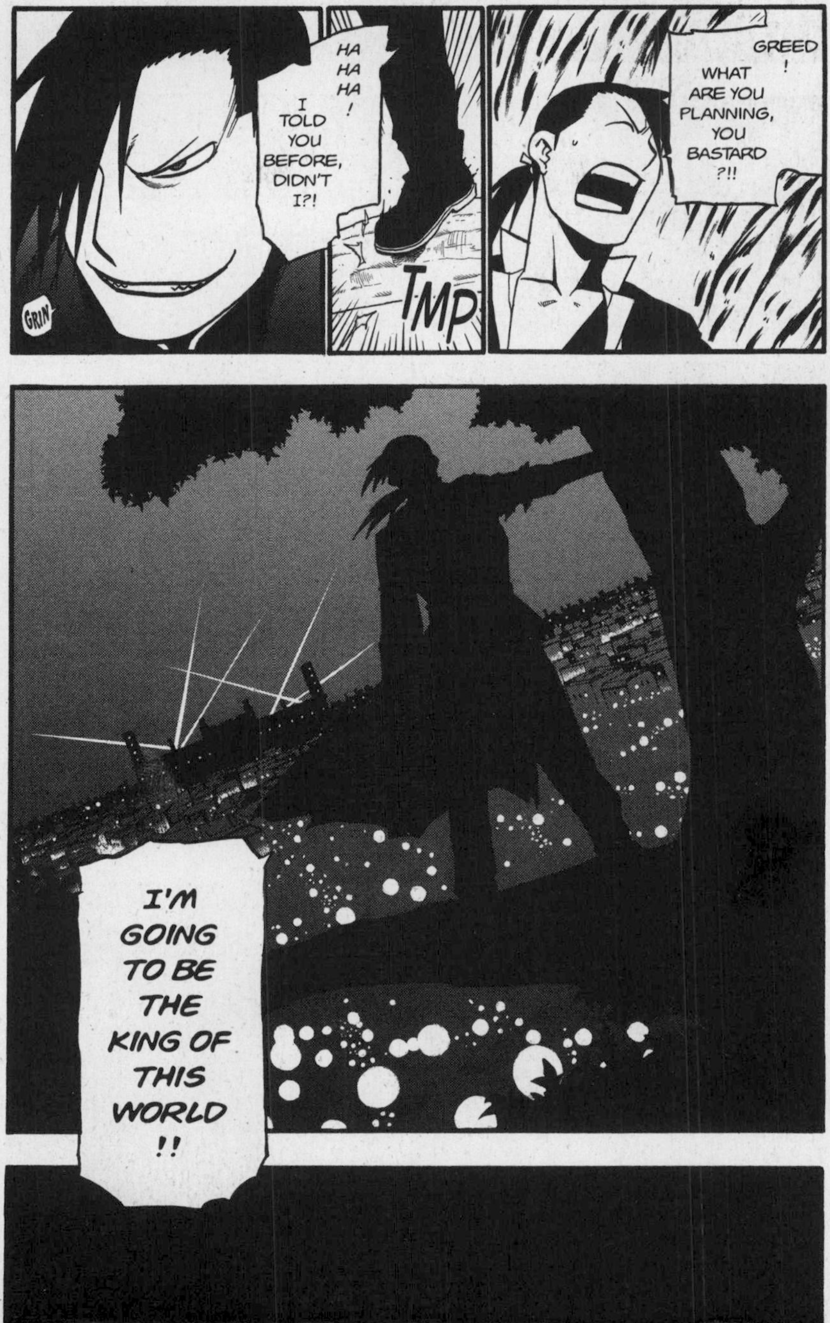
GREED!
WHAT ARE YOU PLANNING, YOU BASTARD?!!
HA HA HA!
I TOLD YOU BEFORE, DIDN'T I?!
TMP
GRIN
I'M GOING TO BE THE KING OF THIS WORLD!!

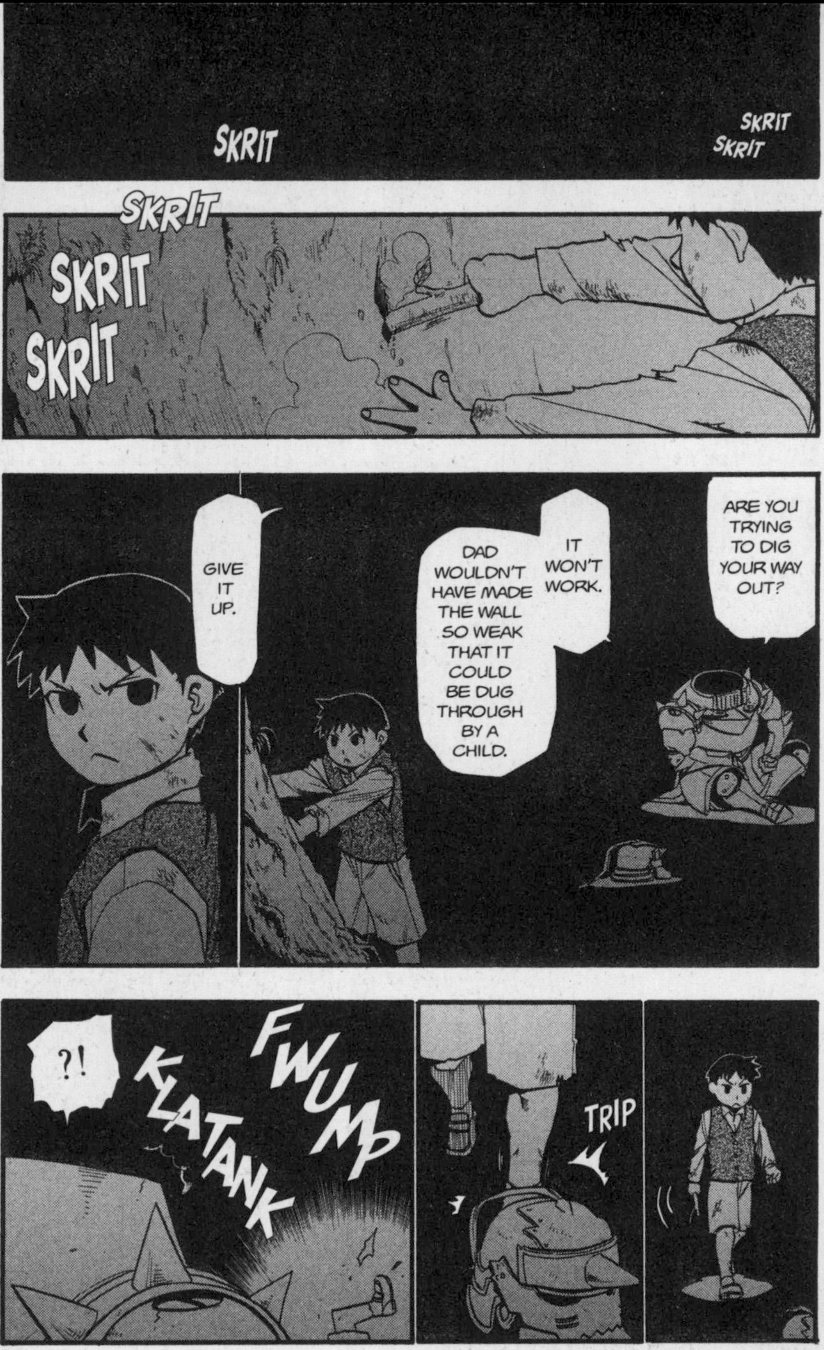
SKRIT
SKRIT
SKRIT
SKRIT
SKRIT
SKRIT
ARE YOU TRYING TO DIG YOUR WAY OUT?
IT WON'T WORK.
DAD WOULDN'T HAVE MADE THE WALL SO WEAK THAT IT COULD BE DUG THROUGH BY A CHILD.
GIVE IT UP.
TRIP
FWUMP
KLATANK
?!

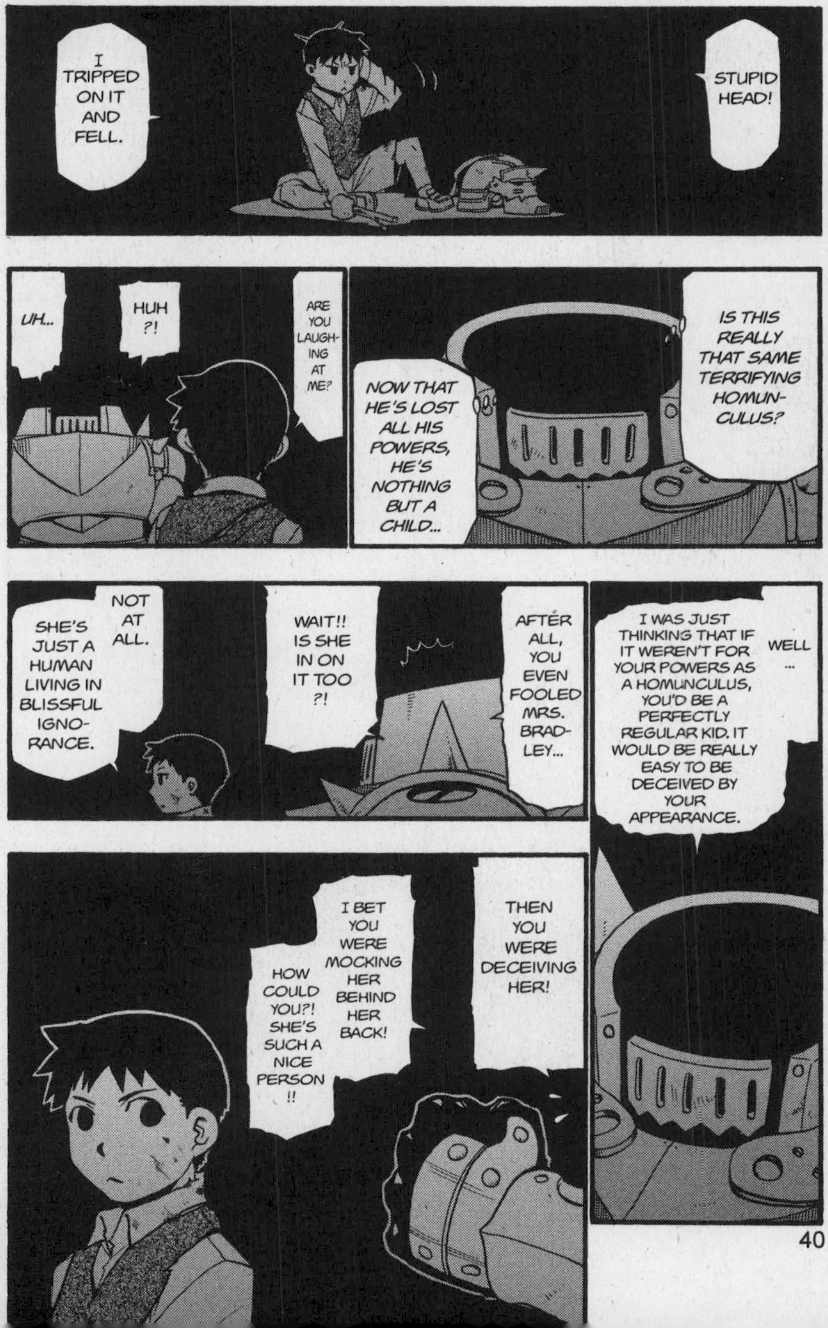
STUPID HEAD!
I TRIPPED ON IT AND FELL.
IS THIS REALLY THAT SAME TERRIFYING HOMUNCULUS?
NOW THAT HE'S LOST ALL HIS POWERS, HE'S NOTHING BUT A CHILD...
ARE YOU LAUGHING AT ME?
HUH?!
UH...
WELL...
I WAS JUST THINKING THAT IF IT WEREN'T FOR YOUR POWERS AS A HOMUNCULUS, YOU'D BE A PERFECTLY REGULAR KID. IT WOULD BE REALLY EASY TO BE DECEIVED BY YOUR APPEARANCE.
AFTER ALL, YOU EVEN FOOLED MRS. BRADLEY...
WAIT!! IS SHE IN ON IT TOO?!
NOT AT ALL.
SHE'S JUST A HUMAN LIVING IN BLISSFUL IGNORANCE.
THEN YOU WERE DECEIVING HER!
I BET YOU WERE MOCKING HER BEHIND HER BACK!
HOW COULD YOU?! SHE'S SUCH A NICE PERSON!!

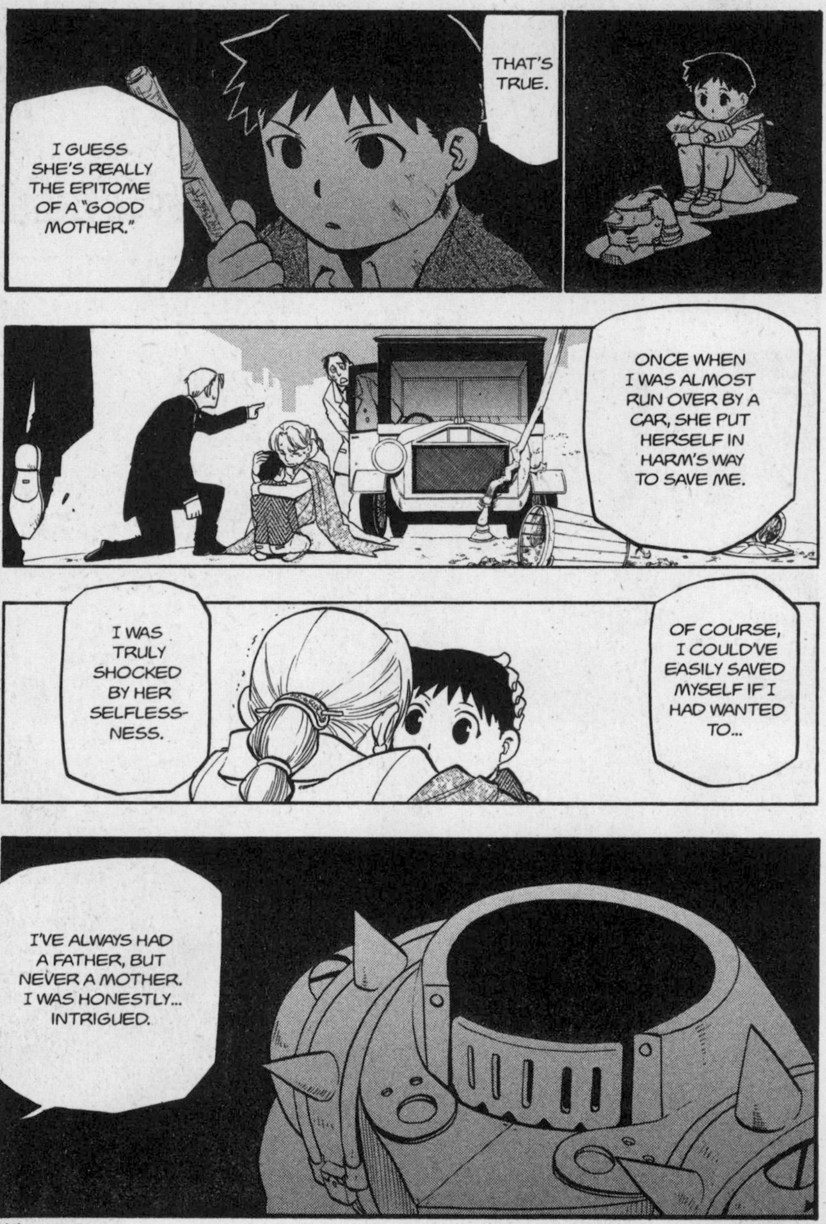
THAT'S TRUE.
I GUESS SHE'S REALLY THE EPITOME OF A "GOOD MOTHER."
ONCE WHEN I WAS ALMOST RUN OVER BY A CAR, SHE PUT HERSELF IN HARM'S WAY TO SAVE ME.
OF COURSE, I COULD'VE EASILY SAVED MYSELF IF I HAD WANTED TO...
I WAS TRULY SHOCKED BY HER SELFLESS-NESS.
I'VE ALWAYS HAD A FATHER, BUT NEVER A MOTHER. I WAS HONESTLY... INTRIGUED.

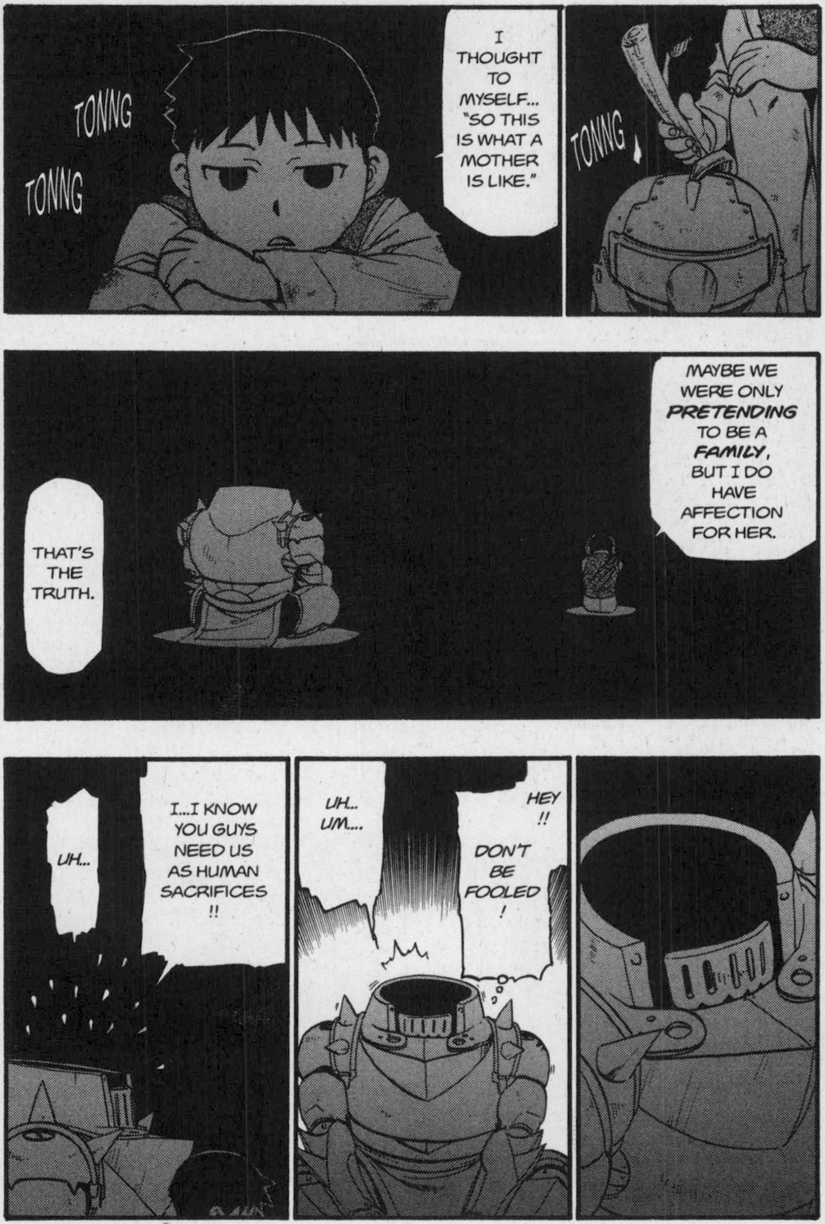
TONNG
I THOUGHT TO MYSELF... "SO THIS IS WHAT A MOTHER IS LIKE."
TONNG
TONNG
MAYBE WE WERE ONLY **PRETENDING** TO BE A **FAMILY**, BUT I DO HAVE AFFECTION FOR HER.
THAT'S THE TRUTH.
HEY !! DON'T BE FOOLED !
UH... UM....
I...I KNOW YOU GUYS NEED US AS HUMAN SACRIFICES !!
UH...

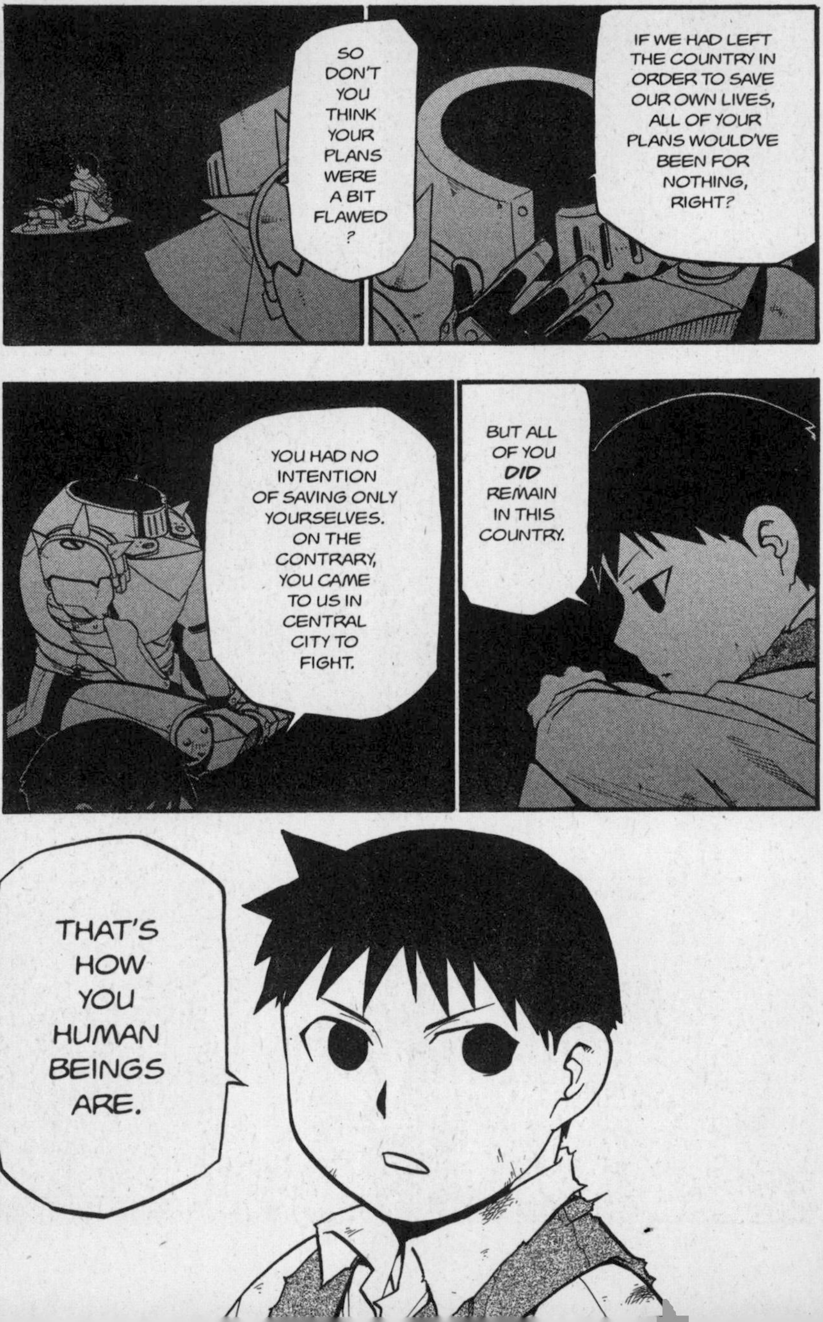
IF WE HAD LEFT THE COUNTRY IN ORDER TO SAVE OUR OWN LIVES, ALL OF YOUR PLANS WOULD'VE BEEN FOR NOTHING, RIGHT?
SO DON'T YOU THINK YOUR PLANS WERE A BIT FLAWED ?
BUT ALL OF YOU *DID* REMAIN IN THIS COUNTRY.
YOU HAD NO INTENTION OF SAVING ONLY YOURSELVES. ON THE CONTRARY, YOU CAME TO US IN CENTRAL CITY TO FIGHT.
THAT'S HOW YOU HUMAN BEINGS ARE.

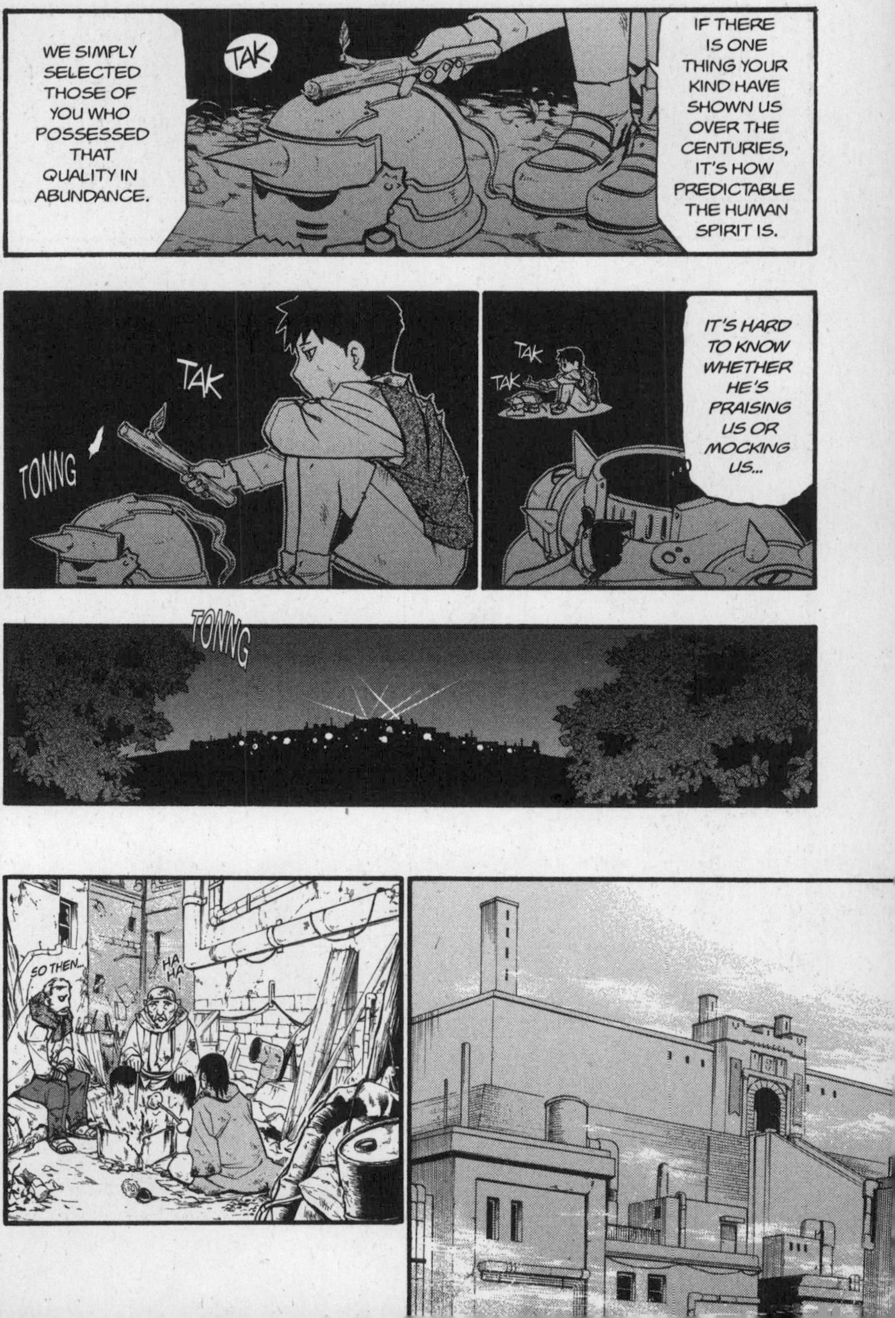
IF THERE IS ONE THING YOUR KIND HAVE SHOWN US OVER THE CENTURIES, IT'S HOW PREDICTABLE THE HUMAN SPIRIT IS.
TAK
WE SIMPLY SELECTED THOSE OF YOU WHO POSSESSED THAT QUALITY IN ABUNDANCE.
IT'S HARD TO KNOW WHETHER HE'S PRAISING US OR MOCKING US...
TAK
TAK
TAK
TONNG
TONNG
HA HA!
SO THEN...

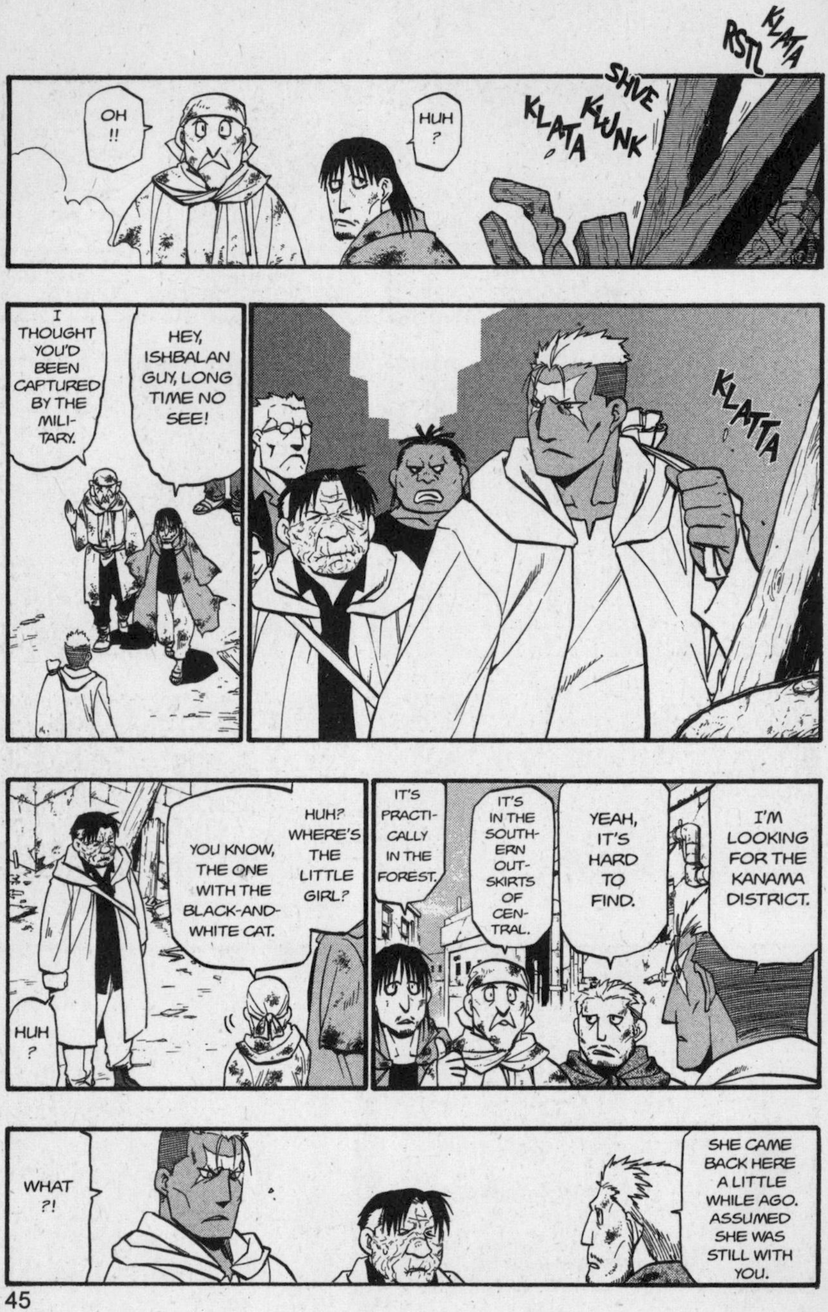
RSTL
KLATA
SHVE
KLUNK
KLATA
HUH?
OH!!
KLATTA
HEY, ISHBALAN GUY, LONG TIME NO SEE!
I THOUGHT YOU'D BEEN CAPTURED BY THE MILITARY.
I'M LOOKING FOR THE KANAMA DISTRICT.
YEAH, IT'S HARD TO FIND.
IT'S IN THE SOUTHERN OUTSKIRTS OF CENTRAL.
IT'S PRACTICALLY IN THE FOREST.
HUH? WHERE'S THE LITTLE GIRL?
YOU KNOW, THE ONE WITH THE BLACK-AND-WHITE CAT.
HUH?
SHE CAME BACK HERE A LITTLE WHILE AGO. ASSUMED SHE WAS STILL WITH YOU.
WHAT?!

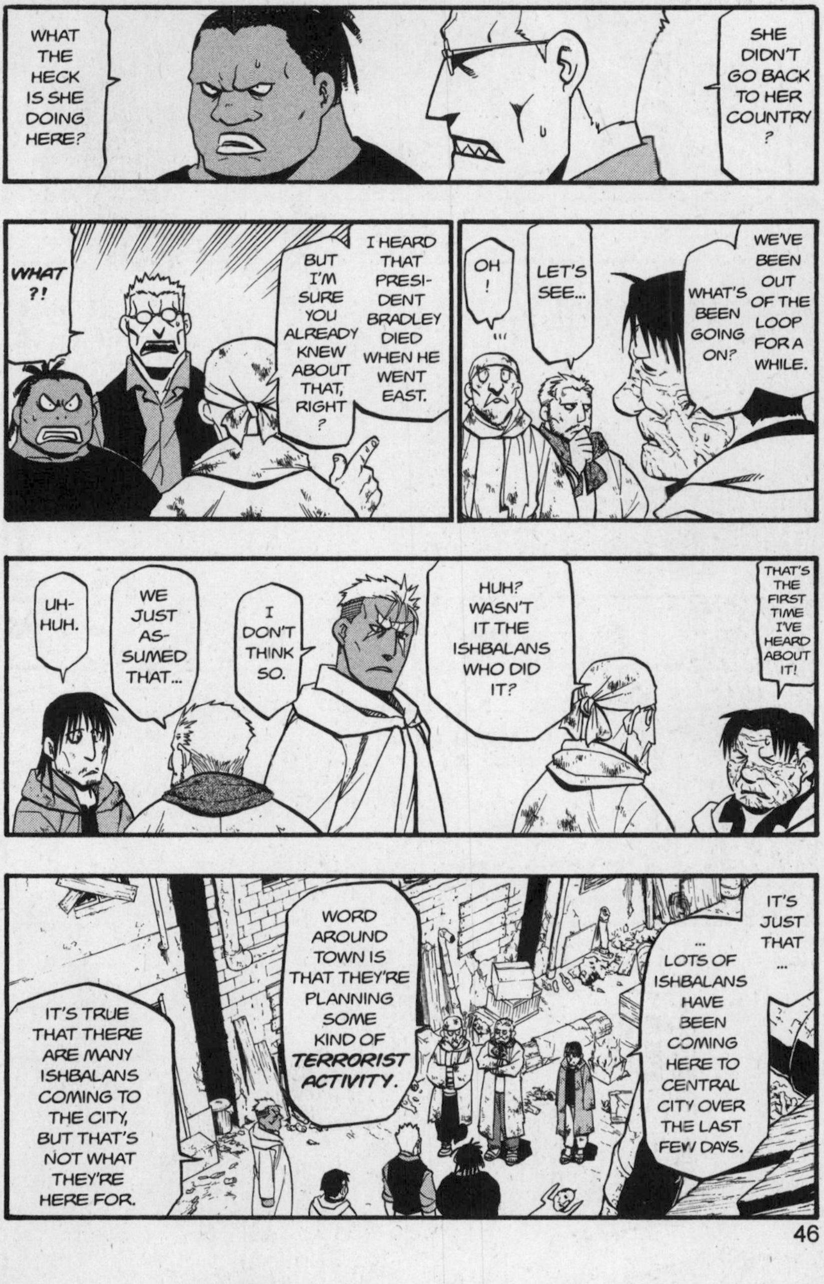
SHE DIDN'T GO BACK TO HER COUNTRY?
WHAT THE HECK IS SHE DOING HERE?
WE'VE BEEN OUT OF THE LOOP FOR A WHILE.
WHAT'S BEEN GOING ON?
LET'S SEE...
OH!
I HEARD THAT PRESIDENT BRADLEY DIED WHEN HE WENT EAST.
BUT I'M SURE YOU ALREADY KNEW ABOUT THAT, RIGHT?
WHAT?!
THAT'S THE FIRST TIME I'VE HEARD ABOUT IT!
HUH? WASN'T IT THE ISHBALANS WHO DID IT?
I DON'T THINK SO.
WE JUST ASSUMED THAT...
UH-HUH.
IT'S JUST THAT...
...LOTS OF ISHBALANS HAVE BEEN COMING HERE TO CENTRAL CITY OVER THE LAST FEW DAYS.
WORD AROUND TOWN IS THAT THEY'RE PLANNING SOME KIND OF **TERRORIST ACTIVITY**.
IT'S TRUE THAT THERE ARE MANY ISHBALANS COMING TO THE CITY, BUT THAT'S NOT WHAT THEY'RE HERE FOR.

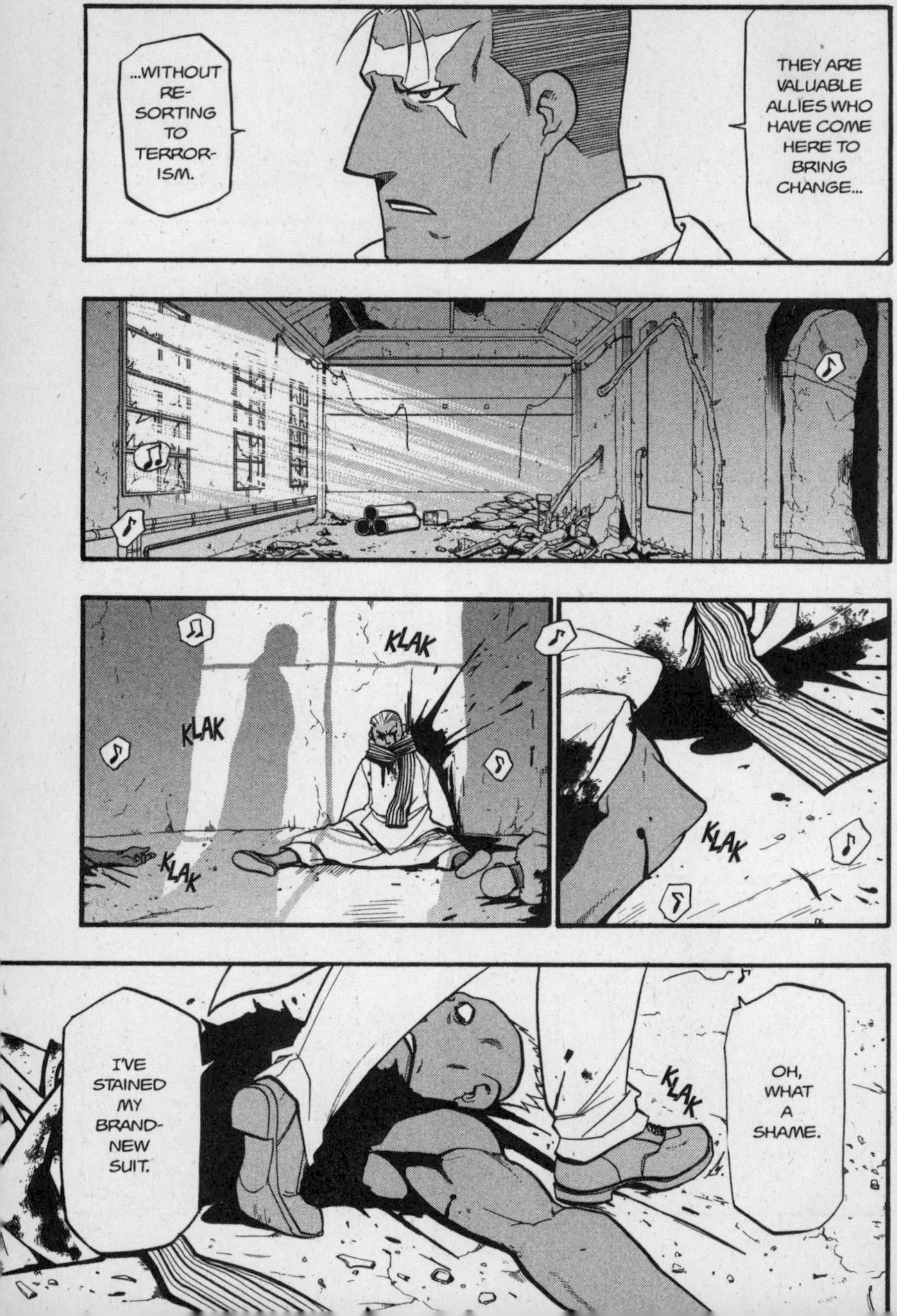
THEY ARE VALUABLE ALLIES WHO HAVE COME HERE TO BRING CHANGE...
...WITHOUT RE-SORTING TO TERROR-ISM.
KLAK
KLAK
KLAK
KLAK
OH, WHAT A SHAME.
KLAK
I'VE STAINED MY BRAND-NEW SUIT.

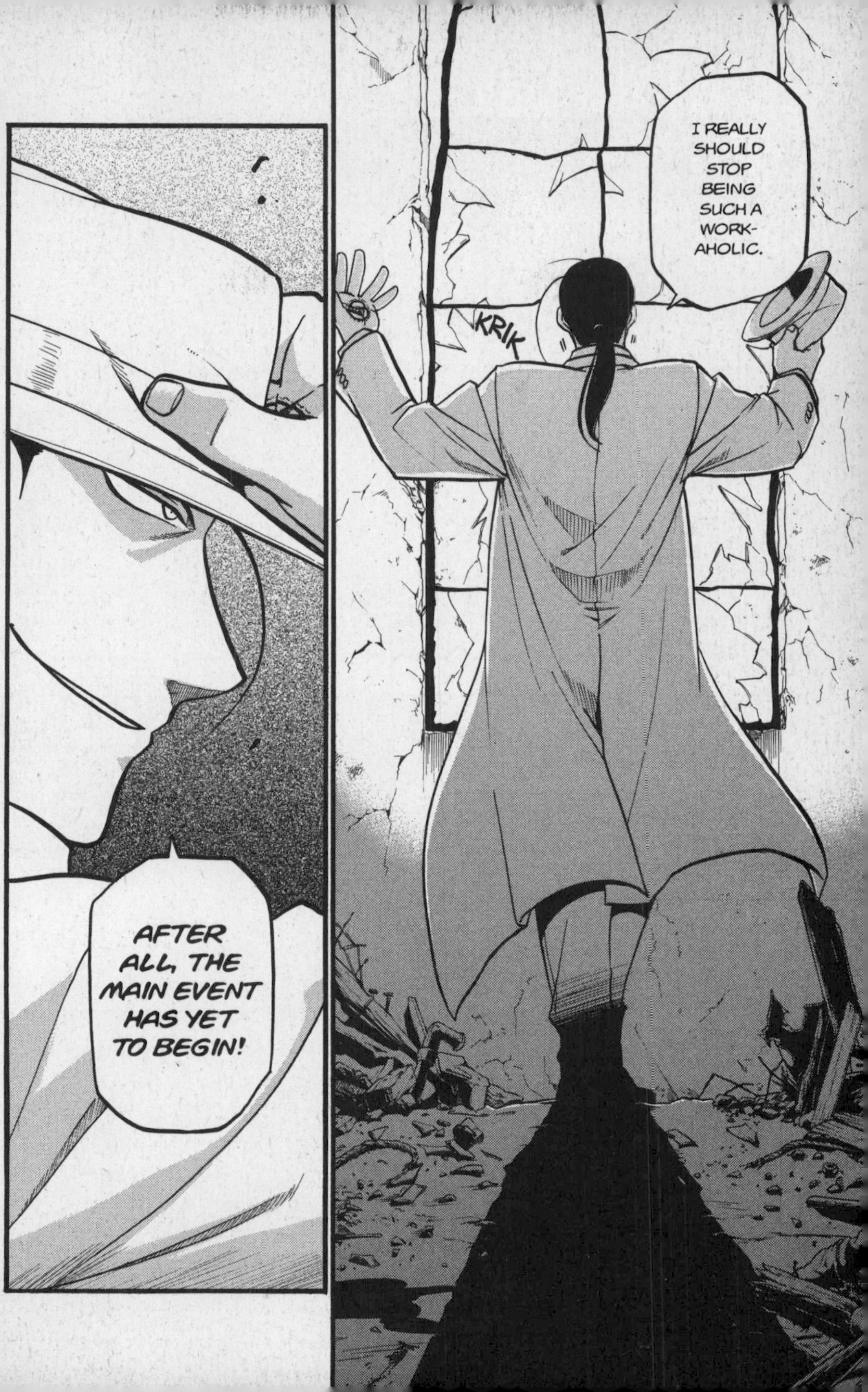
I REALLY SHOULD STOP BEING SUCH A WORK-AHOLIC.
KRIK
AFTER ALL, THE MAIN EVENT HAS YET TO BEGIN!

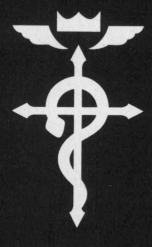

FULLMETAL
ALCHEMIST

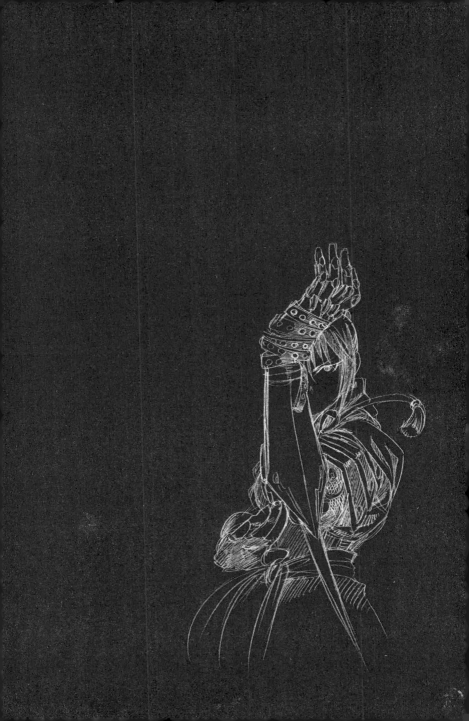

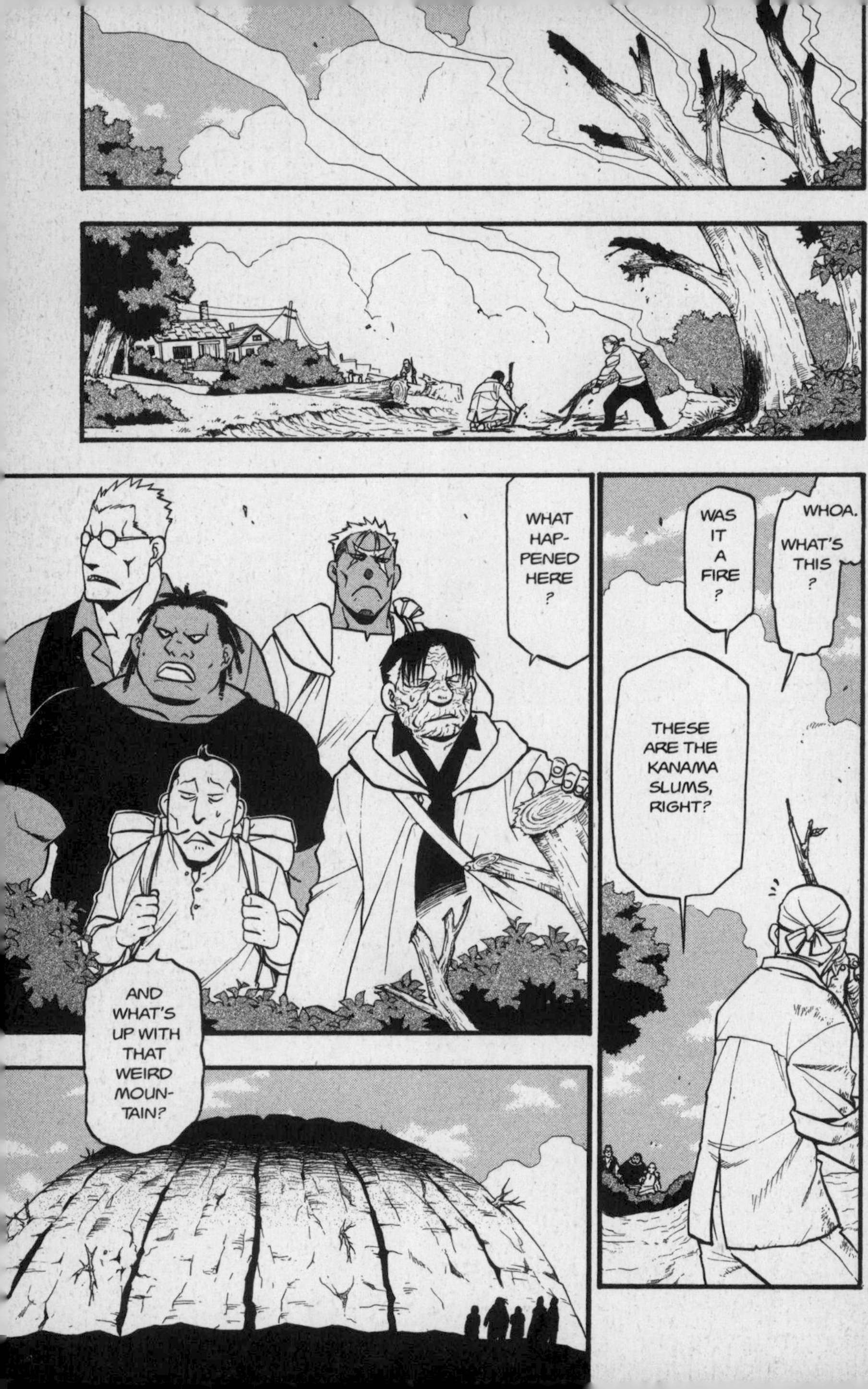
WHOA. WHAT'S THIS?
WAS IT A FIRE?
THESE ARE THE KANAMA SLUMS, RIGHT?
WHAT HAP-PENED HERE?
AND WHAT'S UP WITH THAT WEIRD MOUN-TAIN?

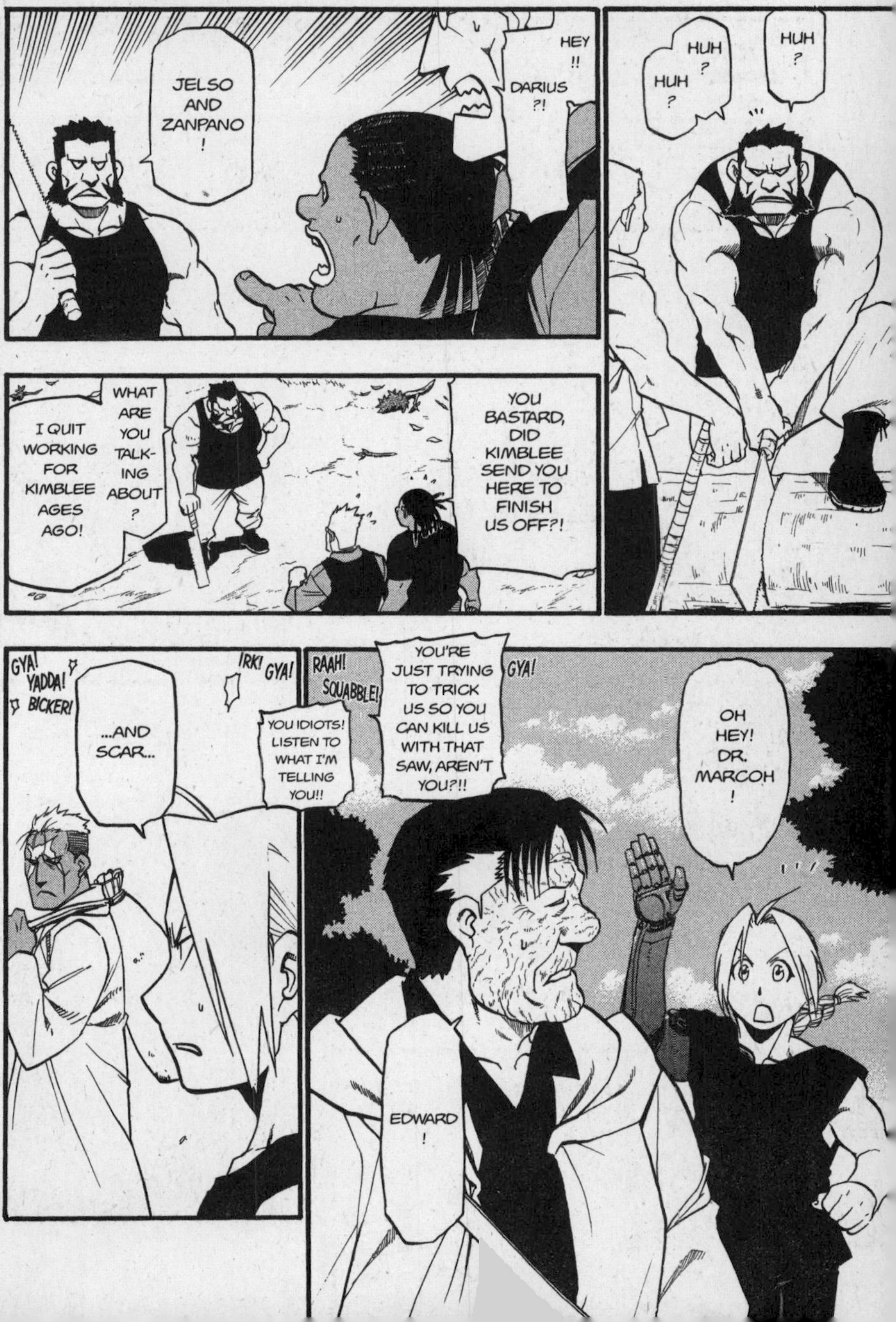
HUH?
HUH?
HUH?
HEY!! DARIUS?!
JELSO AND ZANPANO!
YOU BASTARD, DID KIMBLEE SEND YOU HERE TO FINISH US OFF?!
WHAT ARE YOU TALKING ABOUT?
I QUIT WORKING FOR KIMBLEE AGES AGO!
OH HEY! DR. MARCOH!
GYA!
YOU'RE JUST TRYING TO TRICK US SO YOU CAN KILL US WITH THAT SAW, AREN'T YOU?!!
RAAH! SQUABBLE!
EDWARD!
IRK! GYA!
YOU IDIOTS! LISTEN TO WHAT I'M TELLING YOU!!
...AND SCAR...
GYA! YADDA! BICKER!

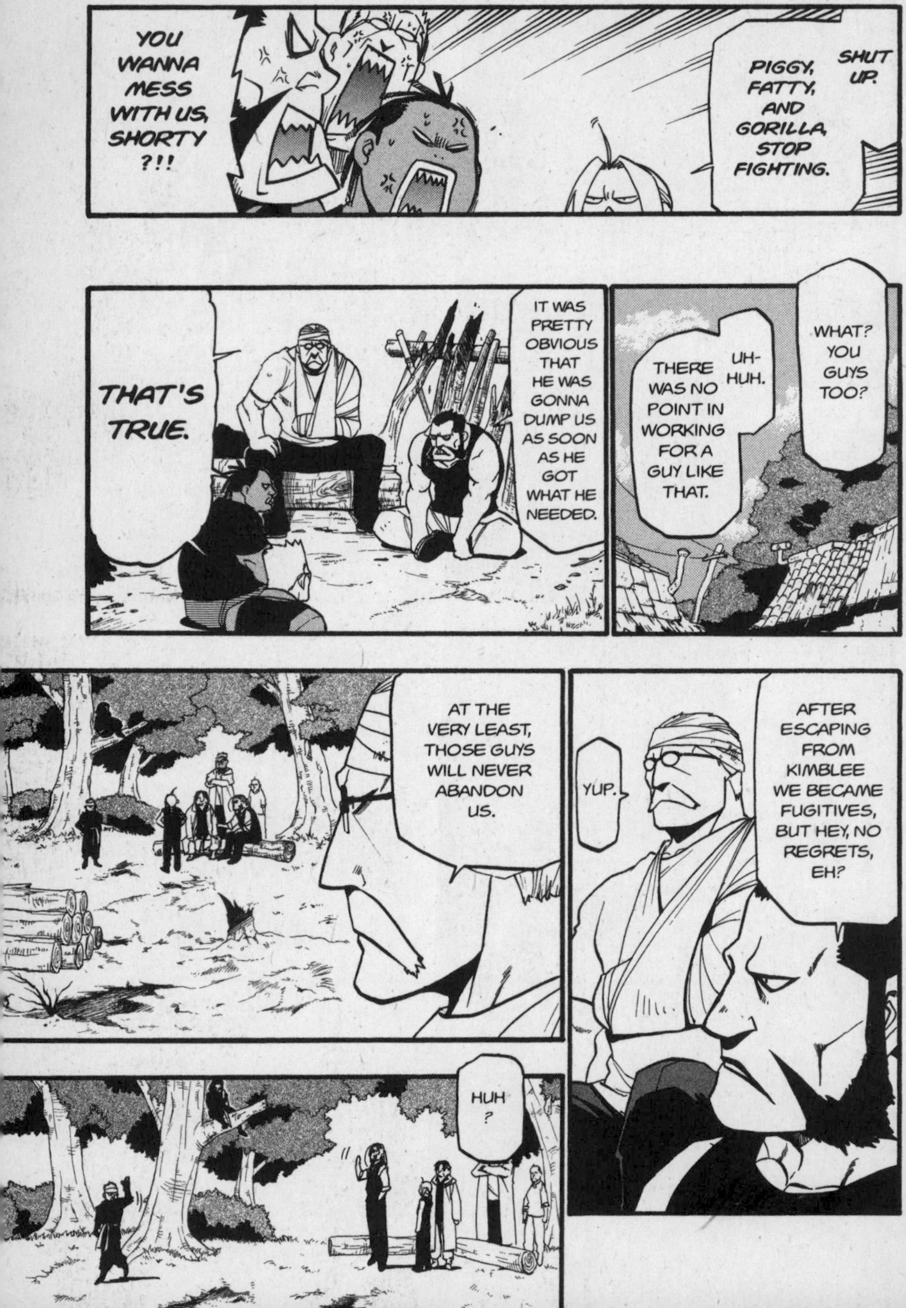
SHUT UP.
PIGGY, FATTY, AND GORILLA, STOP FIGHTING.
YOU WANNA MESS WITH US, SHORTY?!!
WHAT? YOU GUYS TOO?
UH-HUH.
THERE WAS NO POINT IN WORKING FOR A GUY LIKE THAT.
IT WAS PRETTY OBVIOUS THAT HE WAS GONNA DUMP US AS SOON AS HE GOT WHAT HE NEEDED.
THAT'S TRUE.
AFTER ESCAPING FROM KIMBLEE WE BECAME FUGITIVES, BUT HEY, NO REGRETS, EH?
YUP.
AT THE VERY LEAST, THOSE GUYS WILL NEVER ABANDON US.
HUH?

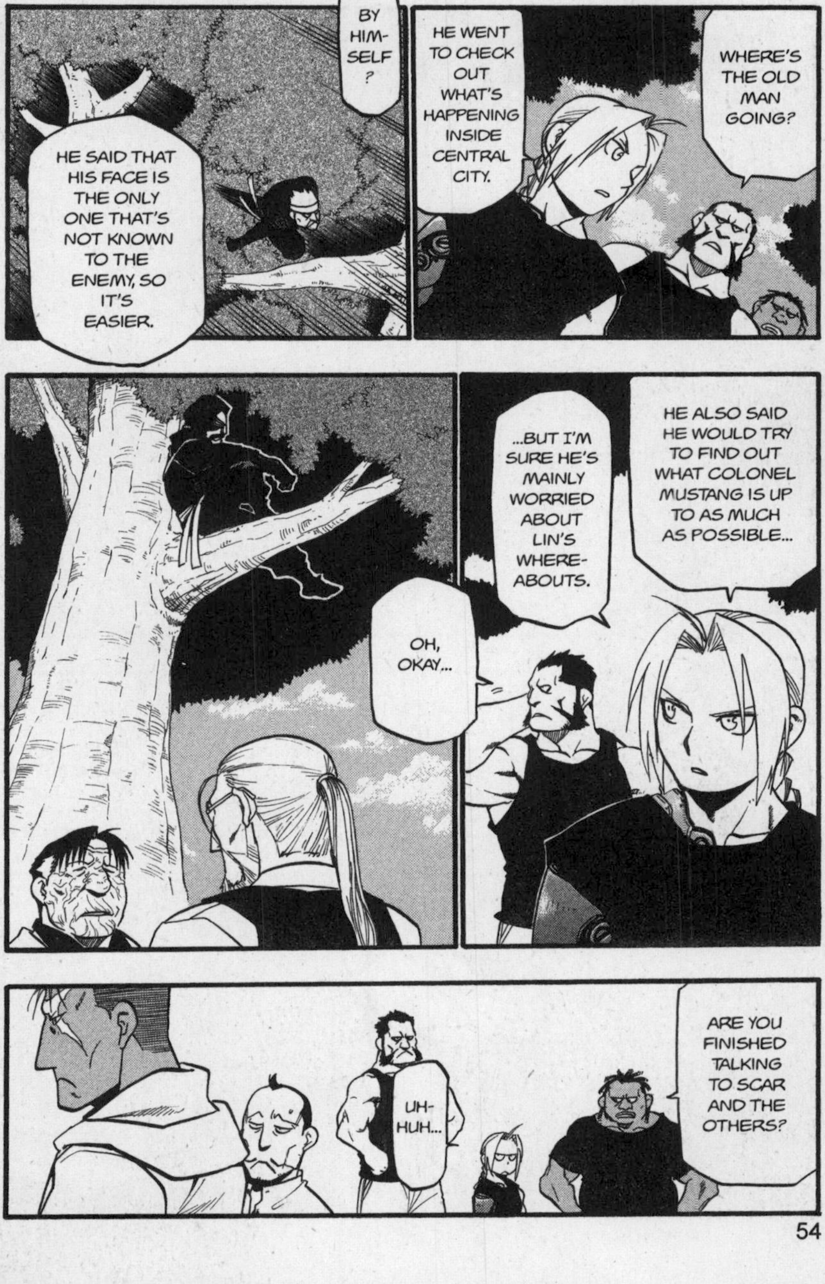
WHERE'S THE OLD MAN GOING?
HE WENT TO CHECK OUT WHAT'S HAPPENING INSIDE CENTRAL CITY.
BY HIM-SELF?
HE SAID THAT HIS FACE IS THE ONLY ONE THAT'S NOT KNOWN TO THE ENEMY, SO IT'S EASIER.
HE ALSO SAID HE WOULD TRY TO FIND OUT WHAT COLONEL MUSTANG IS UP TO AS MUCH AS POSSIBLE...
...BUT I'M SURE HE'S MAINLY WORRIED ABOUT LIN'S WHERE-ABOUTS.
OH, OKAY...
ARE YOU FINISHED TALKING TO SCAR AND THE OTHERS?
UH-HUH...

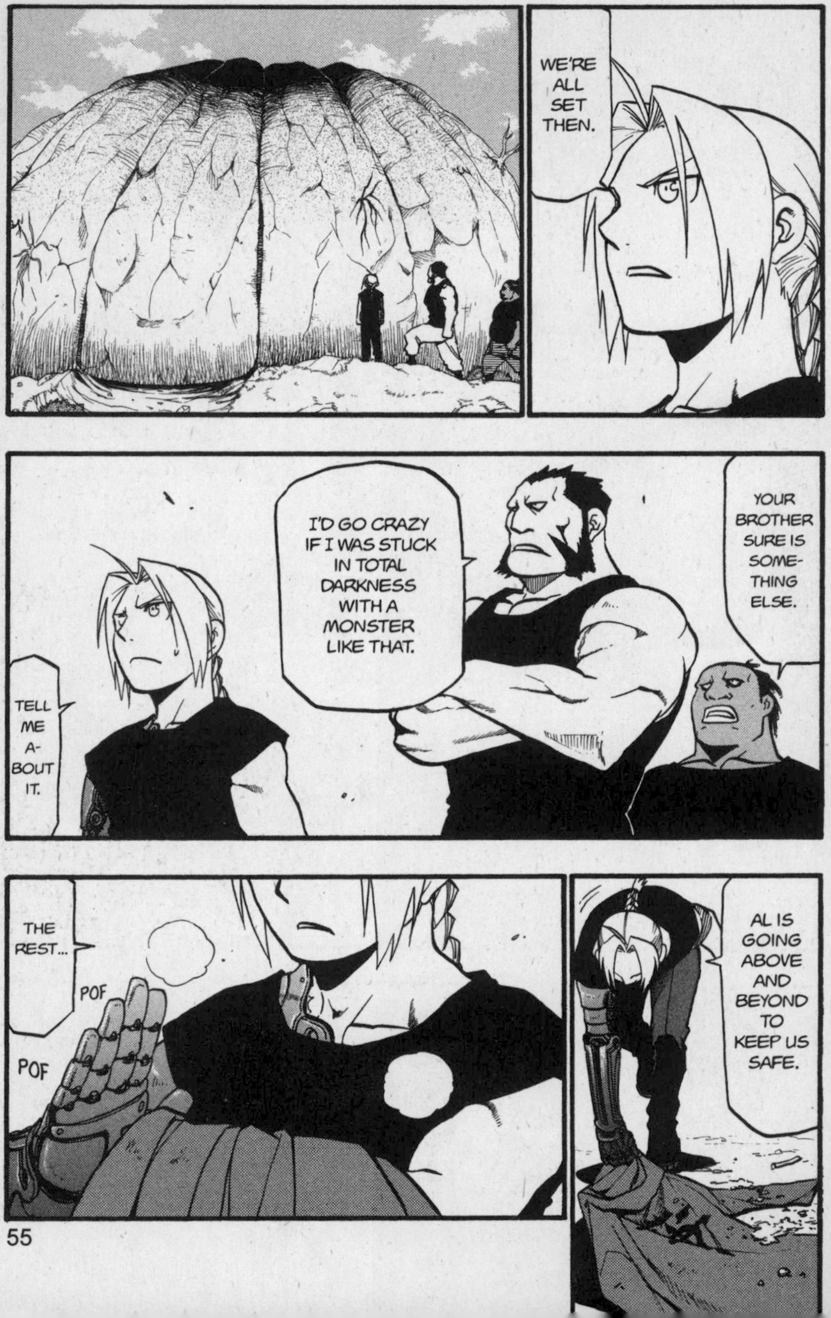
WE'RE ALL SET THEN.
YOUR BROTHER SURE IS SOME-THING ELSE.
I'D GO CRAZY IF I WAS STUCK IN TOTAL DARKNESS WITH A MONSTER LIKE THAT.
TELL ME A-BOUT IT.
AL IS GOING ABOVE AND BEYOND TO KEEP US SAFE.
THE REST...
POF
POF

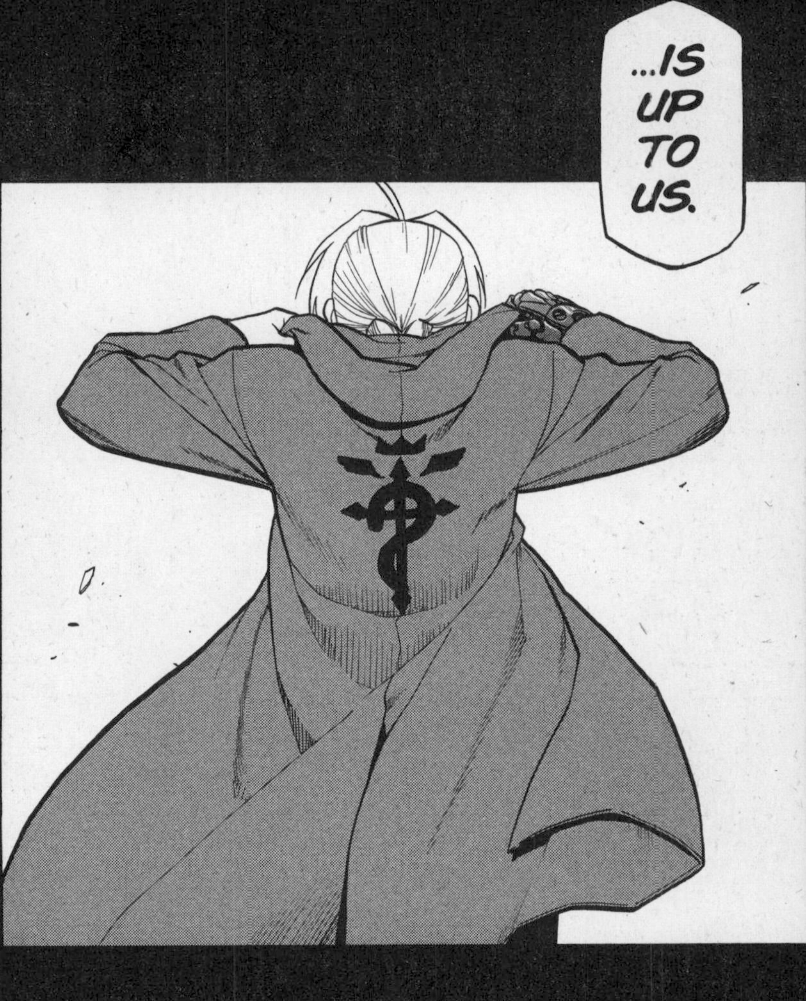

...IS UP TO US.

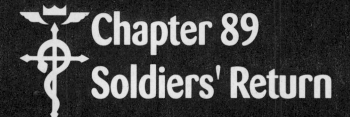

Chapter 89
Soldiers' Return

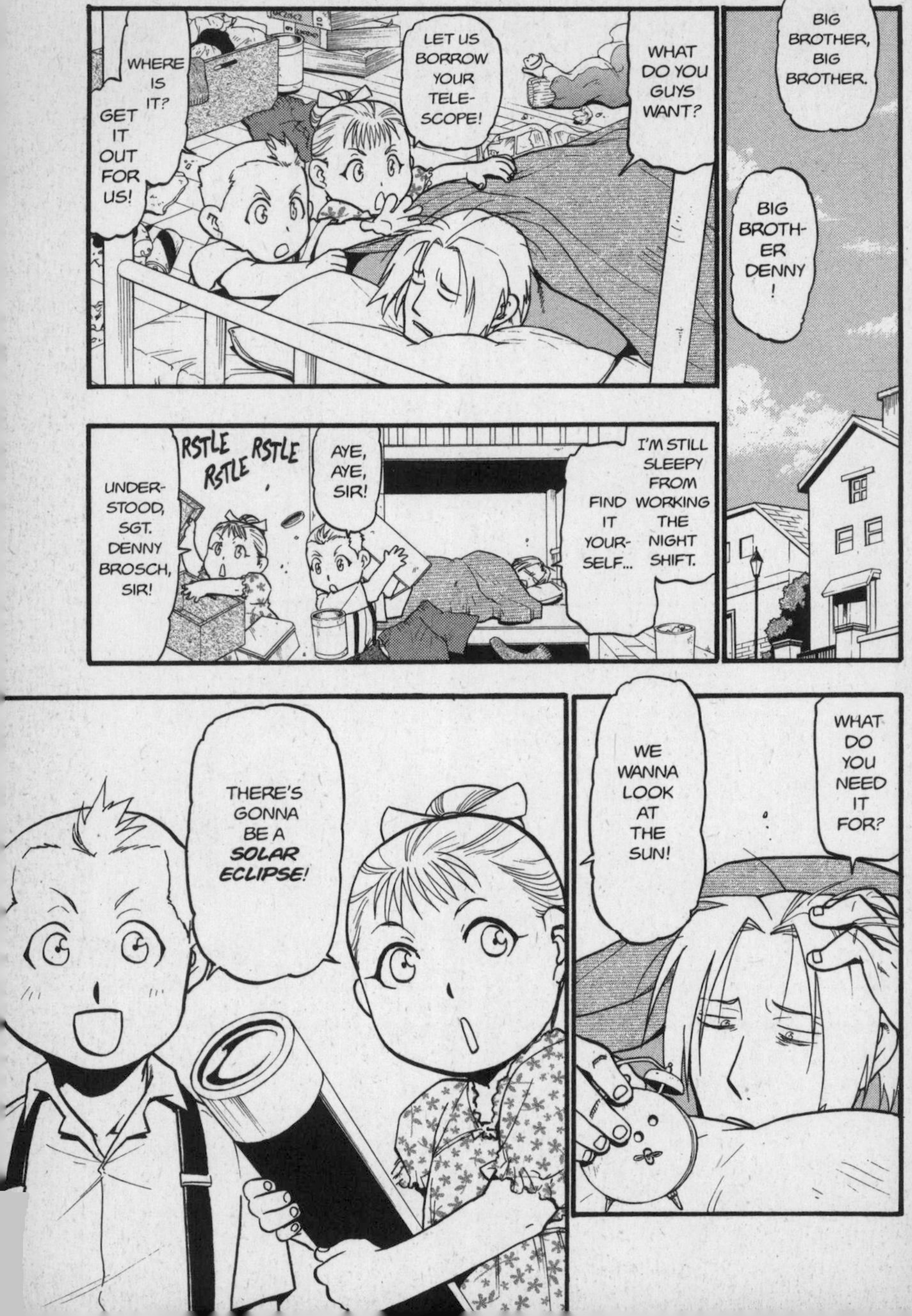
BIG BROTHER, BIG BROTHER.
BIG BROTHER DENNY!
WHAT DO YOU GUYS WANT?
LET US BORROW YOUR TELESCOPE!
WHERE IS IT?
GET IT OUT FOR US!
I'M STILL SLEEPY FROM WORKING THE NIGHT SHIFT.
FIND IT YOURSELF...
AYE, AYE, SIR!
RSTLE RSTLE RSTLE
UNDERSTOOD, SGT. DENNY BROSCH, SIR!
WHAT DO YOU NEED IT FOR?
WE WANNA LOOK AT THE SUN!
THERE'S GONNA BE A *SOLAR ECLIPSE!*

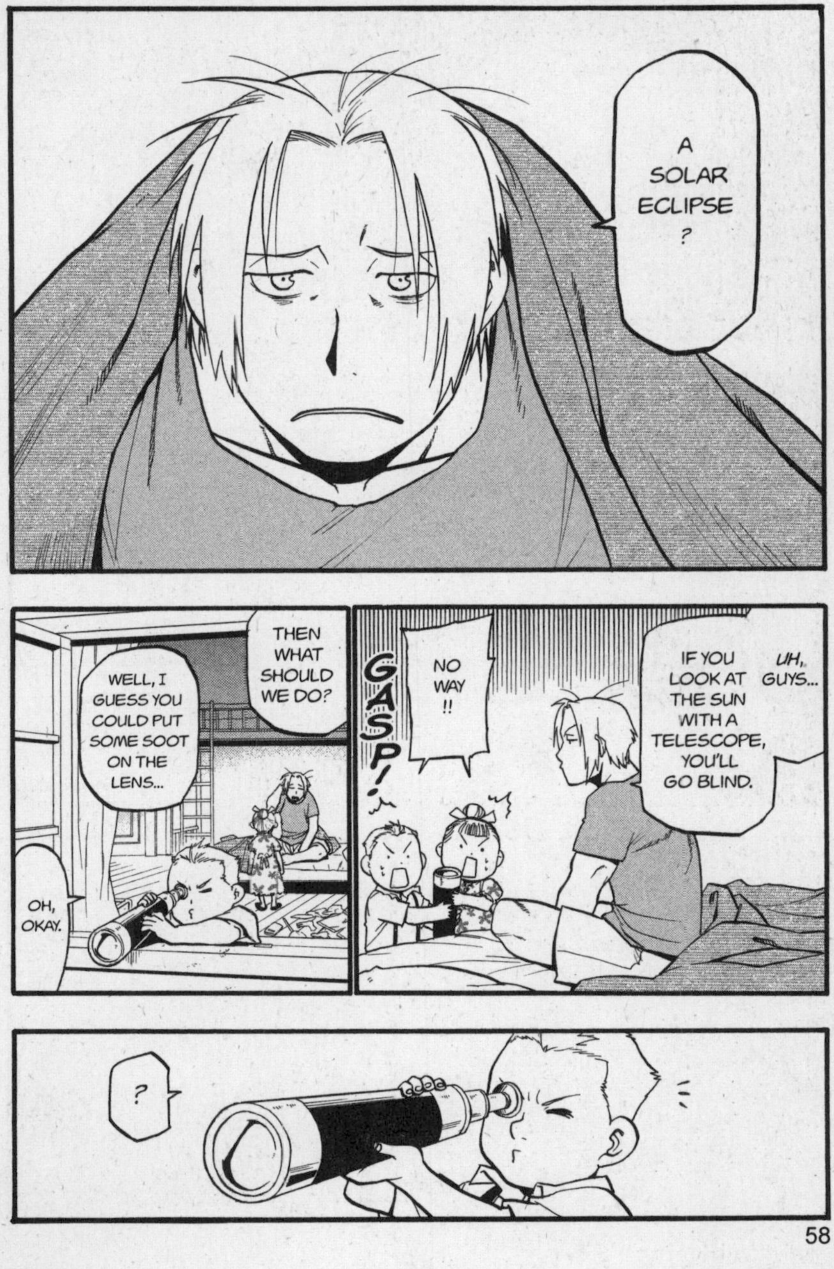
A SOLAR ECLIPSE ?
UH, GUYS...
IF YOU LOOK AT THE SUN WITH A TELESCOPE, YOU'LL GO BLIND.
NO WAY !!
GASP!
THEN WHAT SHOULD WE DO?
WELL, I GUESS YOU COULD PUT SOME SOOT ON THE LENS...
OH, OKAY.
?

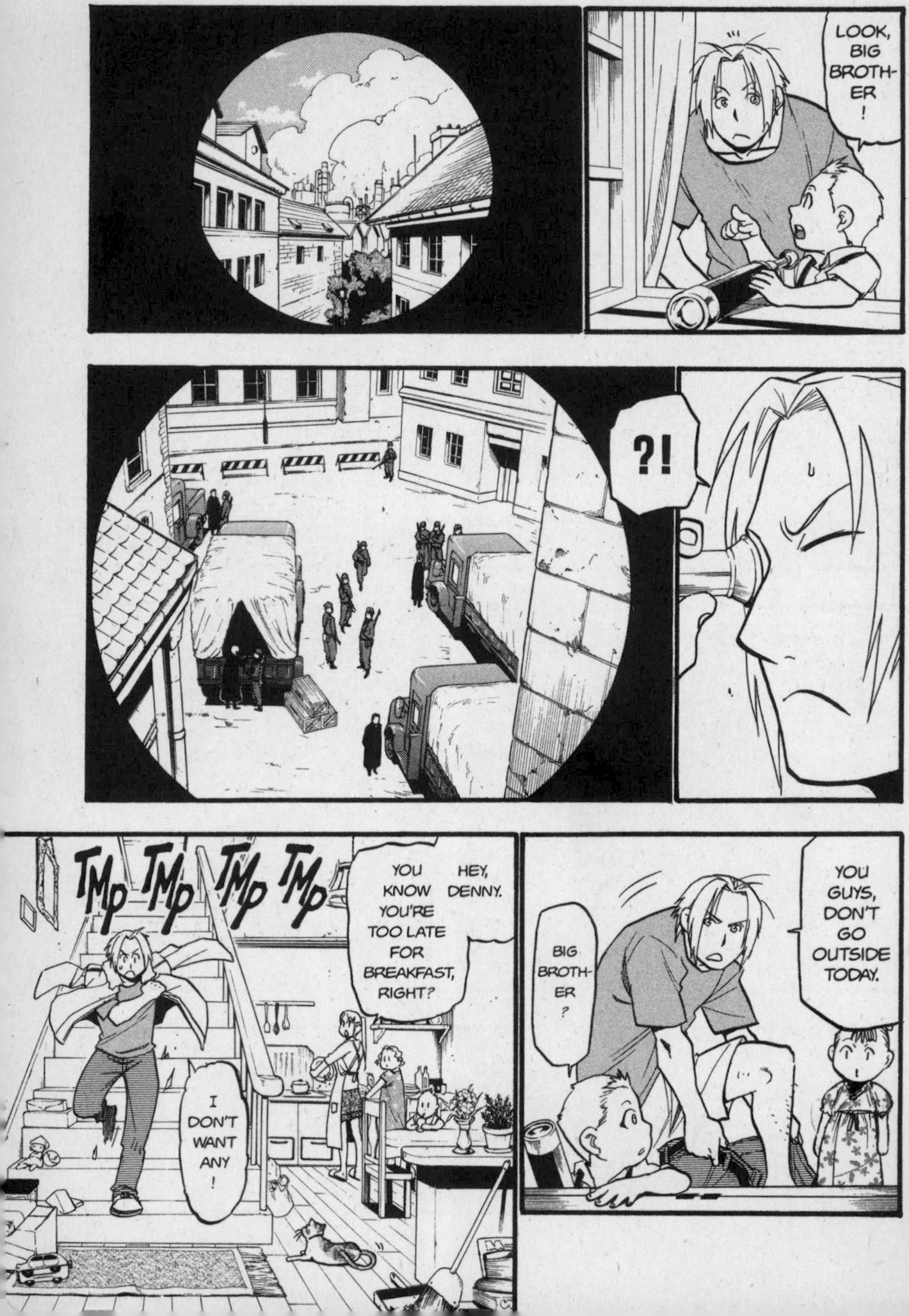
LOOK, BIG BROTH-ER!
?!
YOU GUYS, DON'T GO OUTSIDE TODAY.
BIG BROTH-ER?
HEY, DENNY.
YOU KNOW YOU'RE TOO LATE FOR BREAKFAST, RIGHT?
TMP TMP TMP TMP
I DON'T WANT ANY!

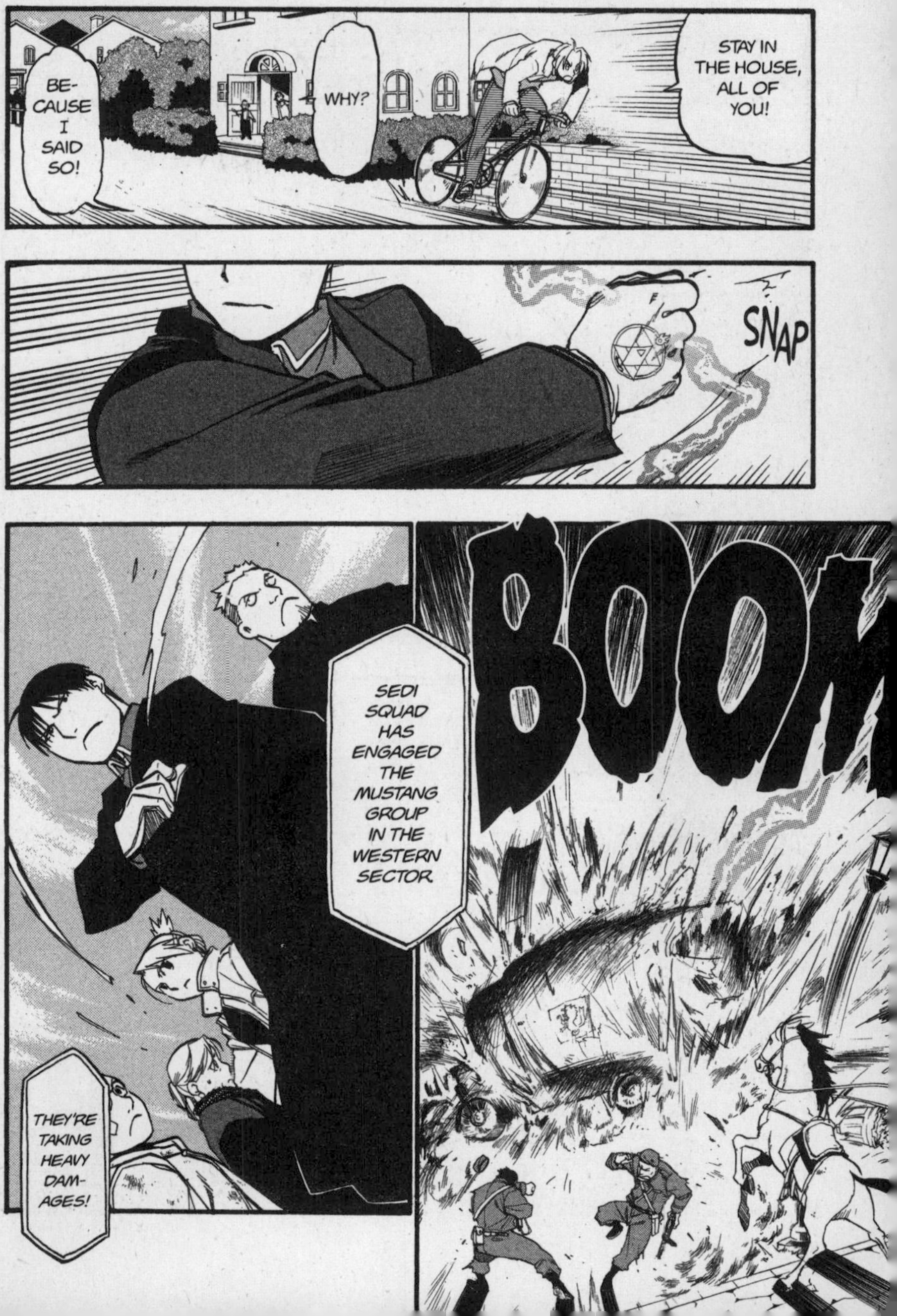
STAY IN THE HOUSE, ALL OF YOU!
WHY?
BE-CAUSE I SAID SO!
SNAP
BOOM
SEDI SQUAD HAS ENGAGED THE MUSTANG GROUP IN THE WESTERN SECTOR.
THEY'RE TAKING HEAVY DAM-AGES!

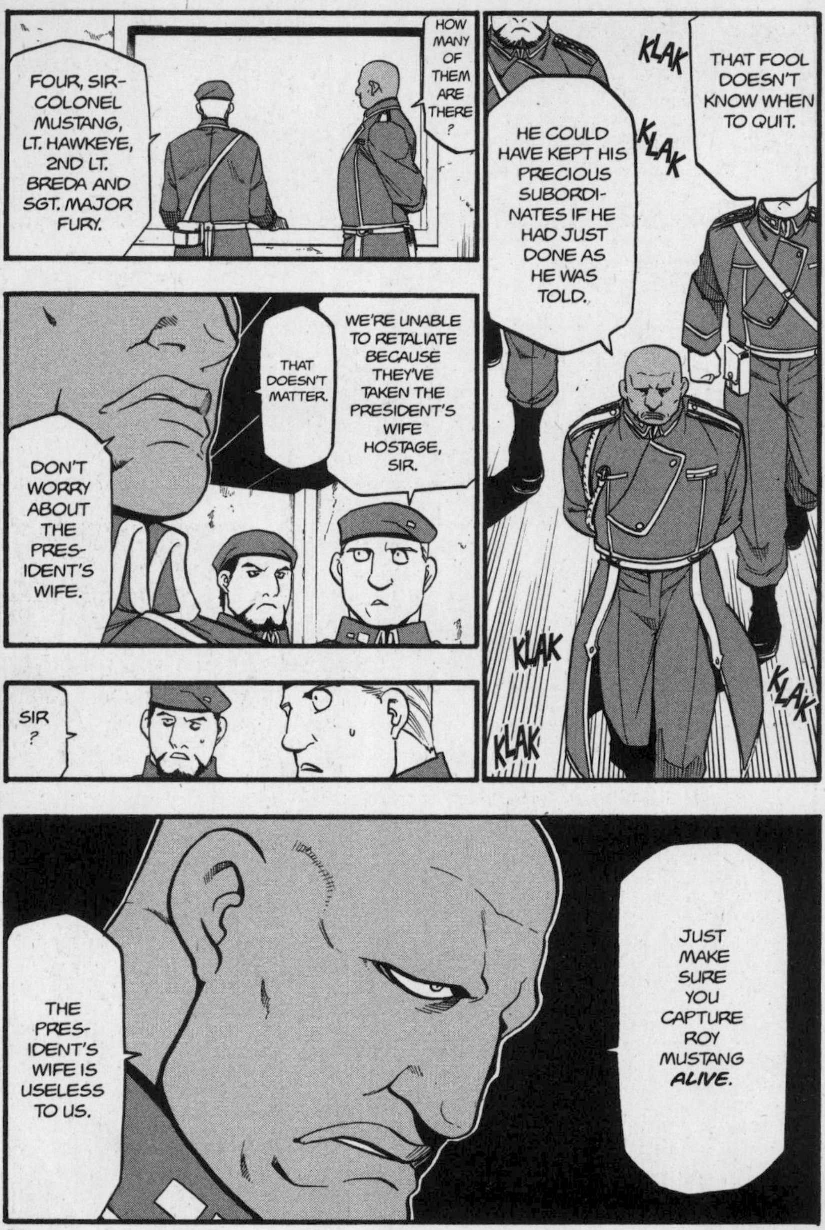

KLAK
THAT FOOL DOESN'T KNOW WHEN TO QUIT.
KLAK
HE COULD HAVE KEPT HIS PRECIOUS SUBORDINATES IF HE HAD JUST DONE AS HE WAS TOLD.
KLAK
KLAK
KLAK
HOW MANY OF THEM ARE THERE?
FOUR, SIR-COLONEL MUSTANG, LT. HAWKEYE, 2ND LT. BREDA AND SGT. MAJOR FURY.
WE'RE UNABLE TO RETALIATE BECAUSE THEY'VE TAKEN THE PRESIDENT'S WIFE HOSTAGE, SIR.
THAT DOESN'T MATTER.
DON'T WORRY ABOUT THE PRESIDENT'S WIFE.
SIR?
JUST MAKE SURE YOU CAPTURE ROY MUSTANG **ALIVE**.
THE PRESIDENT'S WIFE IS USELESS TO US.

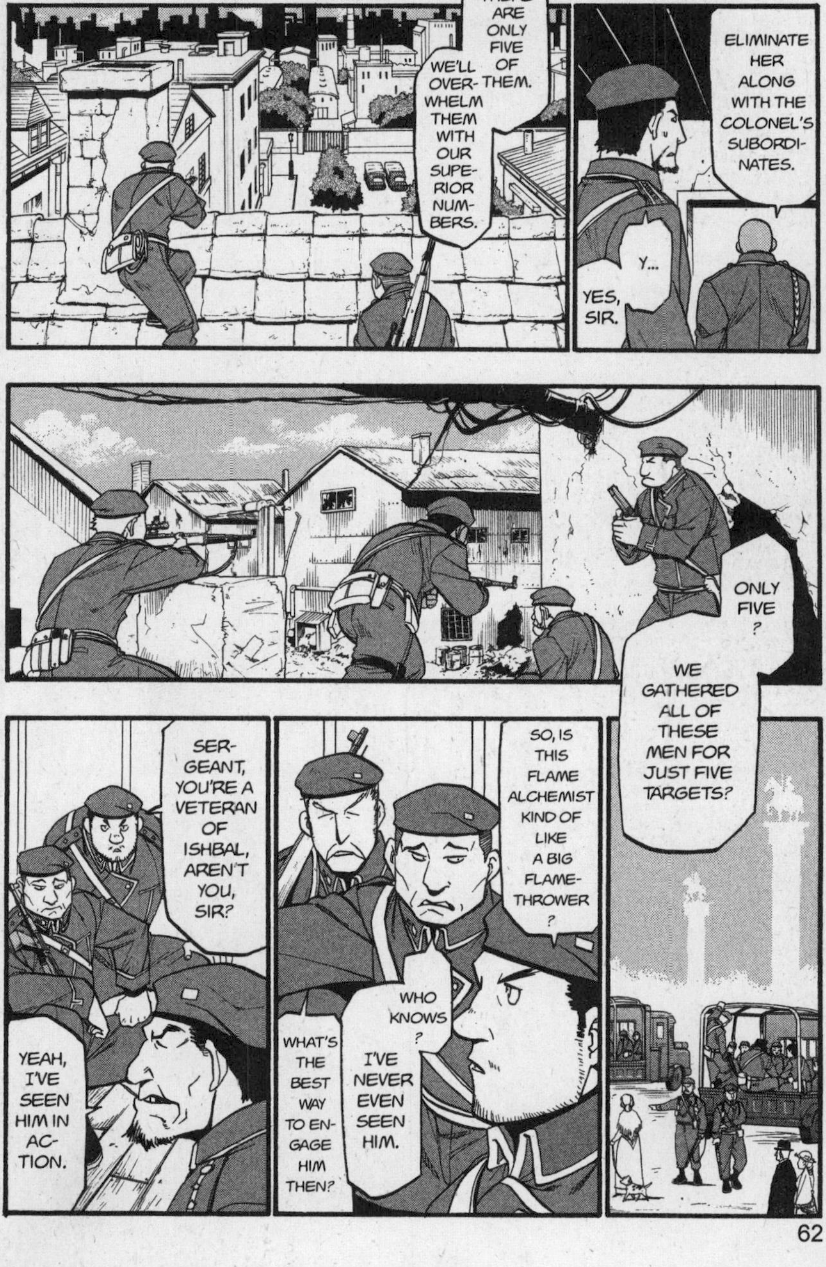
ELIMINATE HER ALONG WITH THE COLONEL'S SUBORDINATES.
Y...
YES, SIR.
THERE ARE ONLY FIVE OF THEM.
WE'LL OVER-WHELM THEM WITH OUR SUPE-RIOR NUM-BERS.
ONLY FIVE ?
WE GATHERED ALL OF THESE MEN FOR JUST FIVE TARGETS?
SO, IS THIS FLAME ALCHEMIST KIND OF LIKE A BIG FLAME-THROWER ?
WHO KNOWS ?
I'VE NEVER EVEN SEEN HIM.
WHAT'S THE BEST WAY TO EN-GAGE HIM THEN?
SER-GEANT, YOU'RE A VETERAN OF ISHBAL, AREN'T YOU, SIR?
YEAH, I'VE SEEN HIM IN AC-TION.

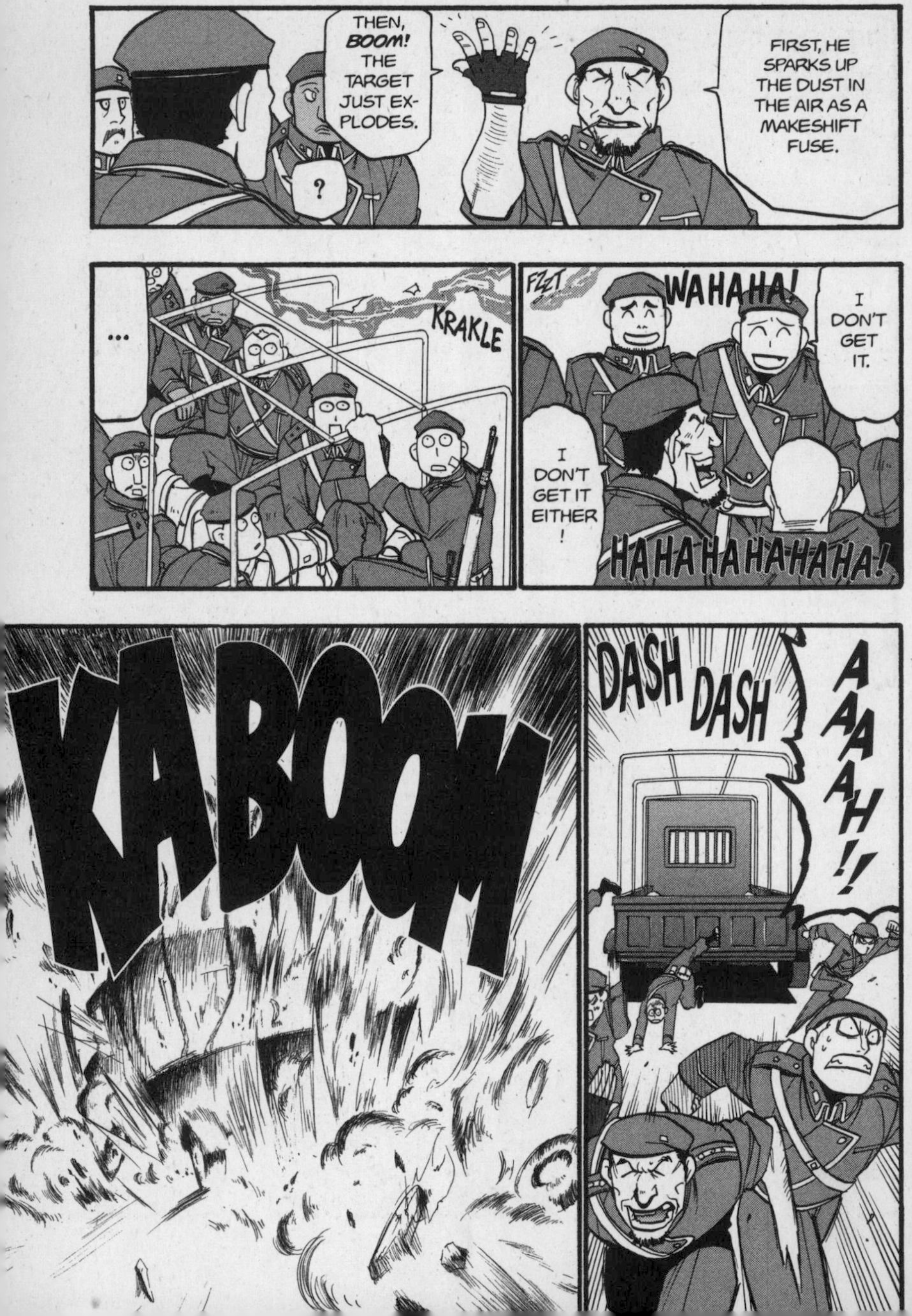
FIRST, HE SPARKS UP THE DUST IN THE AIR AS A MAKESHIFT FUSE.
THEN, *BOOM!* THE TARGET JUST EX-PLODES.
?
I DON'T GET IT.
WAHAHA!
FZZT
I DON'T GET IT EITHER!
HAHAHAHAHAHA!
KRAKLE
...
AAAAH!!
DASH DASH
KABOOM

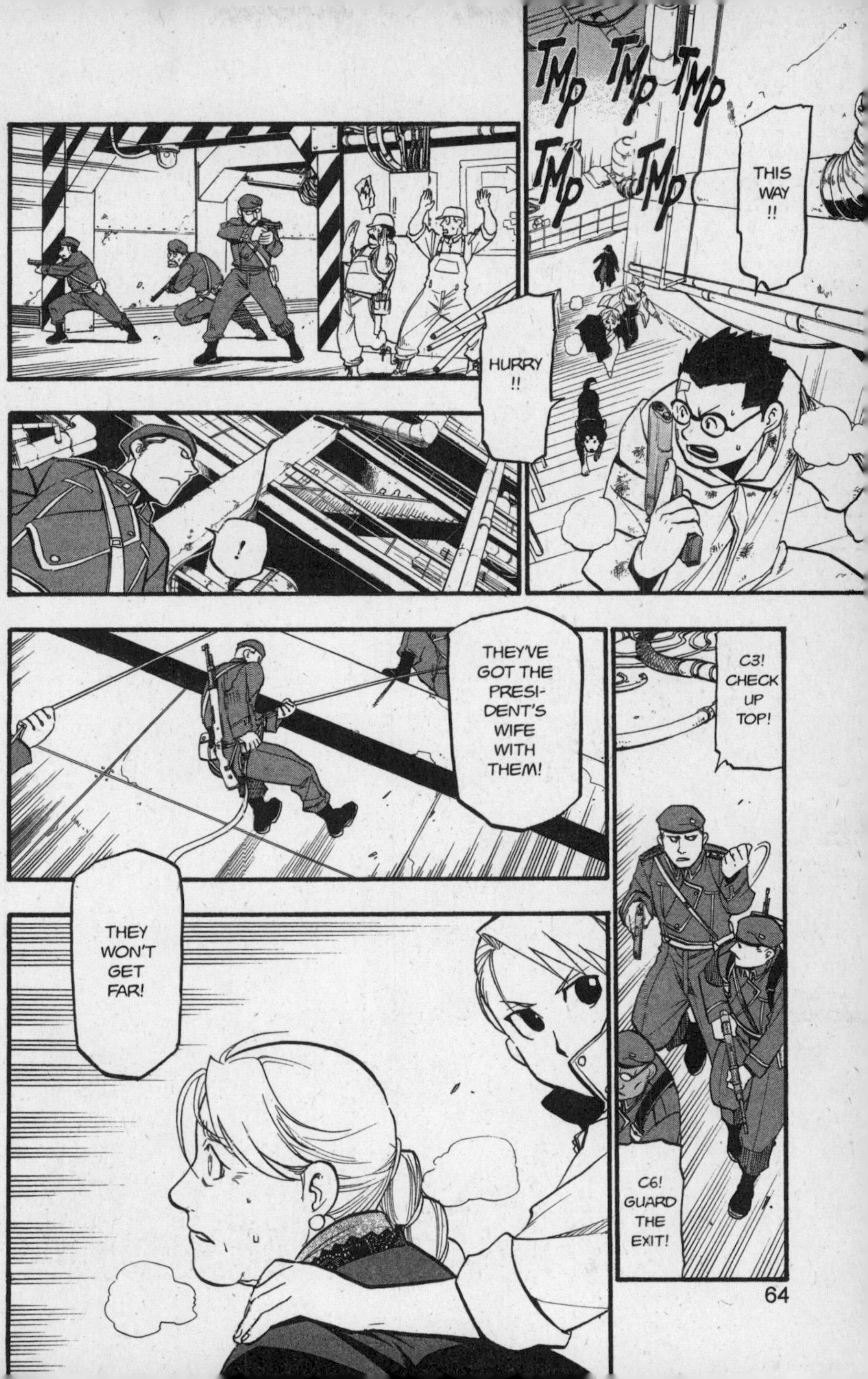
TMP TMP TMP
TMP TMP
THIS WAY !!
HURRY !!
!
C3! CHECK UP TOP!
C6! GUARD THE EXIT!
THEY'VE GOT THE PRESIDENT'S WIFE WITH THEM!
THEY WON'T GET FAR!

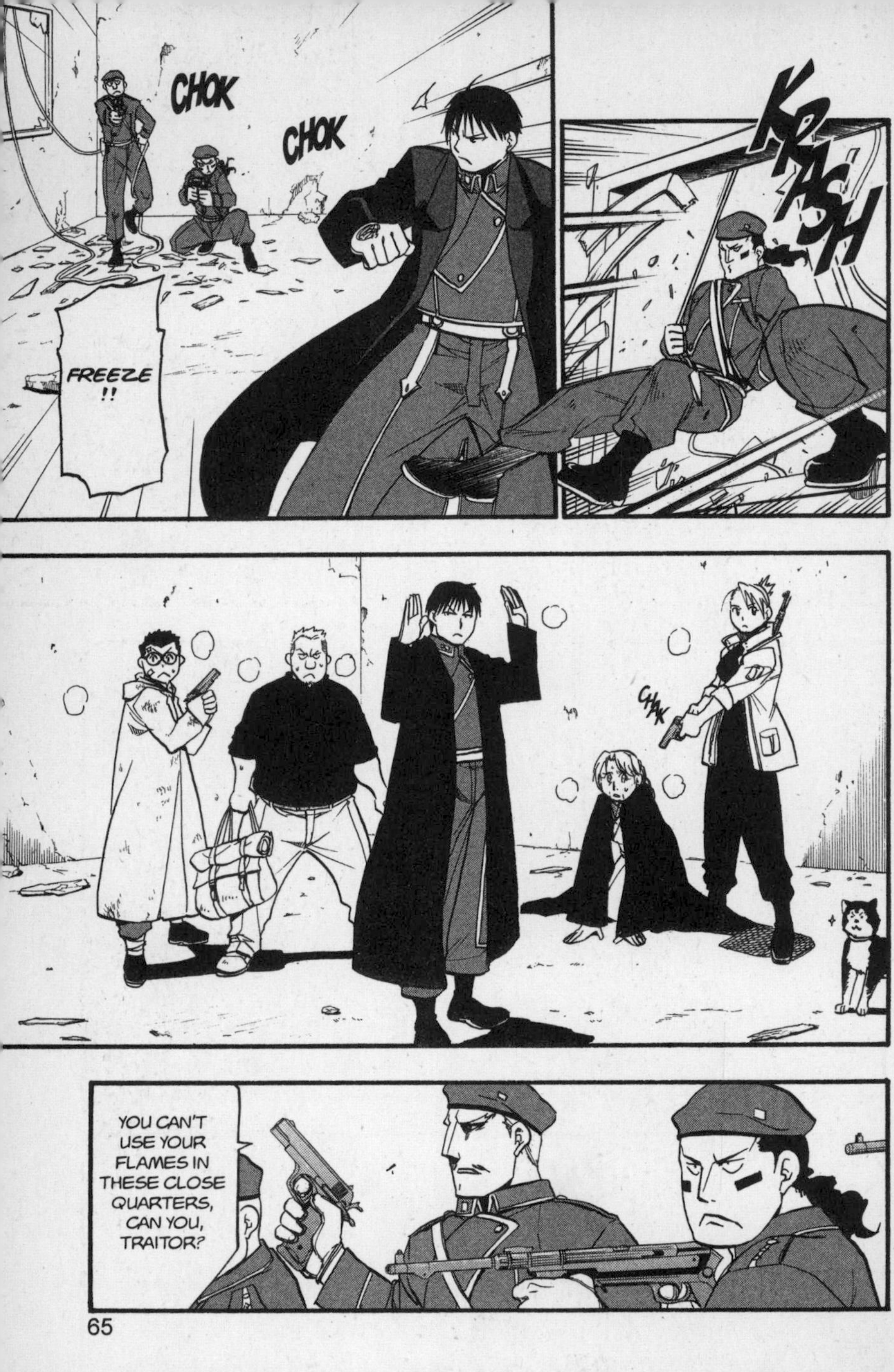
KRASH
CHOK
CHOK
FREEZE !!
CHAK
YOU CAN'T USE YOUR FLAMES IN THESE CLOSE QUARTERS, CAN YOU, TRAITOR?

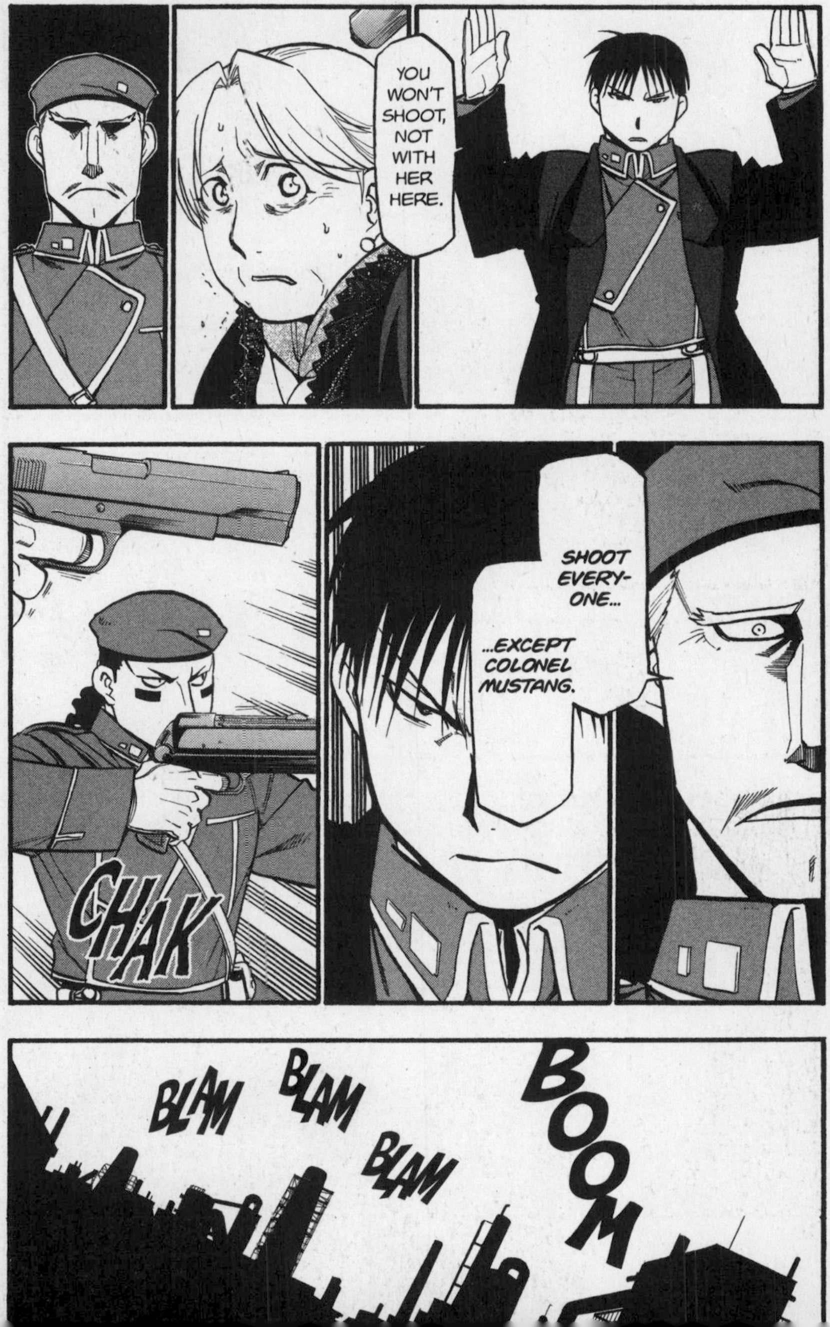
YOU WON'T SHOOT, NOT WITH HER HERE.
SHOOT EVERY-ONE...
...EXCEPT COLONEL MUSTANG.
CHAK
BOOM
BLAM
BLAM
BLAM

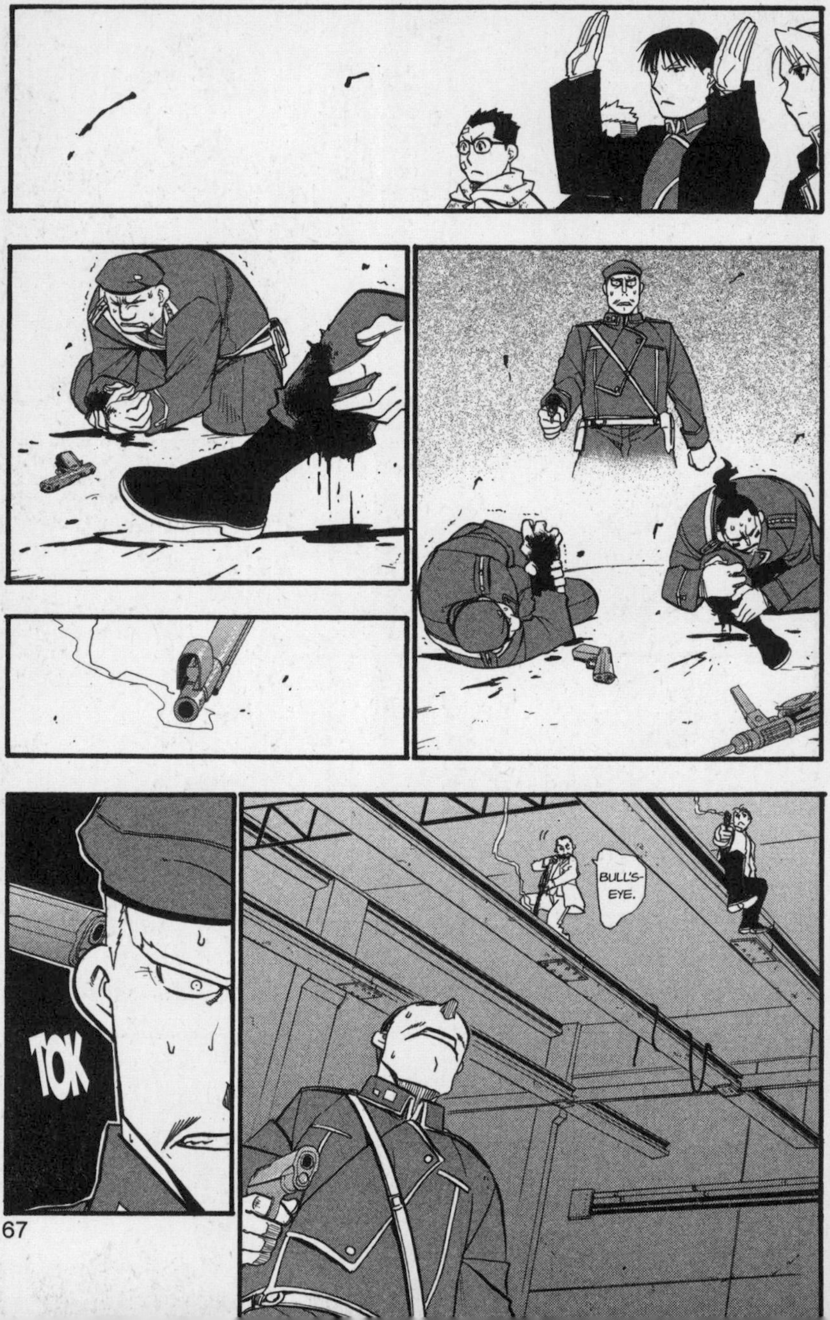
BULL'S-EYE.
TOK

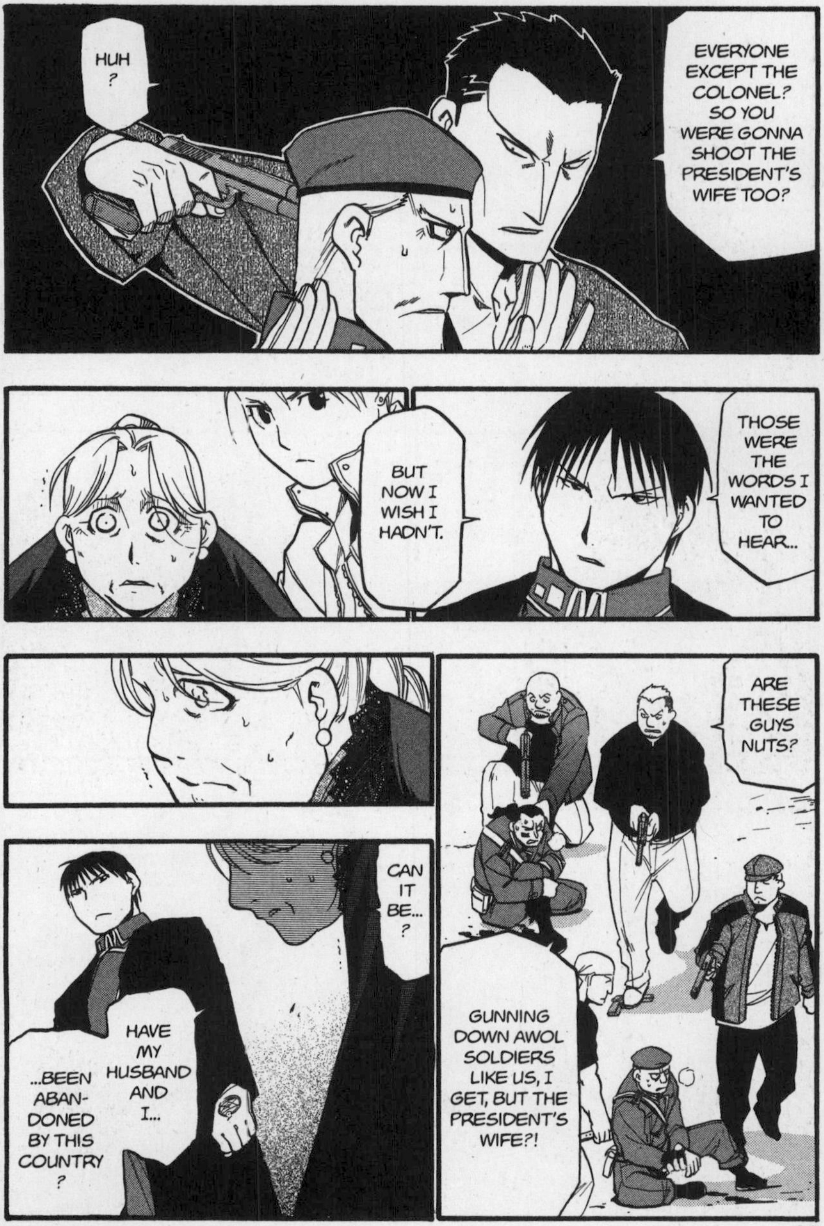
EVERYONE EXCEPT THE COLONEL? SO YOU WERE GONNA SHOOT THE PRESIDENT'S WIFE TOO?
HUH ?
THOSE WERE THE WORDS I WANTED TO HEAR...
BUT NOW I WISH I HADN'T.
ARE THESE GUYS NUTS?
GUNNING DOWN AWOL SOLDIERS LIKE US, I GET, BUT THE PRESIDENT'S WIFE?!
CAN IT BE... ?
HAVE MY HUSBAND AND I...
...BEEN ABAN- DONED BY THIS COUNTRY ?

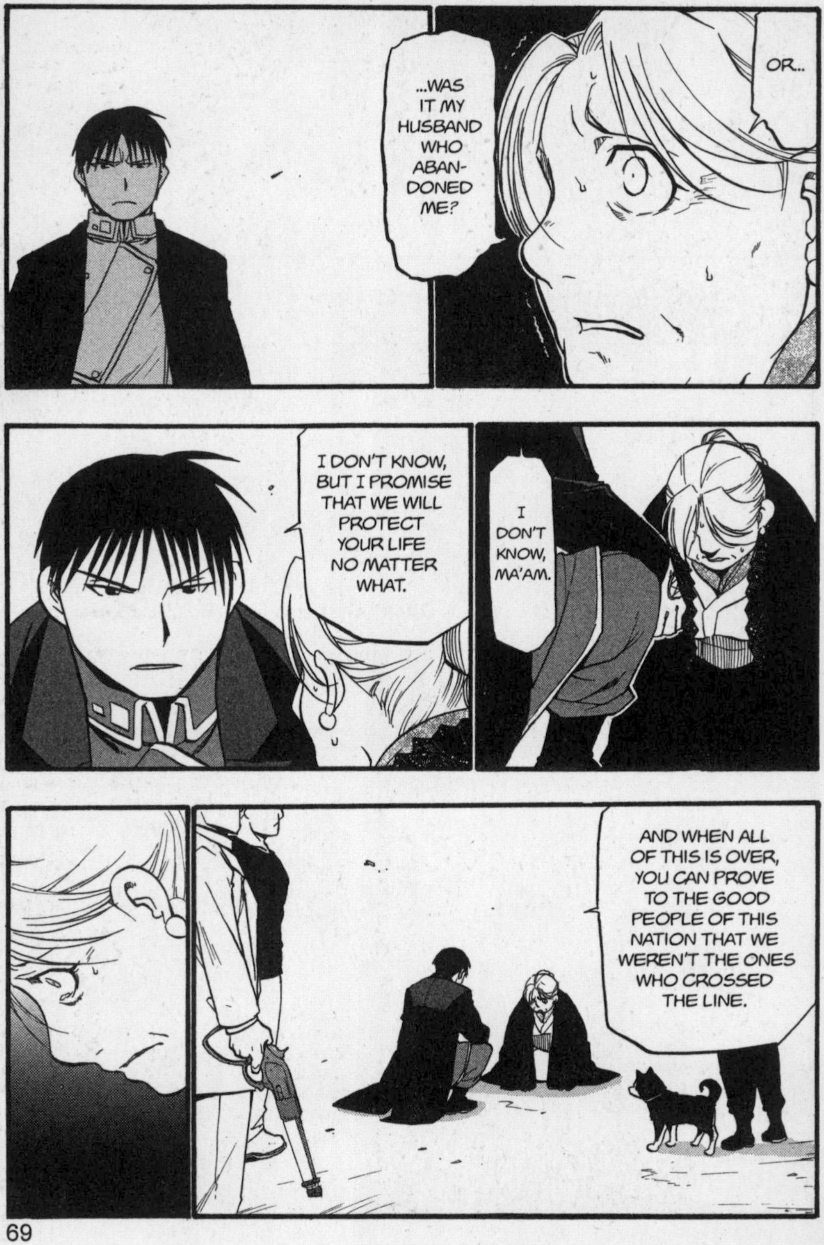
OR...
...WAS IT MY HUSBAND WHO ABANDONED ME?
I DON'T KNOW, MA'AM.
I DON'T KNOW, BUT I PROMISE THAT WE WILL PROTECT YOUR LIFE NO MATTER WHAT.
AND WHEN ALL OF THIS IS OVER, YOU CAN PROVE TO THE GOOD PEOPLE OF THIS NATION THAT WE WEREN'T THE ONES WHO CROSSED THE LINE.

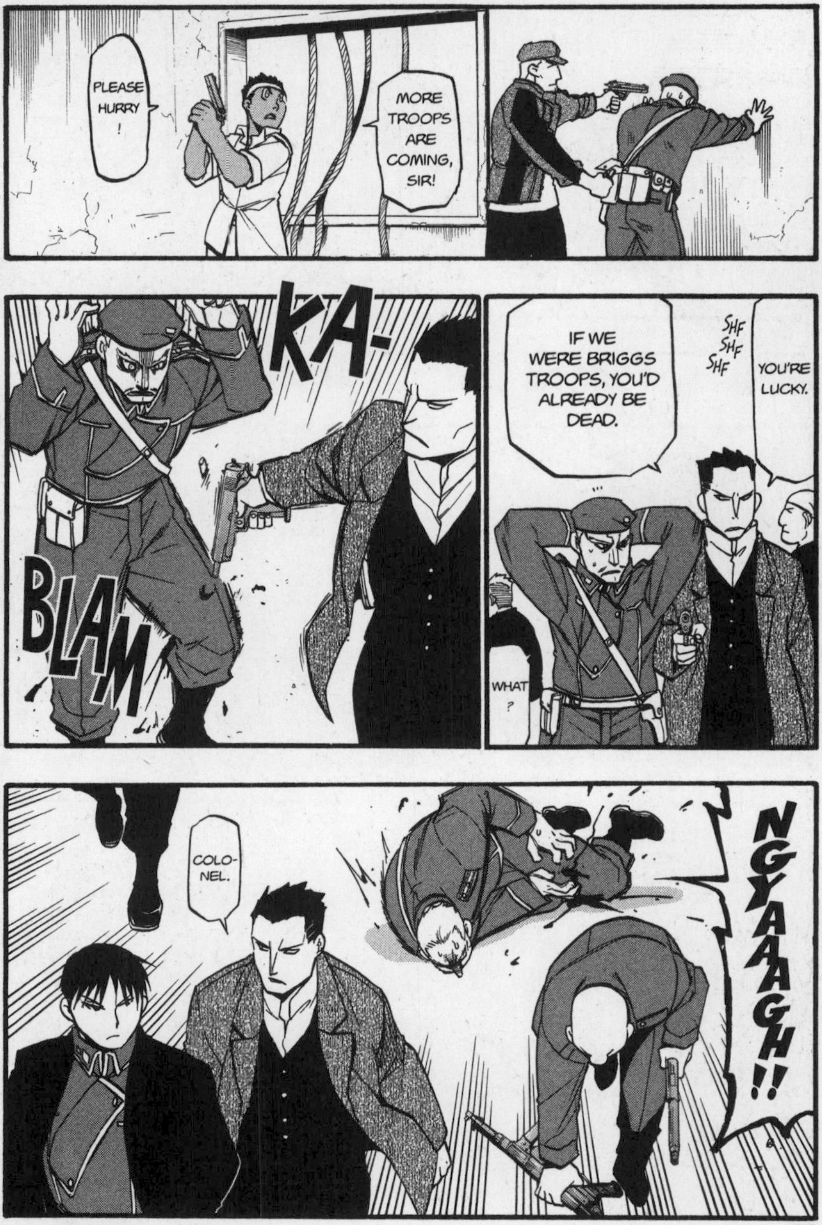
MORE TROOPS ARE COMING, SIR!
PLEASE HURRY!
YOU'RE LUCKY.
SHF SHF SHF
IF WE WERE BRIGGS TROOPS, YOU'D ALREADY BE DEAD.
WHAT?
KA-
BLAM
NGYAAAGH!!
COLONEL.

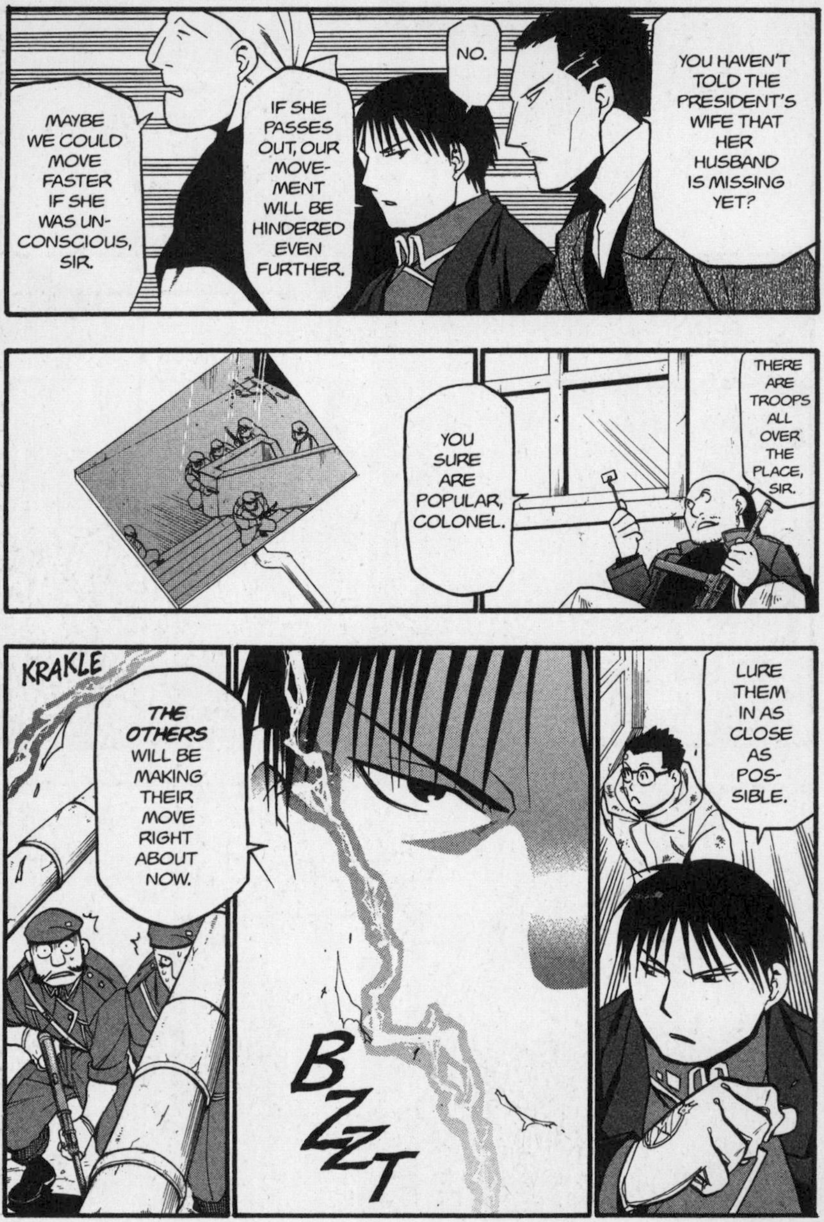
YOU HAVEN'T TOLD THE PRESIDENT'S WIFE THAT HER HUSBAND IS MISSING YET?
NO.
IF SHE PASSES OUT, OUR MOVEMENT WILL BE HINDERED EVEN FURTHER.
MAYBE WE COULD MOVE FASTER IF SHE WAS UNCONSCIOUS, SIR.
THERE ARE TROOPS ALL OVER THE PLACE, SIR.
YOU SURE ARE POPULAR, COLONEL.
LURE THEM IN AS CLOSE AS POSSIBLE.
BZZT
KRAKLE
THE OTHERS WILL BE MAKING THEIR MOVE RIGHT ABOUT NOW.

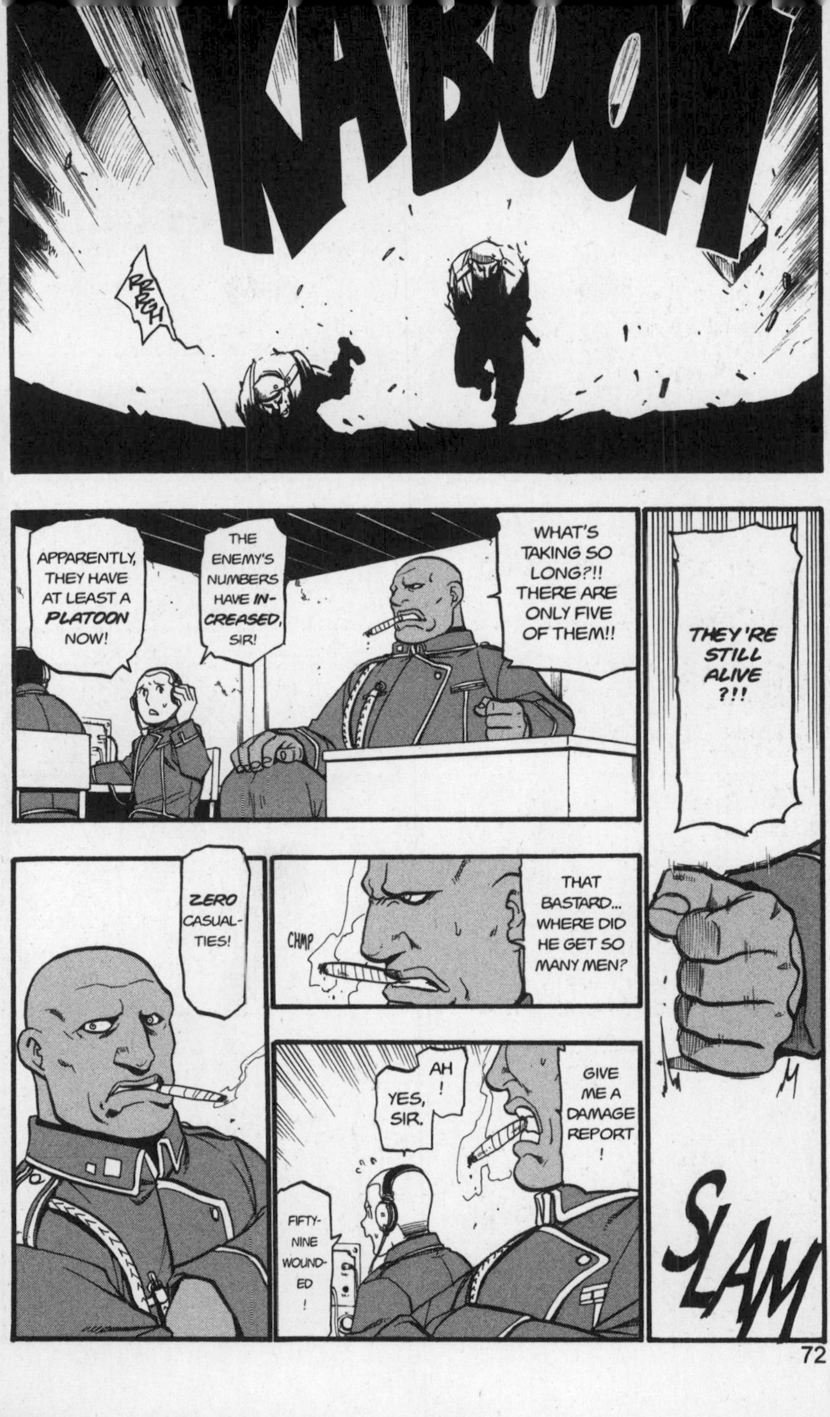
KABOOM
RRRGH
THEY'RE STILL ALIVE?!!
SLAM
WHAT'S TAKING SO LONG?!! THERE ARE ONLY FIVE OF THEM!!
THE ENEMY'S NUMBERS HAVE INCREASED, SIR!
APPARENTLY, THEY HAVE AT LEAST A PLATOON NOW!
THAT BASTARD... WHERE DID HE GET SO MANY MEN?
CHMP
GIVE ME A DAMAGE REPORT!
AH! YES, SIR.
FIFTY-NINE WOUNDED!
ZERO CASUALTIES!

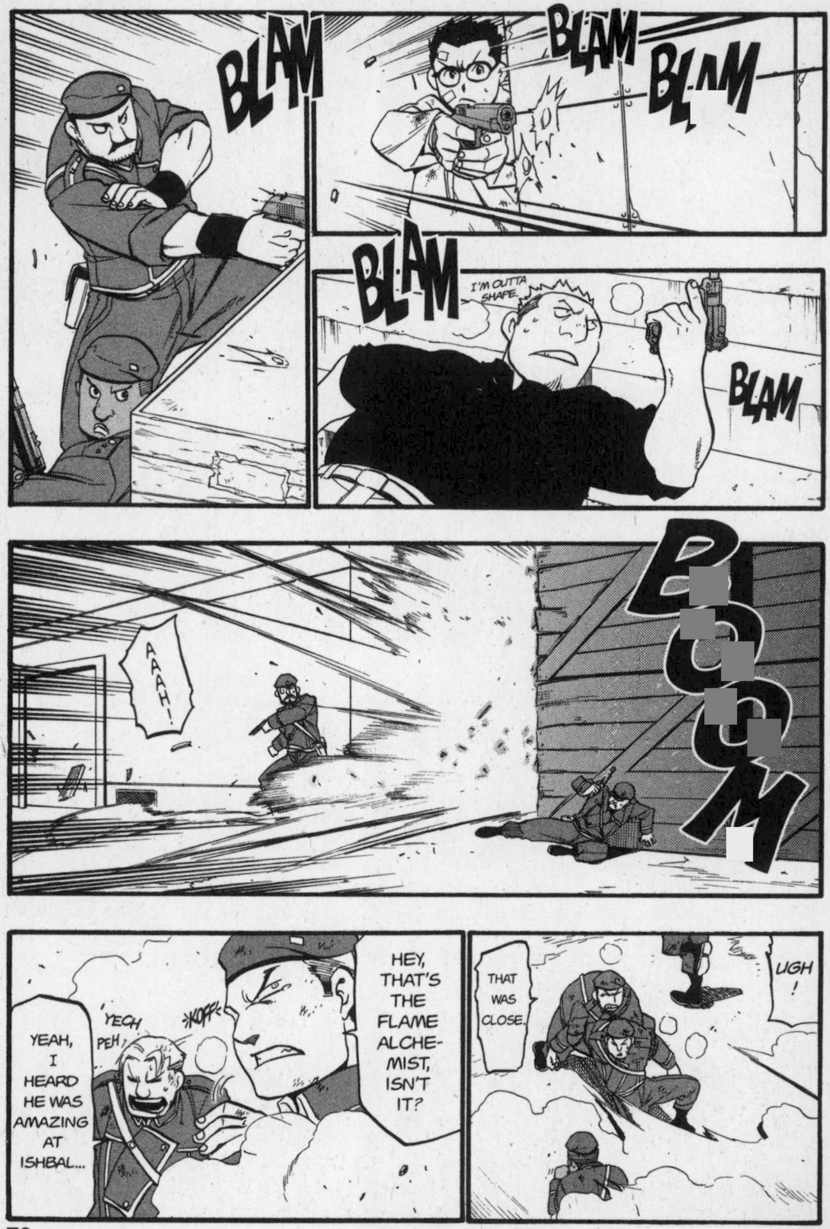
BLAM
BLAM
BLAM
I'M OUTTA SHAPE.
BLAM
BLAM
BOOM
AAAH!
UGH!
THAT WAS CLOSE.
HEY, THAT'S THE FLAME ALCHEMIST, ISN'T IT?
KOFF
YECH
PEH
YEAH, I HEARD HE WAS AMAZING AT ISHBAL...

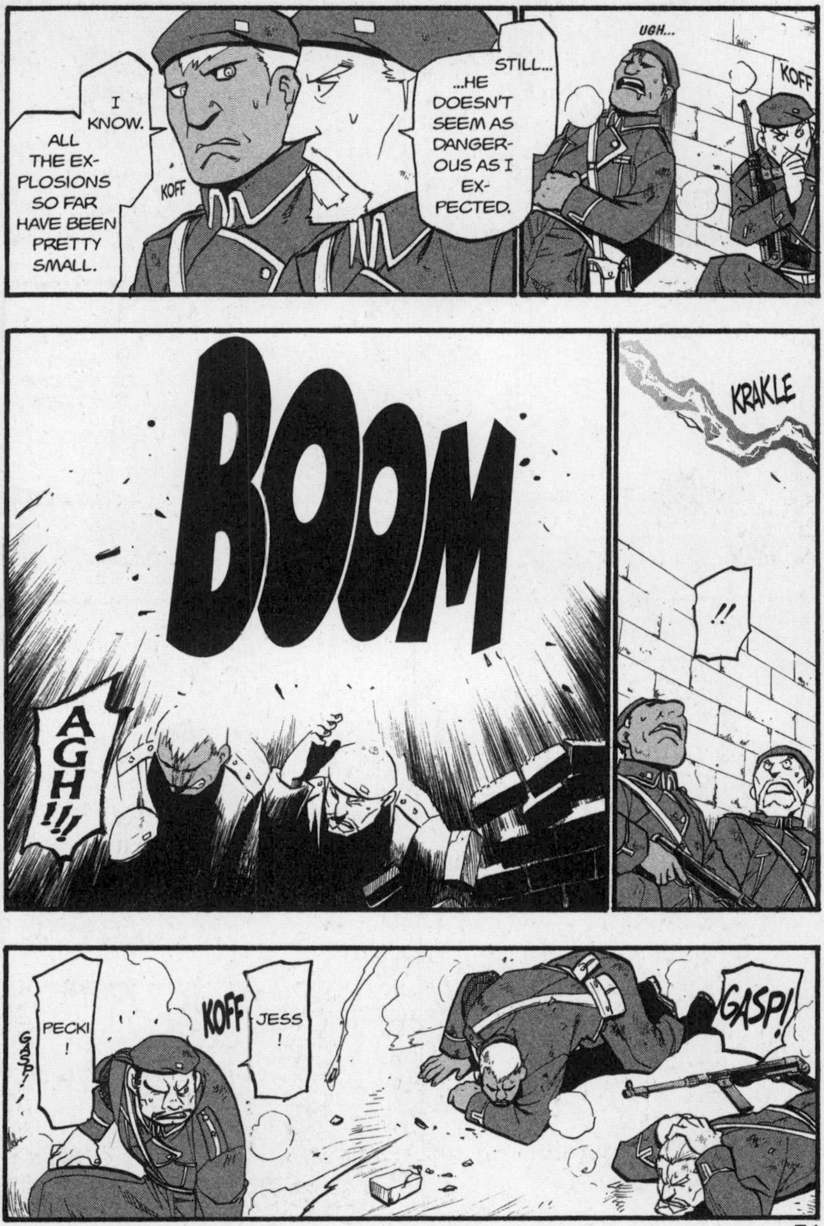

UGH...
KOFF
STILL...
...HE DOESN'T SEEM AS DANGEROUS AS I EXPECTED.
I KNOW.
ALL THE EXPLOSIONS SO FAR HAVE BEEN PRETTY SMALL.
KOFF
KRAKLE
!!
BOOM
AGH!!!
GASP!
JESS!
KOFF
PECKI!
GASP!

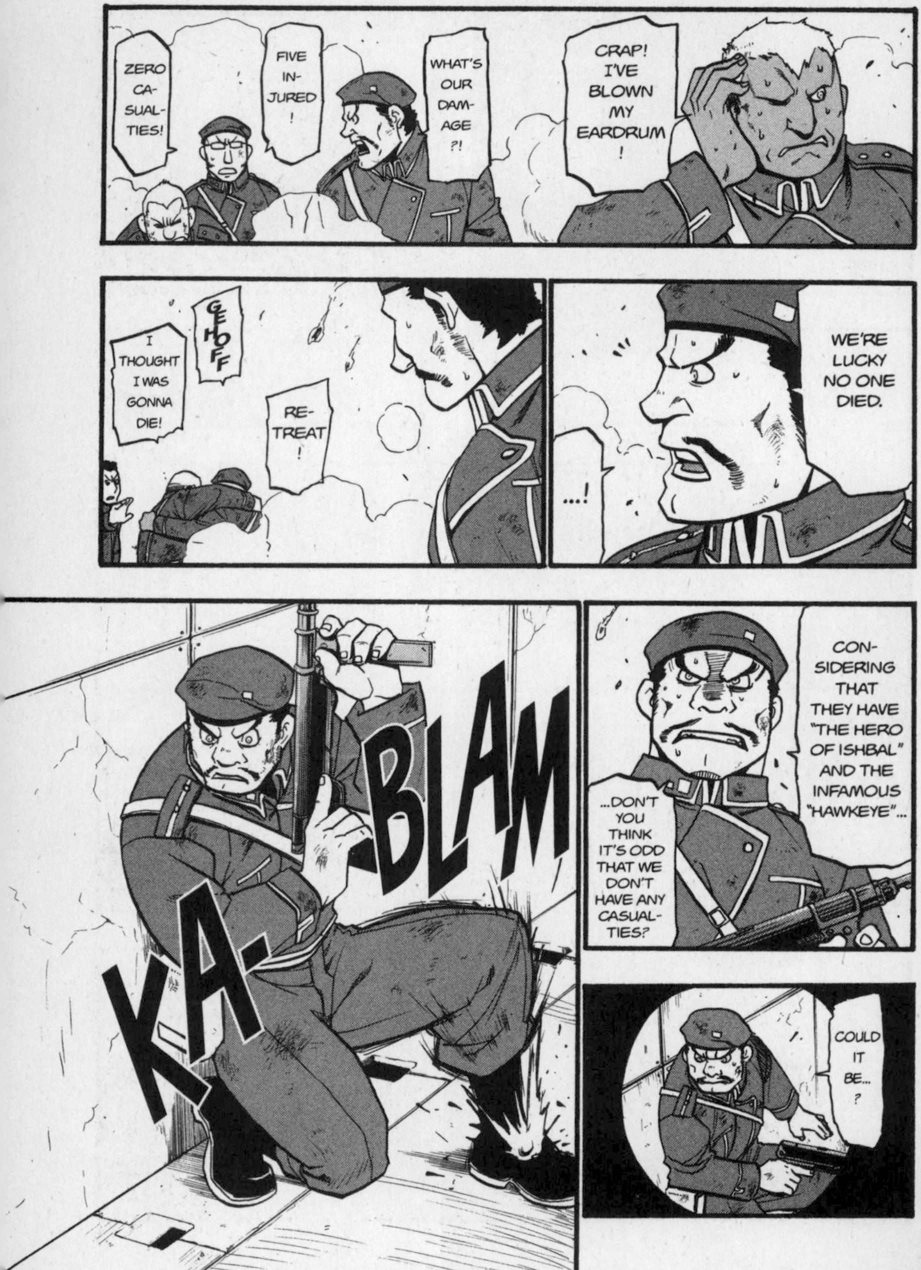
CRAP! I'VE BLOWN MY EARDRUM!
WHAT'S OUR DAMAGE?!
FIVE INJURED!
ZERO CASUALTIES!
WE'RE LUCKY NO ONE DIED.
...!
GEHOFF
I THOUGHT I WAS GONNA DIE!
RETREAT!
CONSIDERING THAT THEY HAVE "THE HERO OF ISHBAL" AND THE INFAMOUS "HAWKEYE"...
...DON'T YOU THINK IT'S ODD THAT WE DON'T HAVE ANY CASUALTIES?
COULD IT BE...?
BLAM
KA-

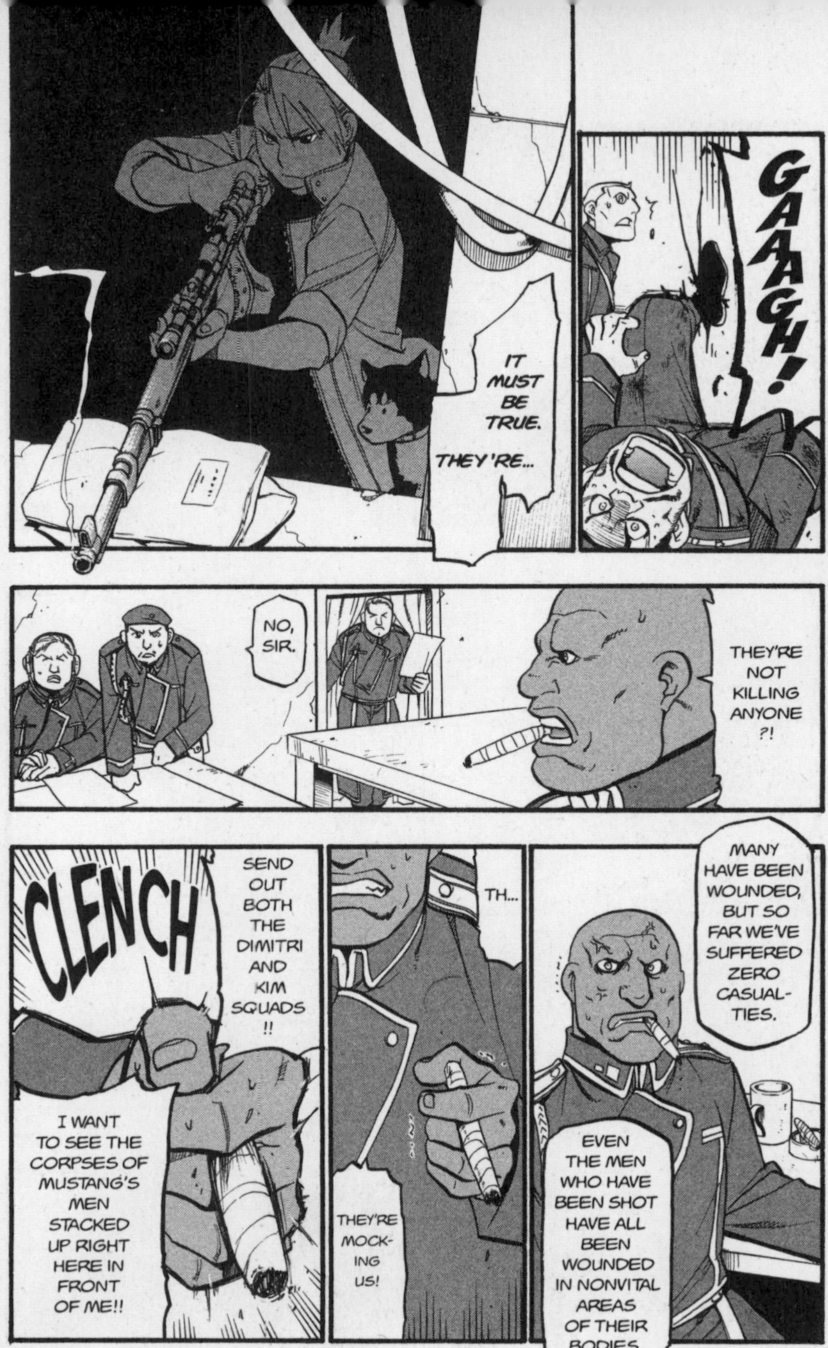
GAAAGH!
IT MUST BE TRUE.
THEY'RE...
THEY'RE NOT KILLING ANYONE?!
NO, SIR.
MANY HAVE BEEN WOUNDED, BUT SO FAR WE'VE SUFFERED ZERO CASUAL-TIES.
EVEN THE MEN WHO HAVE BEEN SHOT HAVE ALL BEEN WOUNDED IN NONVITAL AREAS OF THEIR BODIES.
TH...
THEY'RE MOCK-ING US!
SEND OUT BOTH THE DIMITRI AND KIM SQUADS!!
CLENCH
I WANT TO SEE THE CORPSES OF MUSTANG'S MEN STACKED UP RIGHT HERE IN FRONT OF ME!!

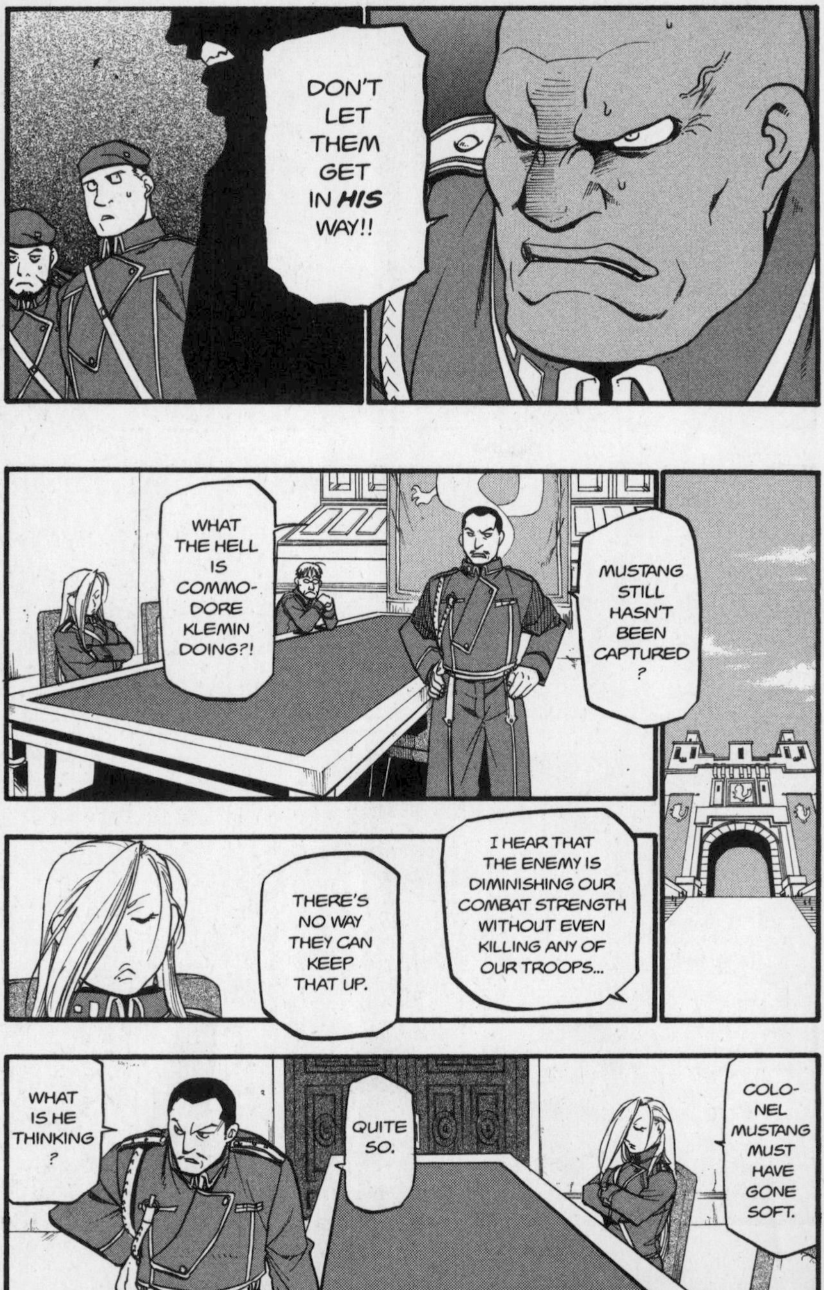
DON'T LET THEM GET IN HIS WAY!!
MUSTANG STILL HASN'T BEEN CAPTURED?
WHAT THE HELL IS COMMODORE KLEMIN DOING?!
I HEAR THAT THE ENEMY IS DIMINISHING OUR COMBAT STRENGTH WITHOUT EVEN KILLING ANY OF OUR TROOPS...
THERE'S NO WAY THEY CAN KEEP THAT UP.
COLONEL MUSTANG MUST HAVE GONE SOFT.
QUITE SO.
WHAT IS HE THINKING?

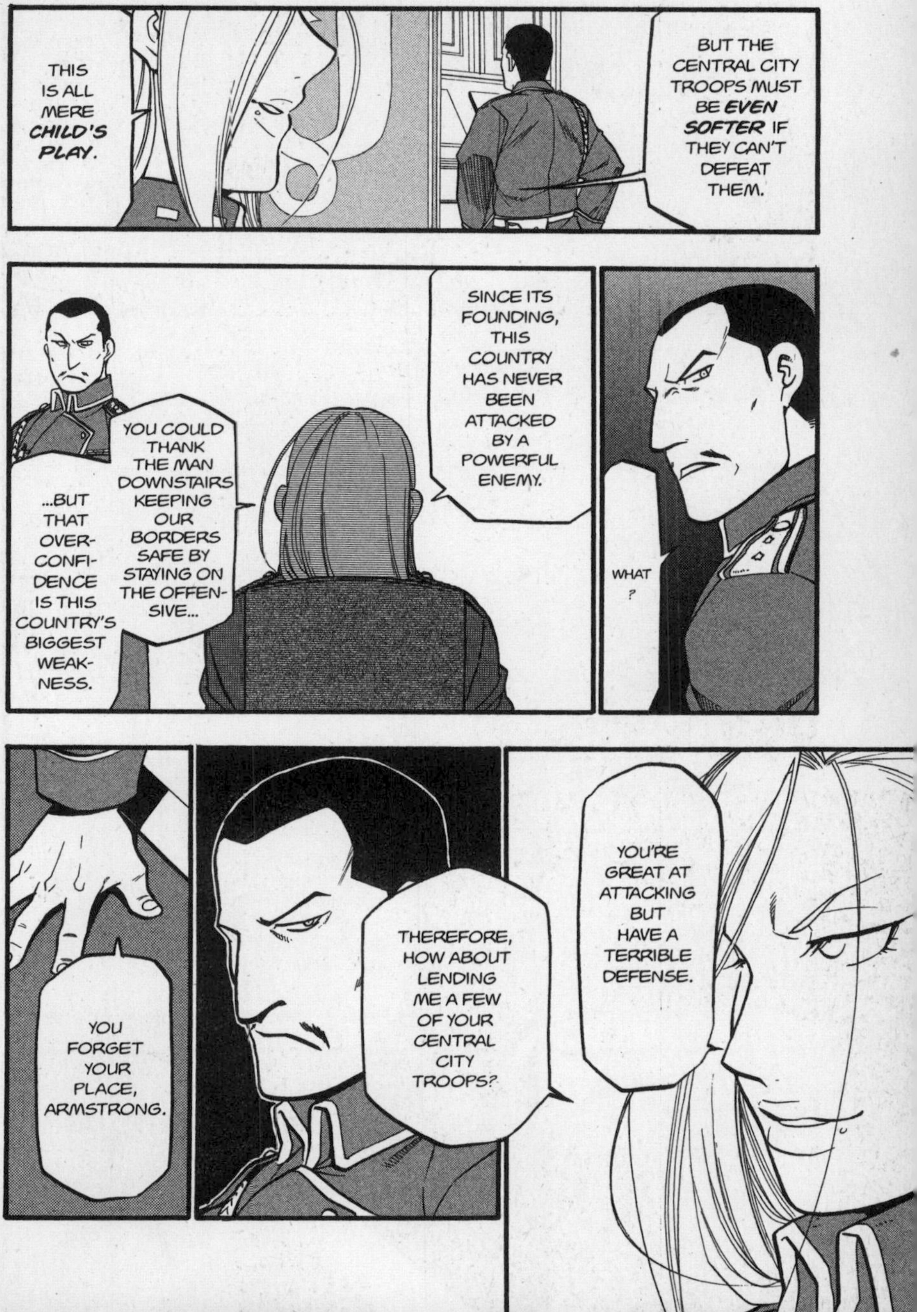
BUT THE CENTRAL CITY TROOPS MUST BE EVEN SOFTER IF THEY CAN'T DEFEAT THEM.
THIS IS ALL MERE CHILD'S PLAY.
WHAT?
SINCE ITS FOUNDING, THIS COUNTRY HAS NEVER BEEN ATTACKED BY A POWERFUL ENEMY.
YOU COULD THANK THE MAN DOWNSTAIRS KEEPING OUR BORDERS SAFE BY STAYING ON THE OFFEN-SIVE...
...BUT THAT OVER-CONFI-DENCE IS THIS COUNTRY'S BIGGEST WEAK-NESS.
YOU'RE GREAT AT ATTACKING BUT HAVE A TERRIBLE DEFENSE.
THEREFORE, HOW ABOUT LENDING ME A FEW OF YOUR CENTRAL CITY TROOPS?
YOU FORGET YOUR PLACE, ARMSTRONG.

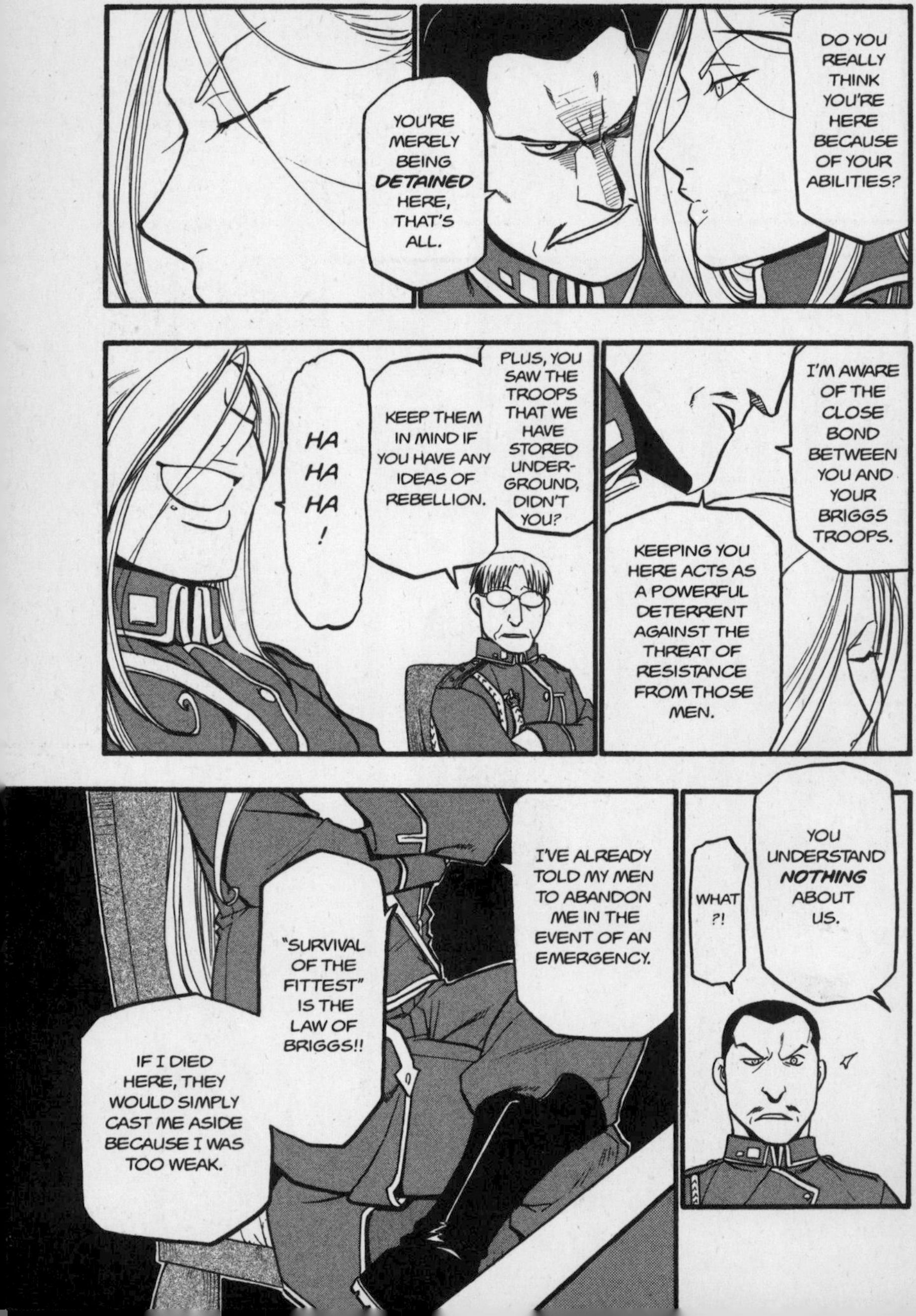
DO YOU REALLY THINK YOU'RE HERE BECAUSE OF YOUR ABILITIES?
YOU'RE MERELY BEING DETAINED HERE, THAT'S ALL.
I'M AWARE OF THE CLOSE BOND BETWEEN YOU AND YOUR BRIGGS TROOPS.
KEEPING YOU HERE ACTS AS A POWERFUL DETERRENT AGAINST THE THREAT OF RESISTANCE FROM THOSE MEN.
PLUS, YOU SAW THE TROOPS THAT WE HAVE STORED UNDERGROUND, DIDN'T YOU?
KEEP THEM IN MIND IF YOU HAVE ANY IDEAS OF REBELLION.
HA HA HA!
YOU UNDERSTAND NOTHING ABOUT US.
WHAT?!
I'VE ALREADY TOLD MY MEN TO ABANDON ME IN THE EVENT OF AN EMERGENCY.
"SURVIVAL OF THE FITTEST" IS THE LAW OF BRIGGS!!
IF I DIED HERE, THEY WOULD SIMPLY CAST ME ASIDE BECAUSE I WAS TOO WEAK.

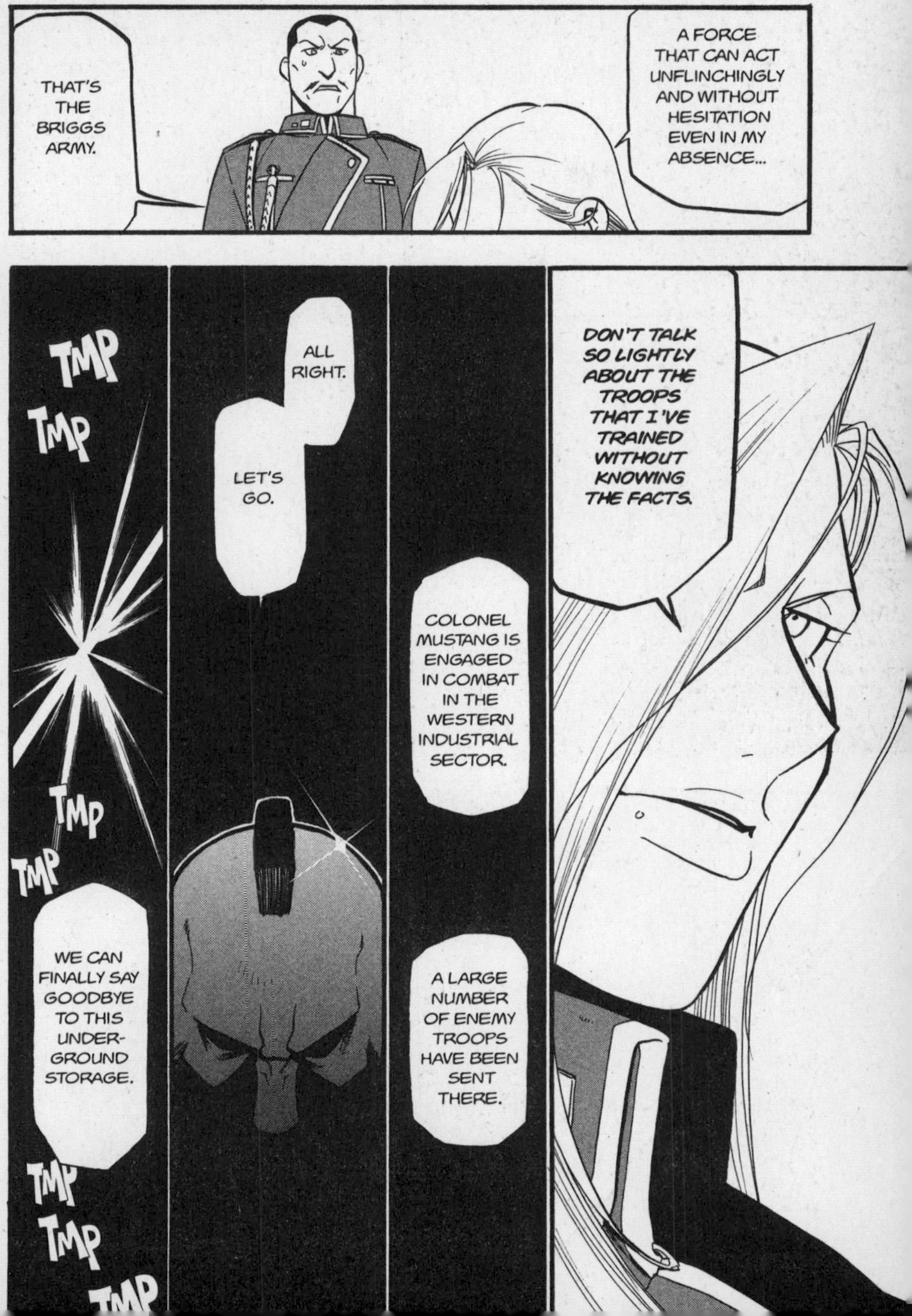
A FORCE THAT CAN ACT UNFLINCHINGLY AND WITHOUT HESITATION EVEN IN MY ABSENCE...
THAT'S THE BRIGGS ARMY.
DON'T TALK SO LIGHTLY ABOUT THE TROOPS THAT I'VE TRAINED WITHOUT KNOWING THE FACTS.
COLONEL MUSTANG IS ENGAGED IN COMBAT IN THE WESTERN INDUSTRIAL SECTOR.
A LARGE NUMBER OF ENEMY TROOPS HAVE BEEN SENT THERE.
ALL RIGHT.
LET'S GO.
TMP
TMP
TMP
TMP
WE CAN FINALLY SAY GOODBYE TO THIS UNDER-GROUND STORAGE.
TMP
TMP
TMP

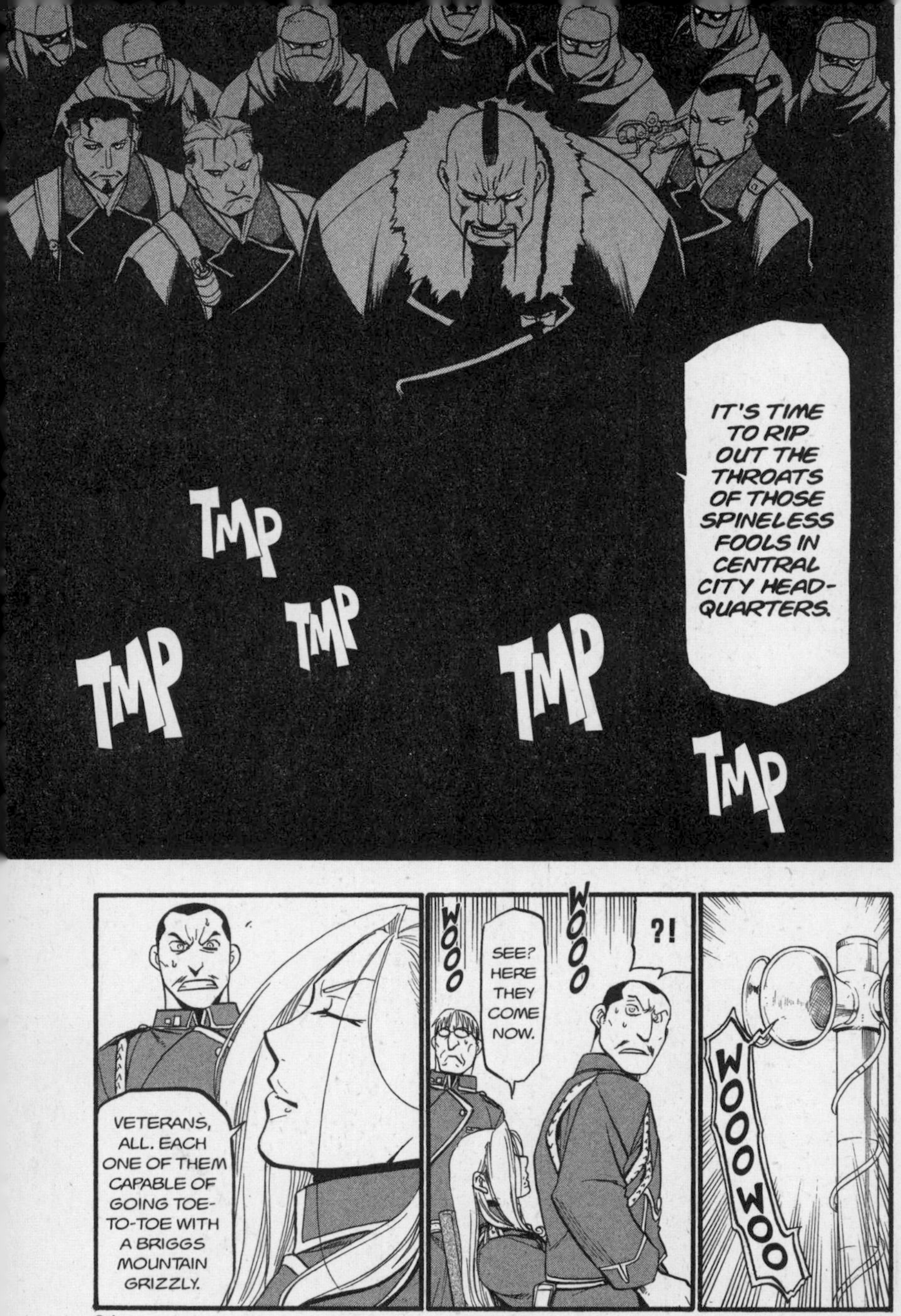
IT'S TIME TO RIP OUT THE THROATS OF THOSE SPINELESS FOOLS IN CENTRAL CITY HEAD-QUARTERS.
TMP
TMP
TMP
TMP
TMP
WOOO WOO
?!
WOOO
SEE? HERE THEY COME NOW.
WOOO
VETERANS, ALL. EACH ONE OF THEM CAPABLE OF GOING TOE-TO-TOE WITH A BRIGGS MOUNTAIN GRIZZLY.

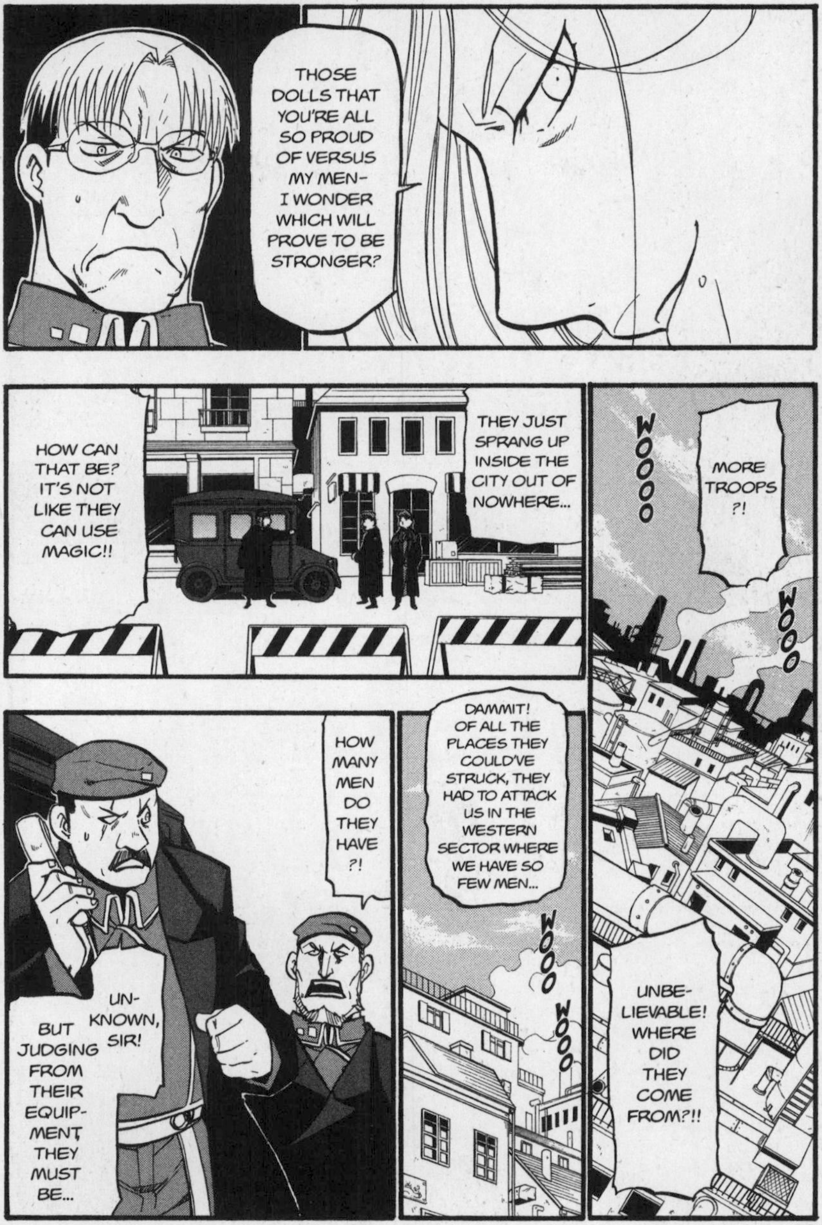
THOSE DOLLS THAT YOU'RE ALL SO PROUD OF VERSUS MY MEN- I WONDER WHICH WILL PROVE TO BE STRONGER?
WOOOO
MORE TROOPS?!
WOOO
UNBE-LIEVABLE! WHERE DID THEY COME FROM?!!
THEY JUST SPRANG UP INSIDE THE CITY OUT OF NOWHERE...
HOW CAN THAT BE? IT'S NOT LIKE THEY CAN USE MAGIC!!
DAMMIT! OF ALL THE PLACES THEY COULD'VE STRUCK, THEY HAD TO ATTACK US IN THE WESTERN SECTOR WHERE WE HAVE SO FEW MEN...
WOOO
WOOO
HOW MANY MEN DO THEY HAVE?!
UN-KNOWN, SIR!
BUT JUDGING FROM THEIR EQUIP-MENT, THEY MUST BE...

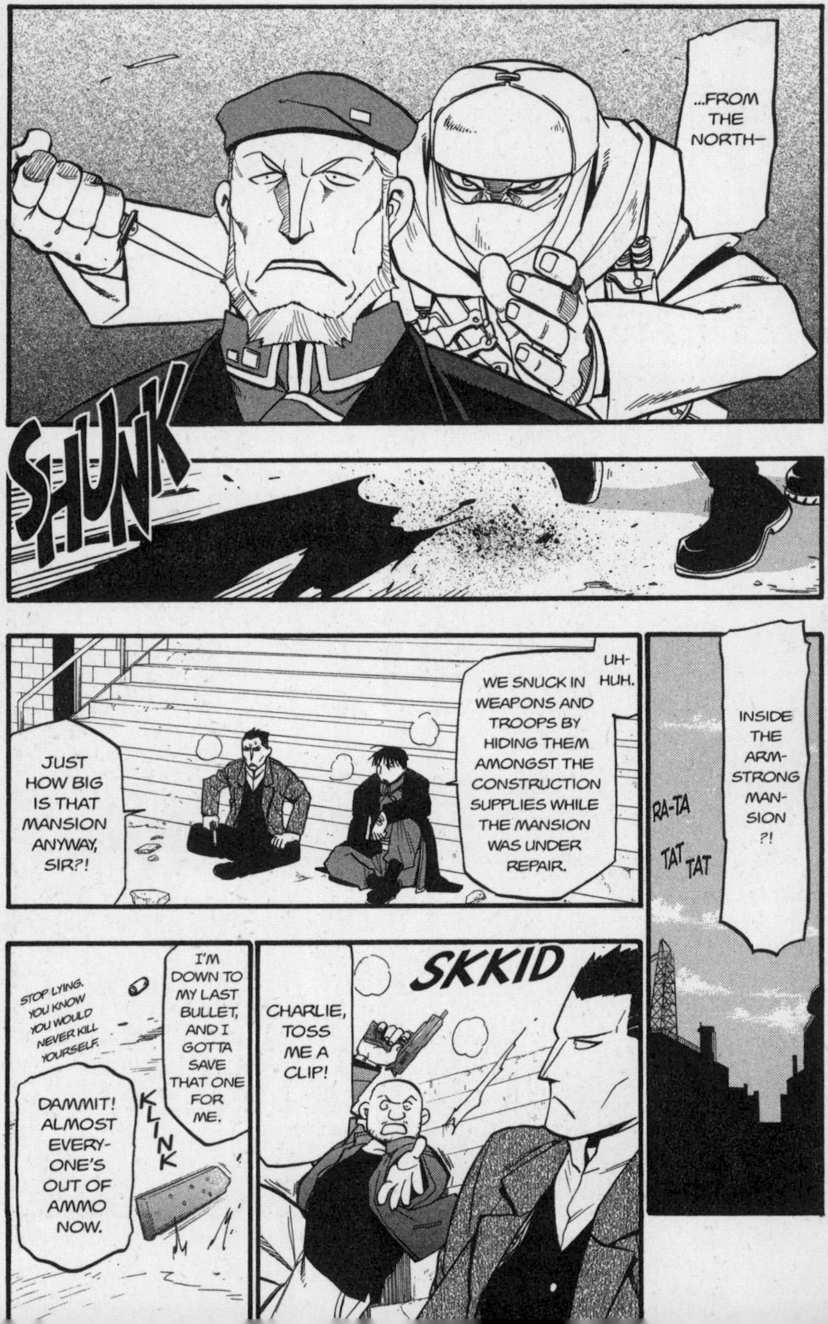
...FROM THE NORTH—
SHUNK
INSIDE THE ARM-STRONG MAN-SION?!
RA-TA TAT TAT
UH-HUH.
WE SNUCK IN WEAPONS AND TROOPS BY HIDING THEM AMONGST THE CONSTRUCTION SUPPLIES WHILE THE MANSION WAS UNDER REPAIR.
JUST HOW BIG IS THAT MANSION ANYWAY, SIR?!
SKKID
CHARLIE, TOSS ME A CLIP!
I'M DOWN TO MY LAST BULLET, AND I GOTTA SAVE THAT ONE FOR ME.
STOP LYING. YOU KNOW YOU WOULD NEVER KILL YOURSELF.
DAMMIT! ALMOST EVERY-ONE'S OUT OF AMMO NOW.
KLINK

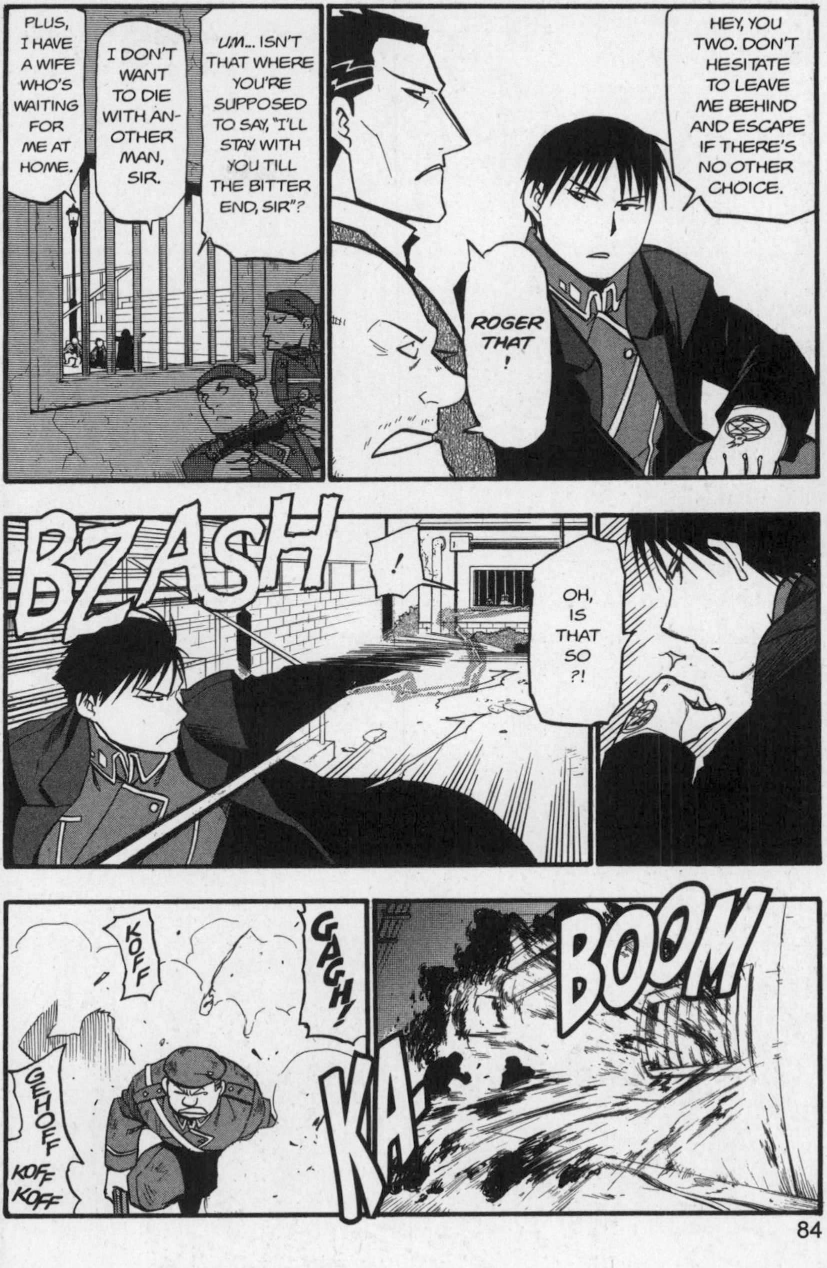
HEY, YOU TWO. DON'T HESITATE TO LEAVE ME BEHIND AND ESCAPE IF THERE'S NO OTHER CHOICE.
ROGER THAT!
UM... ISN'T THAT WHERE YOU'RE SUPPOSED TO SAY, "I'LL STAY WITH YOU TILL THE BITTER END, SIR"?
I DON'T WANT TO DIE WITH AN-OTHER MAN, SIR.
PLUS, I HAVE A WIFE WHO'S WAITING FOR ME AT HOME.
OH, IS THAT SO?!
!
BZASH
KA-BOOM
GAGH!
KOFF
GEHOFF
KOFF KOFF

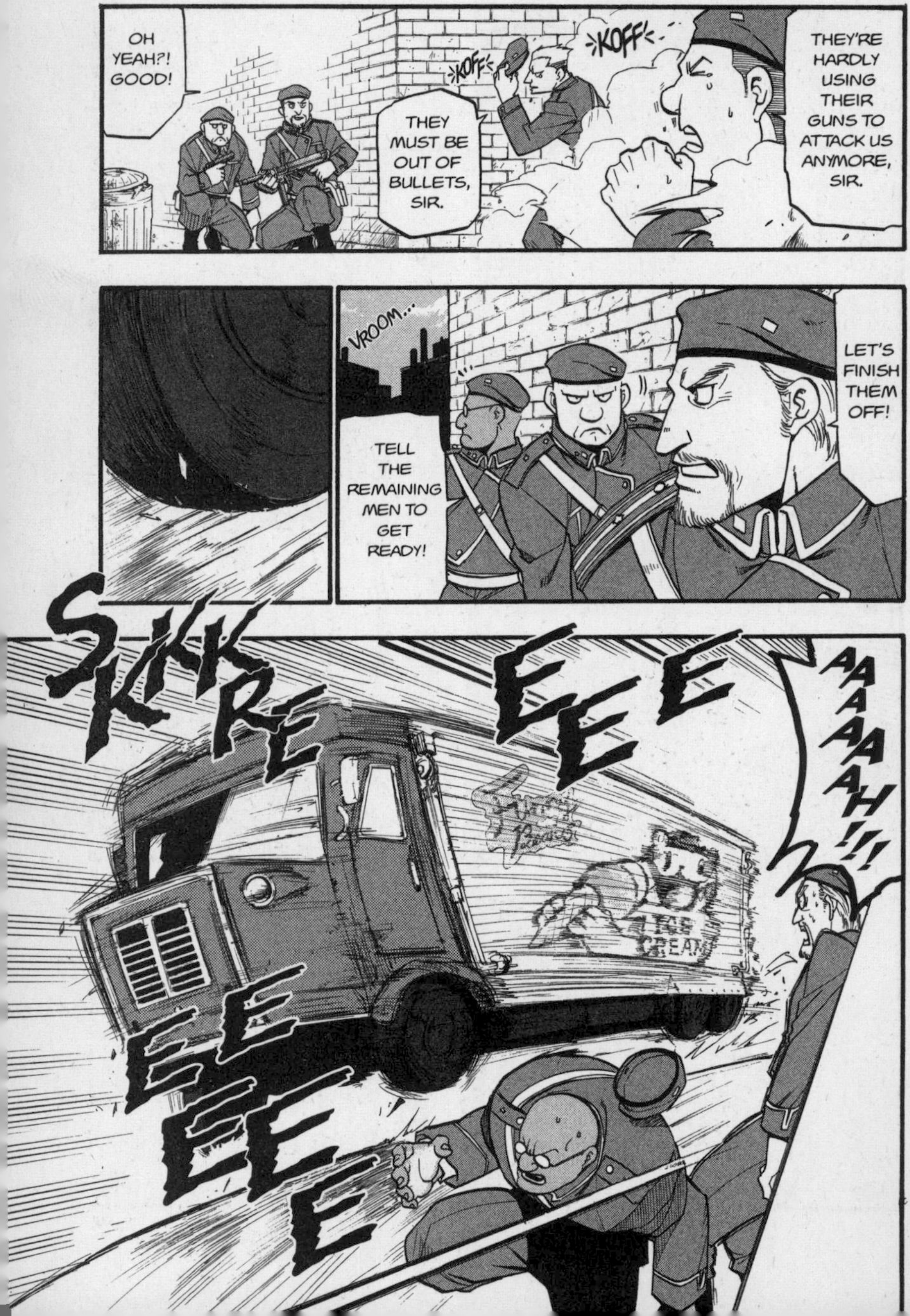
THEY'RE HARDLY USING THEIR GUNS TO ATTACK US ANYMORE, SIR.
KOFF
KOFF
THEY MUST BE OUT OF BULLETS, SIR.
OH YEAH?! GOOD!
LET'S FINISH THEM OFF!
TELL THE REMAINING MEN TO GET READY!
VROOM...
AAAAAH!!!
SKKREEEEEEEEE
ICE CREAM

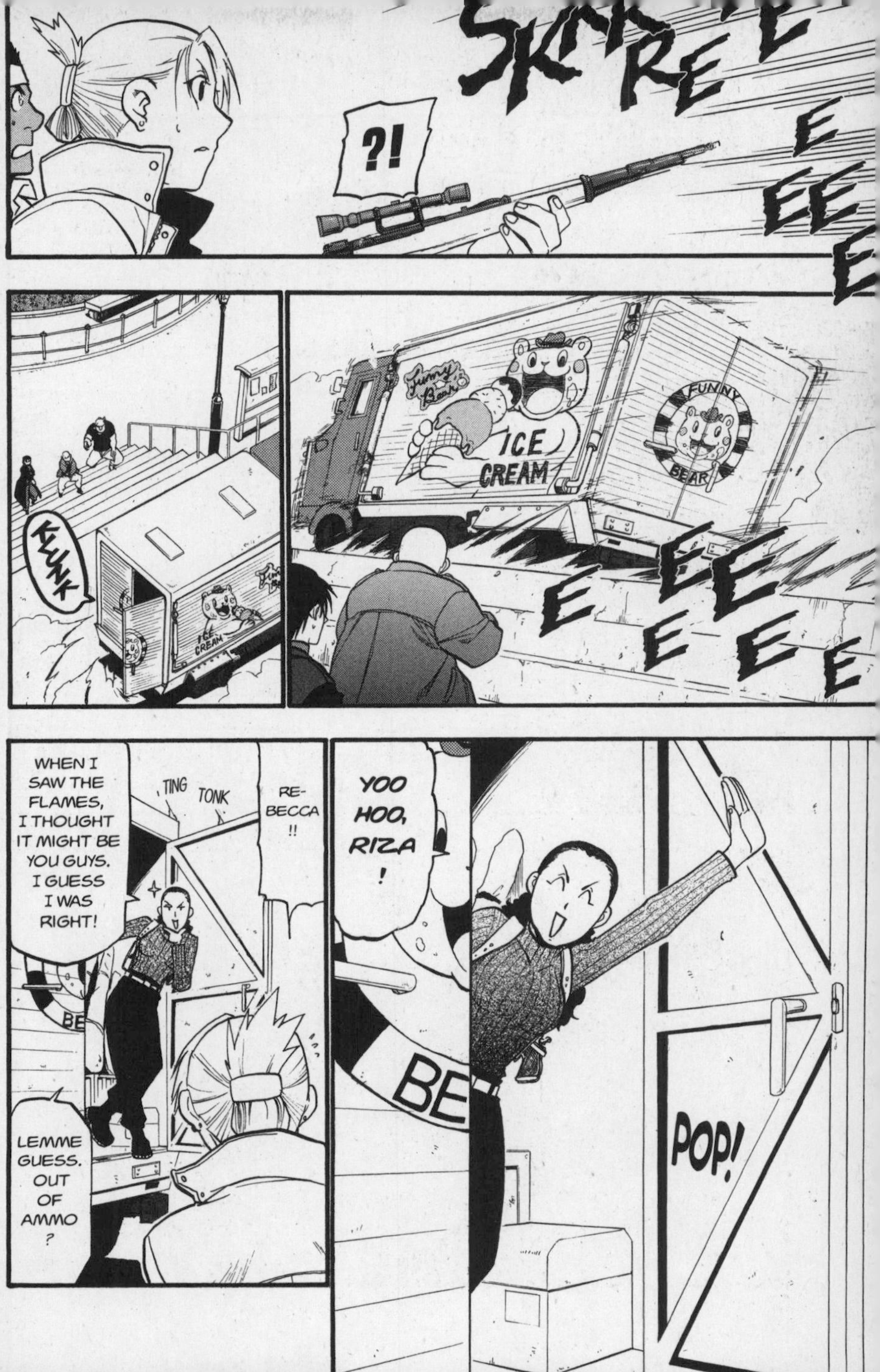
SKREEEEEE
?!
Funny Bear
ICE CREAM
FUNNY BEAR
EEEEEEE
KLUNK
YOO HOO, RIZA!
BE
POP!
RE-BECCA!!
TING
TONK
WHEN I SAW THE FLAMES, I THOUGHT IT MIGHT BE YOU GUYS. I GUESS I WAS RIGHT!
LEMME GUESS. OUT OF AMMO?

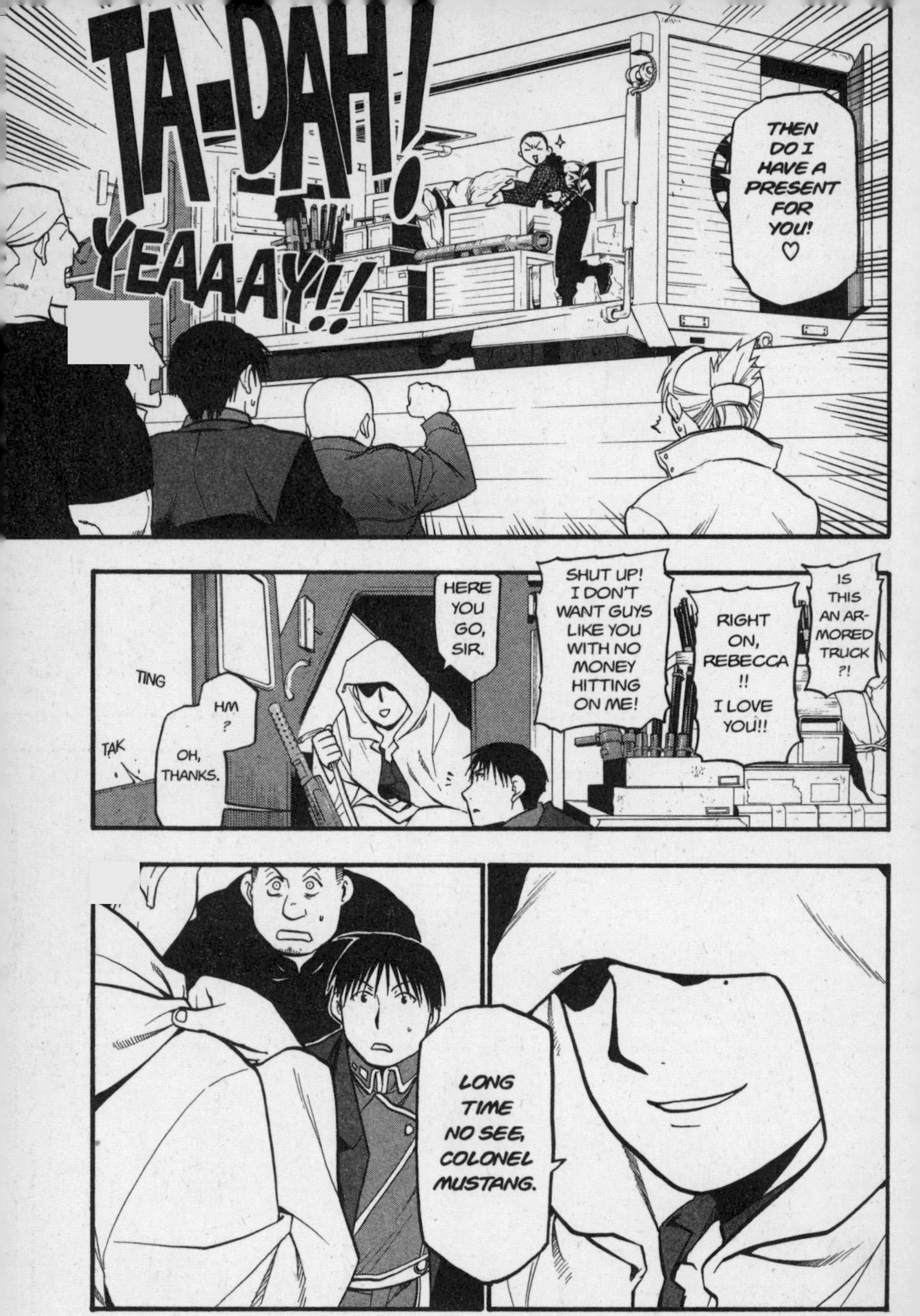
THEN DO I HAVE A PRESENT FOR YOU! ♡
TA-DAH!
YEAAAY!!
IS THIS AN ARMORED TRUCK?!
RIGHT ON, REBECCA!! I LOVE YOU!!
SHUT UP! I DON'T WANT GUYS LIKE YOU WITH NO MONEY HITTING ON ME!
HERE YOU GO, SIR.
TING
HM? OH, THANKS.
TAK
LONG TIME NO SEE, COLONEL MUSTANG.

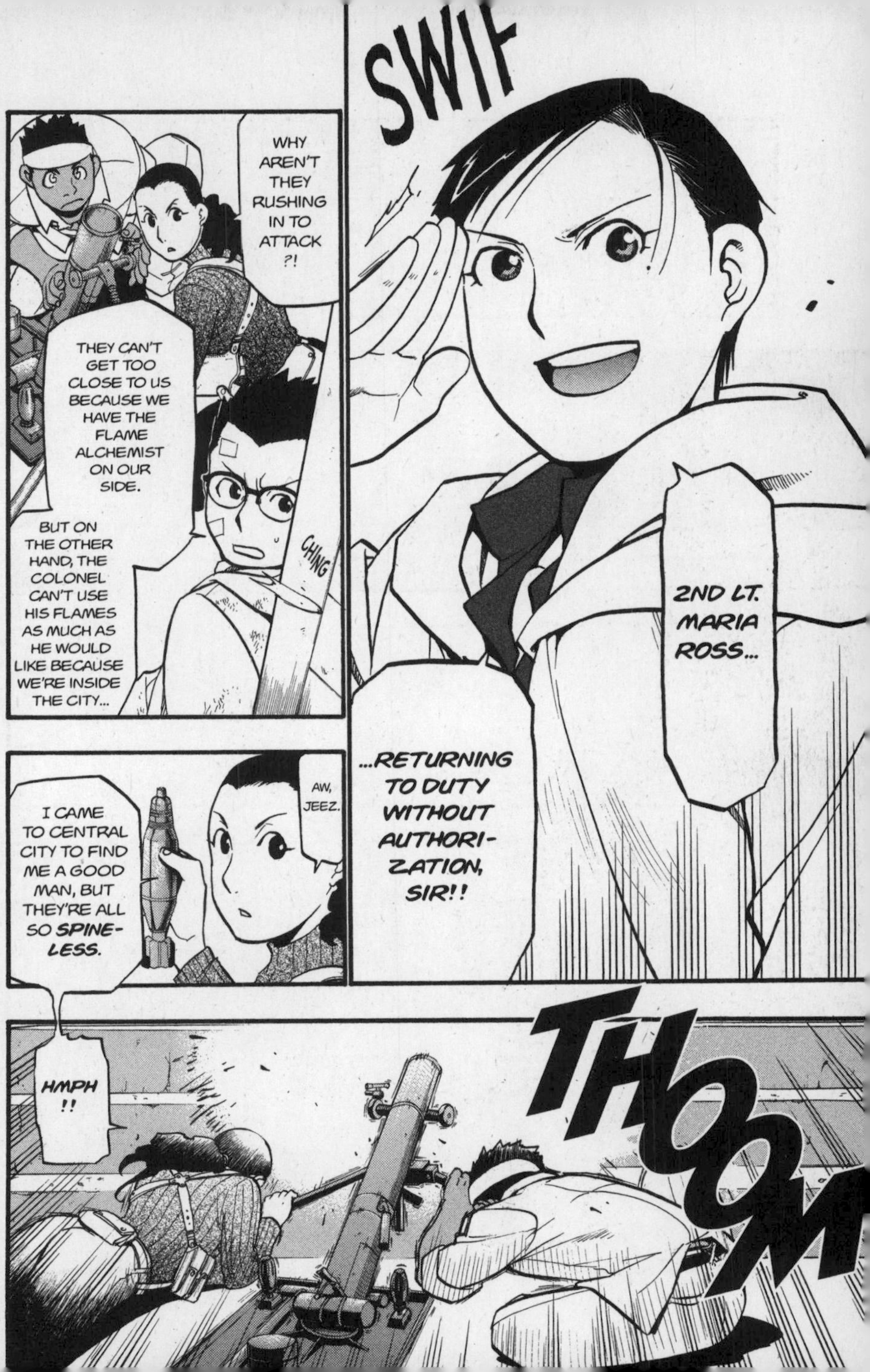
SWIF
2ND LT. MARIA ROSS...
...RETURNING TO DUTY WITHOUT AUTHORI-ZATION, SIR!!
WHY AREN'T THEY RUSHING IN TO ATTACK ?!
THEY CAN'T GET TOO CLOSE TO US BECAUSE WE HAVE THE FLAME ALCHEMIST ON OUR SIDE.
CHING
BUT ON THE OTHER HAND, THE COLONEL CAN'T USE HIS FLAMES AS MUCH AS HE WOULD LIKE BECAUSE WE'RE INSIDE THE CITY...
AW, JEEZ.
I CAME TO CENTRAL CITY TO FIND ME A GOOD MAN, BUT THEY'RE ALL SO SPINE-LESS.
THOOM
HMPH !!

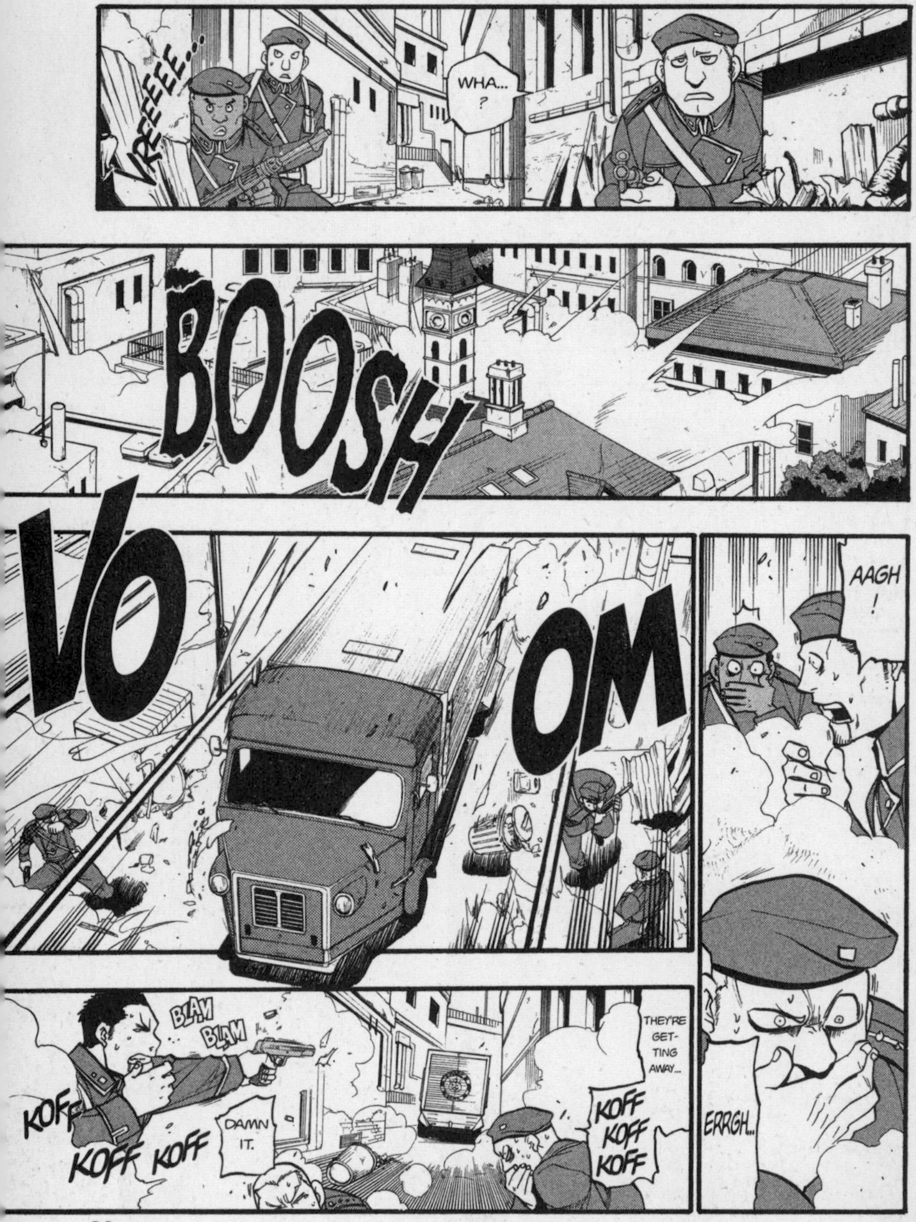
WHA... ?
VREEEEE...
BOOSH
AAGH !
VROOM
ERRGH...
THEY'RE GETTING AWAY...
KOFF KOFF KOFF
DAMN IT.
BLAM BLAM
KOFF KOFF KOFF

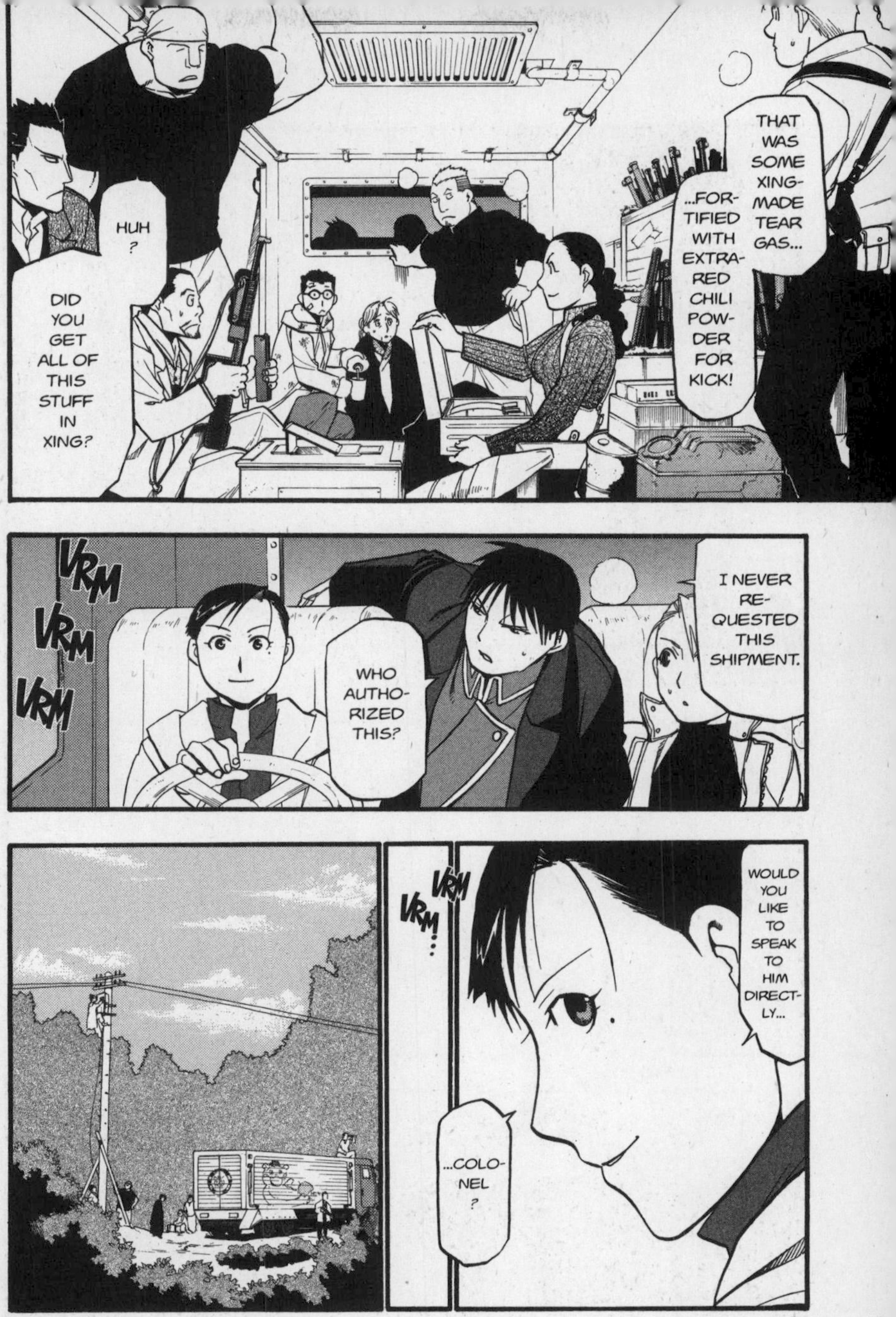
THAT WAS SOME XING-MADE TEAR GAS...
...FORTIFIED WITH EXTRA-RED CHILI POWDER FOR KICK!
HUH?
DID YOU GET ALL OF THIS STUFF IN XING?
I NEVER REQUESTED THIS SHIPMENT.
WHO AUTHORIZED THIS?
VRM VRM VRM
WOULD YOU LIKE TO SPEAK TO HIM DIRECTLY...
...COLONEL?
VRM VRM

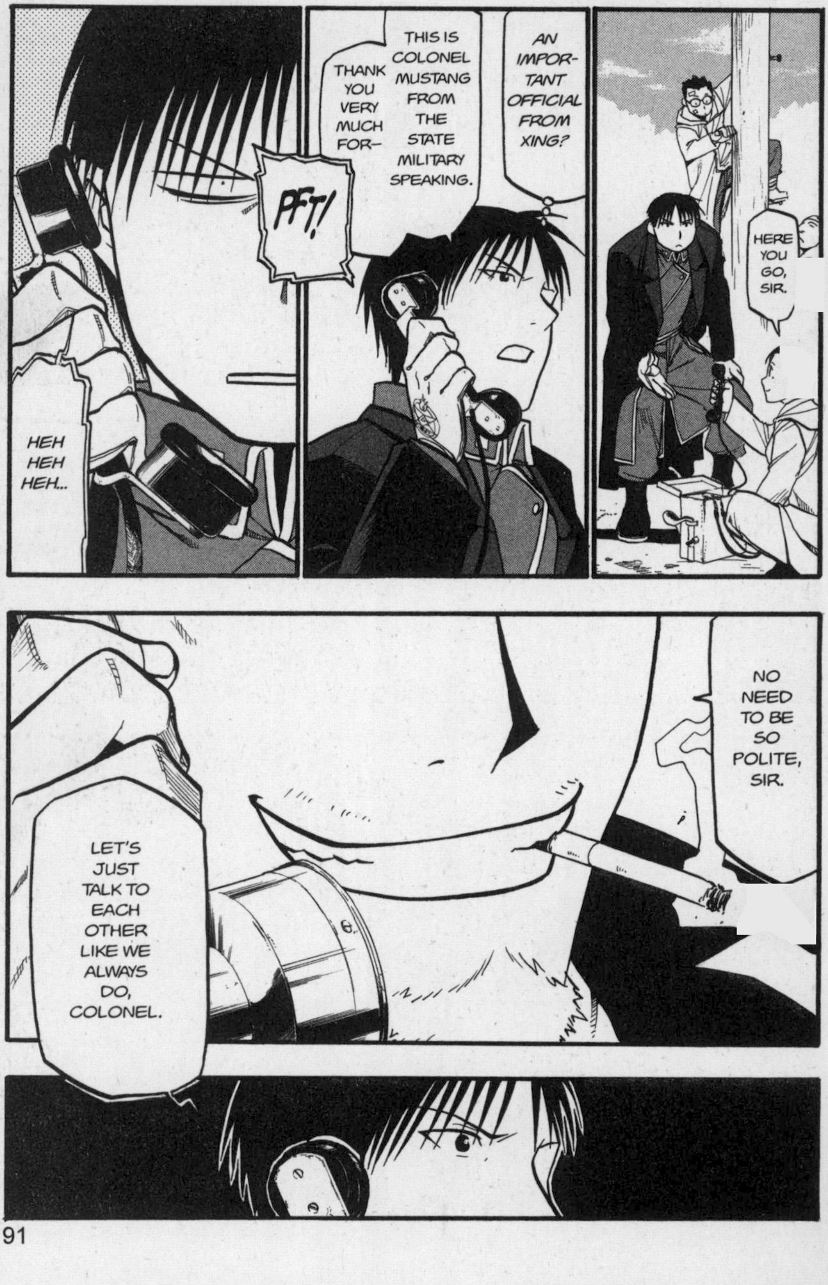
HERE YOU GO, SIR.
AN IMPORTANT OFFICIAL FROM XING?
THIS IS COLONEL MUSTANG FROM THE STATE MILITARY SPEAKING.
THANK YOU VERY MUCH FOR–
PFT!
HEH HEH HEH...
NO NEED TO BE SO POLITE, SIR.
LET'S JUST TALK TO EACH OTHER LIKE WE ALWAYS DO, COLONEL.

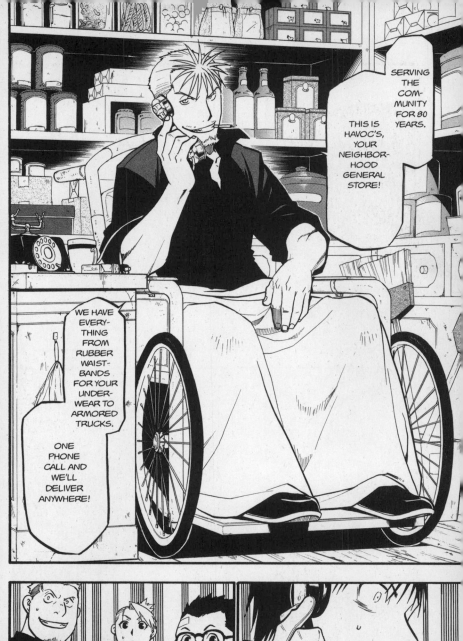

SERVING THE COMMUNITY FOR 80 YEARS.

THIS IS HAVOC'S, YOUR NEIGHBORHOOD GENERAL STORE!

WE HAVE EVERYTHING FROM RUBBER WAISTBANDS FOR YOUR UNDERWEAR TO ARMORED TRUCKS.

ONE PHONE CALL AND WE'LL DELIVER ANYWHERE!

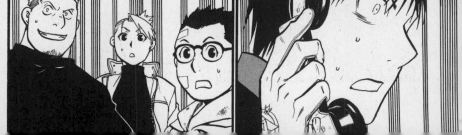

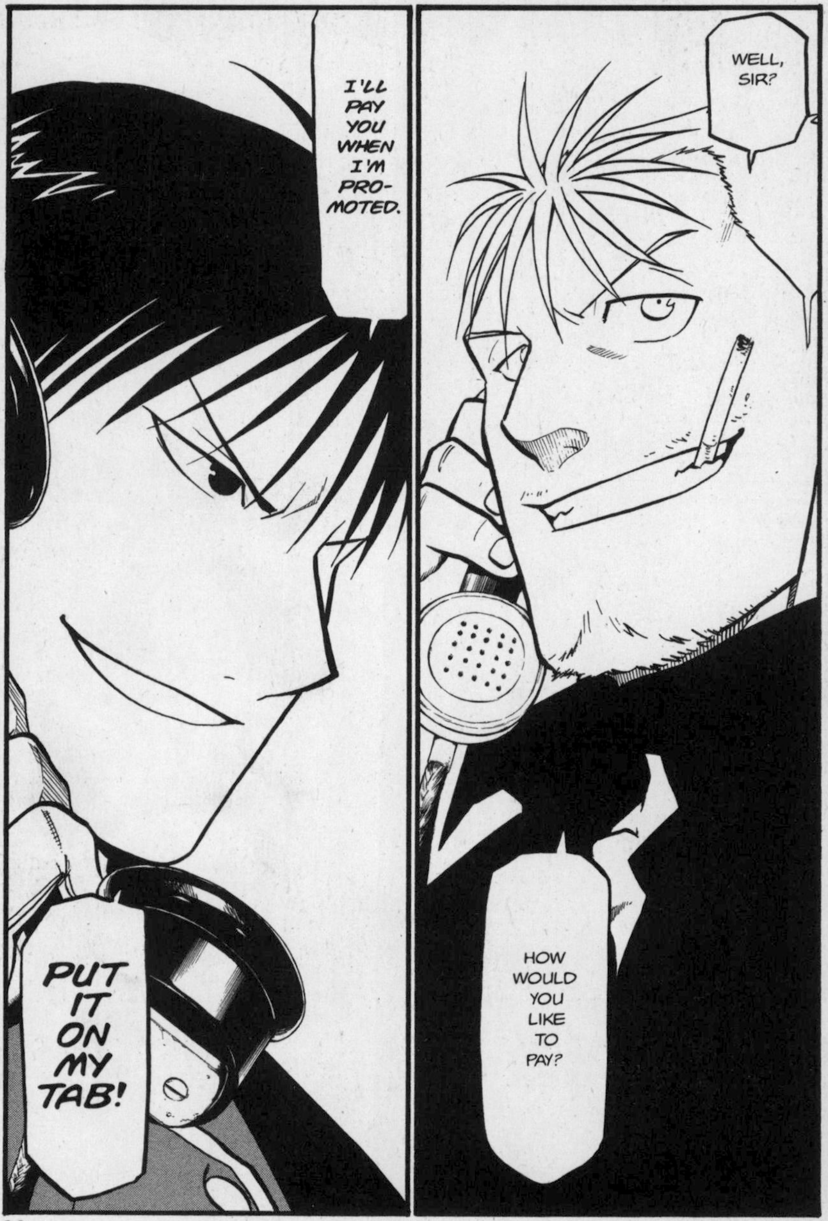
WELL, SIR?
HOW WOULD YOU LIKE TO PAY?
I'LL PAY YOU WHEN I'M PRO-MOTED.
PUT IT ON MY TAB!

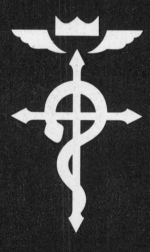

FULLMETAL
ALCHEMIST

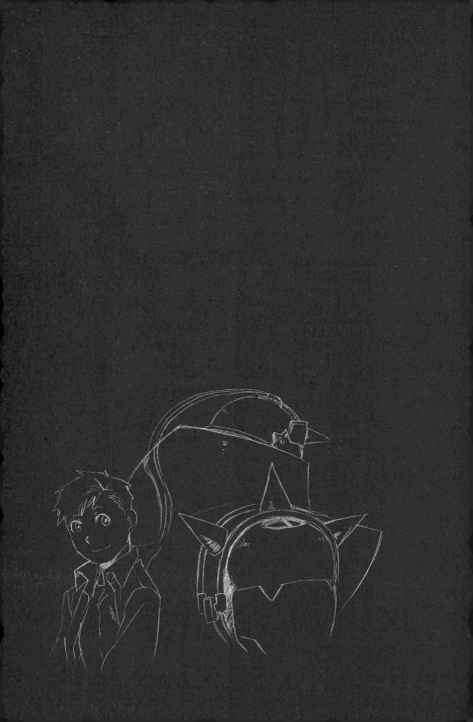

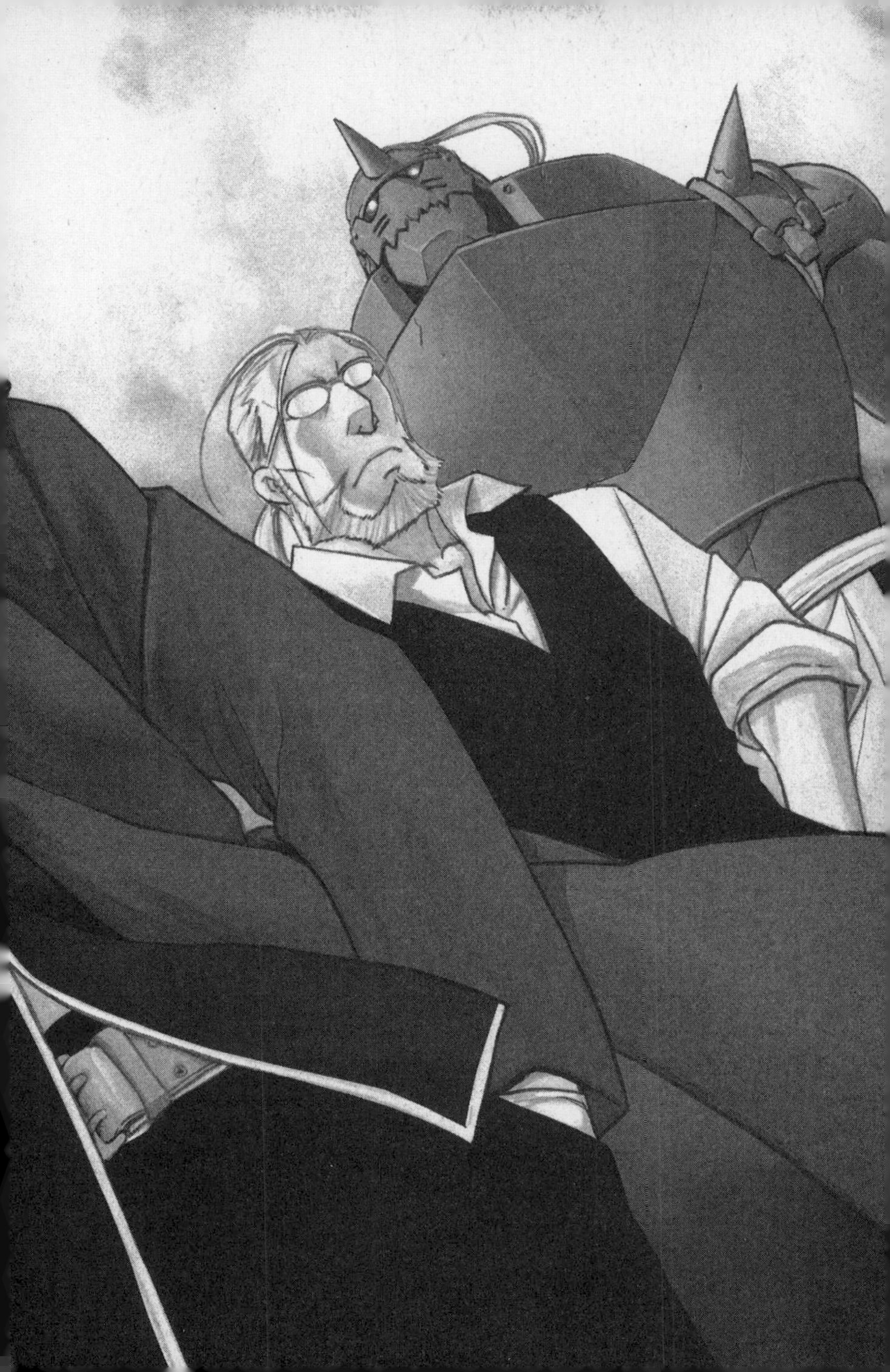

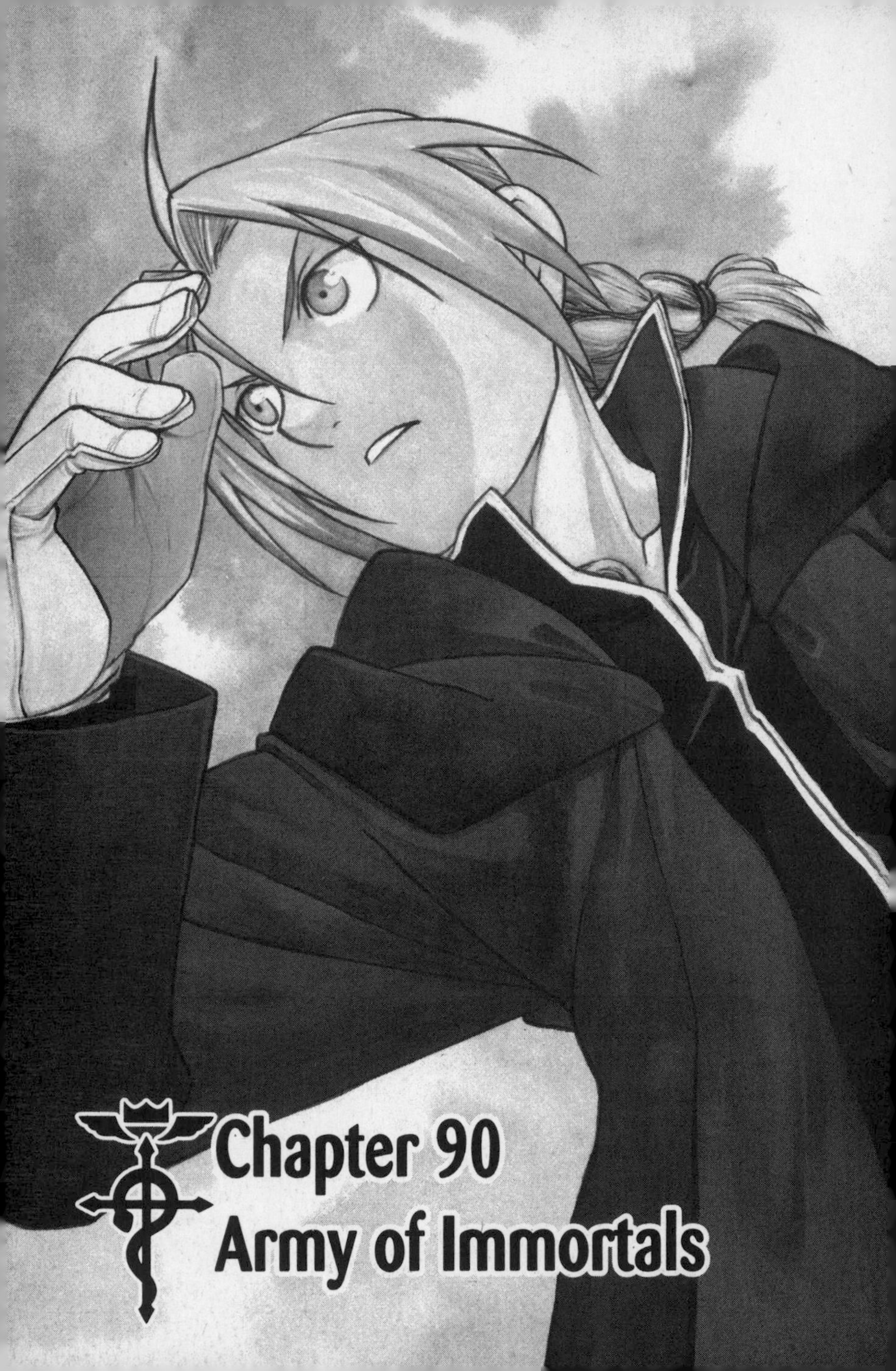
Chapter 90
Army of Immortals

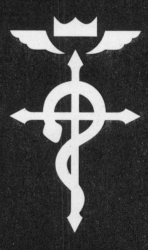

FULLMETAL
ALCHEMIST

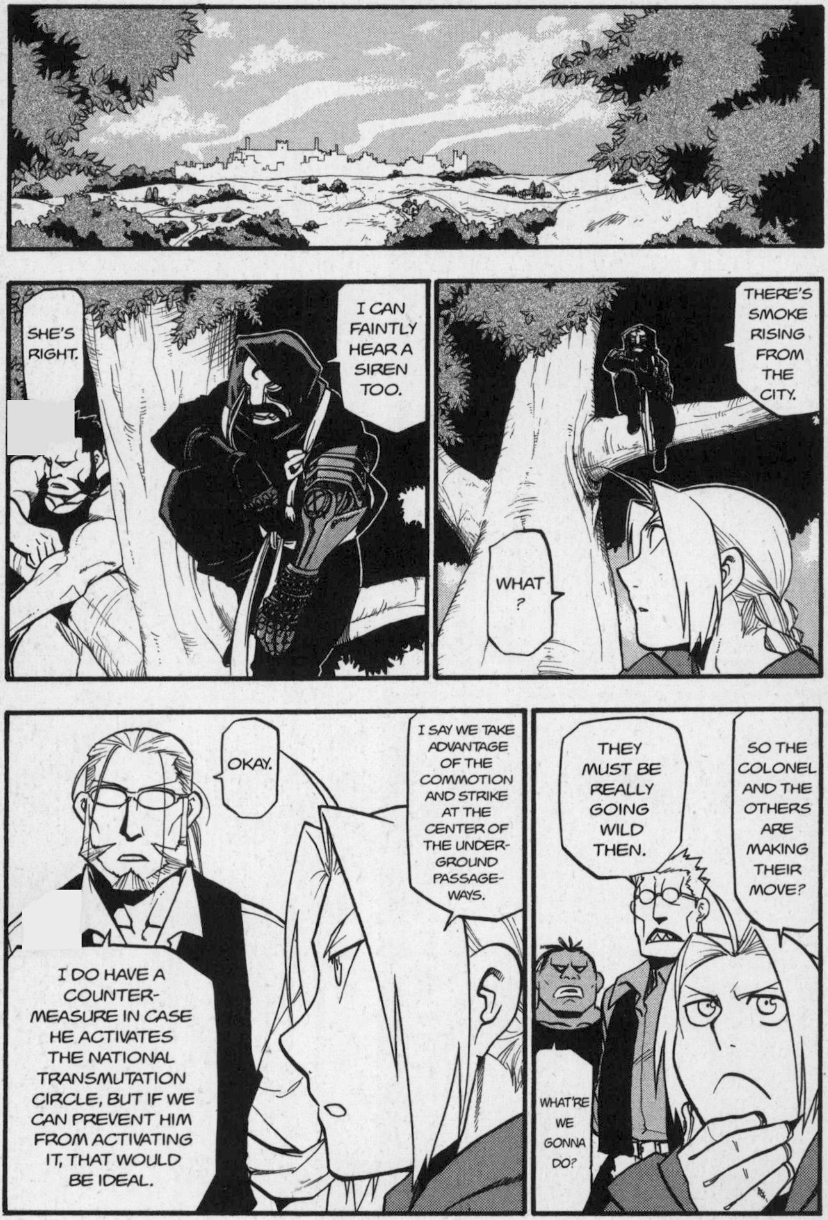
THERE'S SMOKE RISING FROM THE CITY.
WHAT?
I CAN FAINTLY HEAR A SIREN TOO.
SHE'S RIGHT.
SO THE COLONEL AND THE OTHERS ARE MAKING THEIR MOVE?
THEY MUST BE REALLY GOING WILD THEN.
WHAT'RE WE GONNA DO?
I SAY WE TAKE ADVANTAGE OF THE COMMOTION AND STRIKE AT THE CENTER OF THE UNDER-GROUND PASSAGE-WAYS.
OKAY.
I DO HAVE A COUNTER-MEASURE IN CASE HE ACTIVATES THE NATIONAL TRANSMUTATION CIRCLE, BUT IF WE CAN PREVENT HIM FROM ACTIVATING IT, THAT WOULD BE IDEAL.

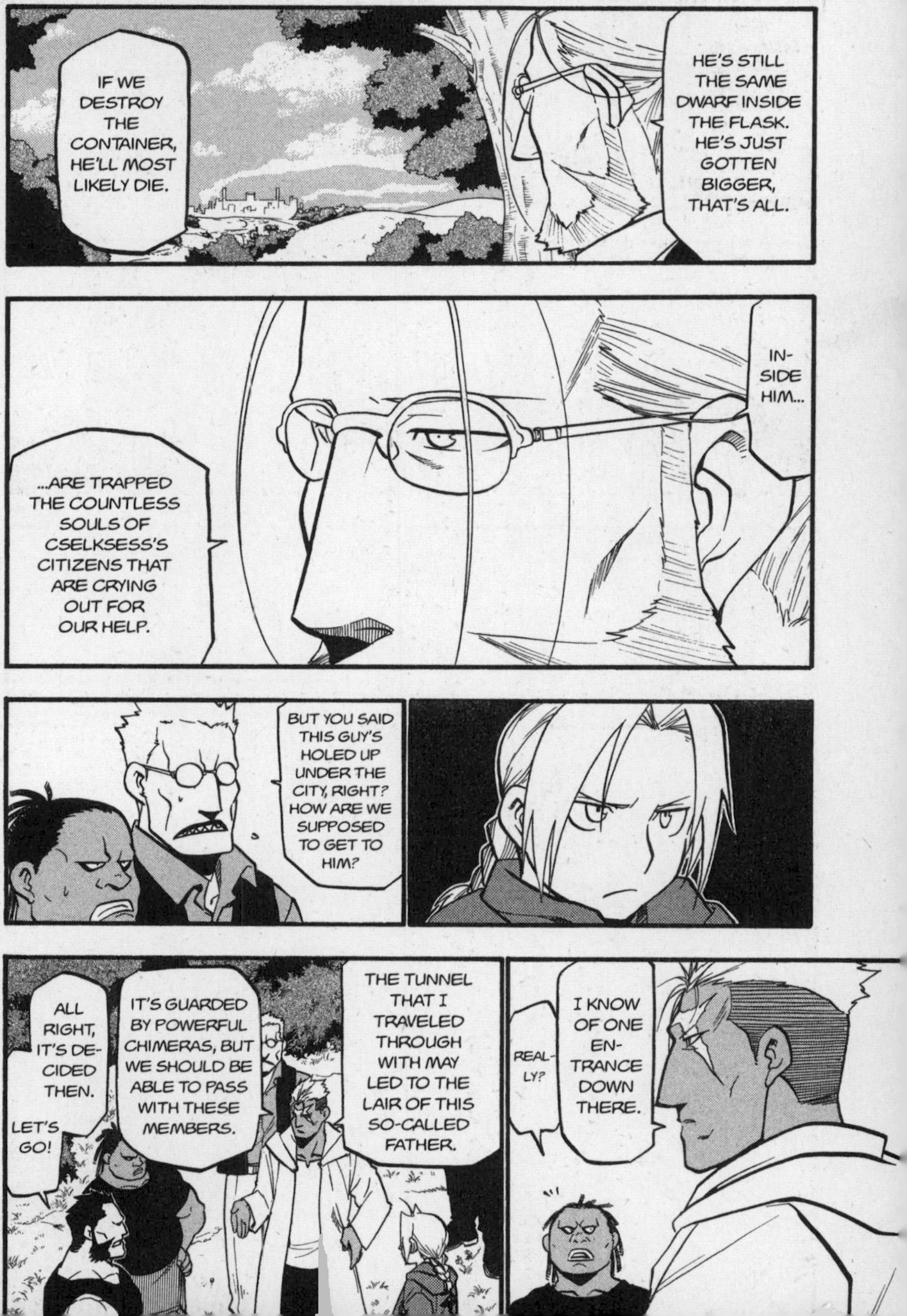
HE'S STILL THE SAME DWARF INSIDE THE FLASK. HE'S JUST GOTTEN BIGGER, THAT'S ALL.
IF WE DESTROY THE CONTAINER, HE'LL MOST LIKELY DIE.
IN-SIDE HIM...
...ARE TRAPPED THE COUNTLESS SOULS OF CSELKSESS'S CITIZENS THAT ARE CRYING OUT FOR OUR HELP.
BUT YOU SAID THIS GUY'S HOLED UP UNDER THE CITY, RIGHT? HOW ARE WE SUPPOSED TO GET TO HIM?
I KNOW OF ONE EN-TRANCE DOWN THERE.
REAL-LY?
THE TUNNEL THAT I TRAVELED THROUGH WITH MAY LED TO THE LAIR OF THIS SO-CALLED FATHER.
IT'S GUARDED BY POWERFUL CHIMERAS, BUT WE SHOULD BE ABLE TO PASS WITH THESE MEMBERS.
ALL RIGHT, IT'S DE-CIDED THEN.
LET'S GO!

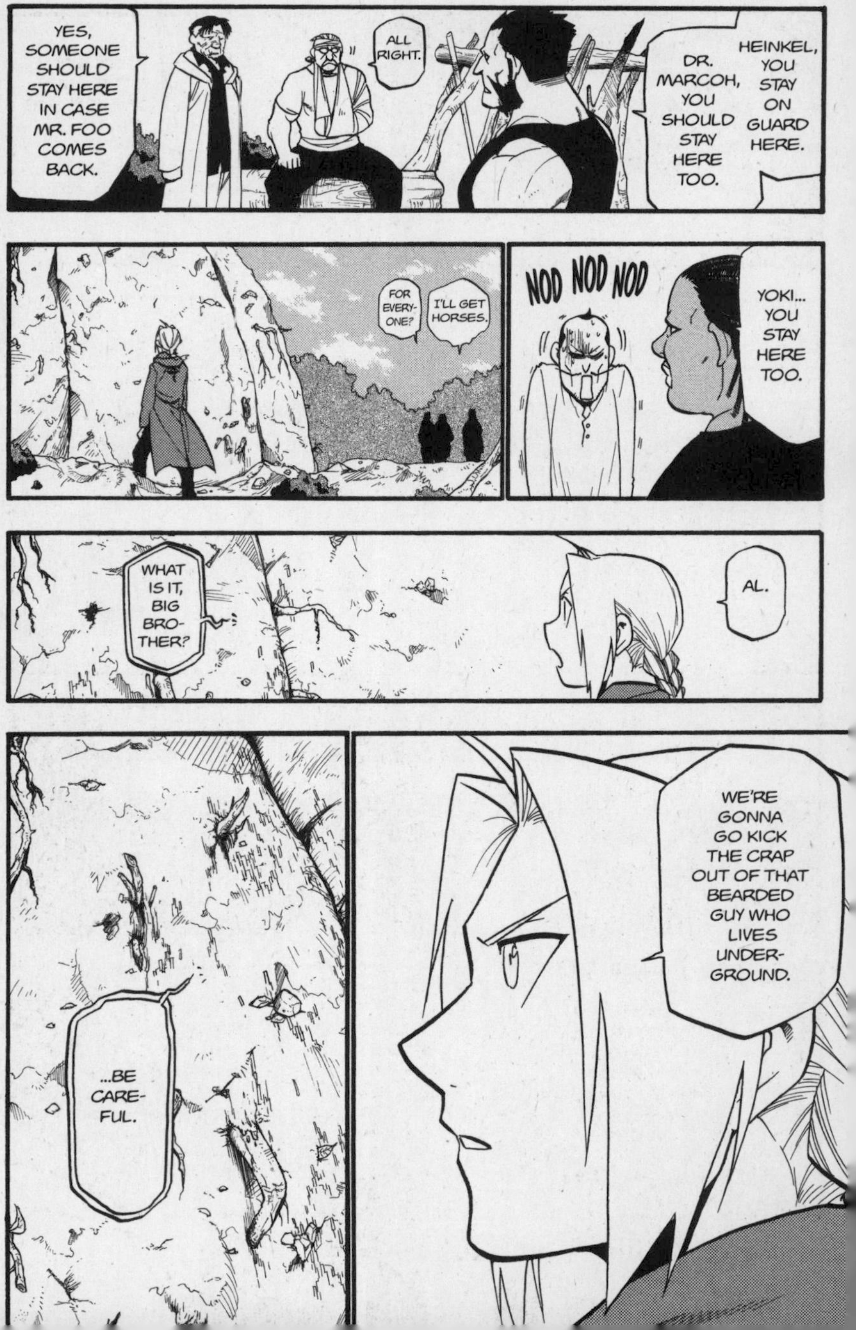
HEINKEL, YOU STAY ON GUARD HERE.
DR. MARCOH, YOU SHOULD STAY HERE TOO.
ALL RIGHT.
YES, SOMEONE SHOULD STAY HERE IN CASE MR. FOO COMES BACK.
YOKI... YOU STAY HERE TOO.
NOD NOD NOD
I'LL GET HORSES.
FOR EVERY-ONE?
AL.
WHAT IS IT, BIG BROTHER?
WE'RE GONNA GO KICK THE CRAP OUT OF THAT BEARDED GUY WHO LIVES UNDER-GROUND.
...BE CARE-FUL.

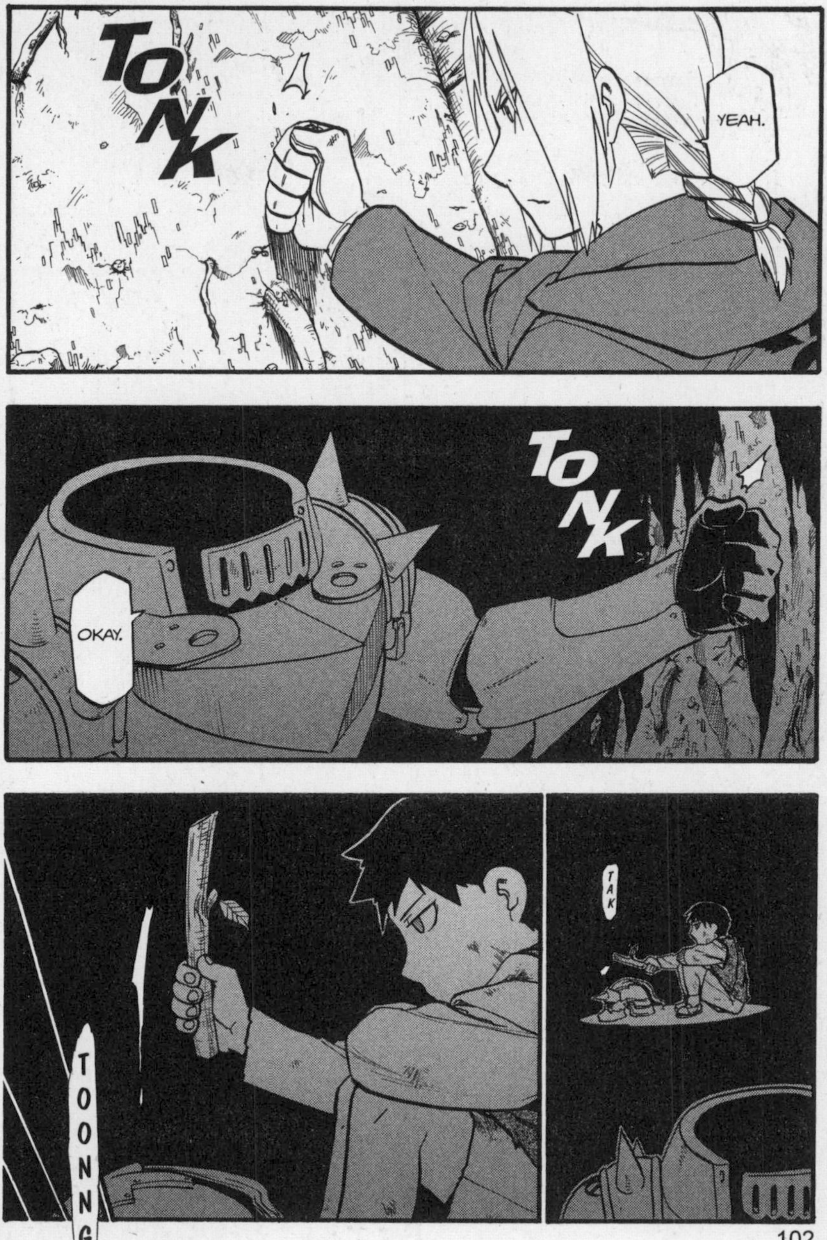
TONK
YEAH.
TONK
OKAY.
TAK
TOONNG

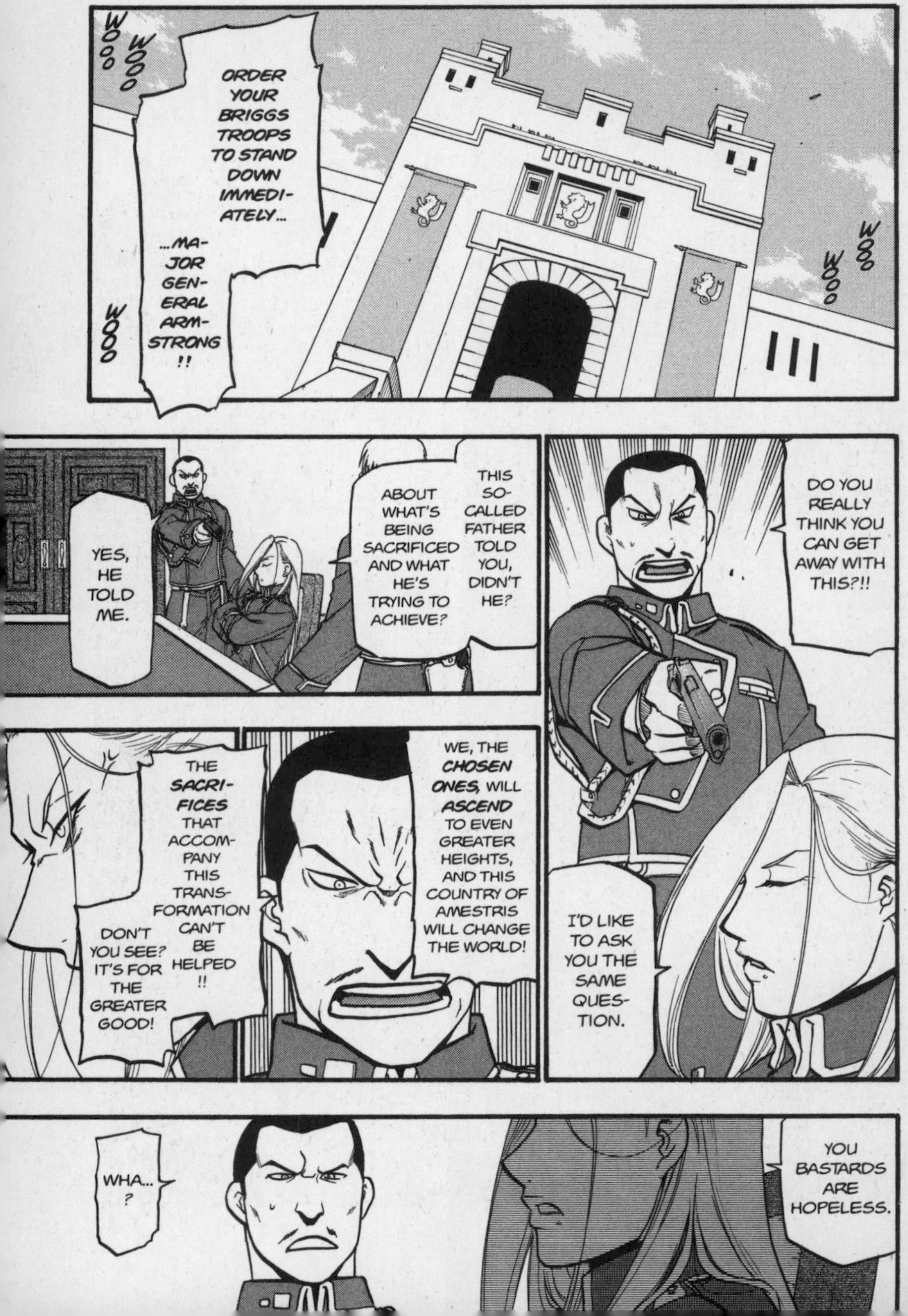
WOOO
WOOO
ORDER YOUR BRIGGS TROOPS TO STAND DOWN IMMEDIATELY...
...MAJOR GENERAL ARMSTRONG!!
WOOO
WOOO
DO YOU REALLY THINK YOU CAN GET AWAY WITH THIS?!!
I'D LIKE TO ASK YOU THE SAME QUESTION.
THIS SO-CALLED FATHER TOLD YOU, DIDN'T HE?
ABOUT WHAT'S BEING SACRIFICED AND WHAT HE'S TRYING TO ACHIEVE?
YES, HE TOLD ME.
WE, THE CHOSEN ONES, WILL ASCEND TO EVEN GREATER HEIGHTS, AND THIS COUNTRY OF AMESTRIS WILL CHANGE THE WORLD!
THE SACRIFICES THAT ACCOMPANY THIS TRANSFORMATION CAN'T BE HELPED!!
DON'T YOU SEE? IT'S FOR THE GREATER GOOD!
YOU BASTARDS ARE HOPELESS.
WHA...?

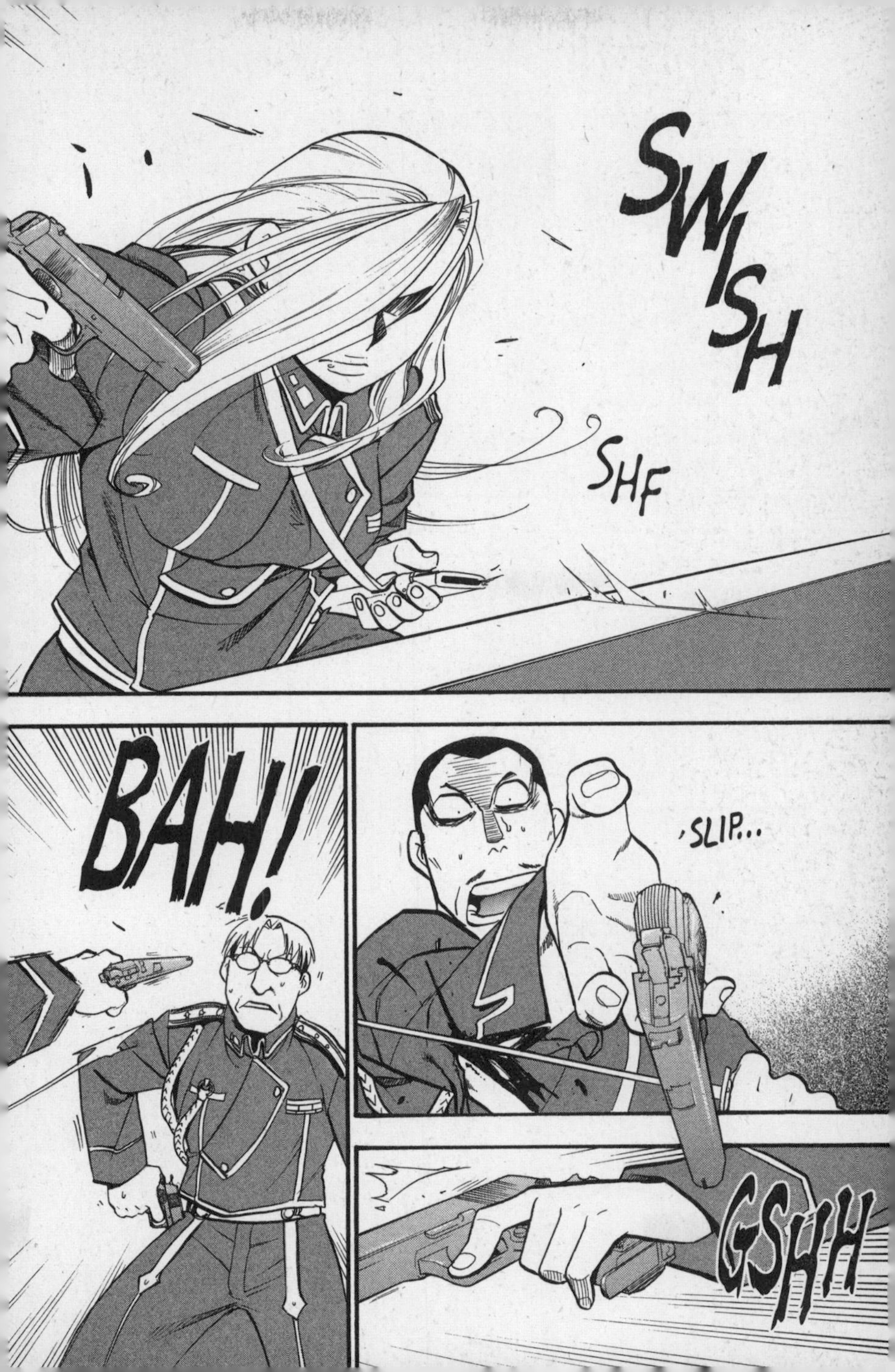
SWISH
SHF
SLIP...
GSHH
BAH!

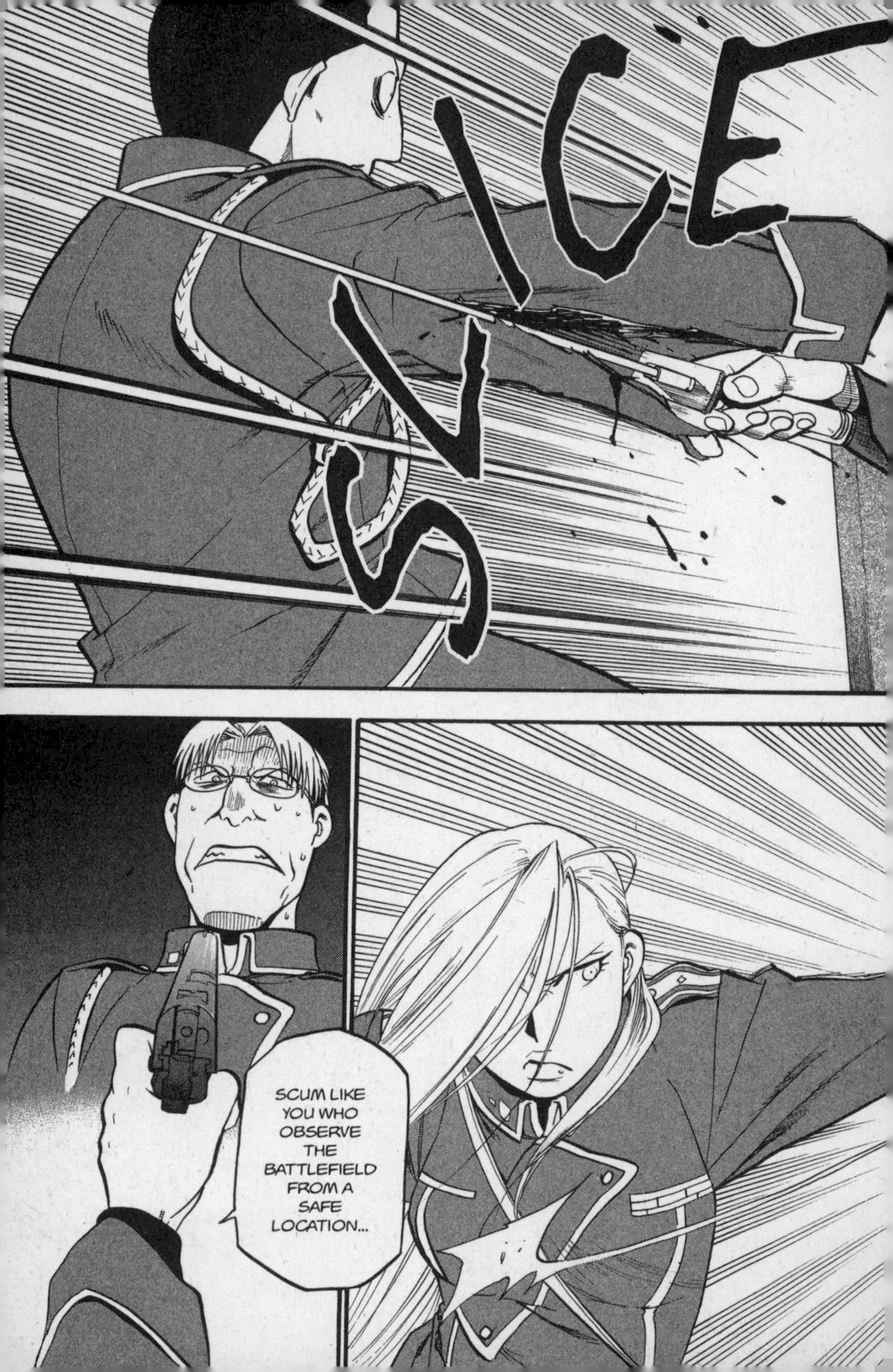
SLICE
SCUM LIKE YOU WHO OBSERVE THE BATTLEFIELD FROM A SAFE LOCATION...

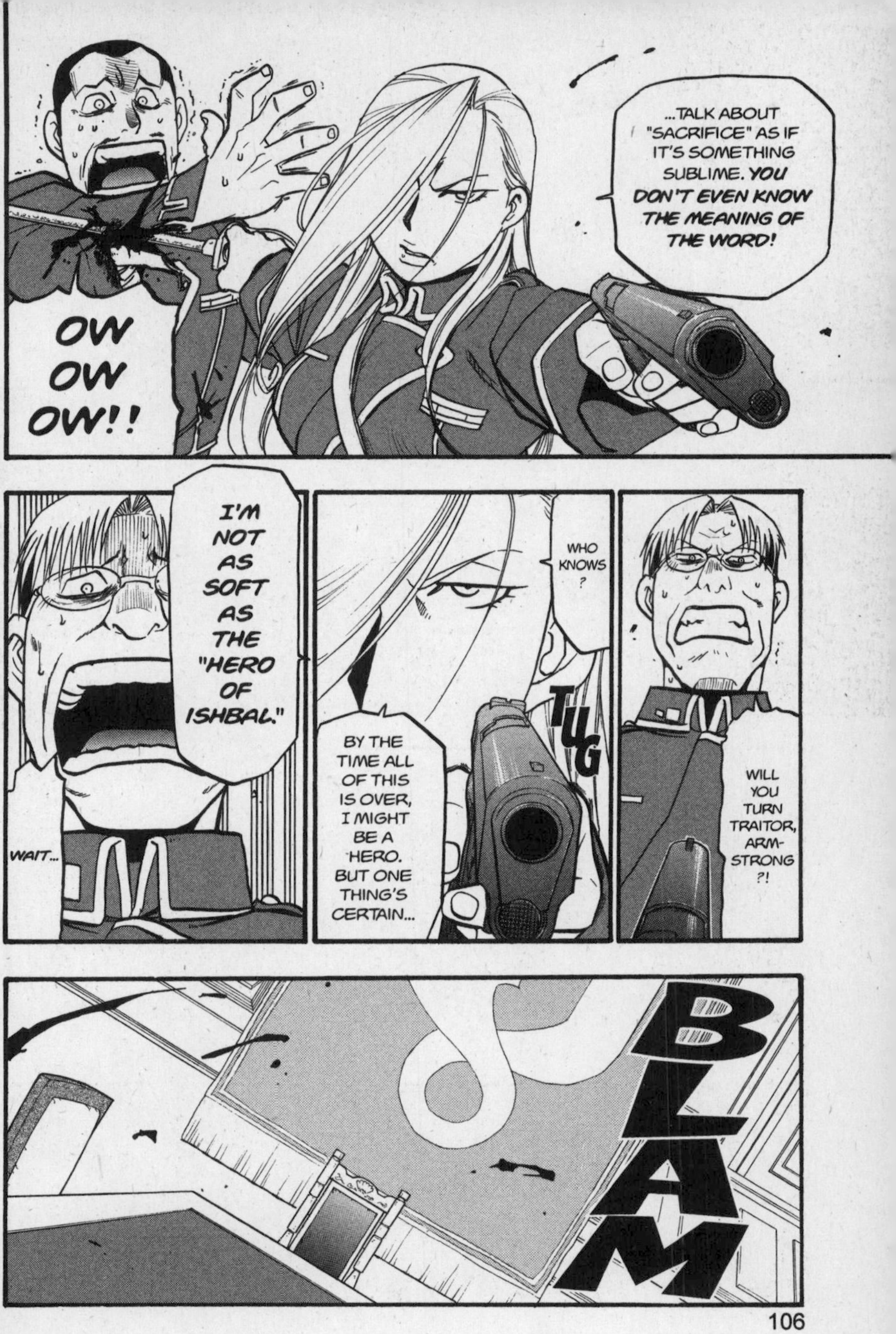
...TALK ABOUT "SACRIFICE" AS IF IT'S SOMETHING SUBLIME. YOU DON'T EVEN KNOW THE MEANING OF THE WORD!
OW OW OW!!
WILL YOU TURN TRAITOR, ARM-STRONG?!
WHO KNOWS?
TUG
BY THE TIME ALL OF THIS IS OVER, I MIGHT BE A HERO. BUT ONE THING'S CERTAIN...
I'M NOT AS SOFT AS THE "HERO OF ISHBAL."
WAIT...
BLAM

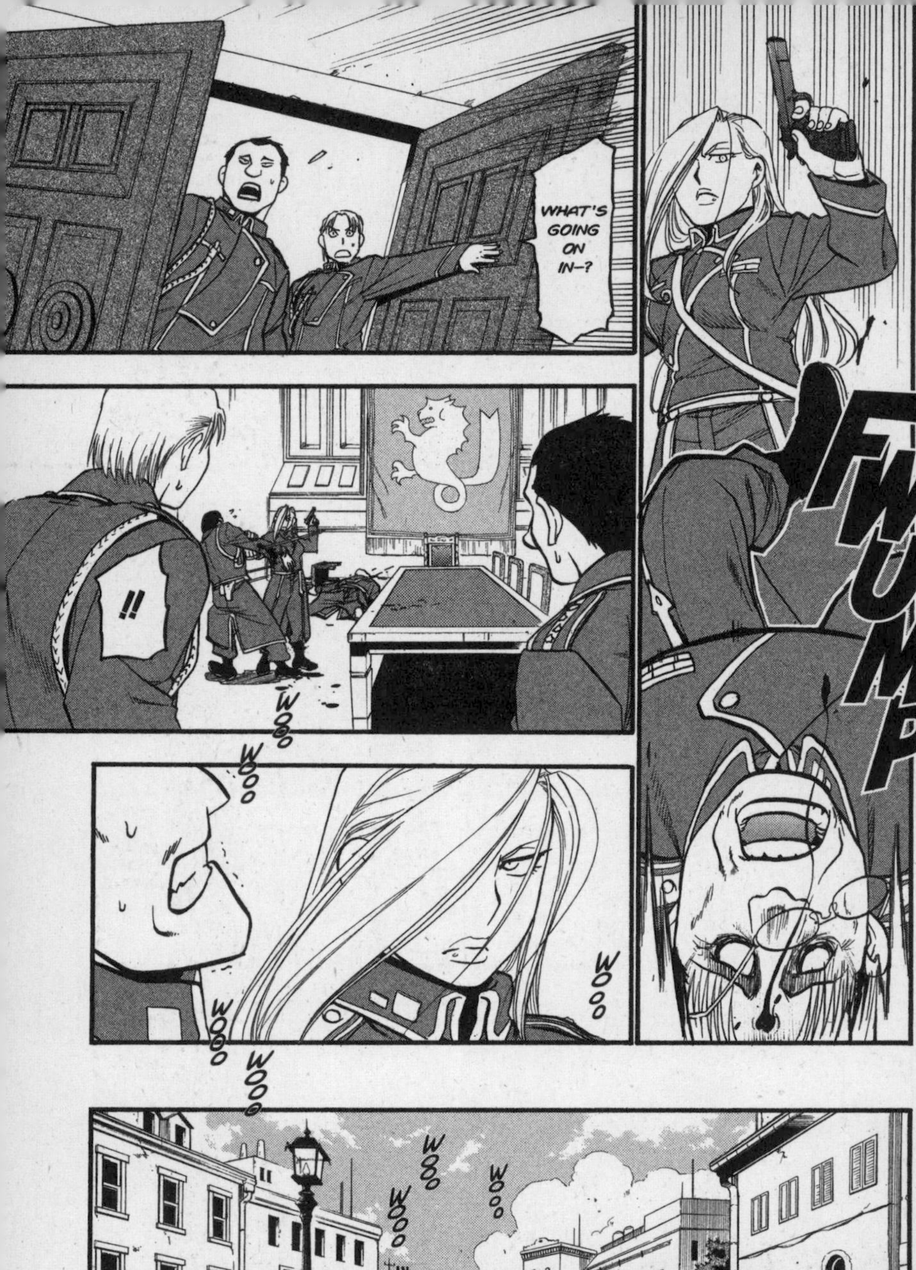
FWUMP
WHAT'S GOING ON IN–?
!!
WOOO
WOOO
WOOO
WOOO
WOOO
WOOO
WOOO
WOOO

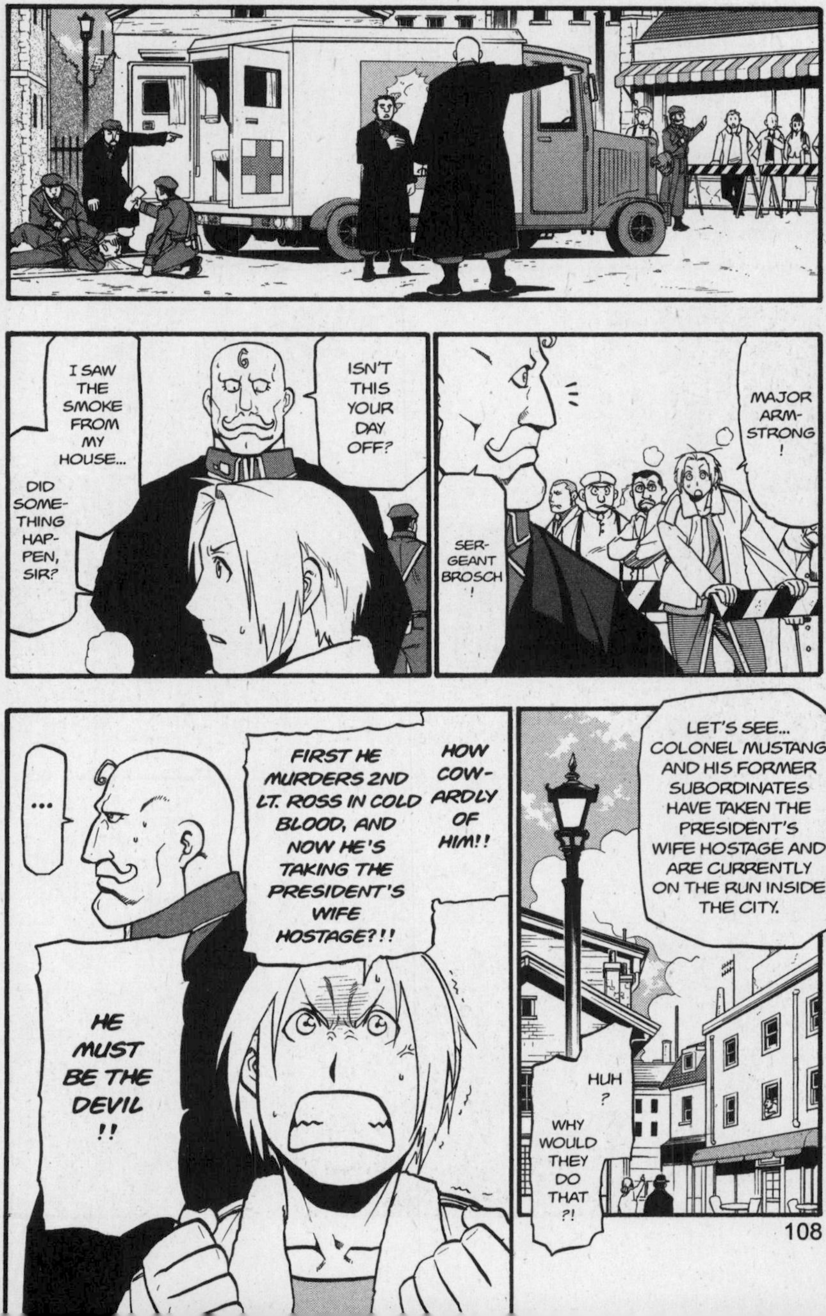

MAJOR ARMSTRONG!
SERGEANT BROSCH!
ISN'T THIS YOUR DAY OFF?
I SAW THE SMOKE FROM MY HOUSE...
DID SOMETHING HAPPEN, SIR?
LET'S SEE... COLONEL MUSTANG AND HIS FORMER SUBORDINATES HAVE TAKEN THE PRESIDENT'S WIFE HOSTAGE AND ARE CURRENTLY ON THE RUN INSIDE THE CITY.
HUH?
WHY WOULD THEY DO THAT?!
HOW COWARDLY OF HIM!!
FIRST HE MURDERS 2ND LT. ROSS IN COLD BLOOD, AND NOW HE'S TAKING THE PRESIDENT'S WIFE HOSTAGE?!!
...
HE MUST BE THE DEVIL!!

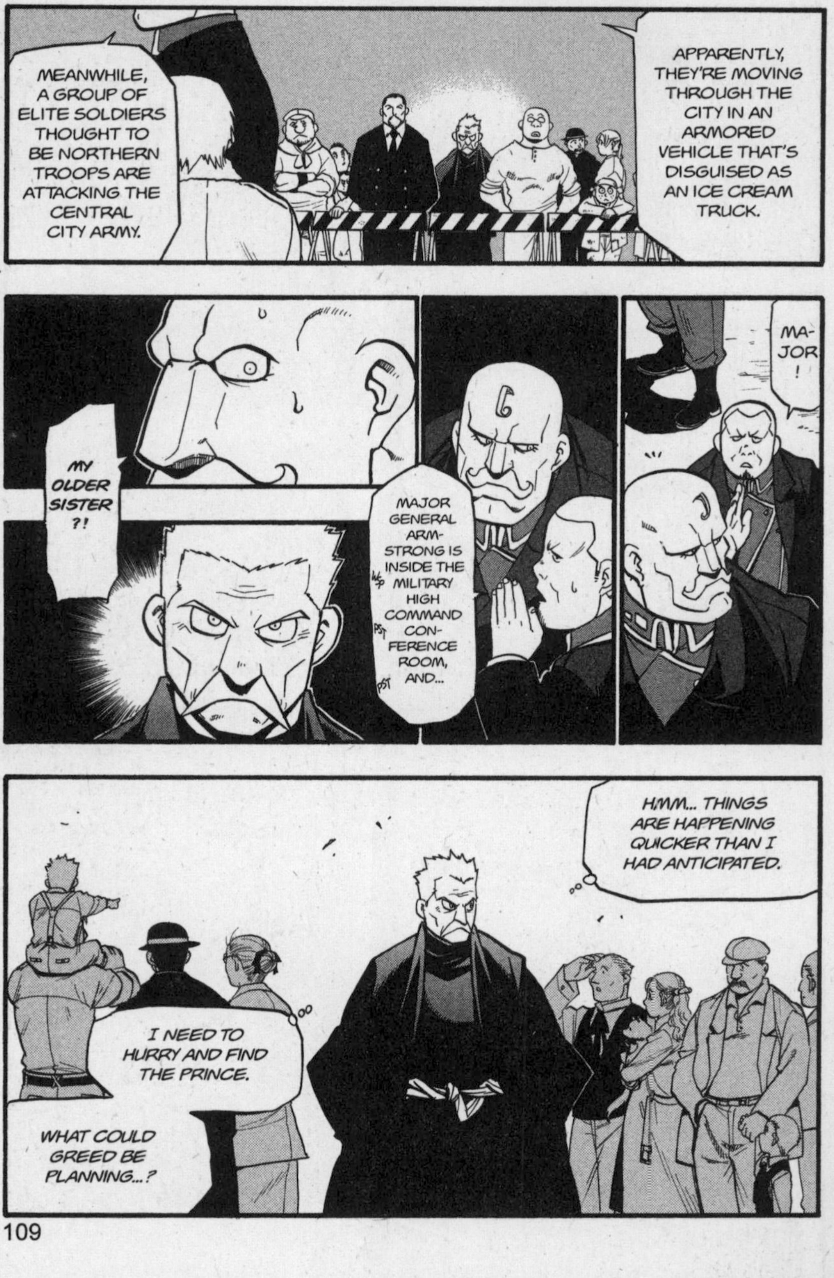
MEANWHILE, A GROUP OF ELITE SOLDIERS THOUGHT TO BE NORTHERN TROOPS ARE ATTACKING THE CENTRAL CITY ARMY.
APPARENTLY, THEY'RE MOVING THROUGH THE CITY IN AN ARMORED VEHICLE THAT'S DISGUISED AS AN ICE CREAM TRUCK.
MA-JOR!
MAJOR GENERAL ARM-STRONG IS INSIDE THE MILITARY HIGH COMMAND CON-FERENCE ROOM, AND...
WSP
PST
PST
MY OLDER SISTER?!
HMM... THINGS ARE HAPPENING QUICKER THAN I HAD ANTICIPATED.
I NEED TO HURRY AND FIND THE PRINCE.
WHAT COULD GREED BE PLANNING...?

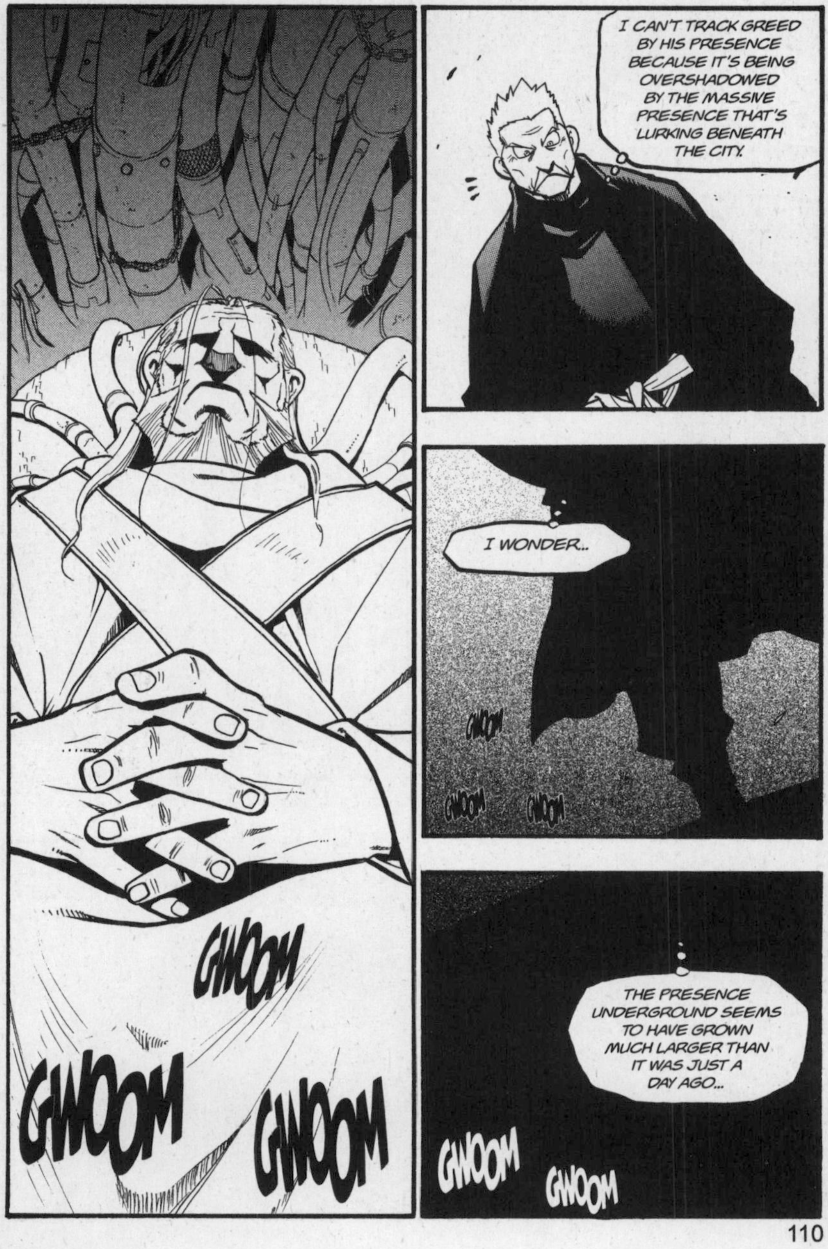
I CAN'T TRACK GREED BY HIS PRESENCE BECAUSE IT'S BEING OVERSHADOWED BY THE MASSIVE PRESENCE THAT'S LURKING BENEATH THE CITY.
I WONDER...
GWOOM
GWOOM
GWOOM
THE PRESENCE UNDERGROUND SEEMS TO HAVE GROWN MUCH LARGER THAN IT WAS JUST A DAY AGO...
GWOOM
GWOOM
GWOOM
GWOOM
GWOOM

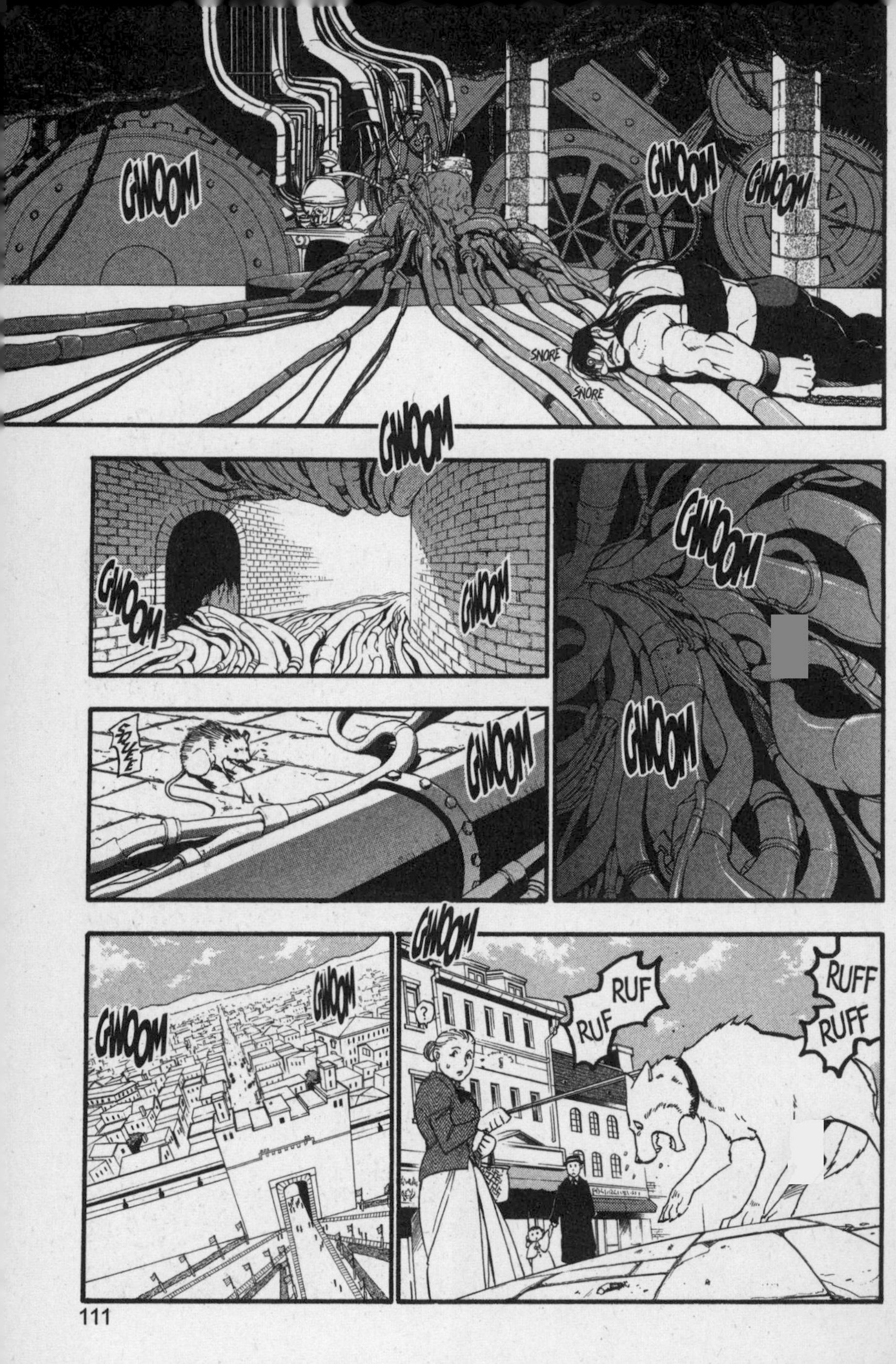
GWOOM
GWOOM
GWOOM
SNORE
SNORE
GWOOM
GWOOM
GWOOM
GWOOM
GWOOM
GWOOM
SQUEE
GWOOM
GWOOM
RUFF RUFF
RUF RUF
?
GWOOM
GWOOM

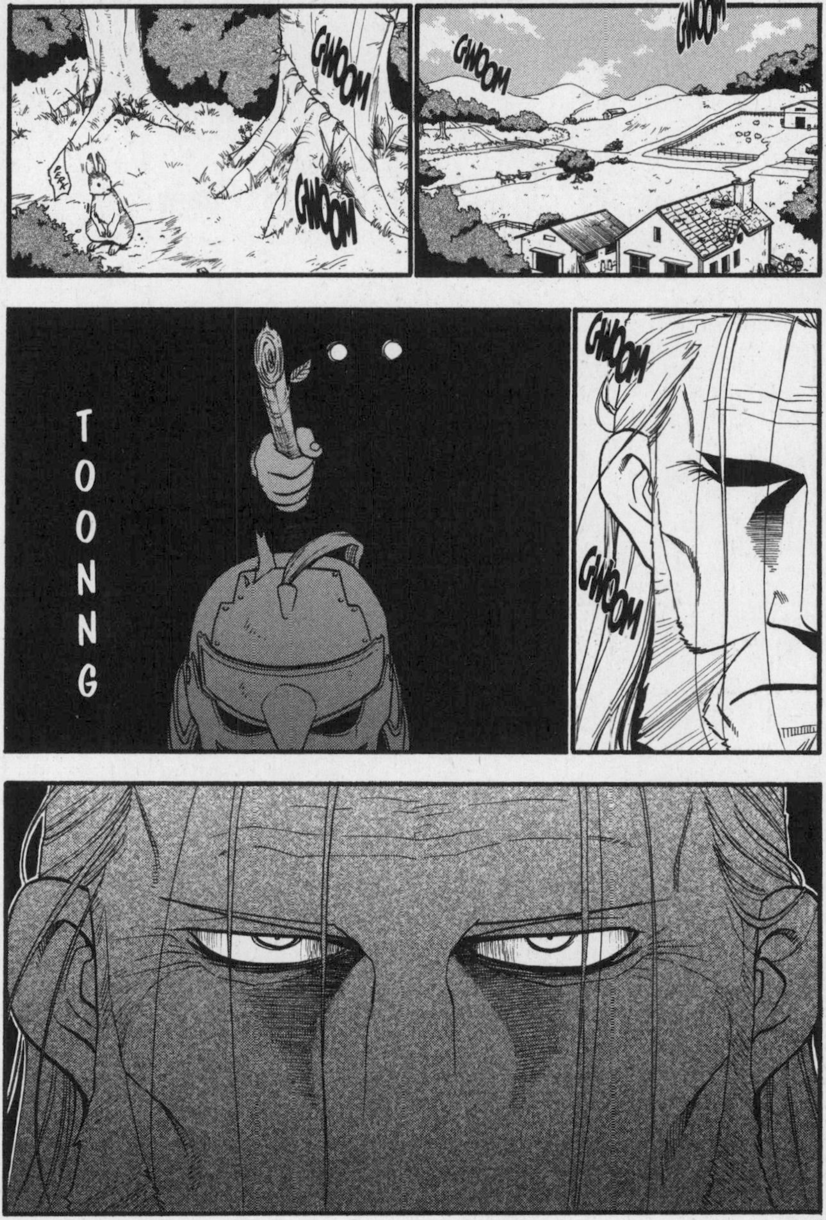
GWOOM
GWOOM
GWOOM
GWOOM
GWOOM
GWOOM
TOONNG

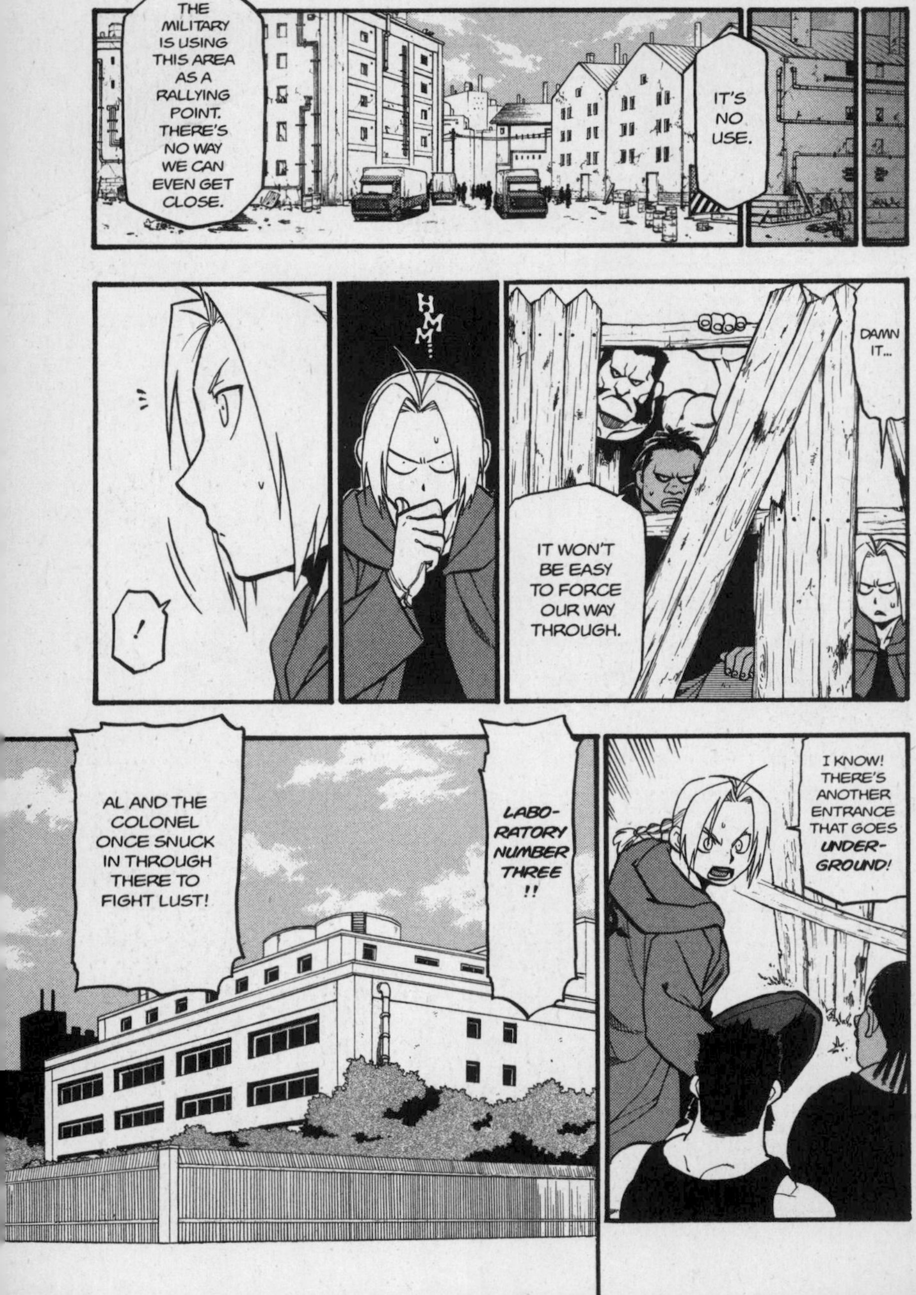
IT'S NO USE.
THE MILITARY IS USING THIS AREA AS A RALLYING POINT. THERE'S NO WAY WE CAN EVEN GET CLOSE.
DAMN IT...
IT WON'T BE EASY TO FORCE OUR WAY THROUGH.
HMM...
!
I KNOW! THERE'S ANOTHER ENTRANCE THAT GOES UNDERGROUND!
LABORATORY NUMBER THREE!!
AL AND THE COLONEL ONCE SNUCK IN THROUGH THERE TO FIGHT LUST!

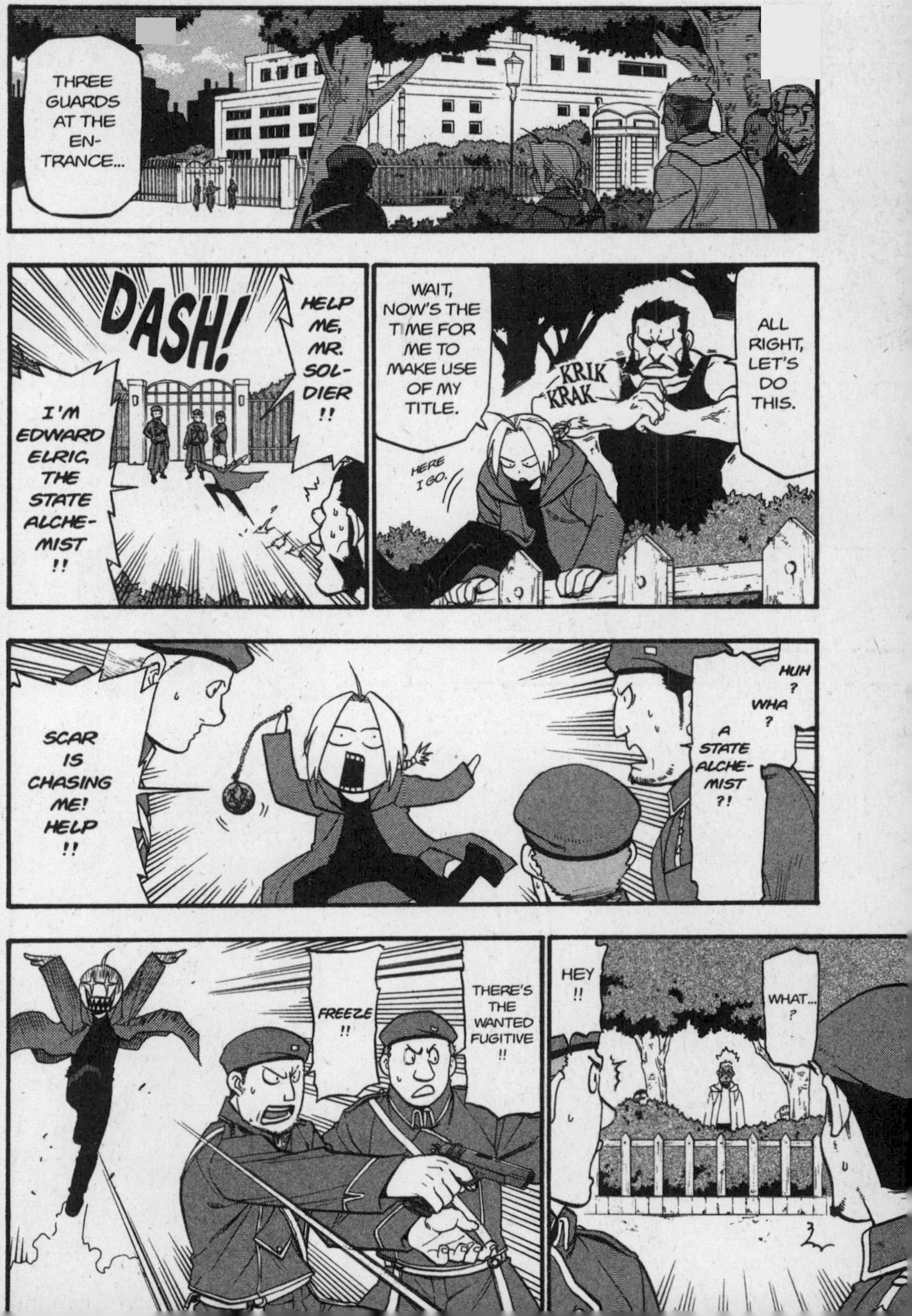
THREE GUARDS AT THE EN- TRANCE...
ALL RIGHT, LET'S DO THIS.
KRIK KRAK
WAIT, NOW'S THE TIME FOR ME TO MAKE USE OF MY TITLE.
HERE I GO.
HELP ME, MR. SOL- DIER !!
DASH!
I'M EDWARD ELRIC, THE STATE ALCHE- MIST !!
HUH ?
WHA ?
A STATE ALCHE- MIST ?!
SCAR IS CHASING ME! HELP !!
WHAT... ?
HEY !!
THERE'S THE WANTED FUGITIVE !!
FREEZE !!

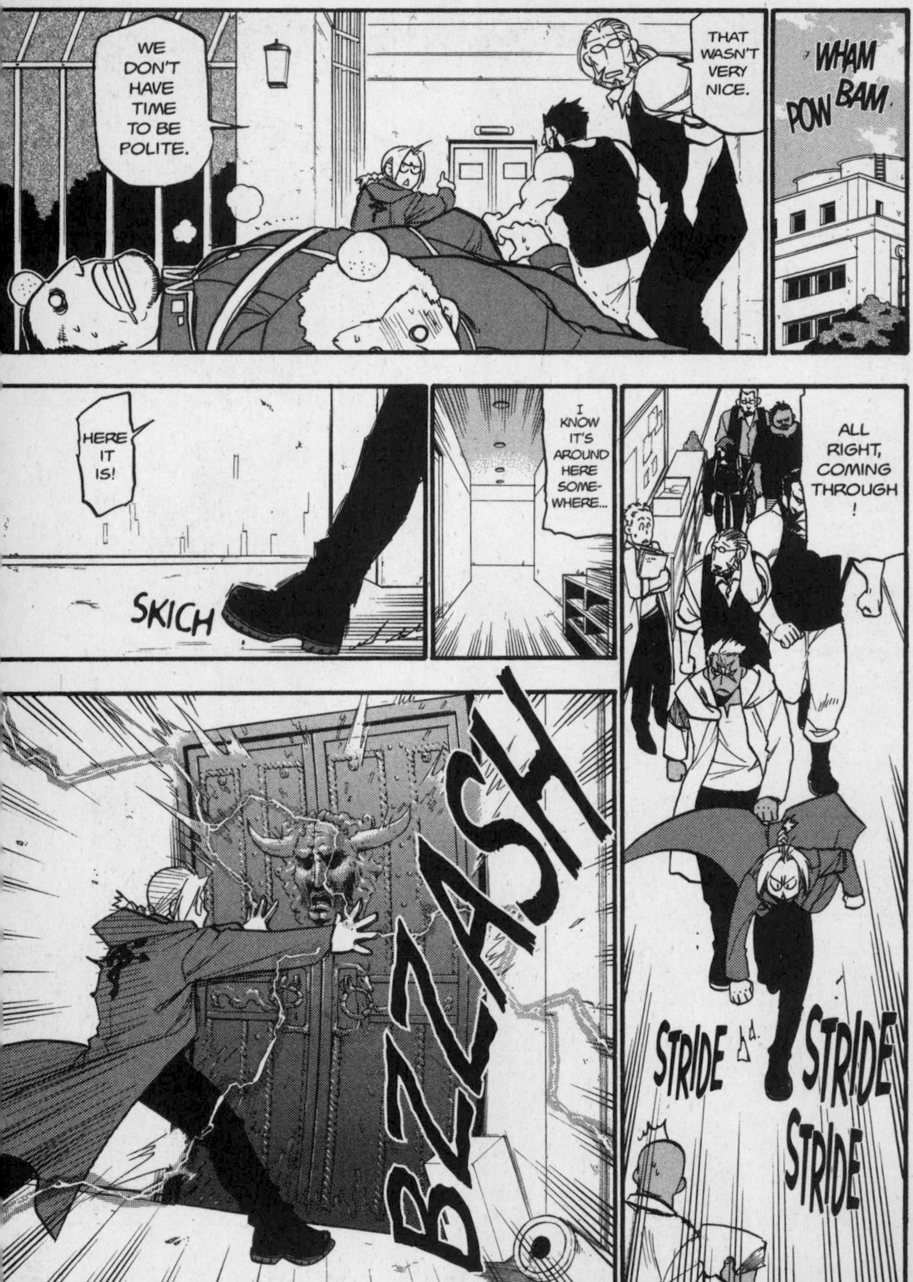
WHAM
BAM
POW
THAT WASN'T VERY NICE.
WE DON'T HAVE TIME TO BE POLITE.
ALL RIGHT, COMING THROUGH!
STRIDE
STRIDE
STRIDE
I KNOW IT'S AROUND HERE SOME-WHERE...
HERE IT IS!
SKICH
BZZASH

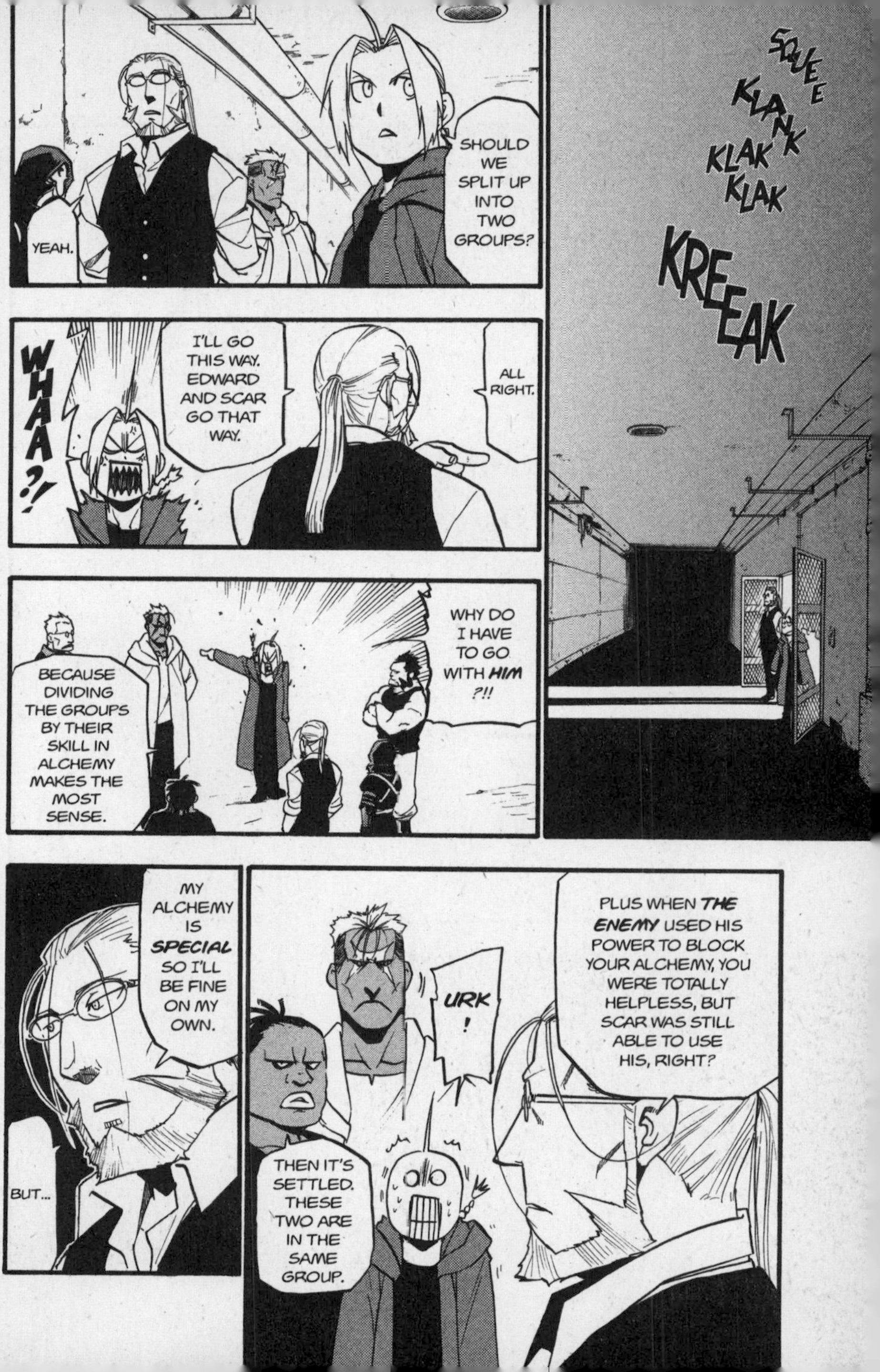
SQUEEE
KLANK
KLAK
KLAK
KREEEAK
SHOULD WE SPLIT UP INTO TWO GROUPS?
YEAH.
ALL RIGHT.
I'LL GO THIS WAY. EDWARD AND SCAR GO THAT WAY.
WHAAA?!
WHY DO I HAVE TO GO WITH HIM?!!
BECAUSE DIVIDING THE GROUPS BY THEIR SKILL IN ALCHEMY MAKES THE MOST SENSE.
PLUS WHEN THE ENEMY USED HIS POWER TO BLOCK YOUR ALCHEMY, YOU WERE TOTALLY HELPLESS, BUT SCAR WAS STILL ABLE TO USE HIS, RIGHT?
URK!
THEN IT'S SETTLED. THESE TWO ARE IN THE SAME GROUP.
MY ALCHEMY IS SPECIAL SO I'LL BE FINE ON MY OWN.
BUT...

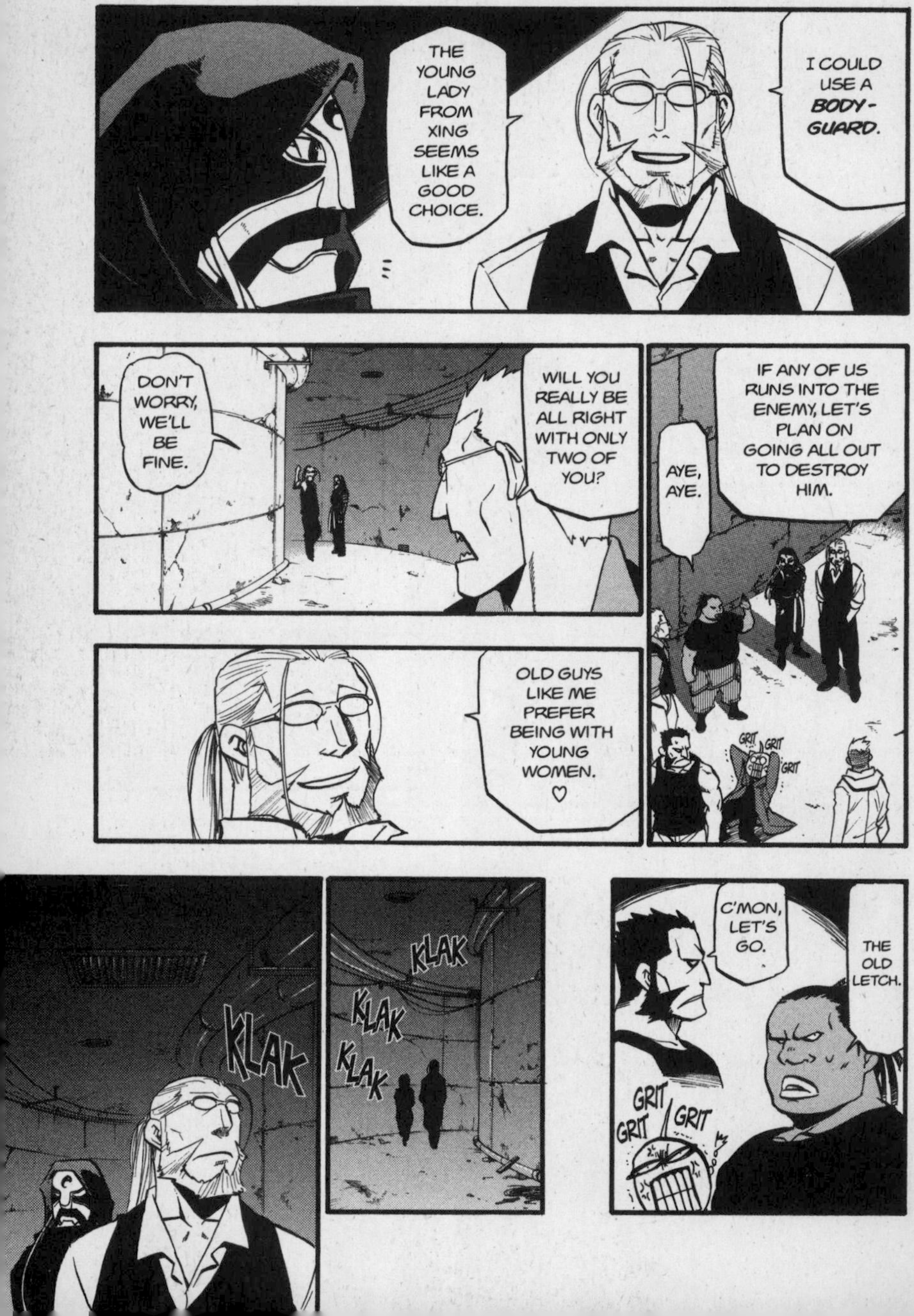
I COULD USE A BODY-GUARD.
THE YOUNG LADY FROM XING SEEMS LIKE A GOOD CHOICE.
IF ANY OF US RUNS INTO THE ENEMY, LET'S PLAN ON GOING ALL OUT TO DESTROY HIM.
AYE, AYE.
GRIT
GRIT
GRIT
WILL YOU REALLY BE ALL RIGHT WITH ONLY TWO OF YOU?
DON'T WORRY, WE'LL BE FINE.
OLD GUYS LIKE ME PREFER BEING WITH YOUNG WOMEN. ♡
THE OLD LETCH.
C'MON, LET'S GO.
GRIT
GRIT
GRIT
KLAK
KLAK
KLAK
KLAK

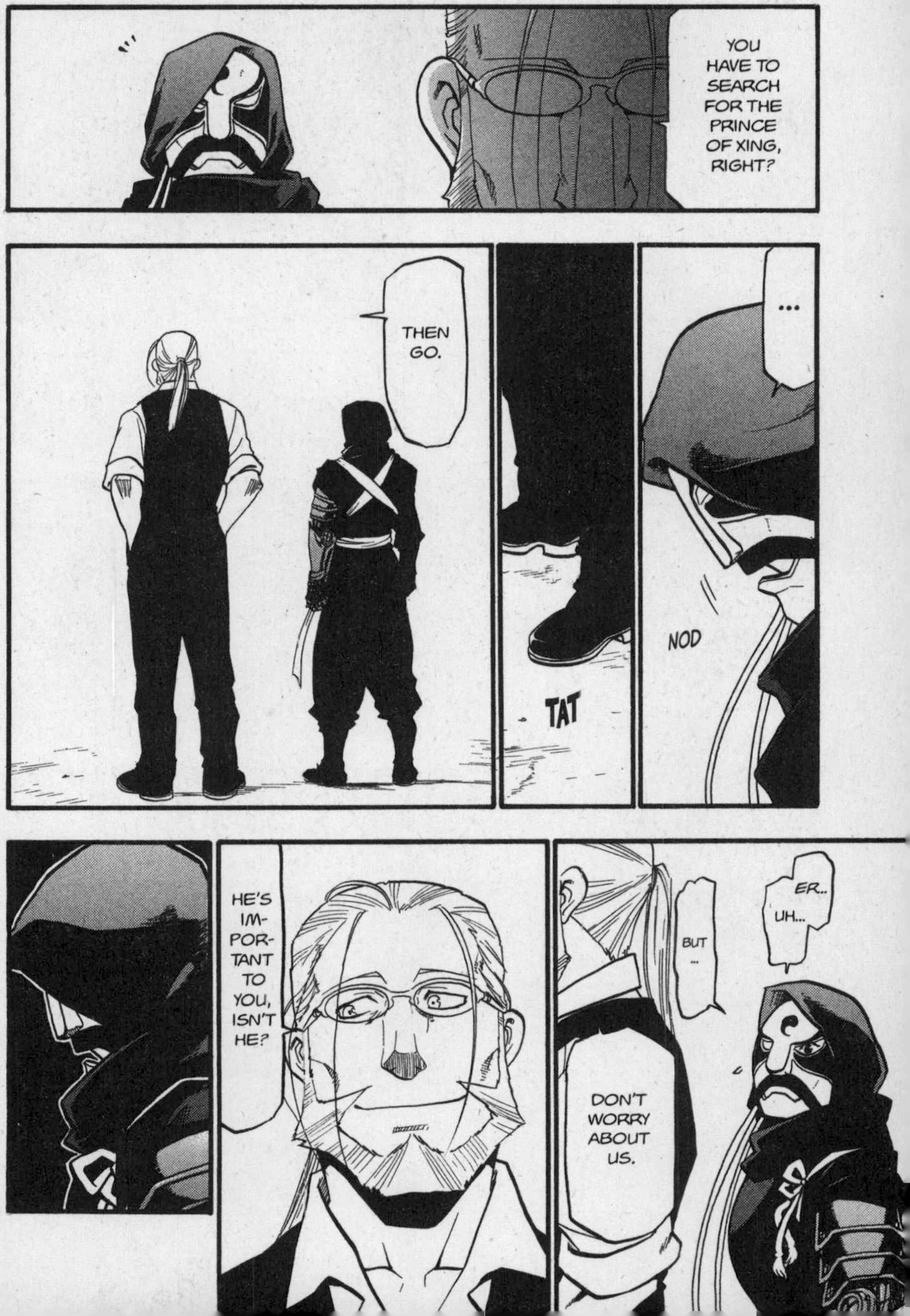
YOU HAVE TO SEARCH FOR THE PRINCE OF XING, RIGHT?
...
NOD
TAT
THEN GO.
ER.. UH...
BUT ...
DON'T WORRY ABOUT US.
HE'S IM-POR-TANT TO YOU, ISN'T HE?

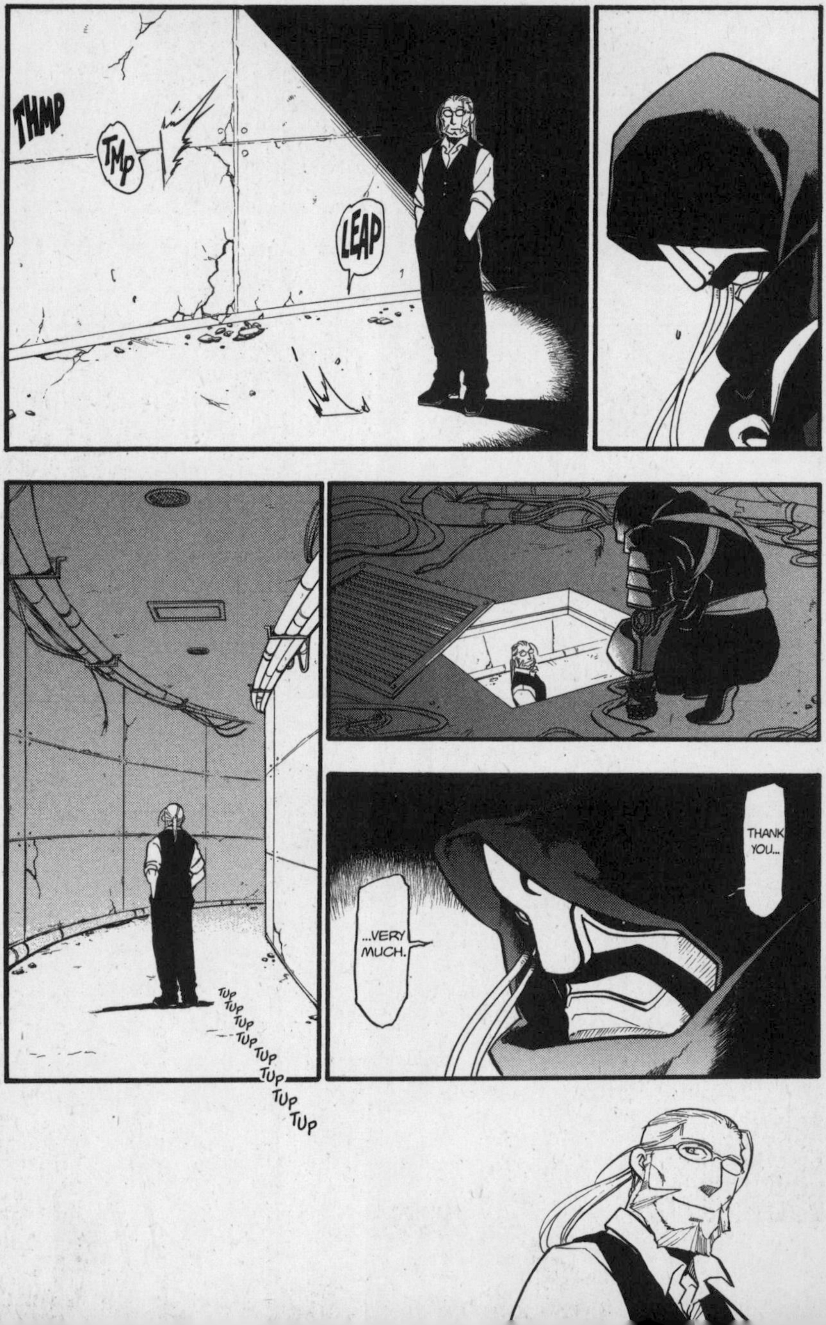
THMP
TMP
LEAP
THANK YOU...
...VERY MUCH.
TUP TUP TUP TUP TUP TUP TUP TUP

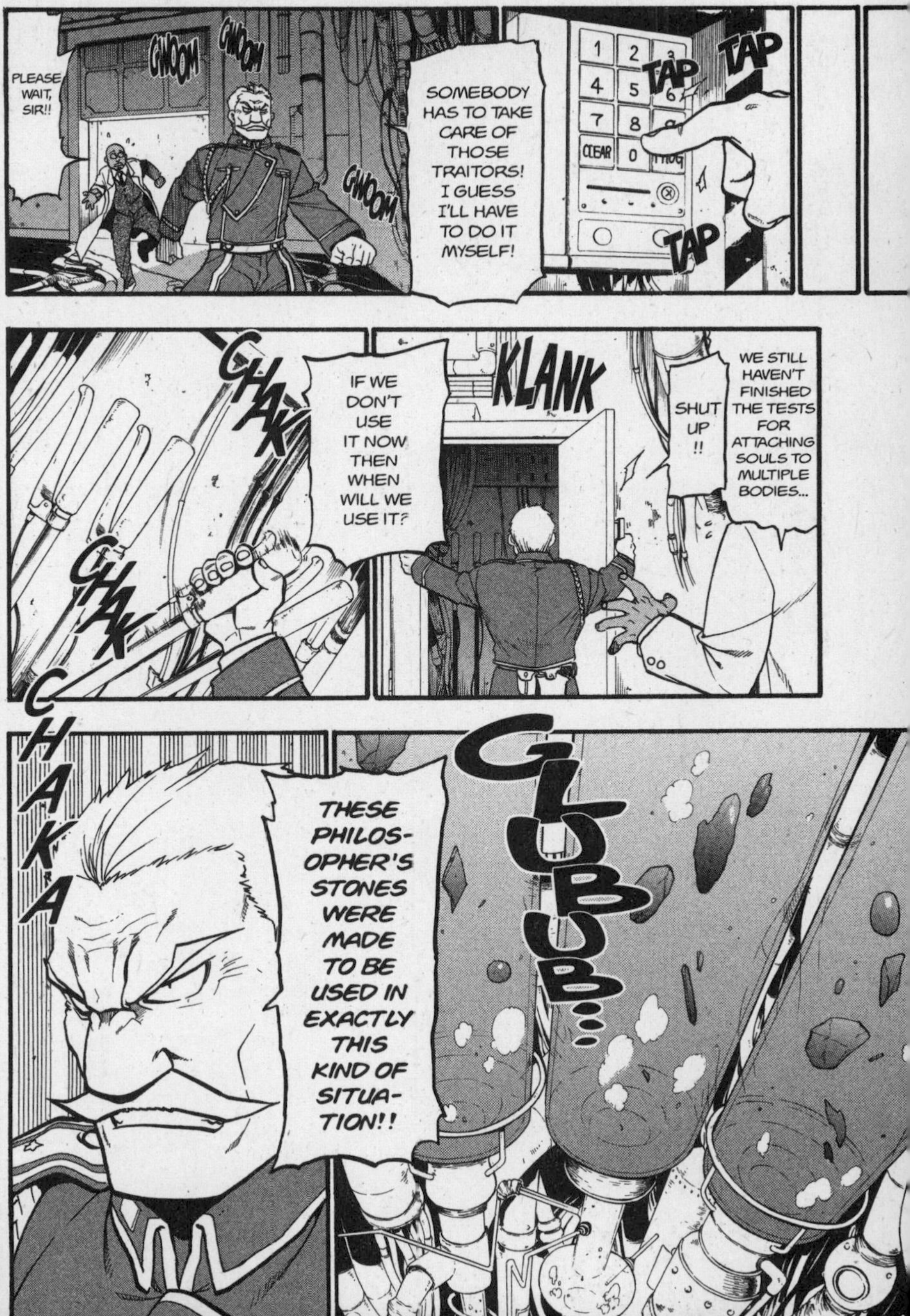
TAP
TAP
TAP
SOMEBODY HAS TO TAKE CARE OF THOSE TRAITORS! I GUESS I'LL HAVE TO DO IT MYSELF!
GWOOM
GWOOM
PLEASE WAIT, SIR!!
GWOOM
WE STILL HAVEN'T FINISHED THE TESTS FOR ATTACHING SOULS TO MULTIPLE BODIES...
SHUT UP!!
KLANK
IF WE DON'T USE IT NOW THEN WHEN WILL WE USE IT?
CHAK
CHAK
CHAK
GLUBUB...
THESE PHILOSOPHER'S STONES WERE MADE TO BE USED IN EXACTLY THIS KIND OF SITUATION!!
CHAKA
CHAKA

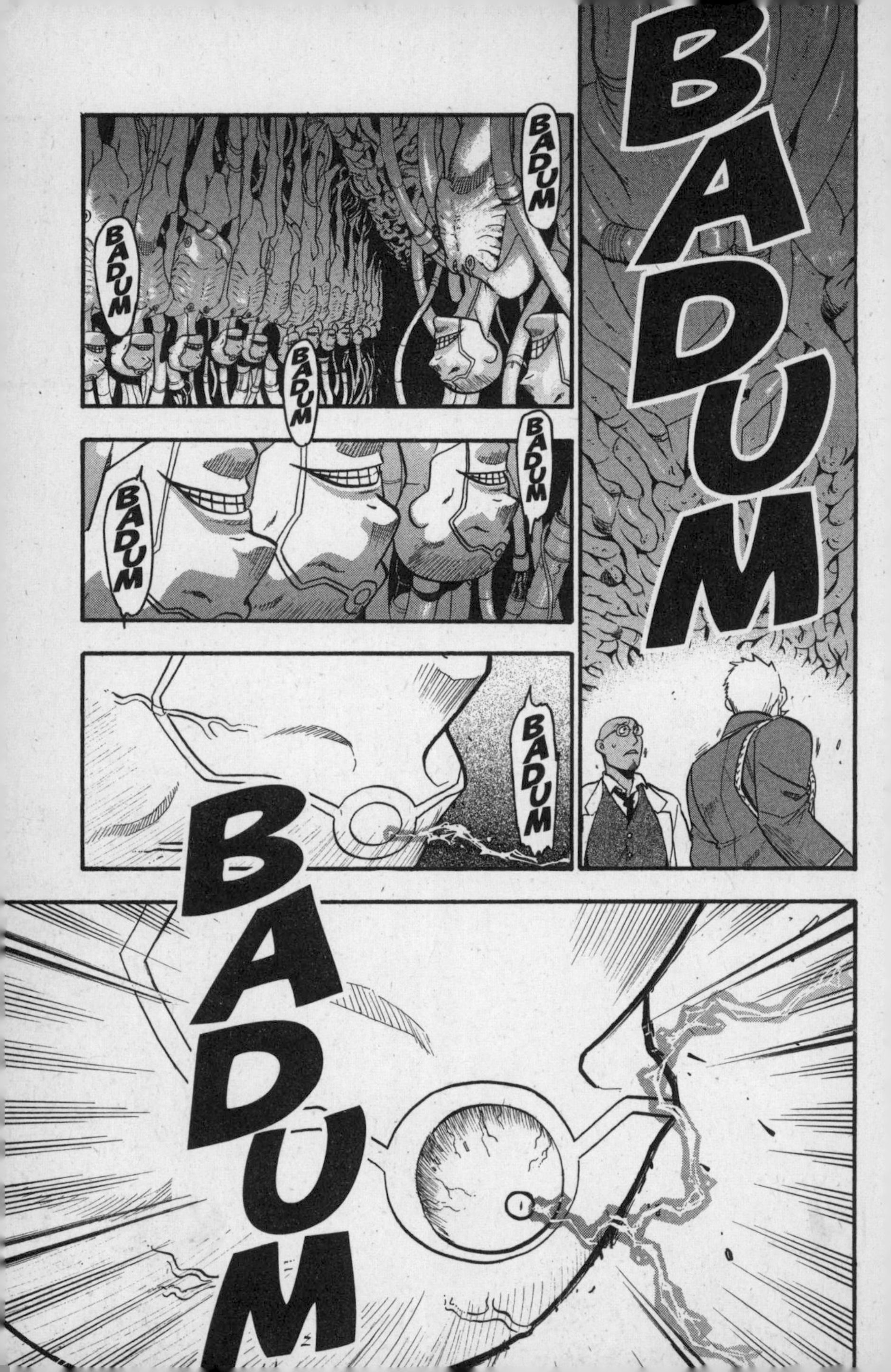
BADUM
BADUM
BADUM
BADUM
BADUM
BADUM
BADUM
BADUM

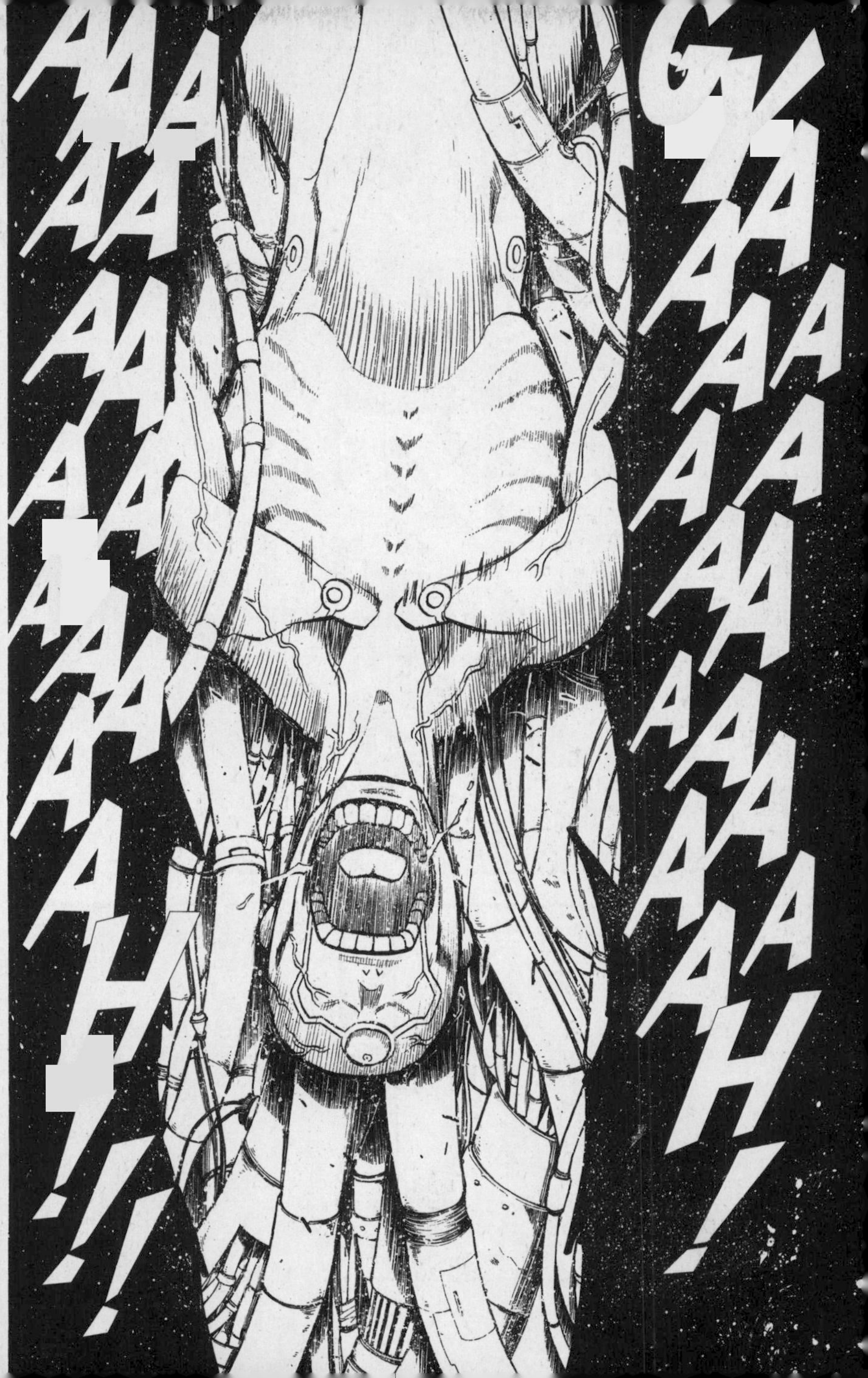
GYAAAAAAAAAAAAAAAAAAAAAH!
AAAAAAAAAAAAAAAAAAAAAAH!!!

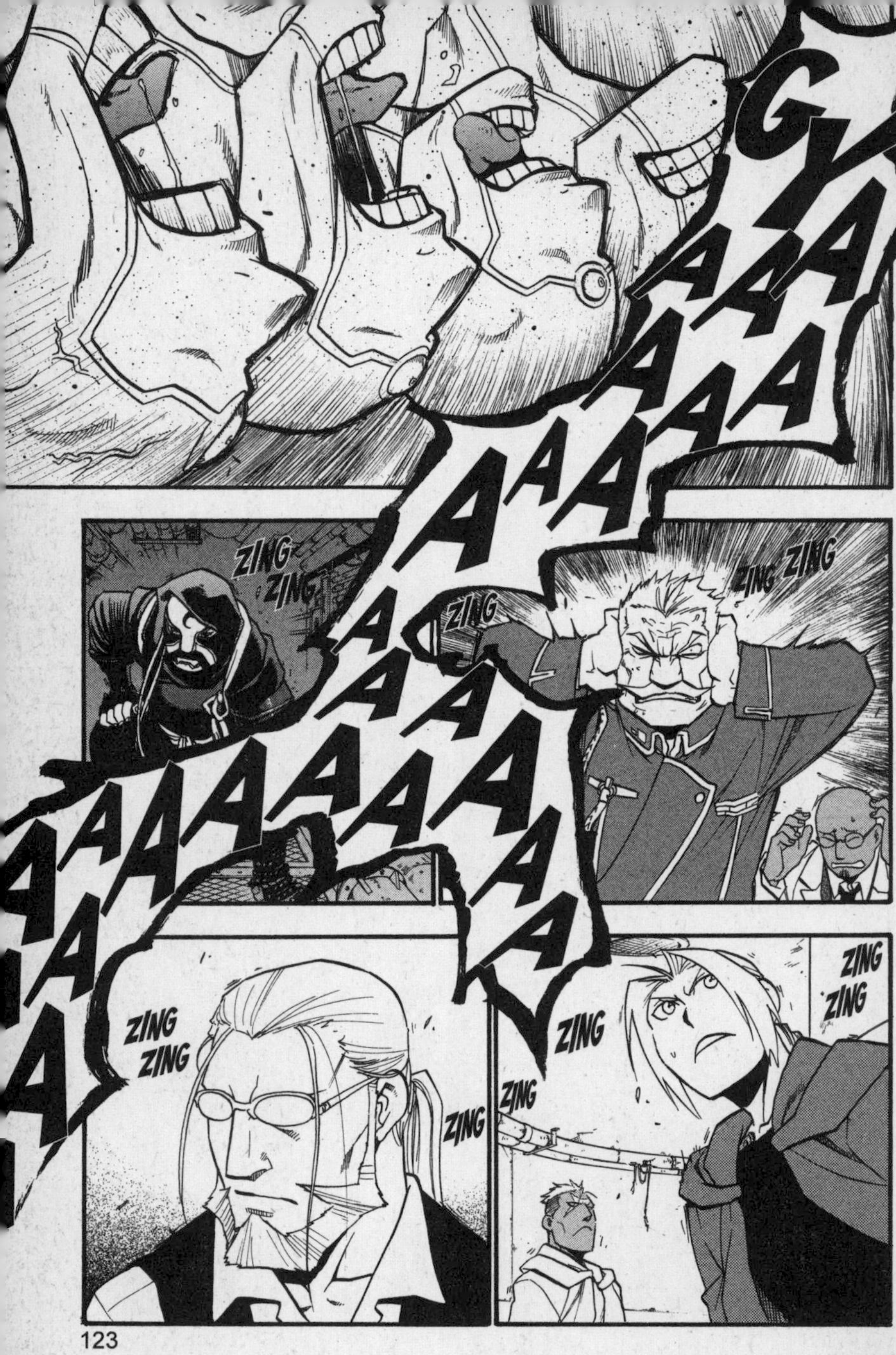
GYAAAAAAAAAAAAAAAAAAAAAAAAAAAAAA
ZING ZING
ZING
ZING
ZING ZING
ZING ZING
ZING
ZING
ZING
ZING ZING

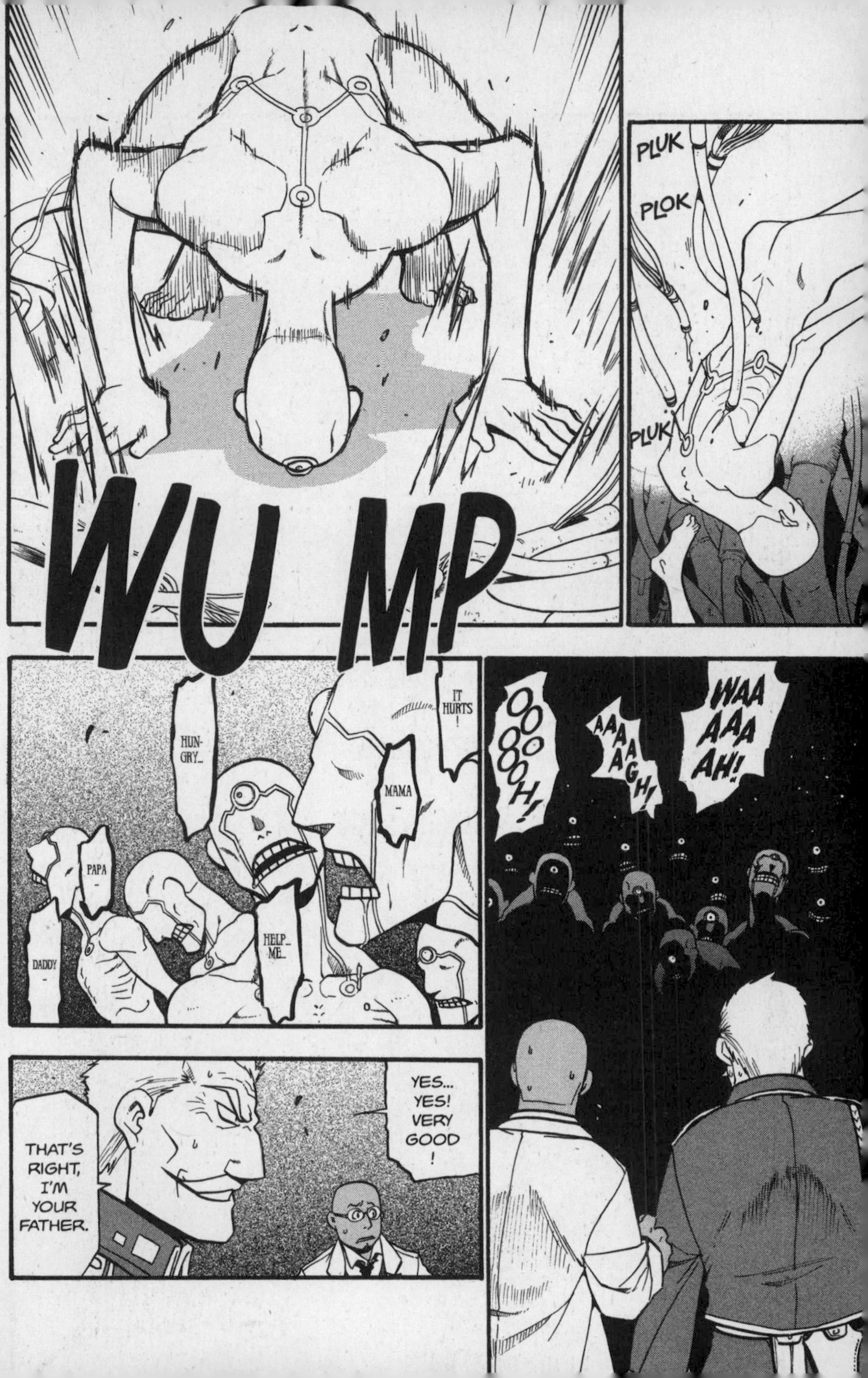
PLUK
PLOK
PLUK
WUMP
WAAAAAAAH!
AAAAAGH!
OOOOOOH!
IT HURTS!
MAMA...
HUNGRY...
HELP ME...
PAPA...
DADDY...
YES... YES! VERY GOOD!
THAT'S RIGHT, I'M YOUR FATHER.

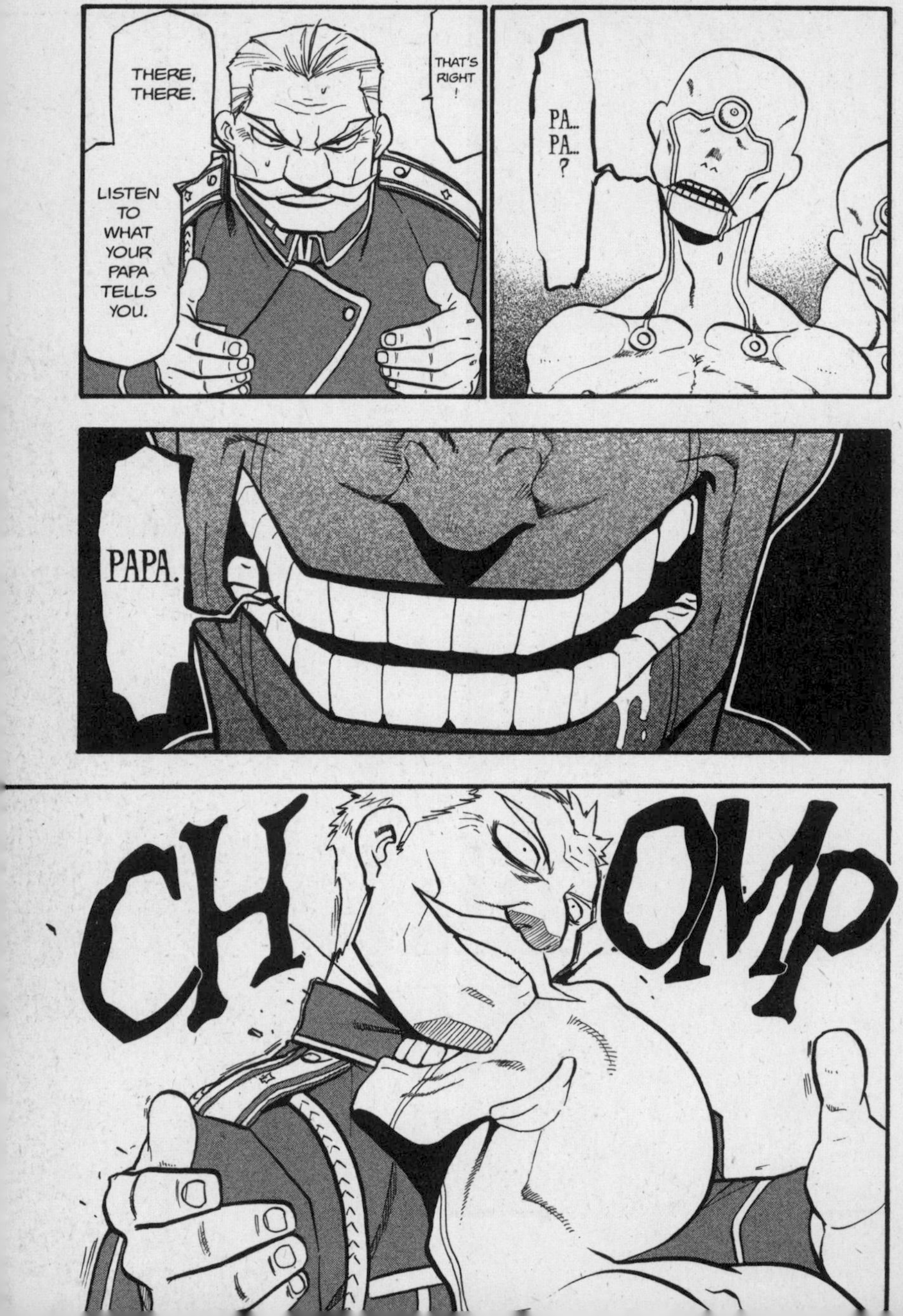
PA.. PA.. ?
THAT'S RIGHT !
THERE, THERE.
LISTEN TO WHAT YOUR PAPA TELLS YOU.
PAPA.
CHOMP

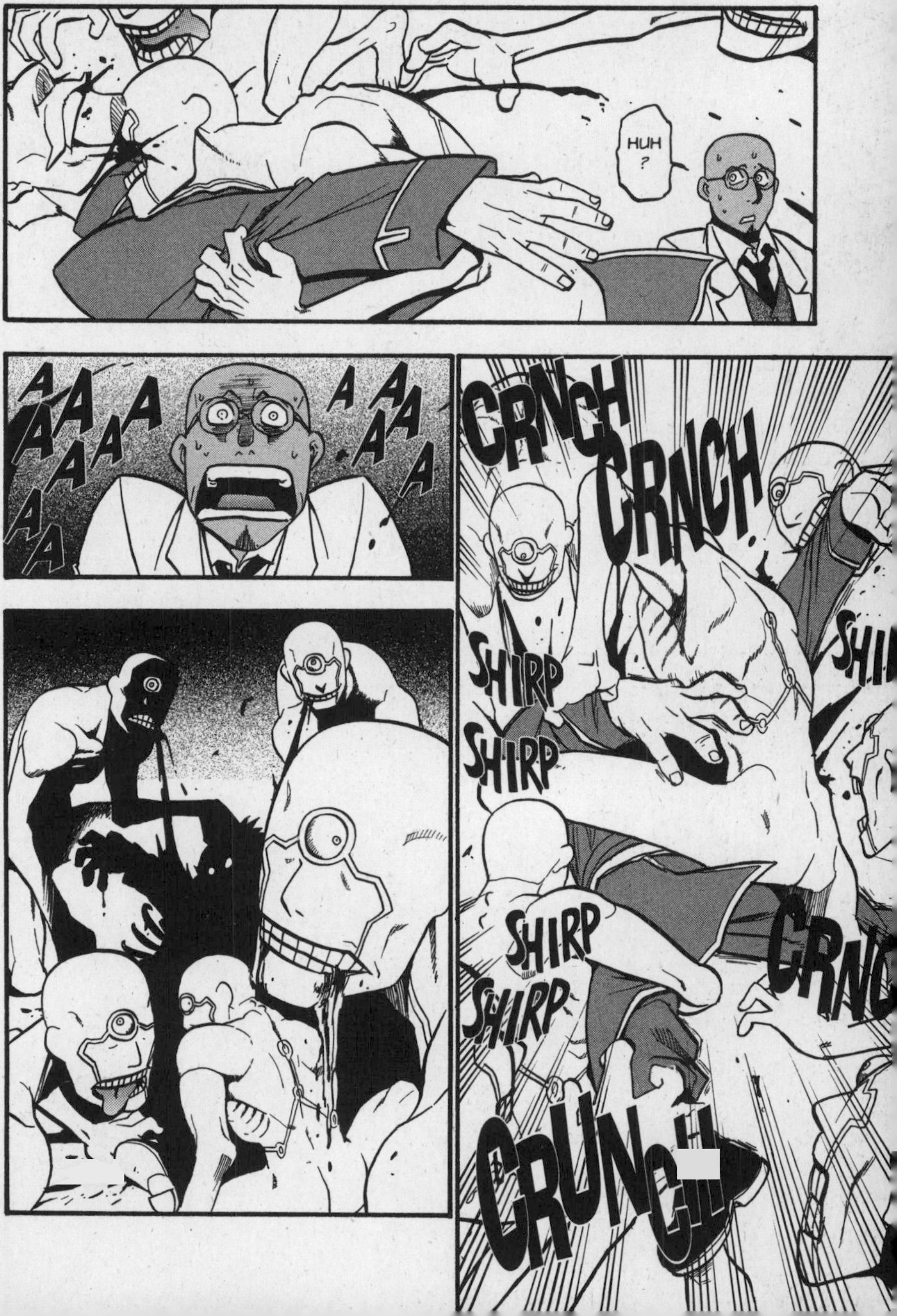
HUH ?
CRNCH
CRNCH
SHIRP
SHIRP
SHIRP
SHIRP
CRUNCH
AAAAAAAAAA
AAAAAAA

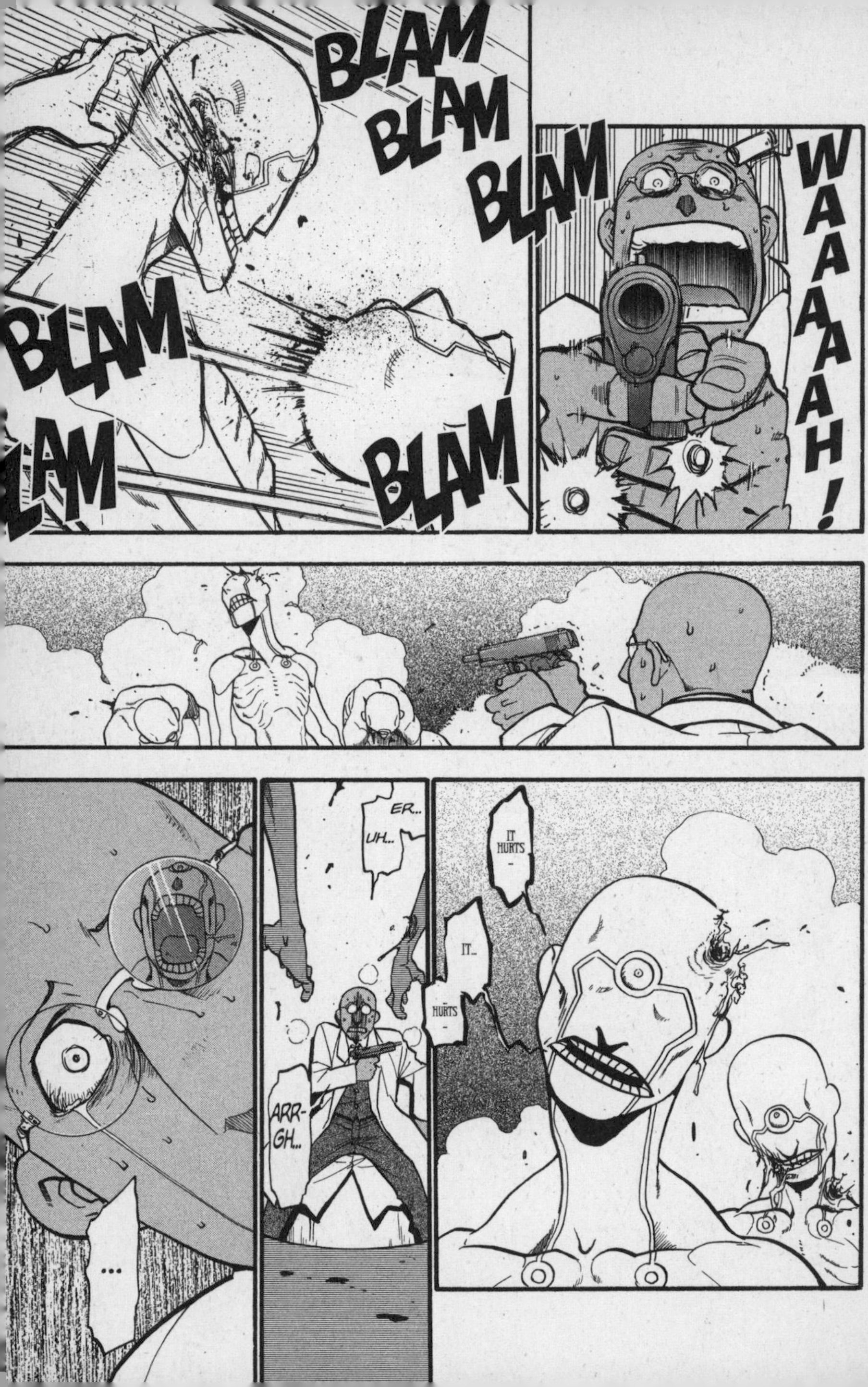
WAAAAAH!
BLAM
BLAM
BLAM
BLAM
BLAM
LAM
IT HURTS—
IT...
HURTS—
ER...
UH...
ARRGH...
...

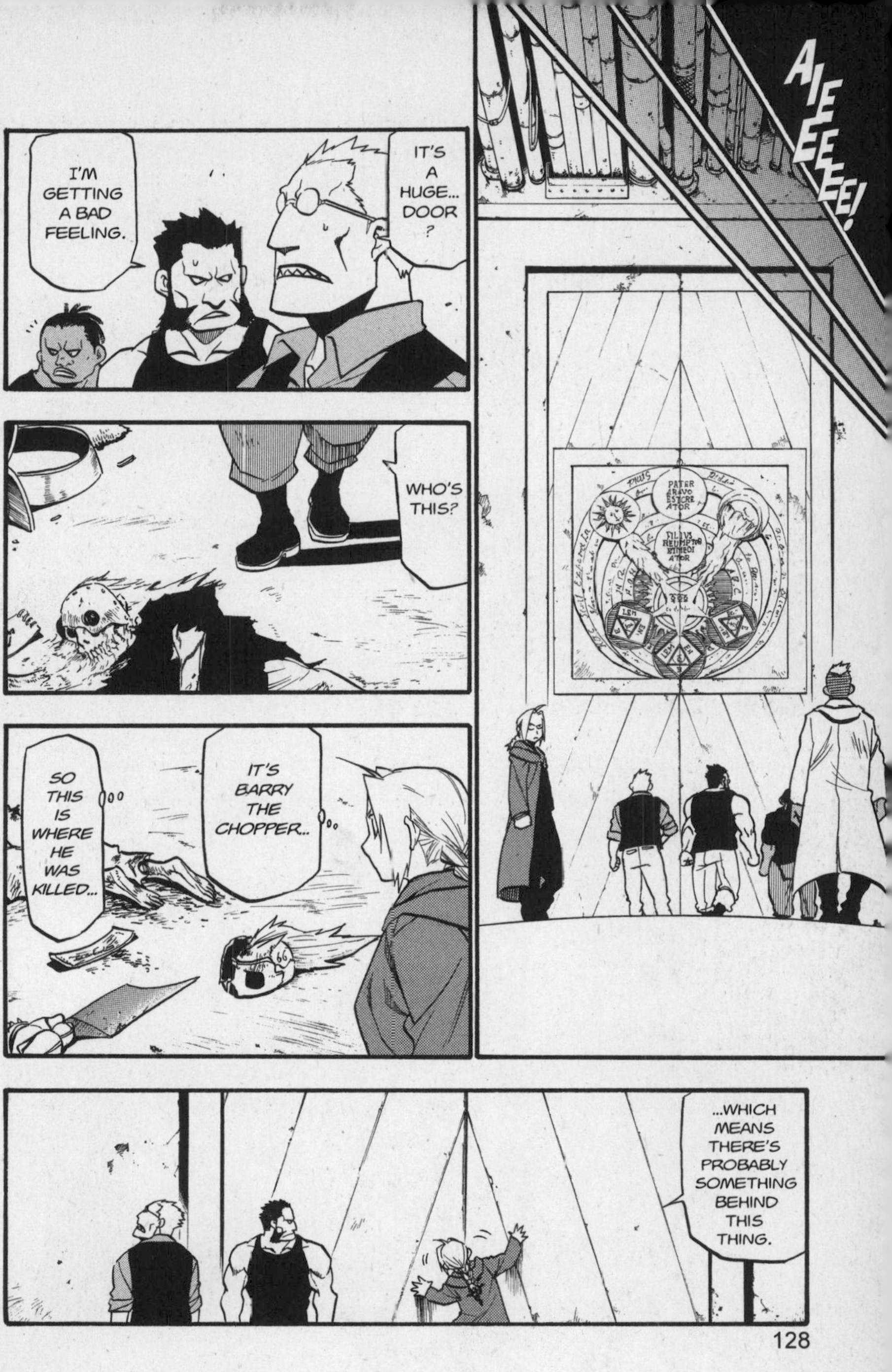
AIEEEEE!
IT'S A HUGE... DOOR?
I'M GETTING A BAD FEELING.
WHO'S THIS?
IT'S BARRY THE CHOPPER...
SO THIS IS WHERE HE WAS KILLED...
...WHICH MEANS THERE'S PROBABLY SOMETHING BEHIND THIS THING.

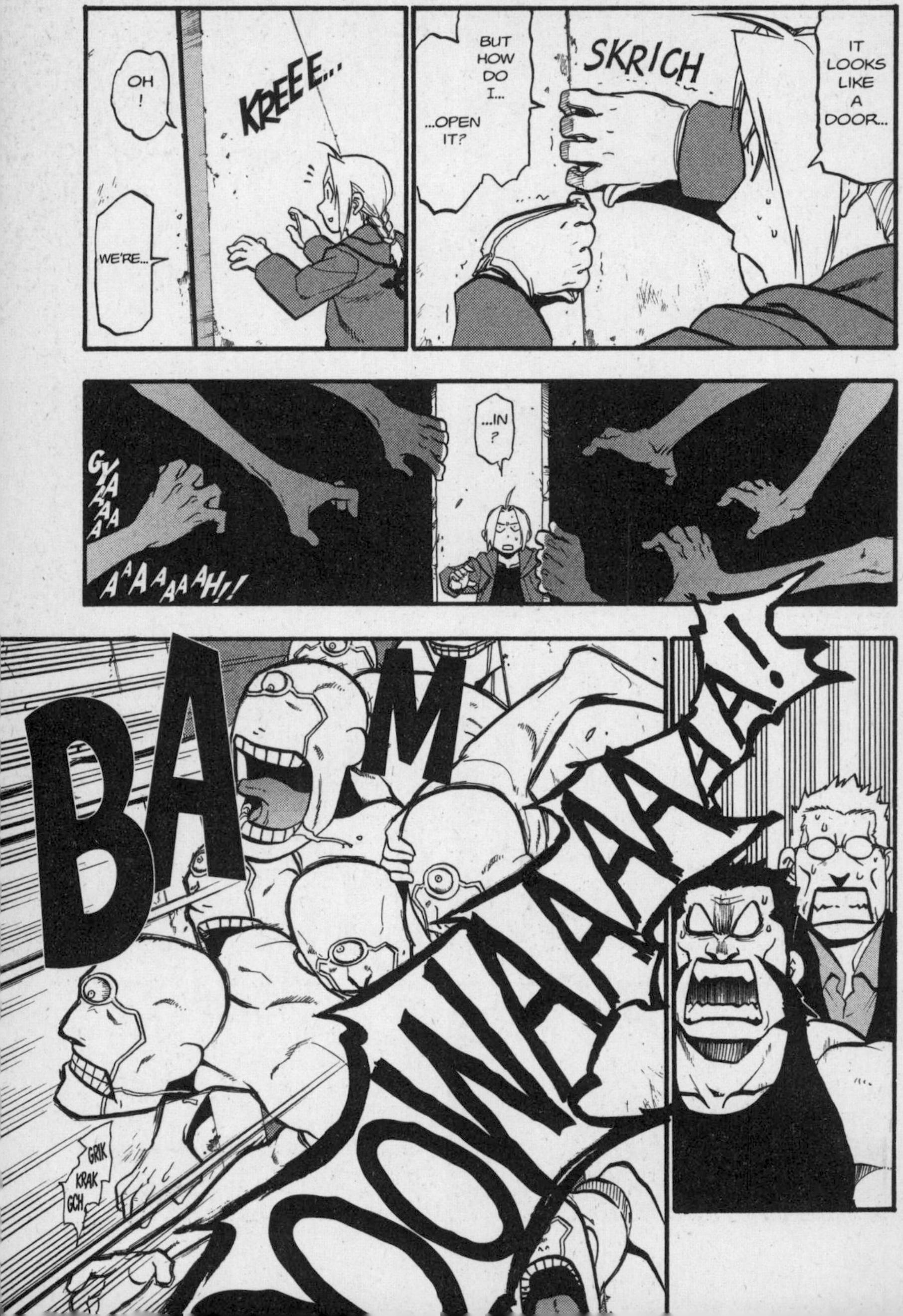
IT LOOKS LIKE A DOOR...
SKRICH
BUT HOW DO I...
...OPEN IT?
KREEE...
OH!
WE'RE...
...IN?
GYAAAAAAAAAAAH!!
BAM
OOWAAAAAAA!
GRIK KRAK GCH

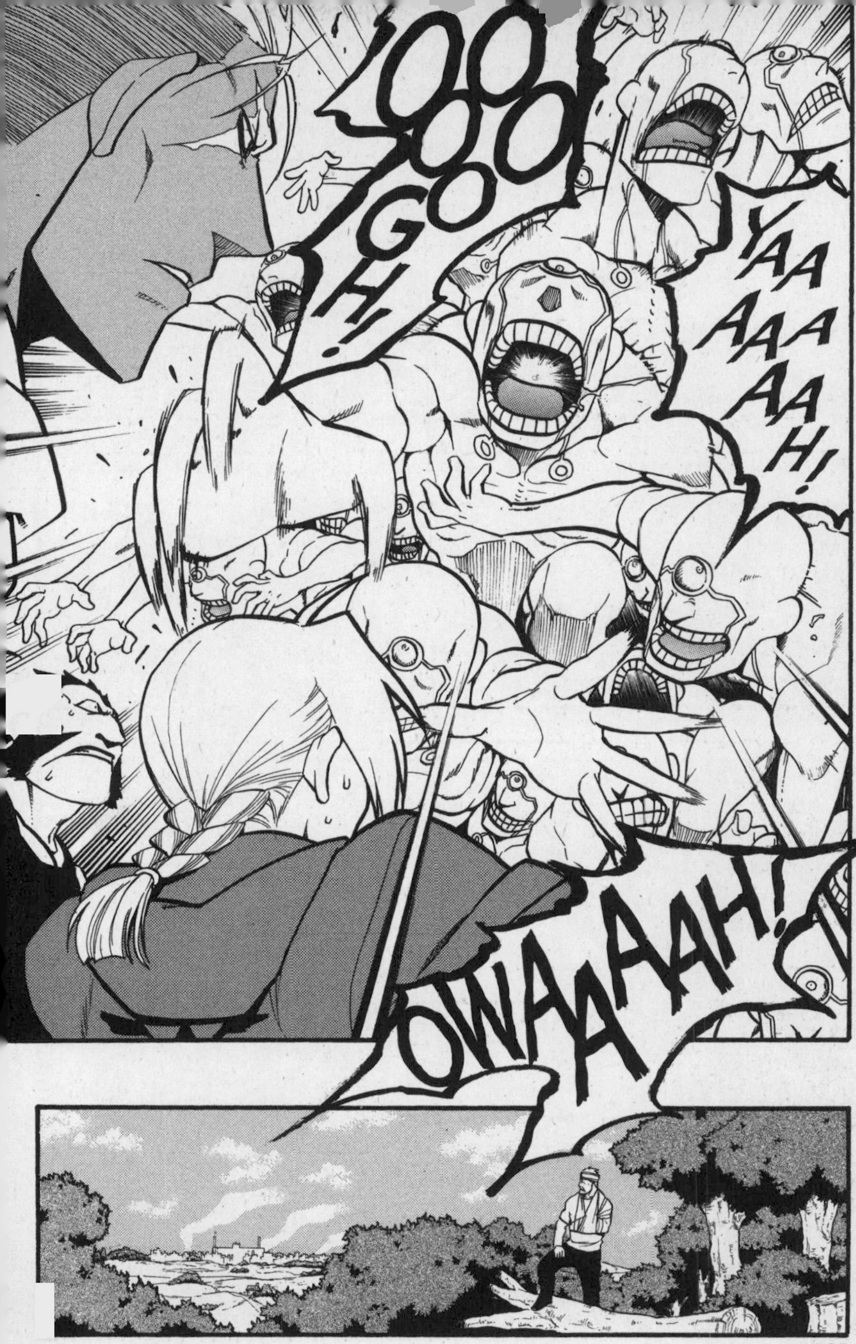
YAAAAAAAH!
OOOOOGH!
OWAAAAH!

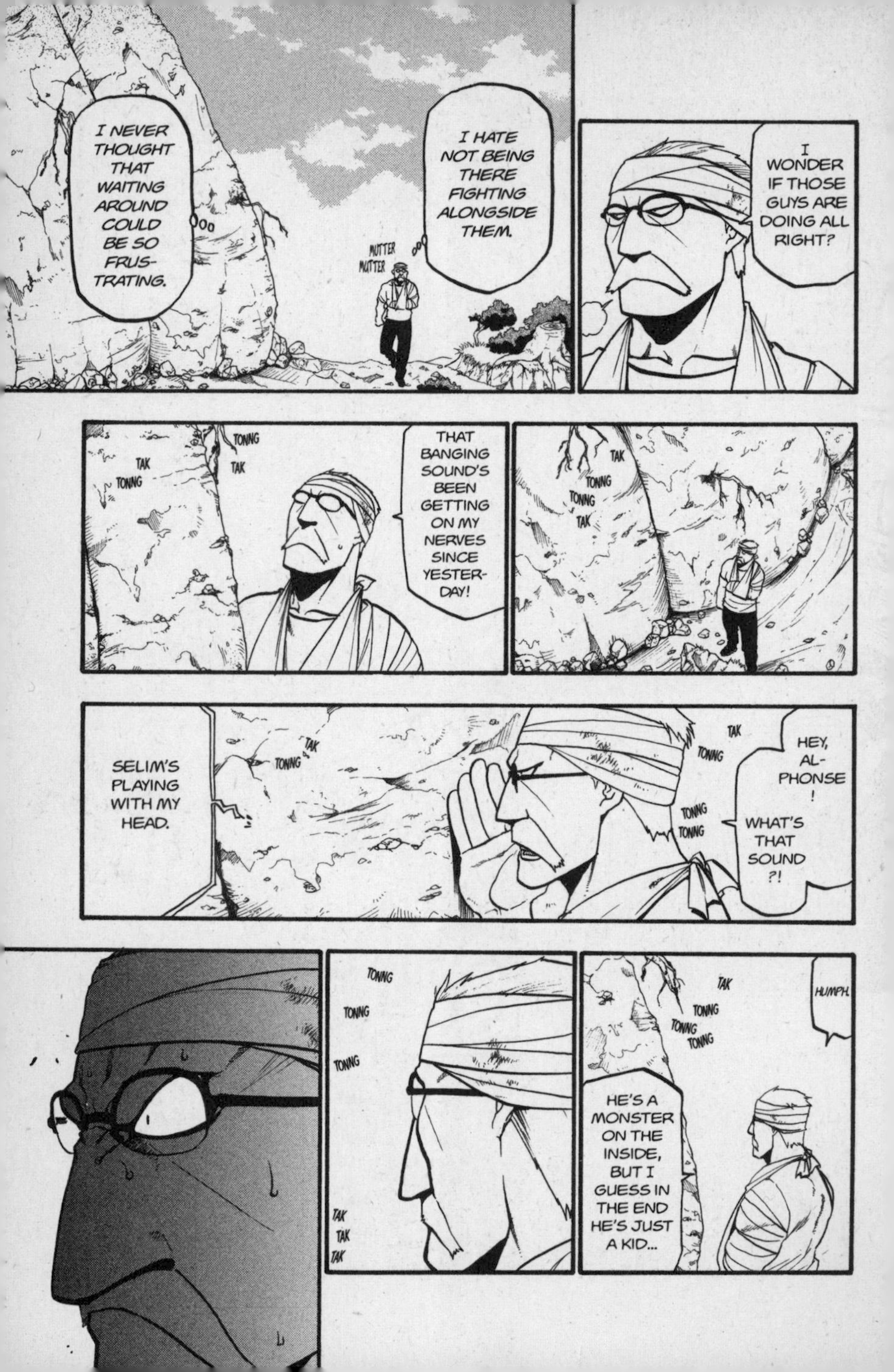
I WONDER IF THOSE GUYS ARE DOING ALL RIGHT?
I HATE NOT BEING THERE FIGHTING ALONGSIDE THEM.
MUTTER
MUTTER
I NEVER THOUGHT THAT WAITING AROUND COULD BE SO FRUS-TRATING.
TAK
TONNG
TONNG
TAK
TONNG
TAK
TAK
TONNG
THAT BANGING SOUND'S BEEN GETTING ON MY NERVES SINCE YESTER-DAY!
TAK
TONNG
HEY, AL-PHONSE!
WHAT'S THAT SOUND?!
TONNG
TONNG
TAK
TONNG
SELIM'S PLAYING WITH MY HEAD.
HUMPH.
TAK
TONNG
TONNG
TONNG
HE'S A MONSTER ON THE INSIDE, BUT I GUESS IN THE END HE'S JUST A KID...
TONNG
TONNG
TONNG
TAK
TAK
TAK

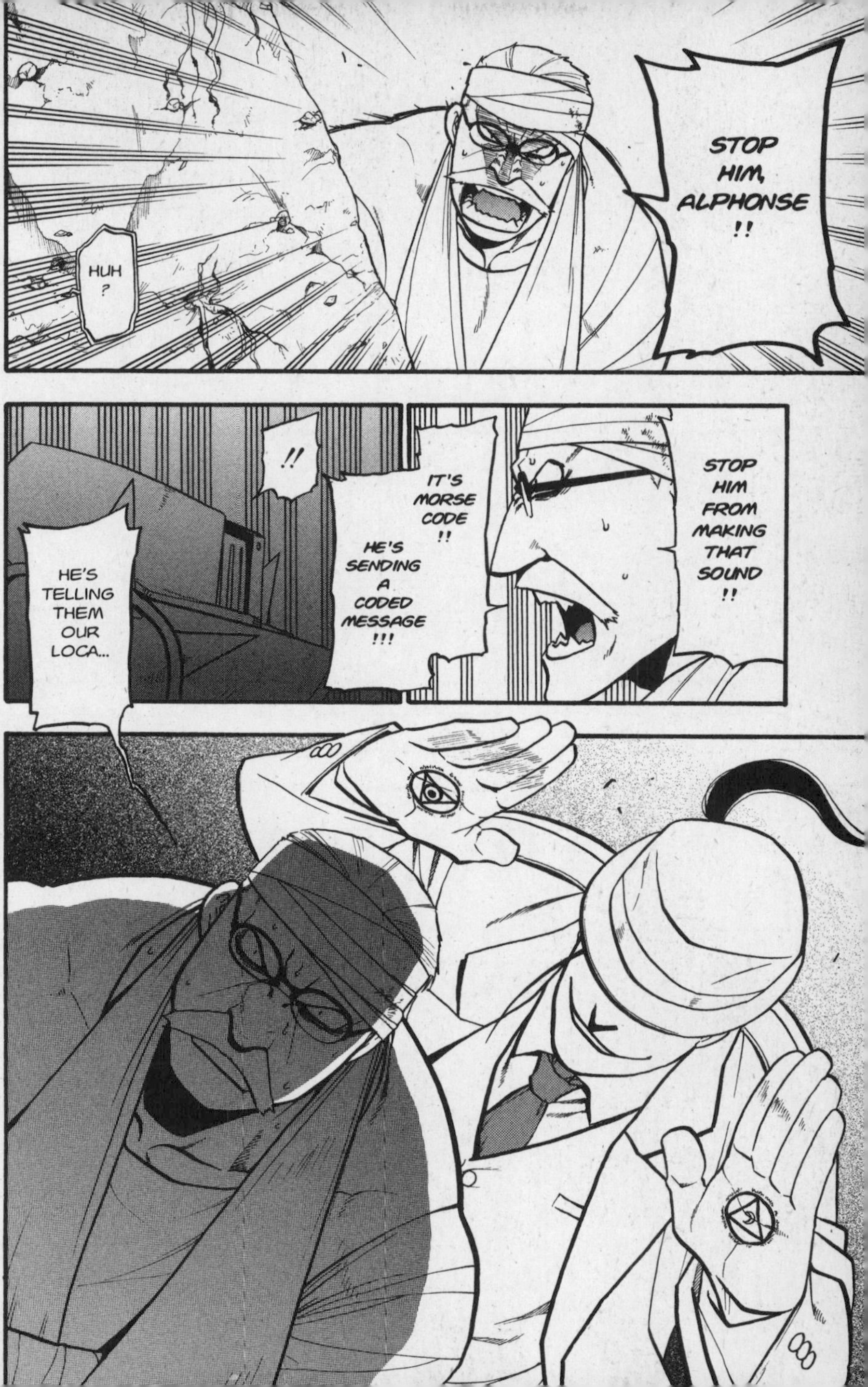
STOP HIM, ALPHONSE !!
HUH ?
STOP HIM FROM MAKING THAT SOUND !!
IT'S MORSE CODE !!
HE'S SENDING A CODED MESSAGE !!!
!!
HE'S TELLING THEM OUR LOCA...

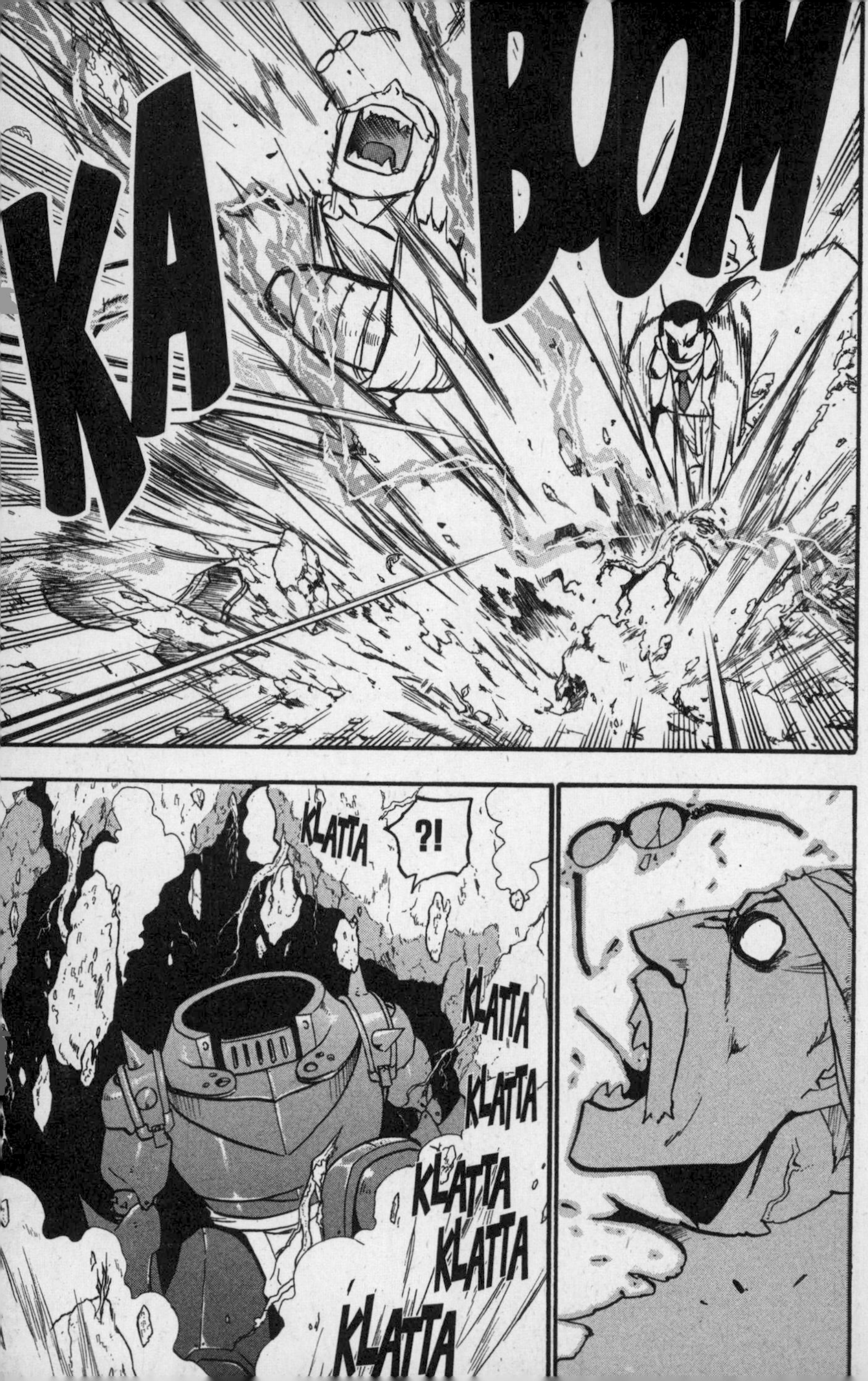
KA BOOM
?!
KLATTA
KLATTA
KLATTA
KLATTA
KLATTA
KLATTA

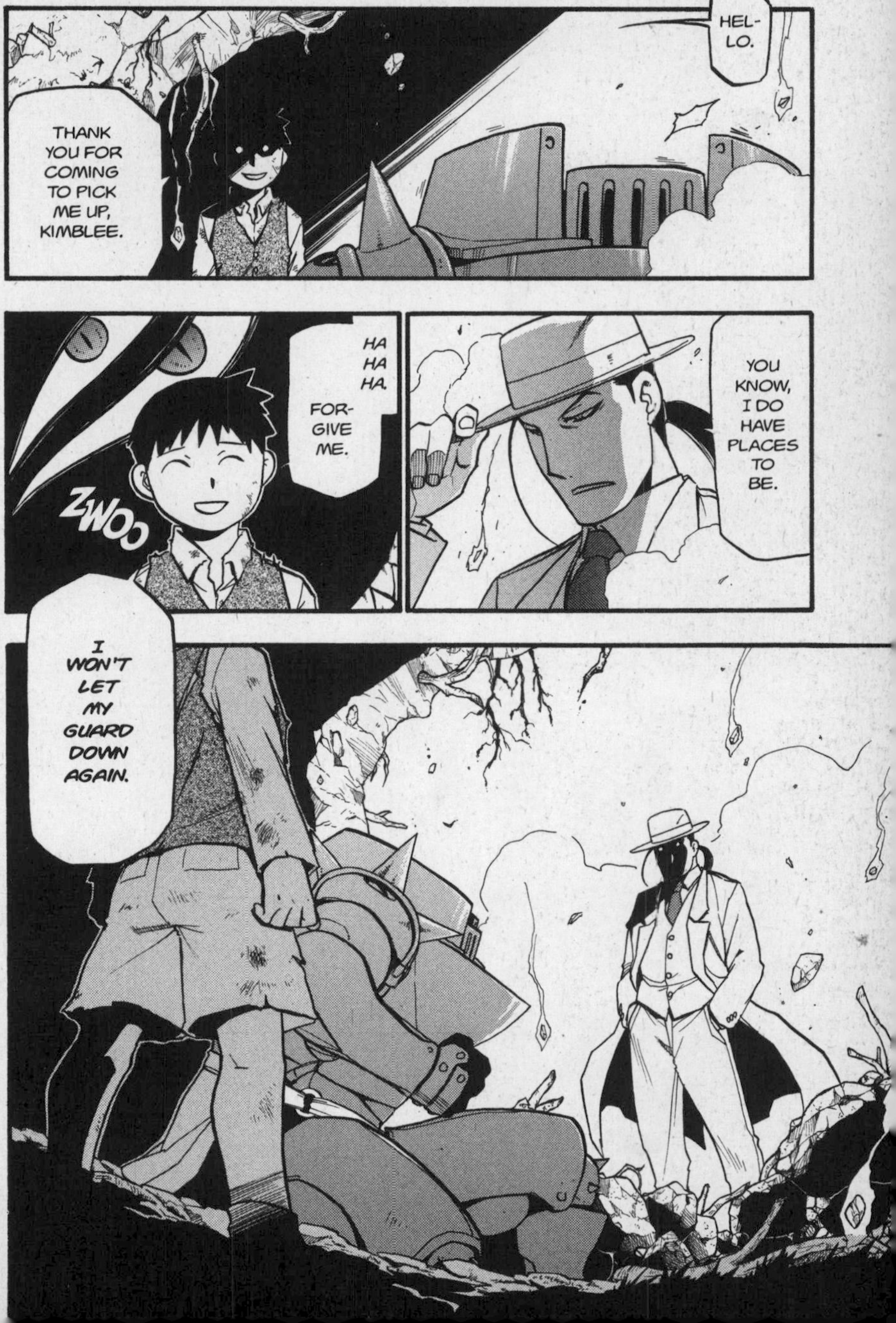
HEL-LO.
THANK YOU FOR COMING TO PICK ME UP, KIMBLEE.
YOU KNOW, I DO HAVE PLACES TO BE.
HA HA HA. FOR-GIVE ME.
ZWOO
I WON'T LET MY GUARD DOWN AGAIN.

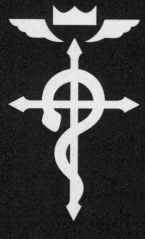

FULLMETAL
ALCHEMIST

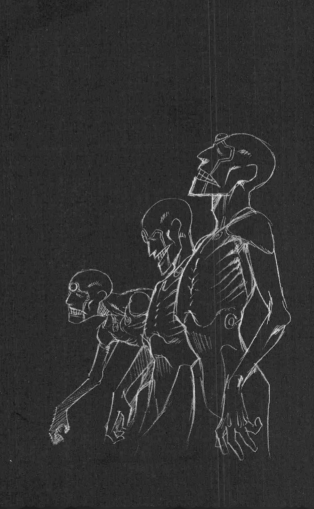

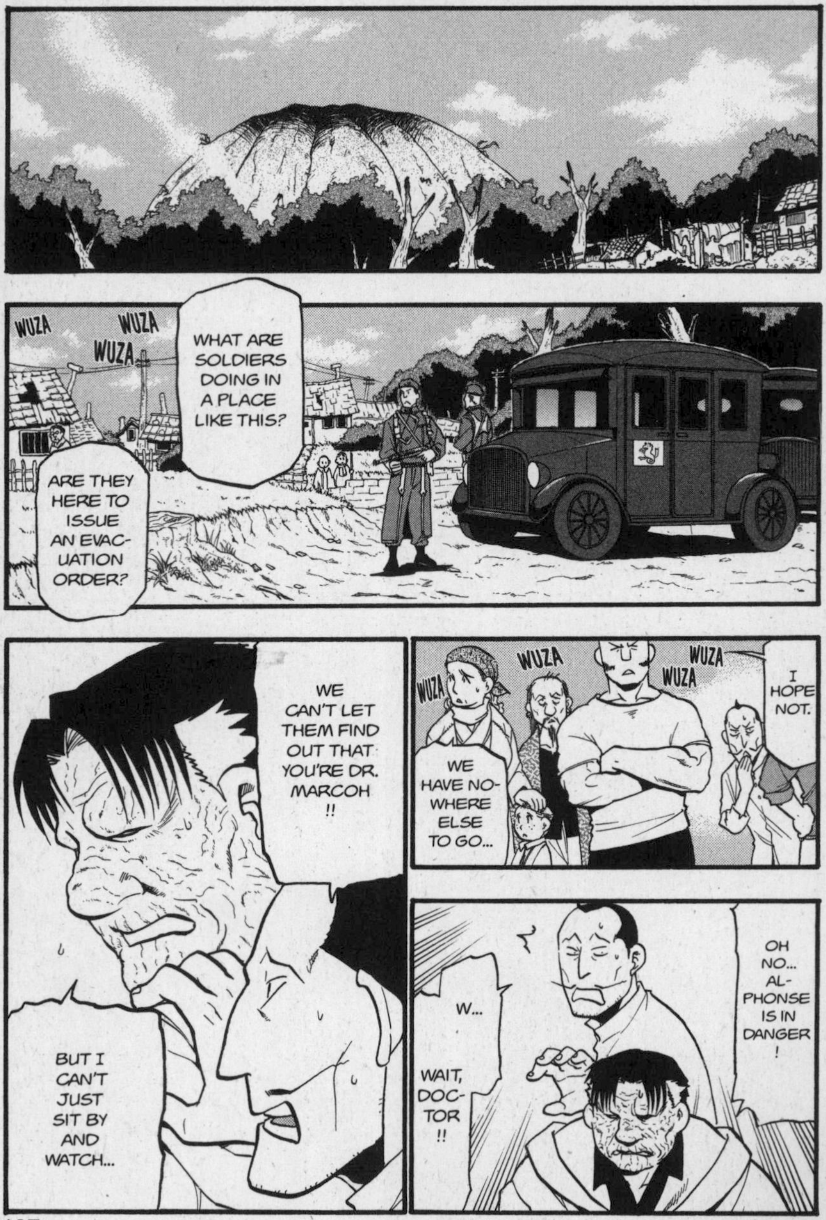
WUZA
WUZA
WUZA
WHAT ARE SOLDIERS DOING IN A PLACE LIKE THIS?
ARE THEY HERE TO ISSUE AN EVACUATION ORDER?
I HOPE NOT.
WUZA
WUZA
WUZA
WUZA
WE HAVE NOWHERE ELSE TO GO...
OH NO... ALPHONSE IS IN DANGER!
W...
WAIT, DOCTOR!!
WE CAN'T LET THEM FIND OUT THAT YOU'RE DR. MARCOH!!
BUT I CAN'T JUST SIT BY AND WATCH...

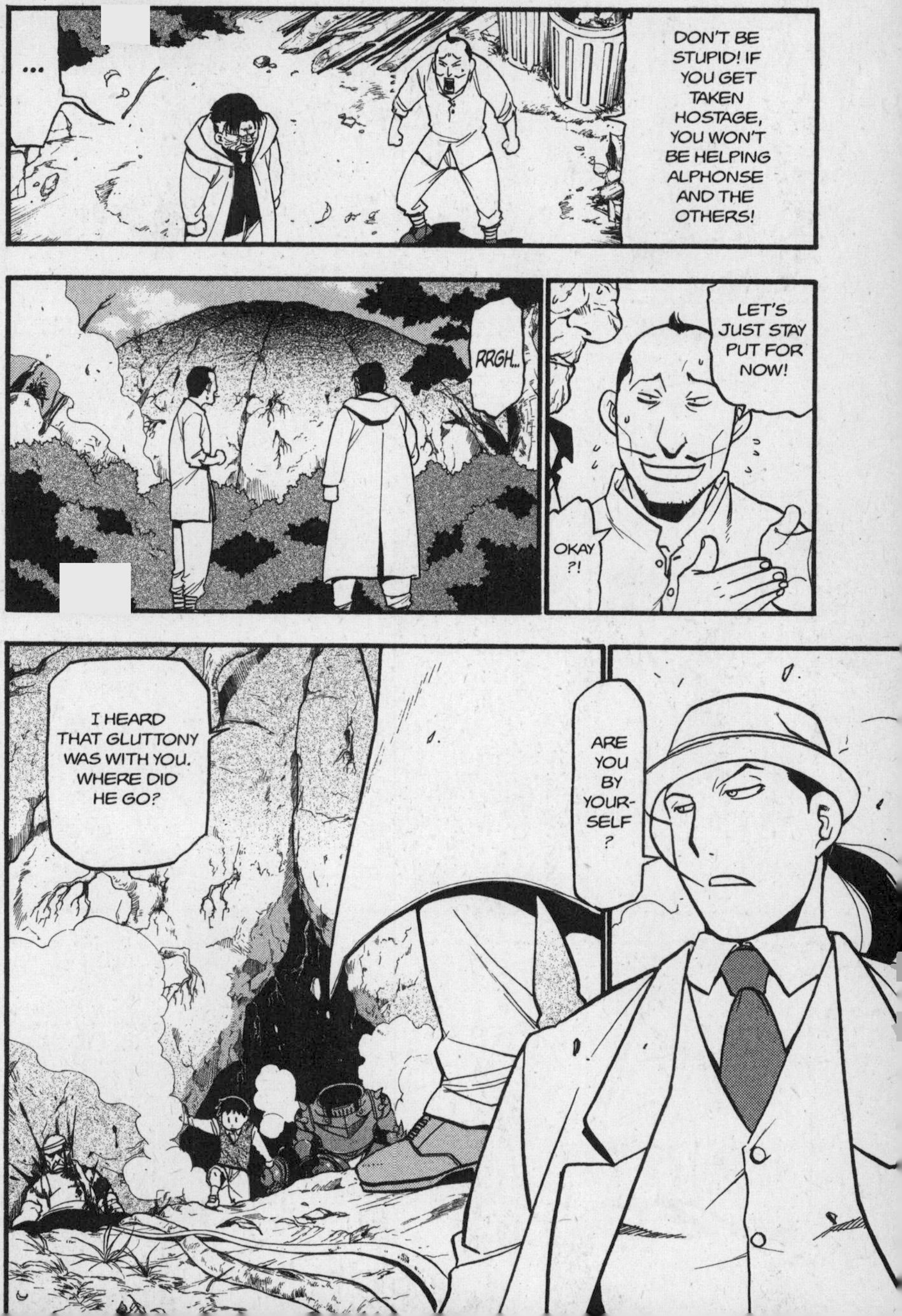
DON'T BE STUPID! IF YOU GET TAKEN HOSTAGE, YOU WON'T BE HELPING ALPHONSE AND THE OTHERS!
...
LET'S JUST STAY PUT FOR NOW!
OKAY?!
RRGH...
ARE YOU BY YOURSELF?
I HEARD THAT GLUTTONY WAS WITH YOU. WHERE DID HE GO?

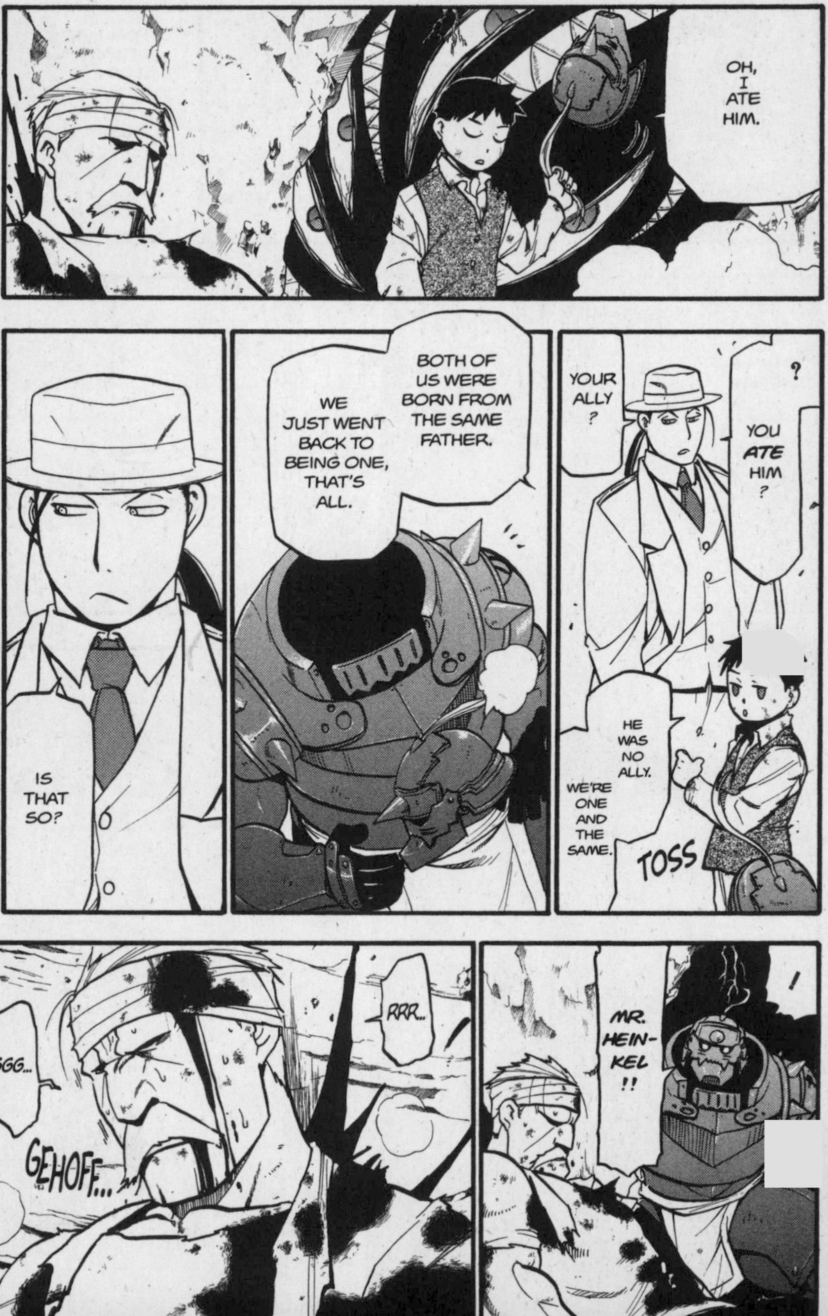
OH, I ATE HIM.
?
YOU ATE HIM?
YOUR ALLY?
HE WAS NO ALLY.
WE'RE ONE AND THE SAME.
TOSS
BOTH OF US WERE BORN FROM THE SAME FATHER.
WE JUST WENT BACK TO BEING ONE, THAT'S ALL.
IS THAT SO?
!
MR. HEIN-KEL!!
RRR...
GGG...
GEHOFF...

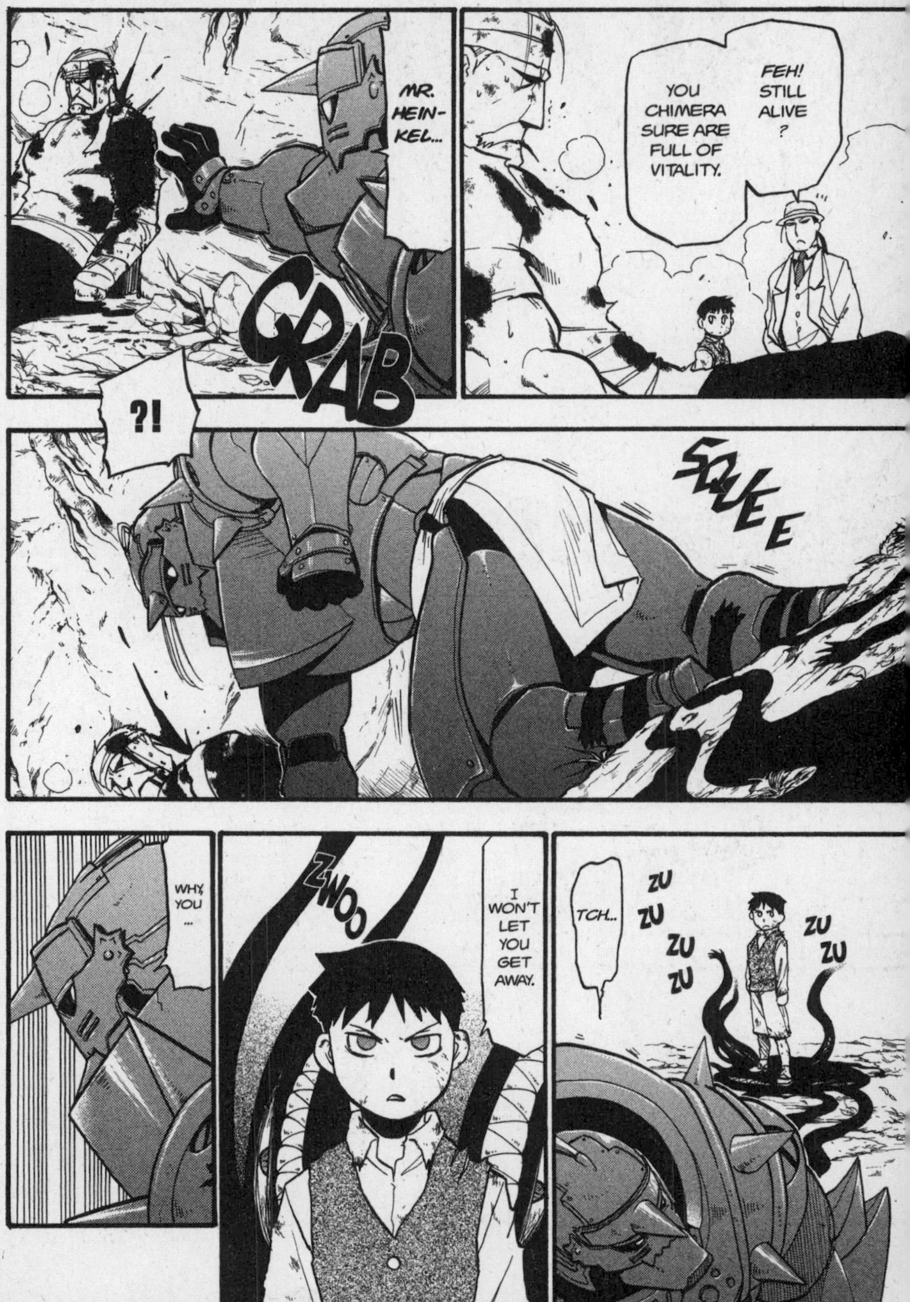
FEH! STILL ALIVE ?
YOU CHIMERA SURE ARE FULL OF VITALITY.
MR. HEIN-KEL...
GRAB
?!
SQUEEE
TCH...
ZU ZU ZU ZU ZU ZU
ZWOO
I WON'T LET YOU GET AWAY.
WHY, YOU ...

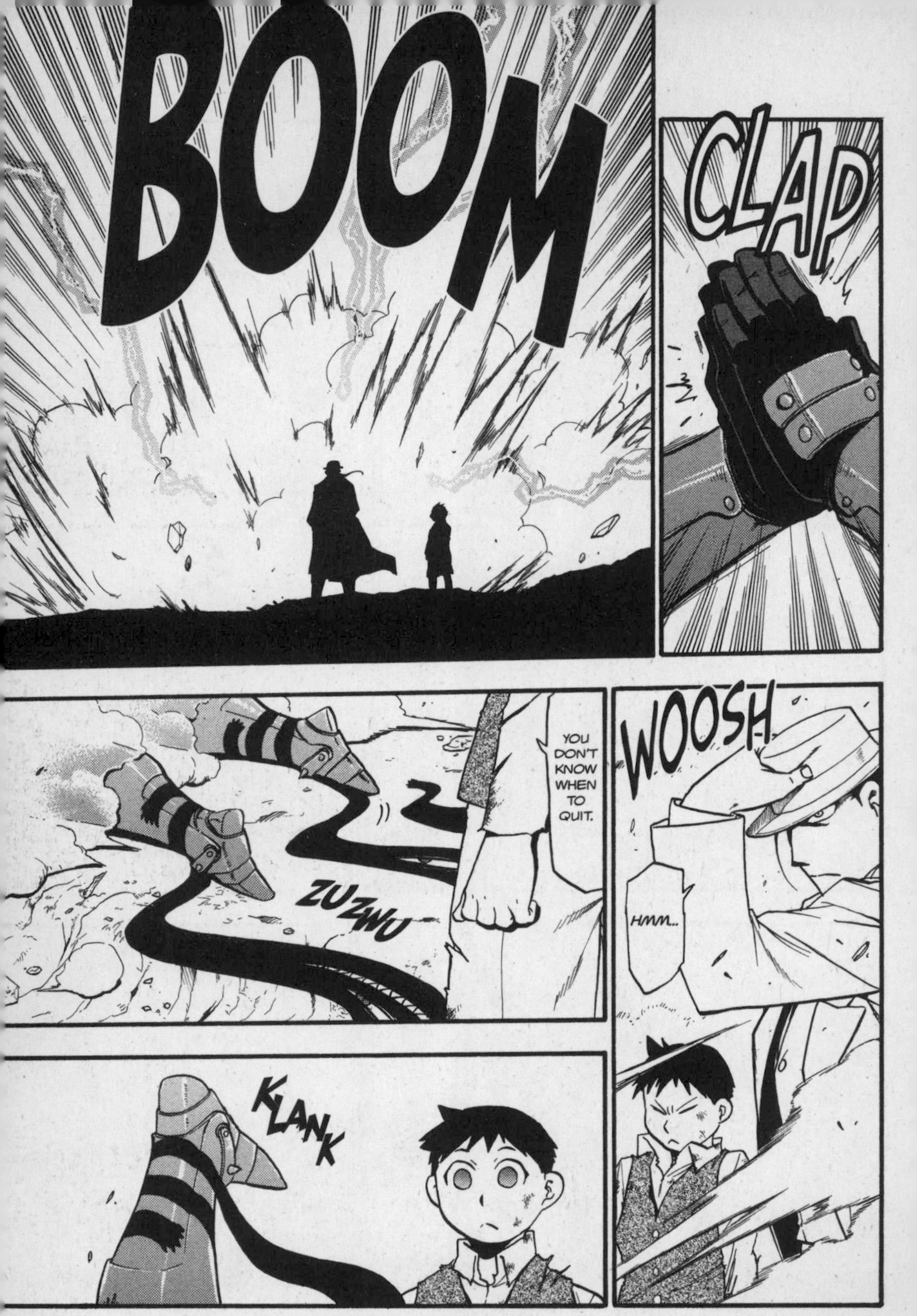
CLAP
BOOM
WOOSH
HMM..
YOU DON'T KNOW WHEN TO QUIT.
ZUZWU
KLANK

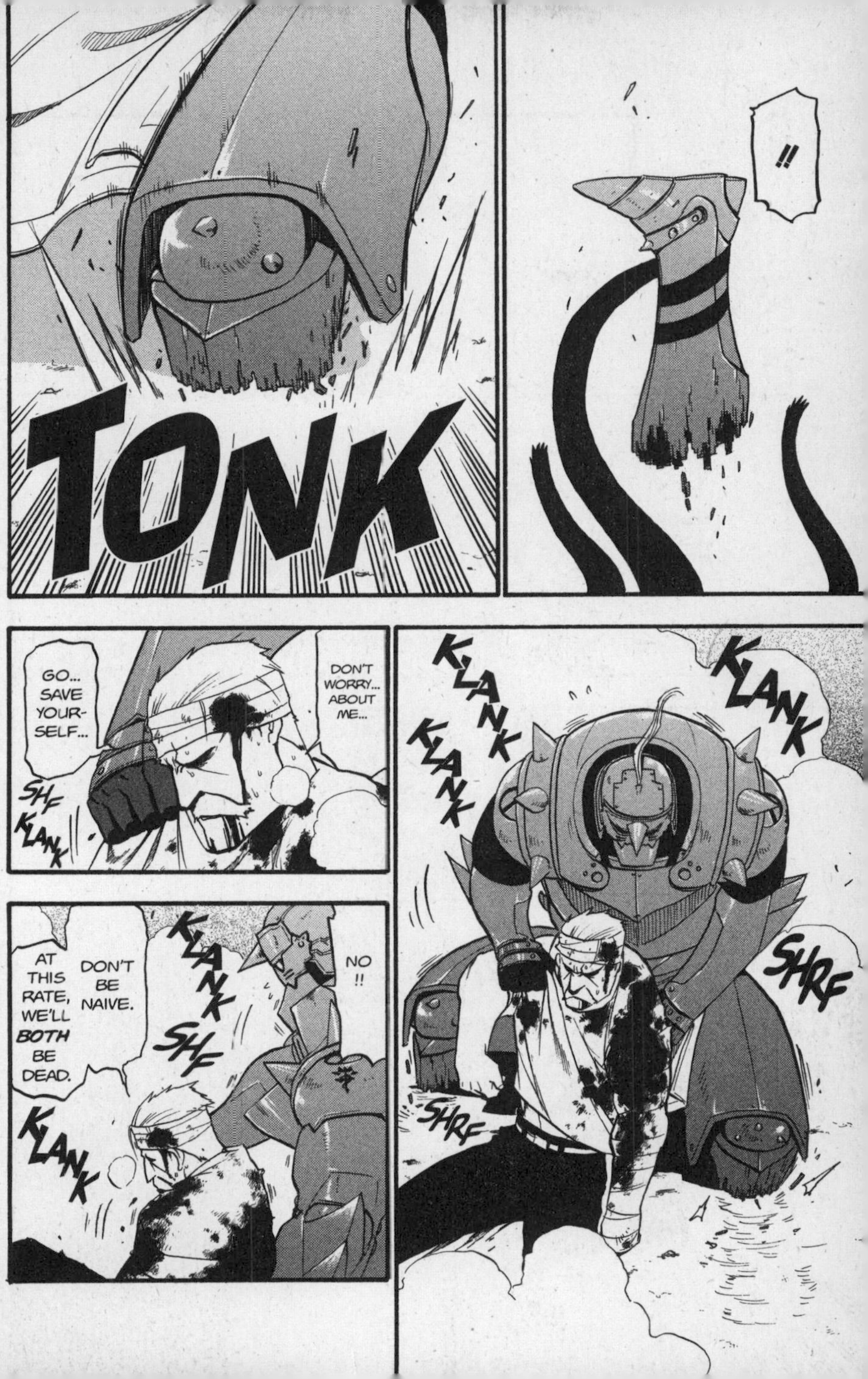
!!
TONK
KLANK
KLANK
KLANK
SHRF
SHRF
DON'T WORRY... ABOUT ME...
GO... SAVE YOURSELF...
SHF
KLANK
NO !!
KLANK
SHF
DON'T BE NAIVE.
AT THIS RATE, WE'LL *BOTH* BE DEAD.
KLANK

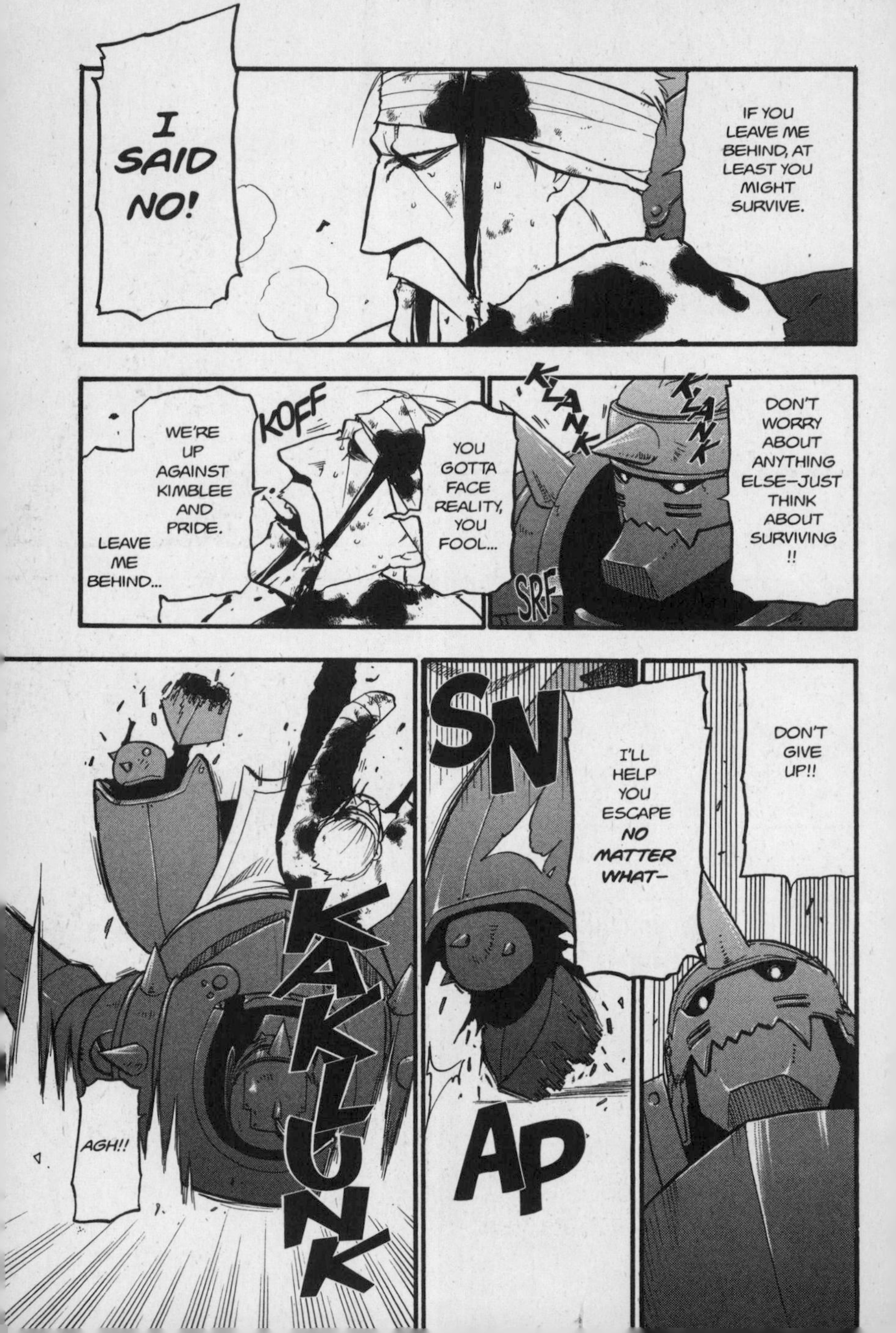
IF YOU LEAVE ME BEHIND, AT LEAST YOU MIGHT SURVIVE.
I SAID NO!
DON'T WORRY ABOUT ANYTHING ELSE—JUST THINK ABOUT SURVIVING!!
KLANK
KLANK
SRF
YOU GOTTA FACE REALITY, YOU FOOL...
KOFF
WE'RE UP AGAINST KIMBLEE AND PRIDE.
LEAVE ME BEHIND...
DON'T GIVE UP!!
I'LL HELP YOU ESCAPE *NO MATTER WHAT*-
SNAP
KAKLUNK
AGH!!

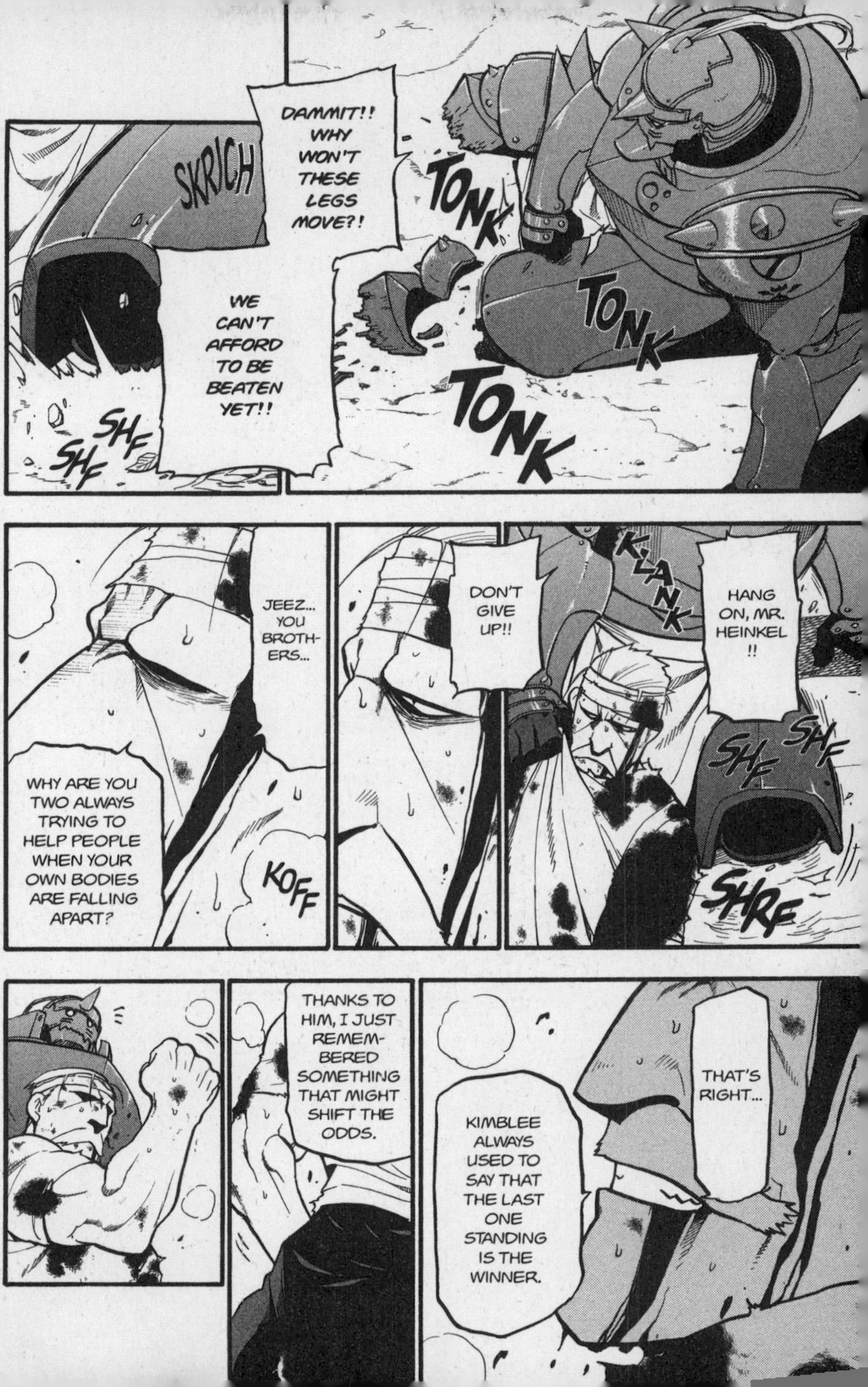
DAMMIT!! WHY WON'T THESE LEGS MOVE?!
TONK
SKRICH
TONK
TONK
WE CAN'T AFFORD TO BE BEATEN YET!!
SHF
SHF
KLANK
HANG ON, MR. HEINKEL!!
SHF
SHF
SHRF
DON'T GIVE UP!!
JEEZ... YOU BROTHERS...
WHY ARE YOU TWO ALWAYS TRYING TO HELP PEOPLE WHEN YOUR OWN BODIES ARE FALLING APART?
KOFF
THAT'S RIGHT...
KIMBLEE ALWAYS USED TO SAY THAT THE LAST ONE STANDING IS THE WINNER.
THANKS TO HIM, I JUST REMEMBERED SOMETHING THAT MIGHT SHIFT THE ODDS.

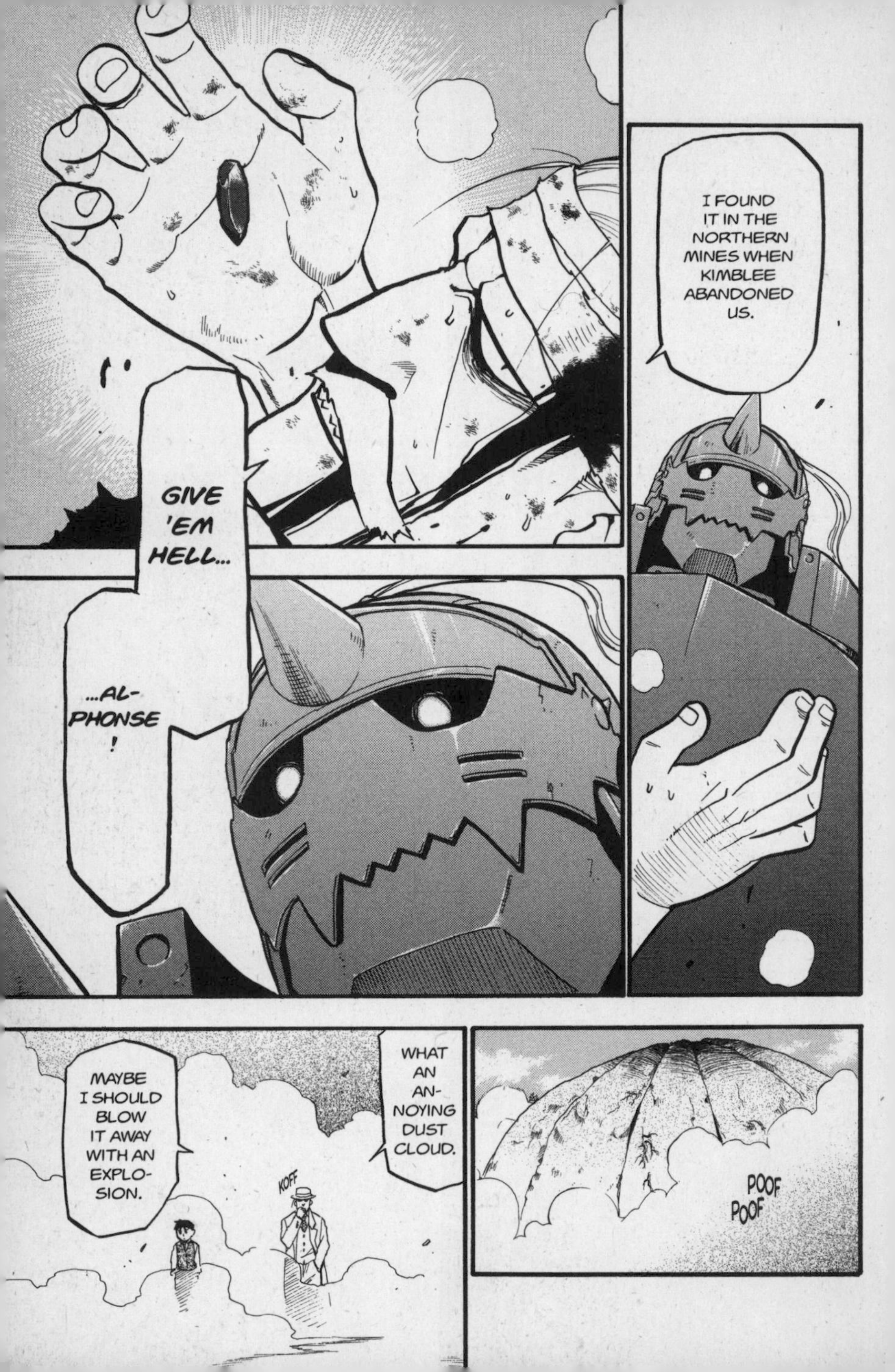
I FOUND IT IN THE NORTHERN MINES WHEN KIMBLEE ABANDONED US.
GIVE 'EM HELL...
...AL-PHONSE!
POOF
POOF
WHAT AN AN-NOYING DUST CLOUD.
KOFF
MAYBE I SHOULD BLOW IT AWAY WITH AN EXPLO-SION.

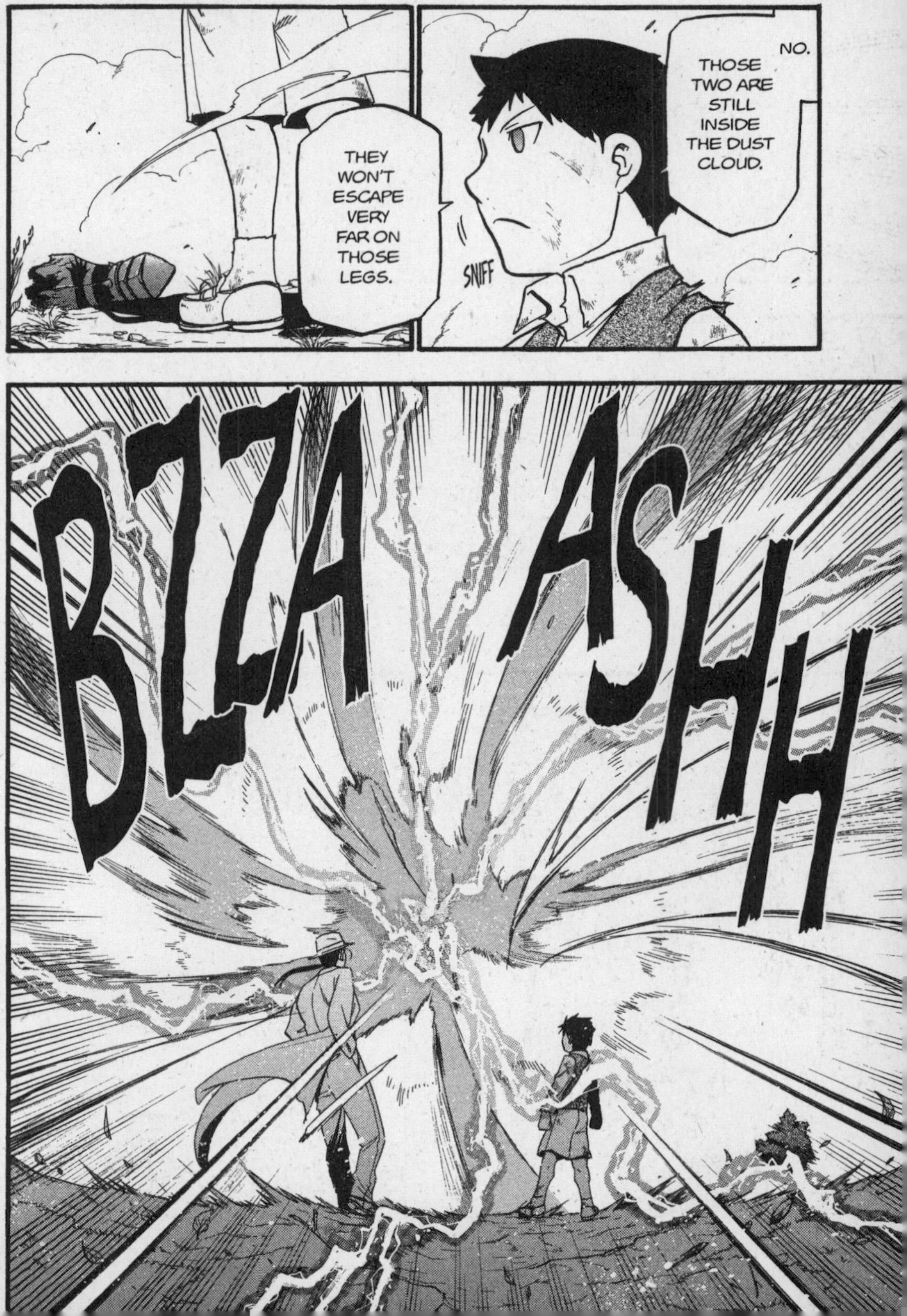
NO.
THOSE TWO ARE STILL INSIDE THE DUST CLOUD.
SNIFF
THEY WON'T ESCAPE VERY FAR ON THOSE LEGS.
BZZA ASHH

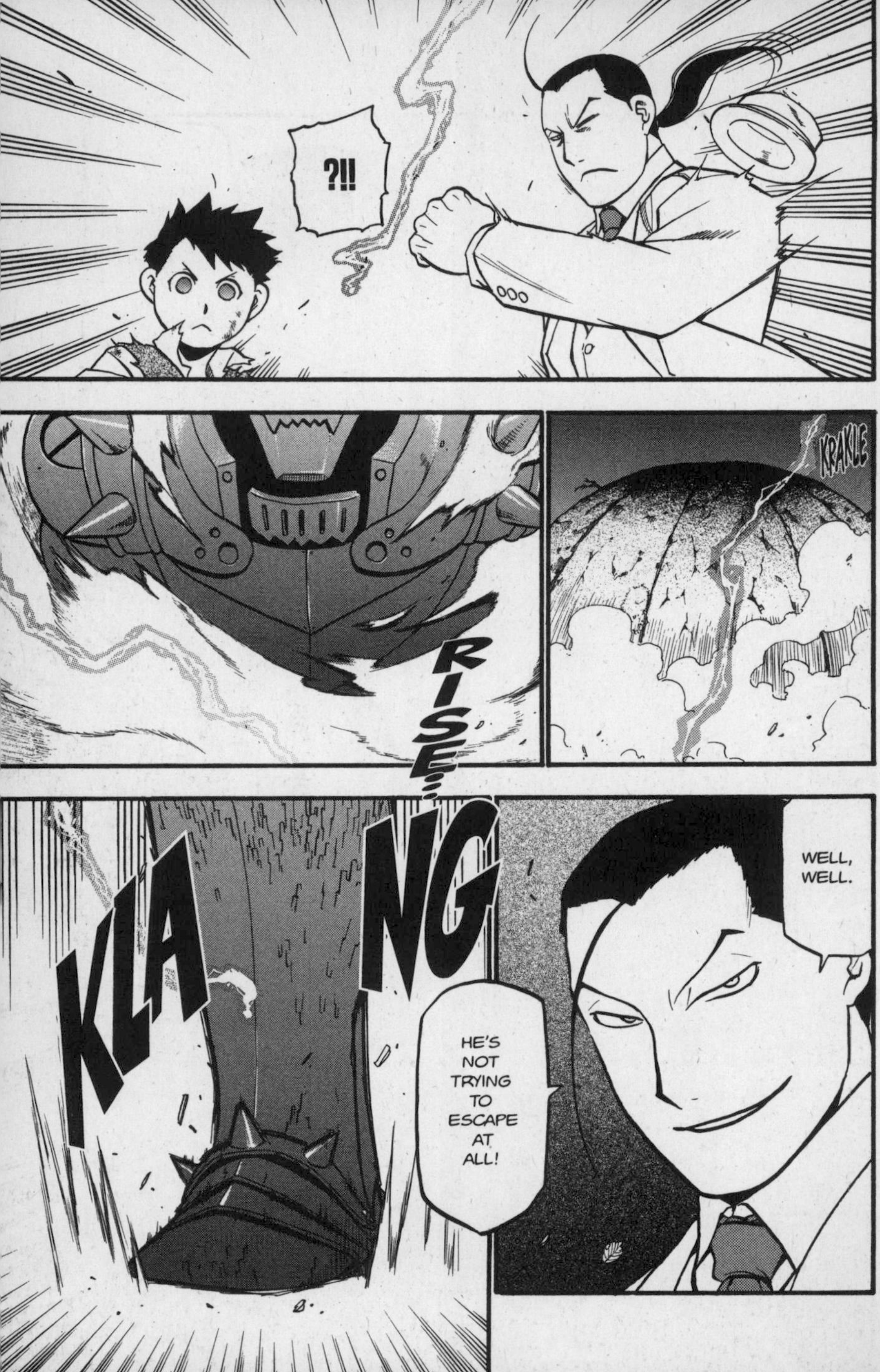
?!!
KRAKLE
RISE...
WELL, WELL.
HE'S NOT TRYING TO ESCAPE AT ALL!
KLANG

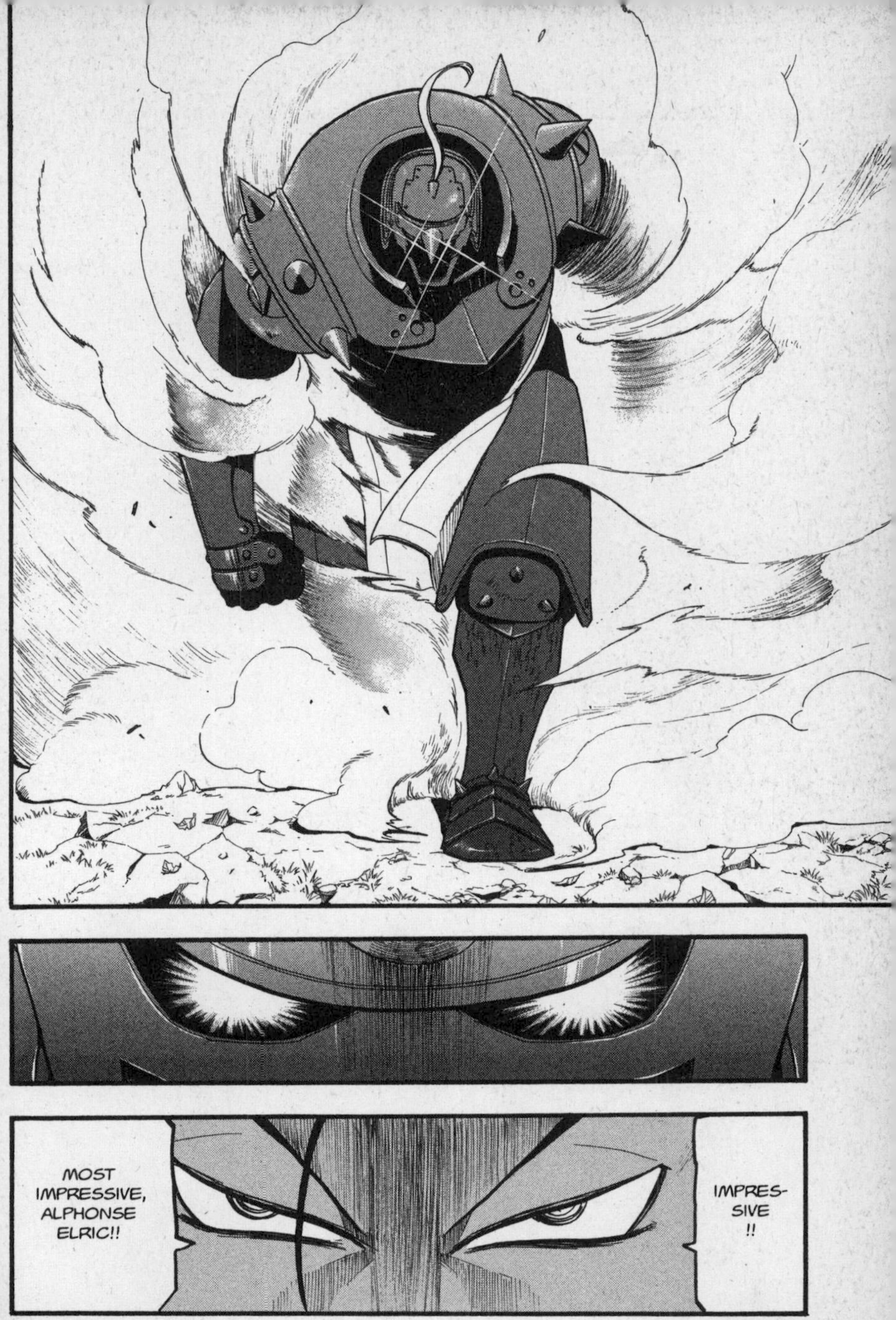
IMPRES-
SIVE
!!
MOST
IMPRESSIVE,
ALPHONSE
ELRIC!!

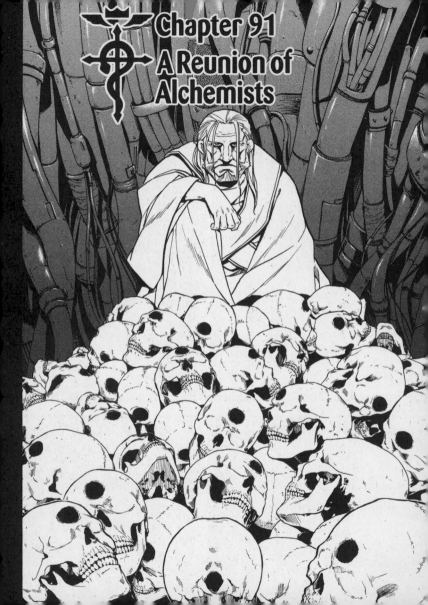

Chapter 91
A Reunion of
Alchemists

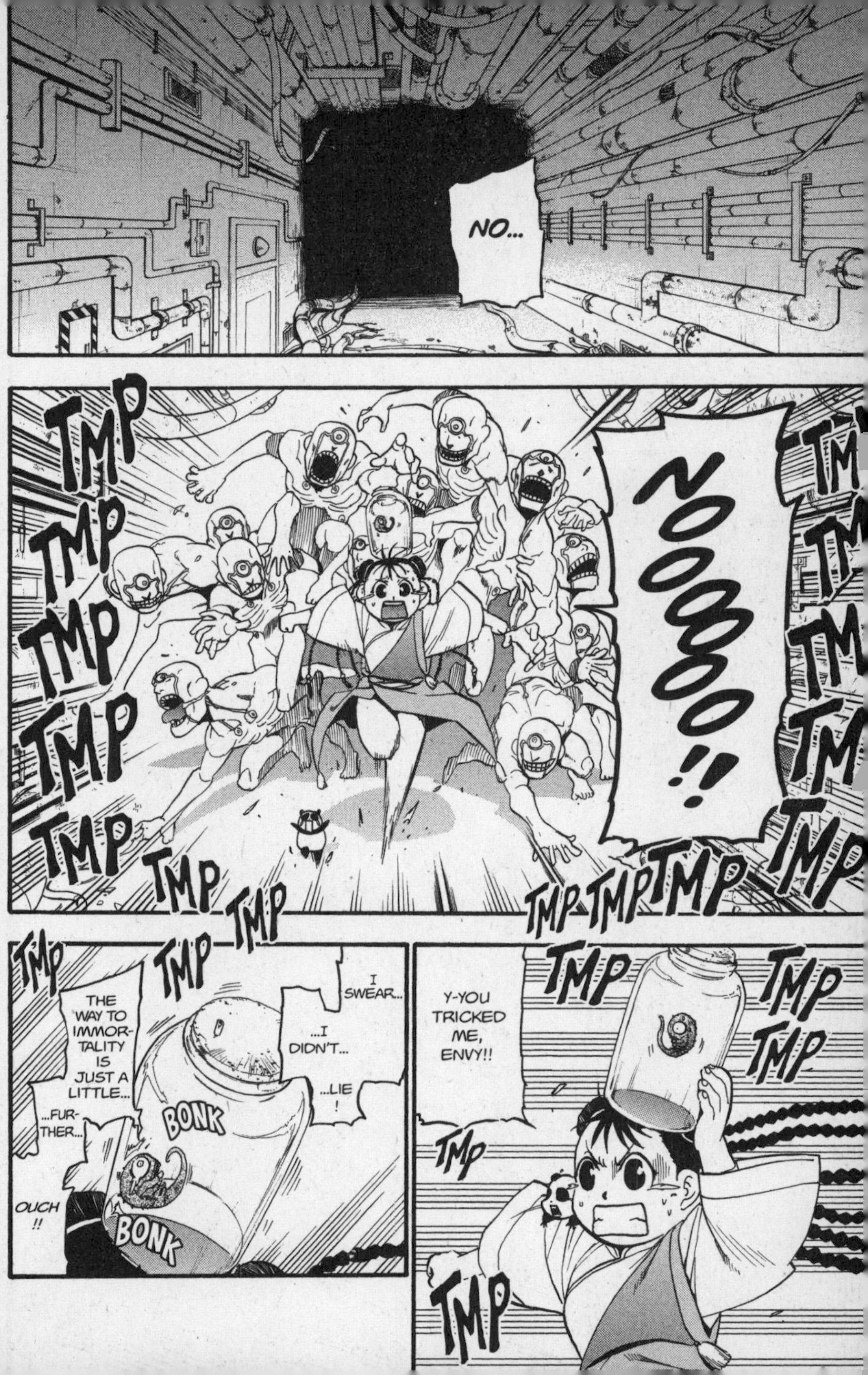
NO...
TMP
TMP
TMP
TMP
NOOOOOO!!
TMP TMP TMP
TMP
TMP
TMP
TMP
TMP
TMP
TMP
TMP
Y-YOU TRICKED ME, ENVY!!
TMP
TMP
TMP
TMP
TMP
TMP
I SWEAR...
...I DIDN'T...
...LIE!
THE WAY TO IMMORTALITY IS JUST A LITTLE...
...FURTHER...
BONK
BONK
OUCH!!
TMP

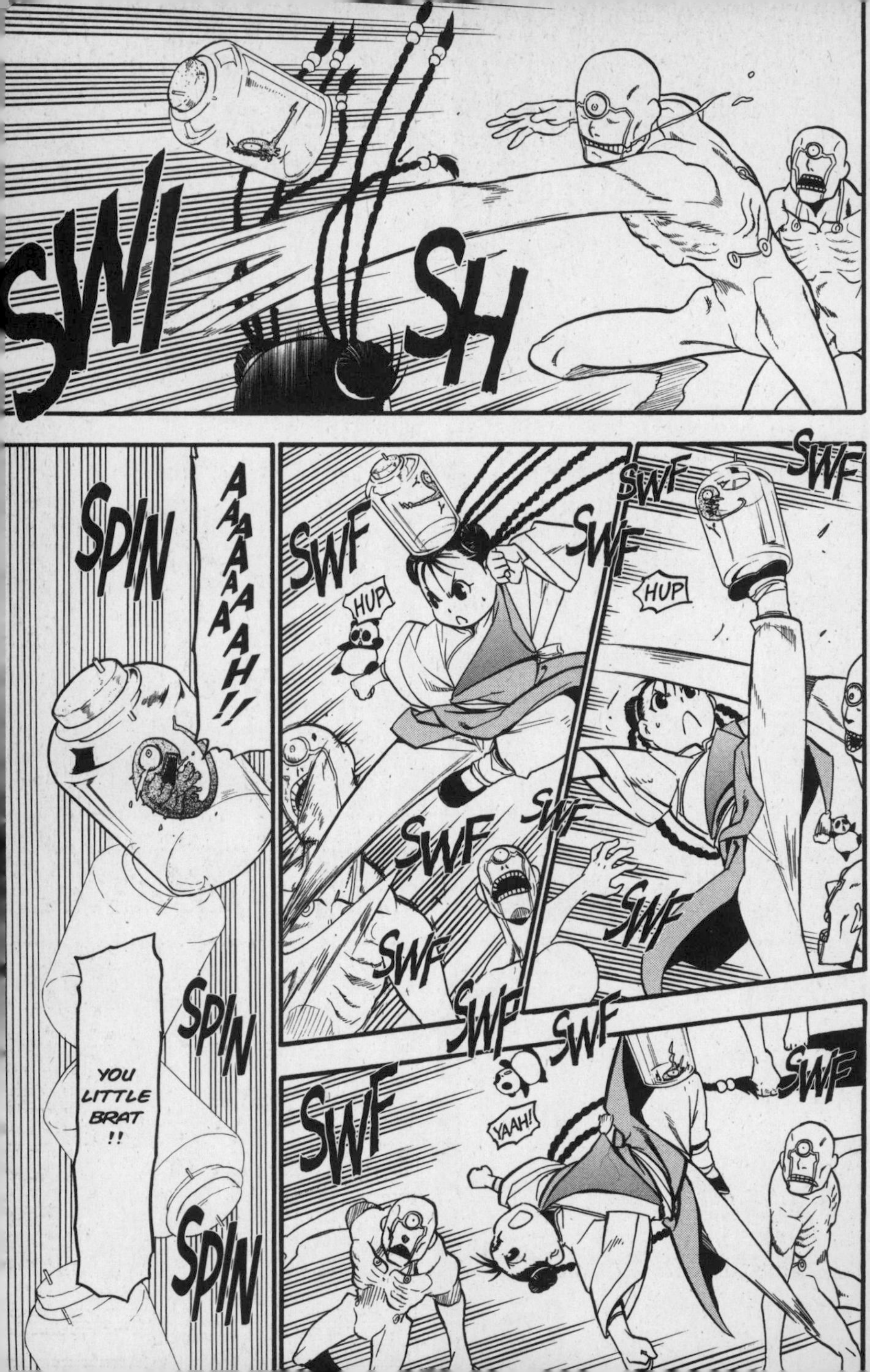

SWI
SH
SWF
SWF
HUP
SWF
SWF
SWF
SWF
HUP
SWF
SWF
SWF
SWF
SWF
YAAH!
SWF
SPIN
AAAAAAAAH!!
YOU LITTLE BRAT !!
SPIN
SPIN

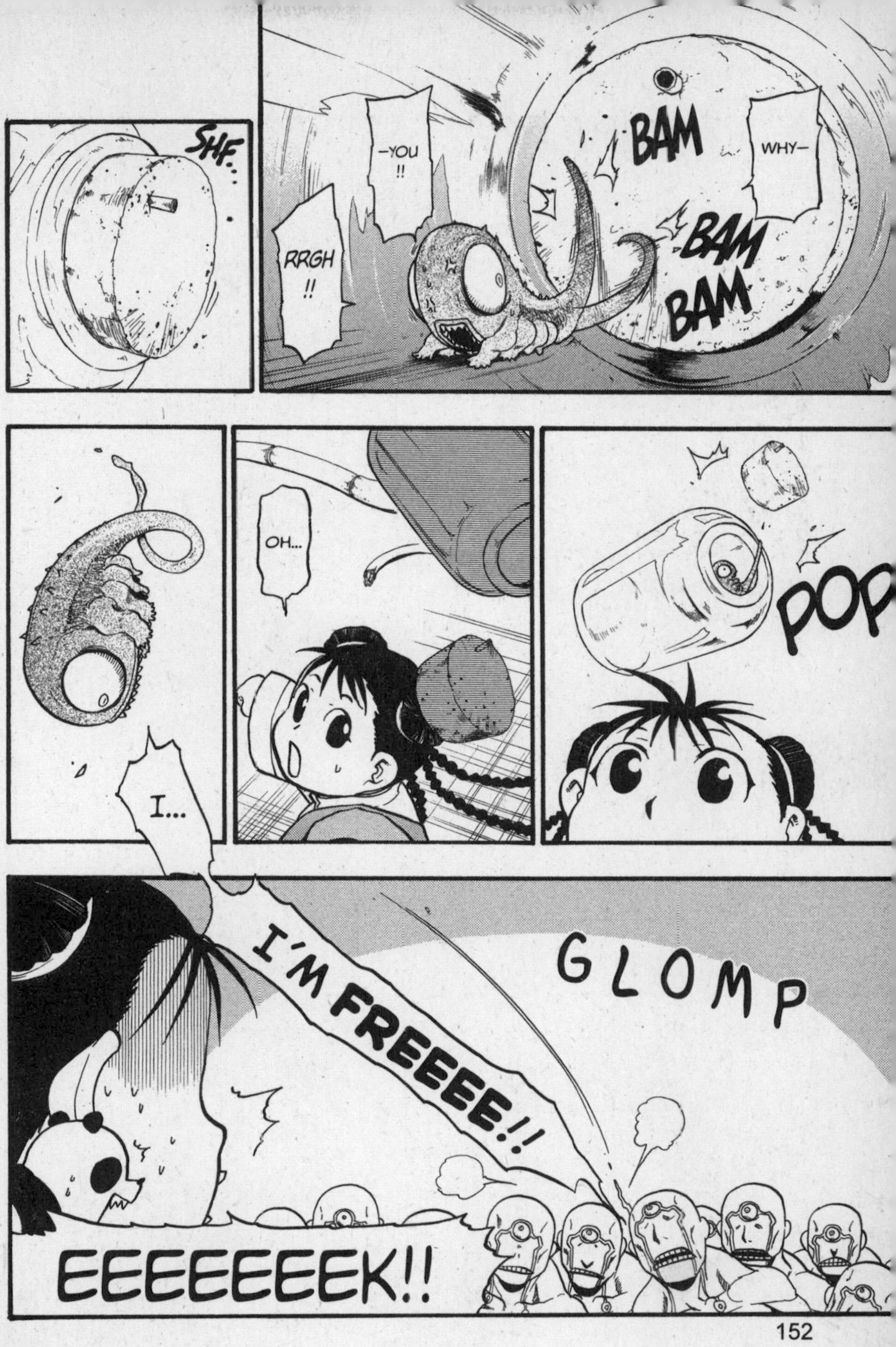

WHY—
BAM
BAM
BAM
—YOU !!
RRGH !!
SHF...
POP
OH...
I...
GLOMP
I'M FREEEEE!!
EEEEEEEEK!!

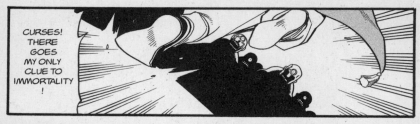

CURSES! THERE GOES MY ONLY CLUE TO IMMORTALITY!

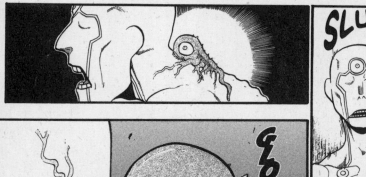

SLUMP

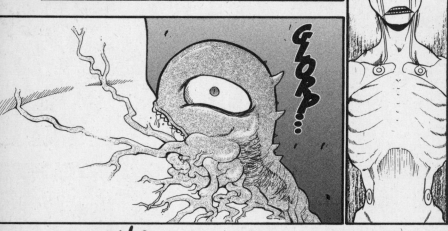

GLORP...

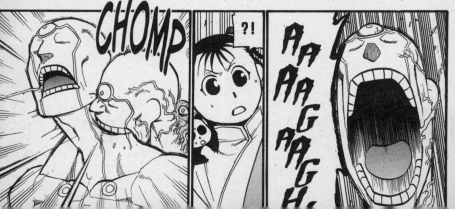

CHOMP

?!

AAAAAGAAAGH

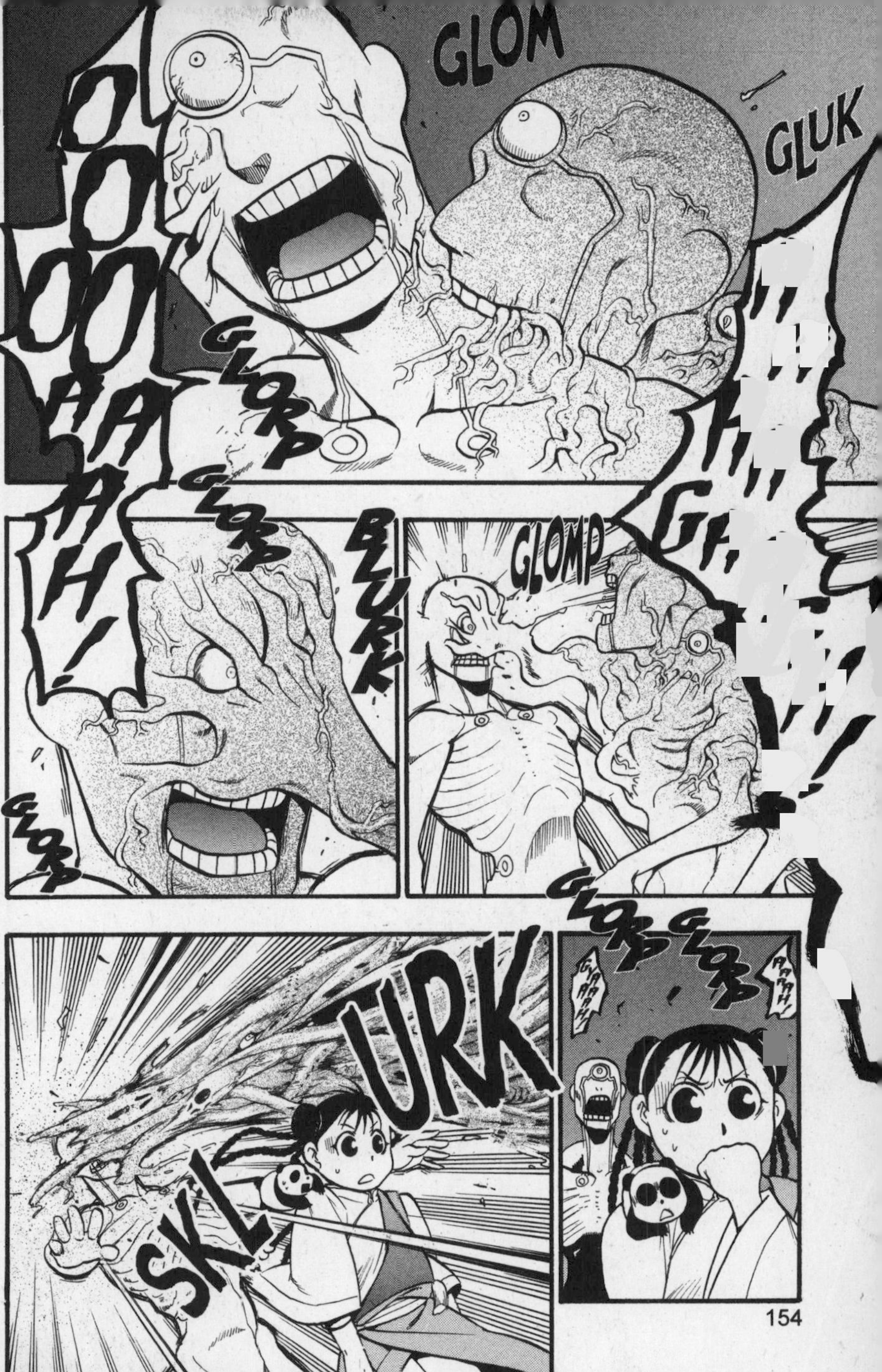
GLUK
GLOM
OOOOAAAAH!
GLORP
GLOMP
GLORP
BLURK
GLORP
GLORP
GLORP
AAAH!
GYAAAAH!
URK
SKL

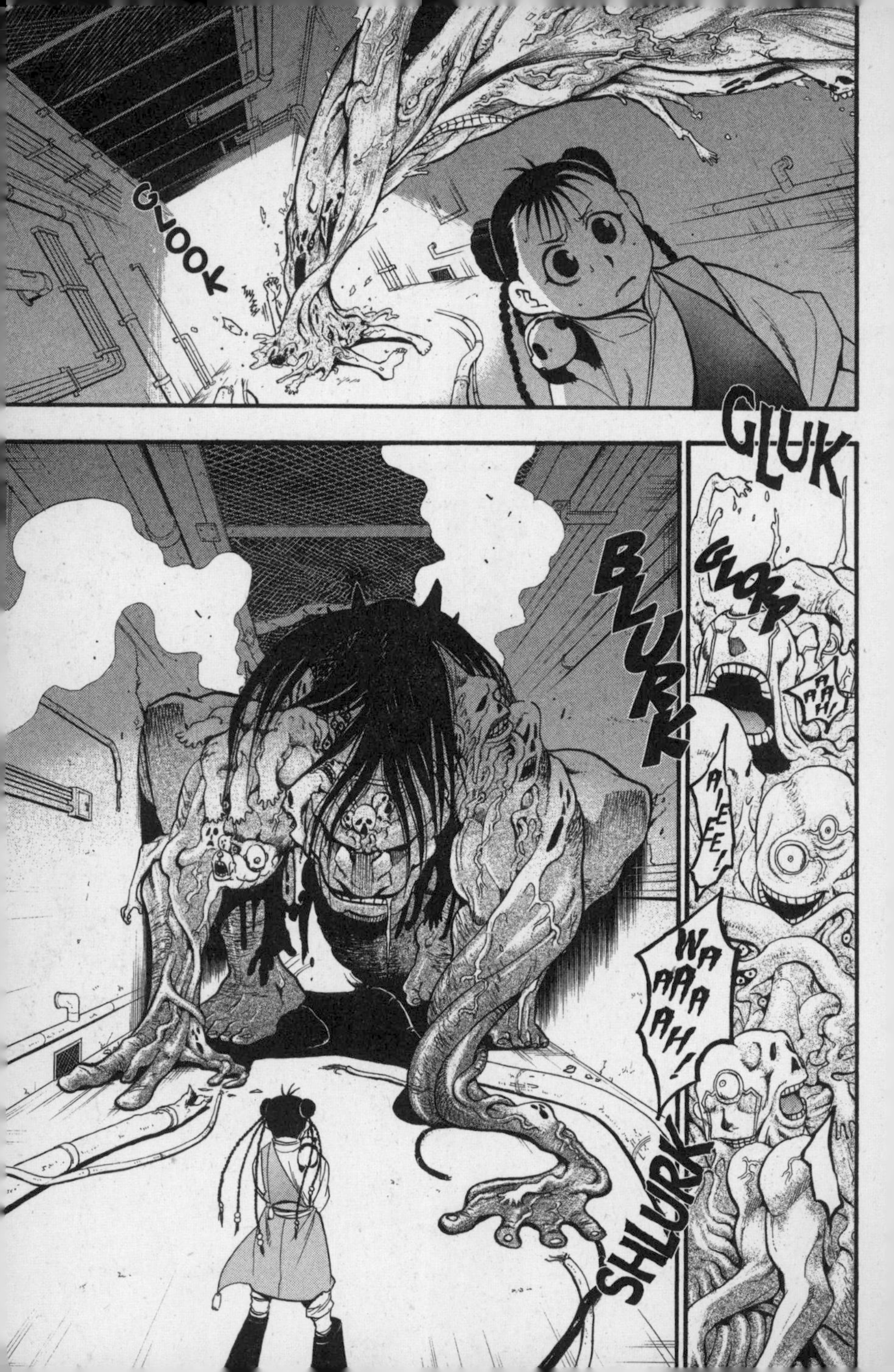
GLOOK
GLUK
GLOOP
AAAH!
AIEEE!
WAAAAAH!
SHLURK
BLURK

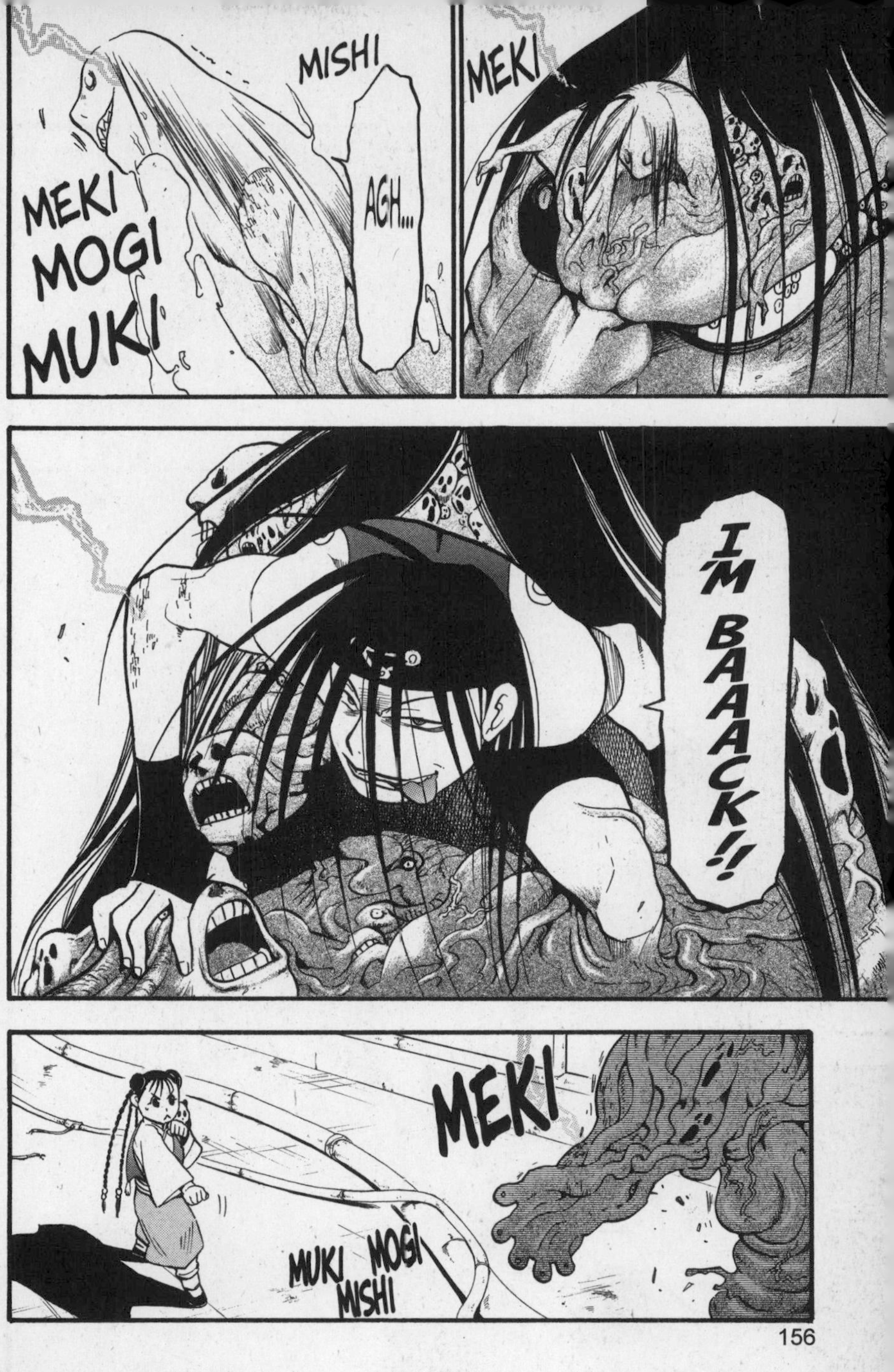
MEKI
MISHI
AGH...
MEKI
MOGI
MUKI
I'M BAAACK!!
MEKI
MUKI MOGI
MISHI

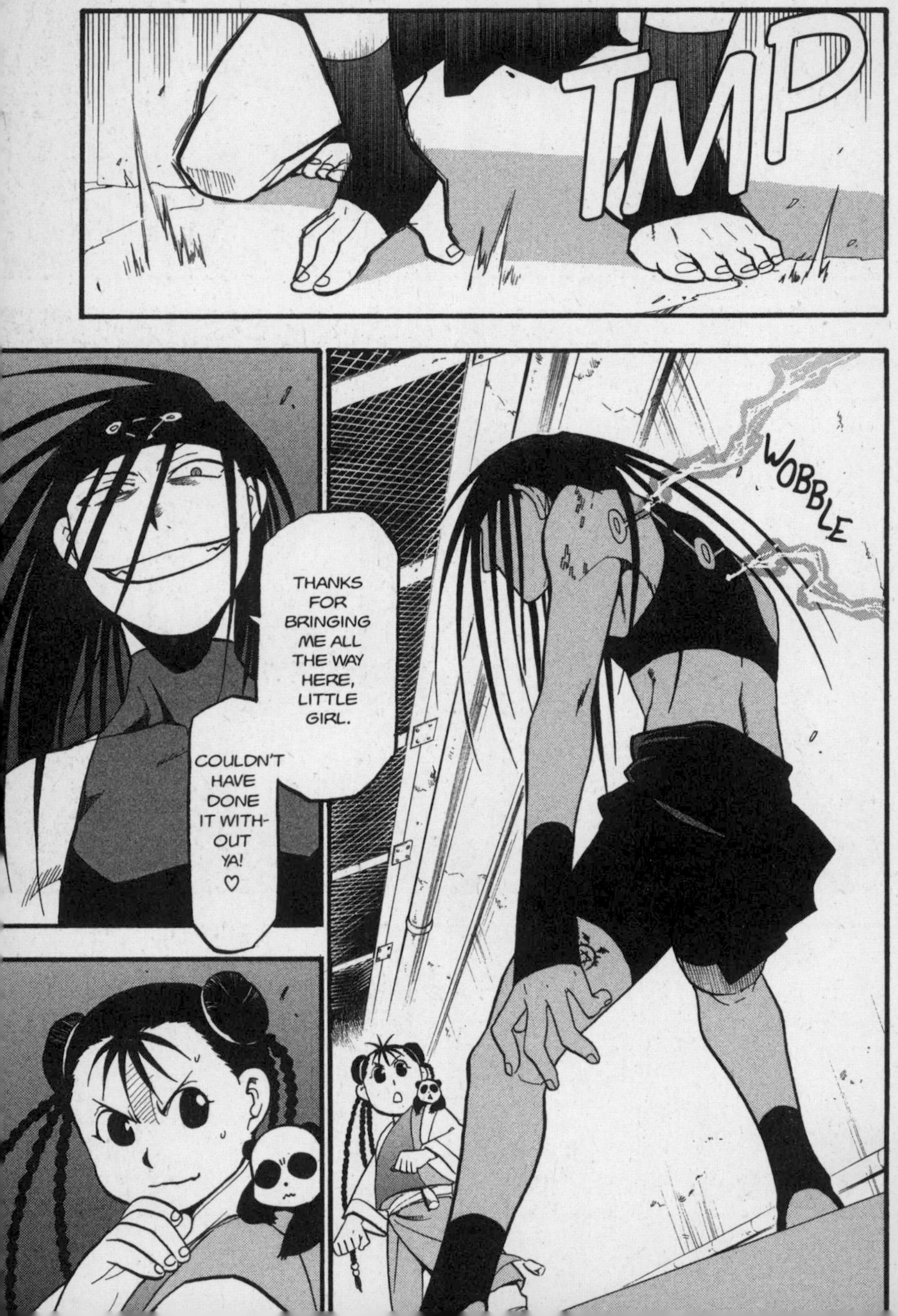
TMP
WOBBLE
THANKS FOR BRINGING ME ALL THE WAY HERE, LITTLE GIRL.
COULDN'T HAVE DONE IT WITH-OUT YA! ♥

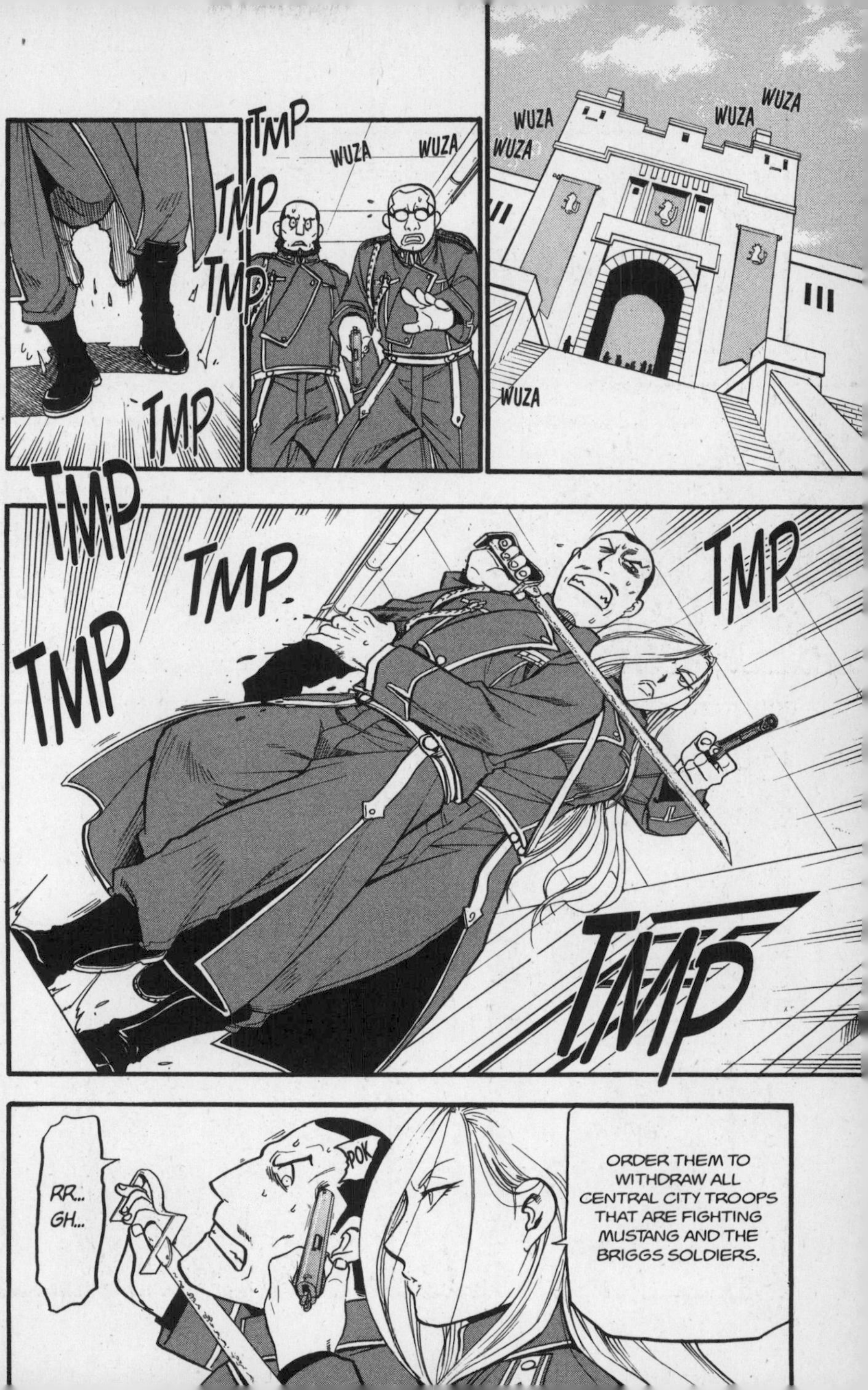
WUZA
WUZA
WUZA
WUZA
WUZA
WUZA
WUZA
TMP
TMP
TMP
TMP
TMP
TMP
TMP
TMP
TMP
ORDER THEM TO WITHDRAW ALL CENTRAL CITY TROOPS THAT ARE FIGHTING MUSTANG AND THE BRIGGS SOLDIERS.
POK
RR... GH...

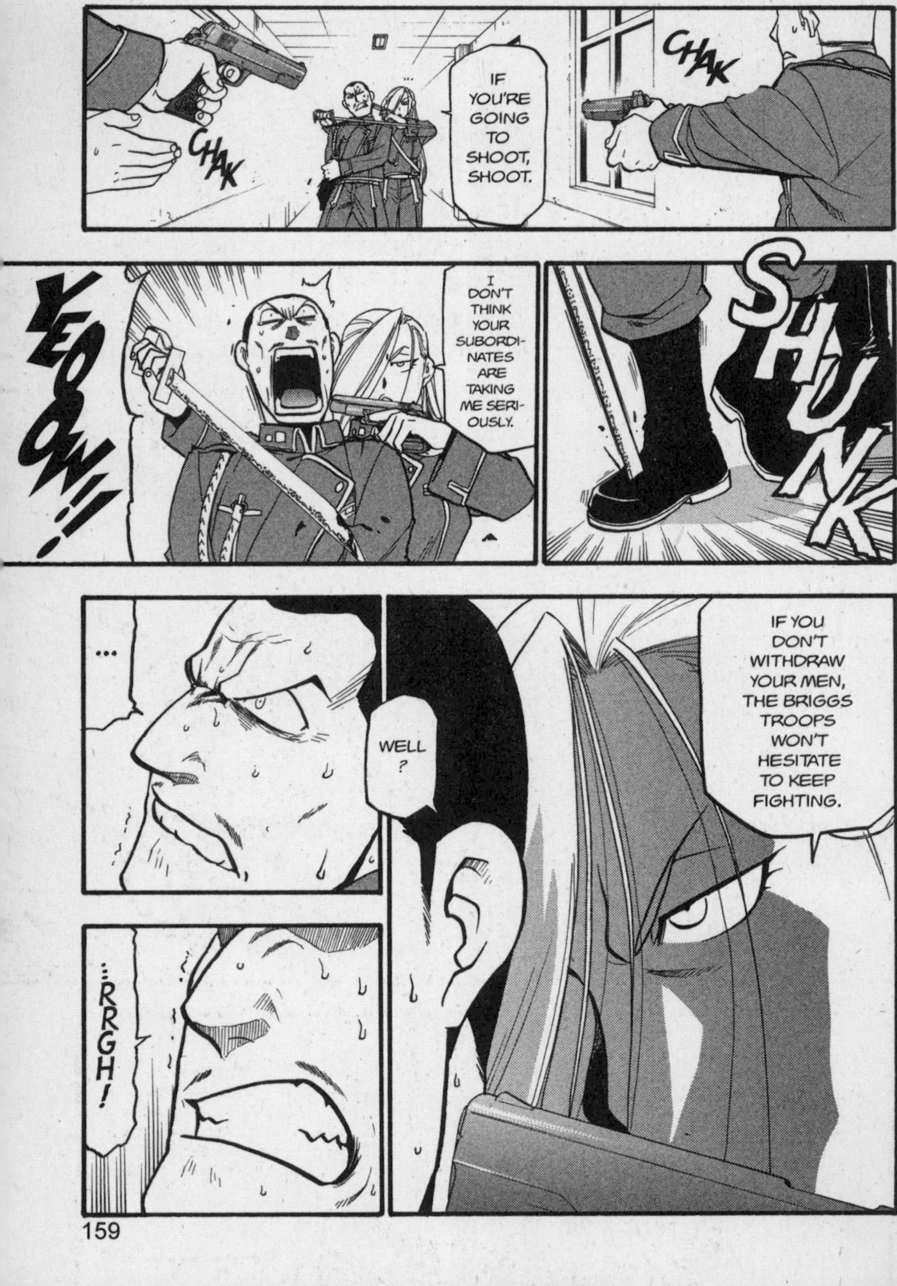
CHAK
IF YOU'RE GOING TO SHOOT, SHOOT.
...
CHAK
SHUNK
I DON'T THINK YOUR SUBORDINATES ARE TAKING ME SERIOUSLY.
YEOOW!!!
IF YOU DON'T WITHDRAW YOUR MEN, THE BRIGGS TROOPS WON'T HESITATE TO KEEP FIGHTING.
WELL?
...
...RRRGH!

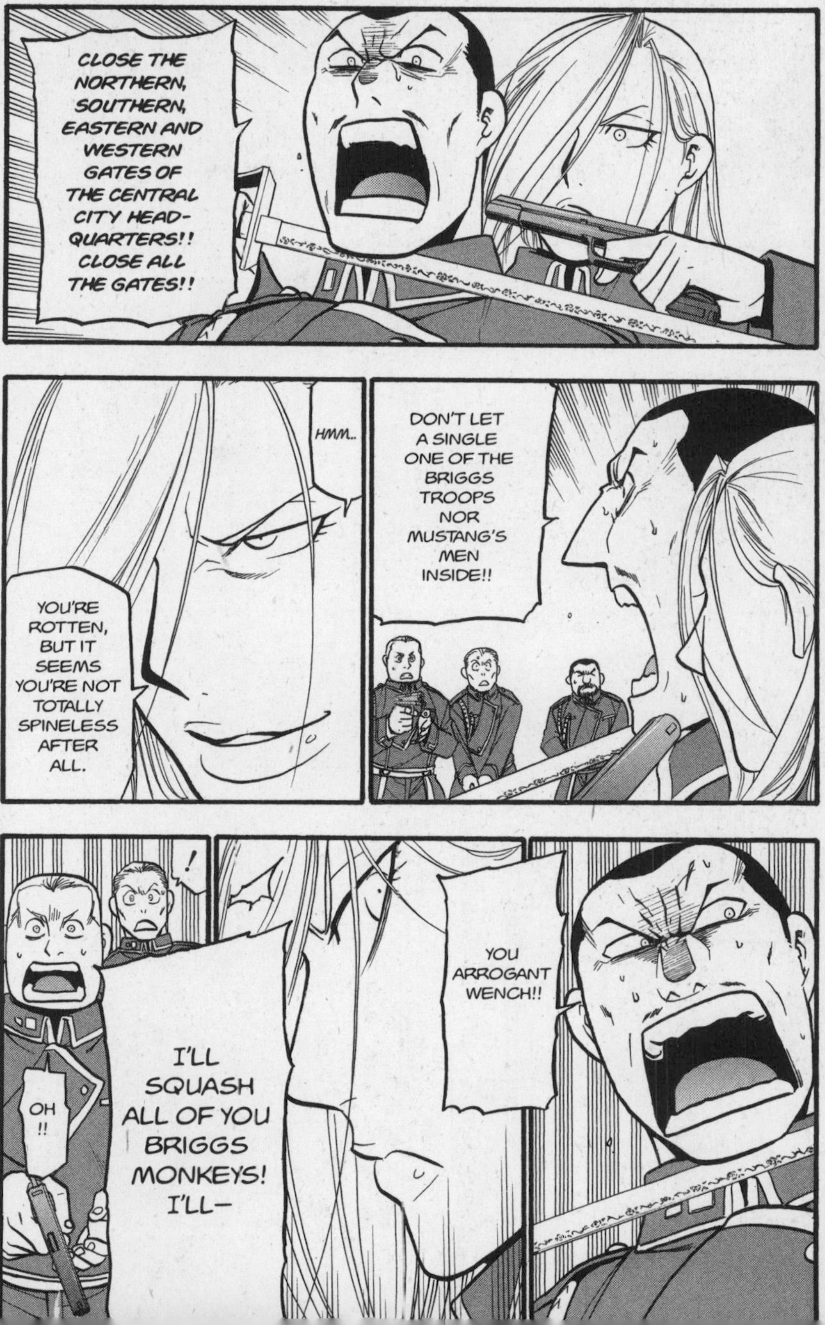
CLOSE THE NORTHERN, SOUTHERN, EASTERN AND WESTERN GATES OF THE CENTRAL CITY HEAD-QUARTERS!! CLOSE ALL THE GATES!!
DON'T LET A SINGLE ONE OF THE BRIGGS TROOPS NOR MUSTANG'S MEN INSIDE!!
HMM..
YOU'RE ROTTEN, BUT IT SEEMS YOU'RE NOT TOTALLY SPINELESS AFTER ALL.
YOU ARROGANT WENCH!!
I'LL SQUASH ALL OF YOU BRIGGS MONKEYS! I'LL—
!
OH !!

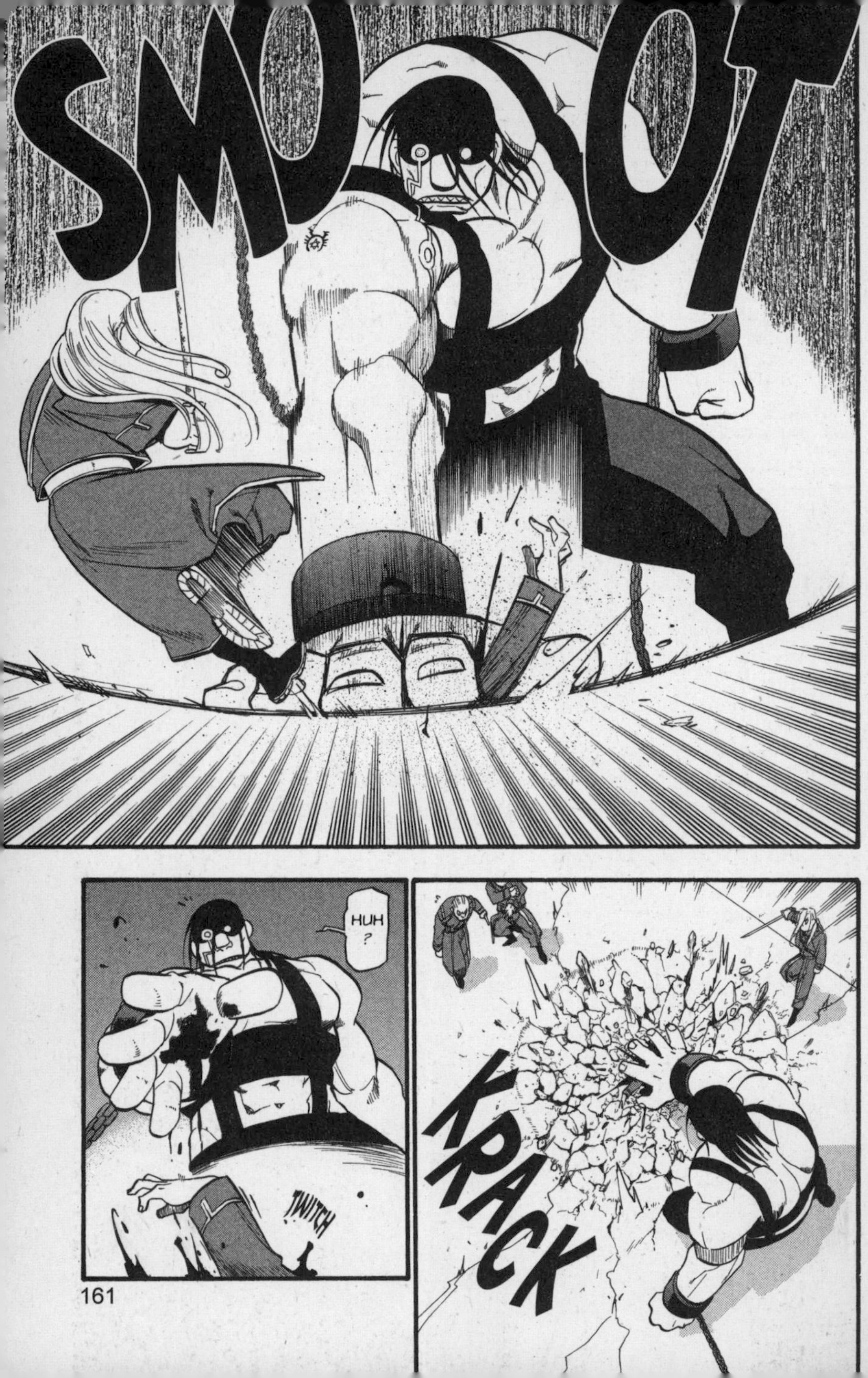
SMOOT
KRACK
HUH?
TWITCH

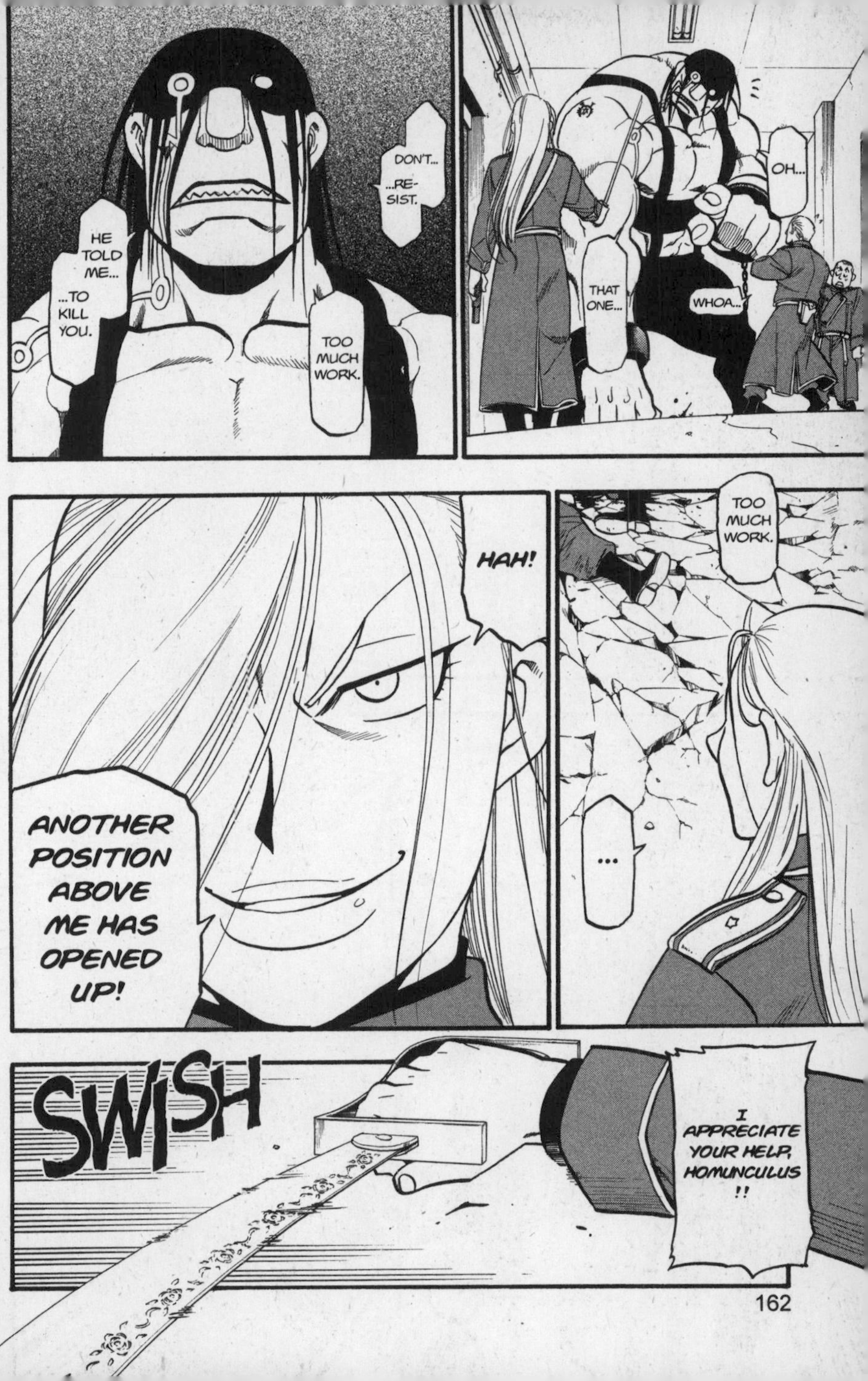
OH...
WHOA...
THAT ONE...
DON'T... ...RE-SIST.
HE TOLD ME... ...TO KILL YOU.
TOO MUCH WORK.
TOO MUCH WORK.
...
HAH!
ANOTHER POSITION ABOVE ME HAS OPENED UP!
I APPRECIATE YOUR HELP, HOMUNCULUS!!
SWISH

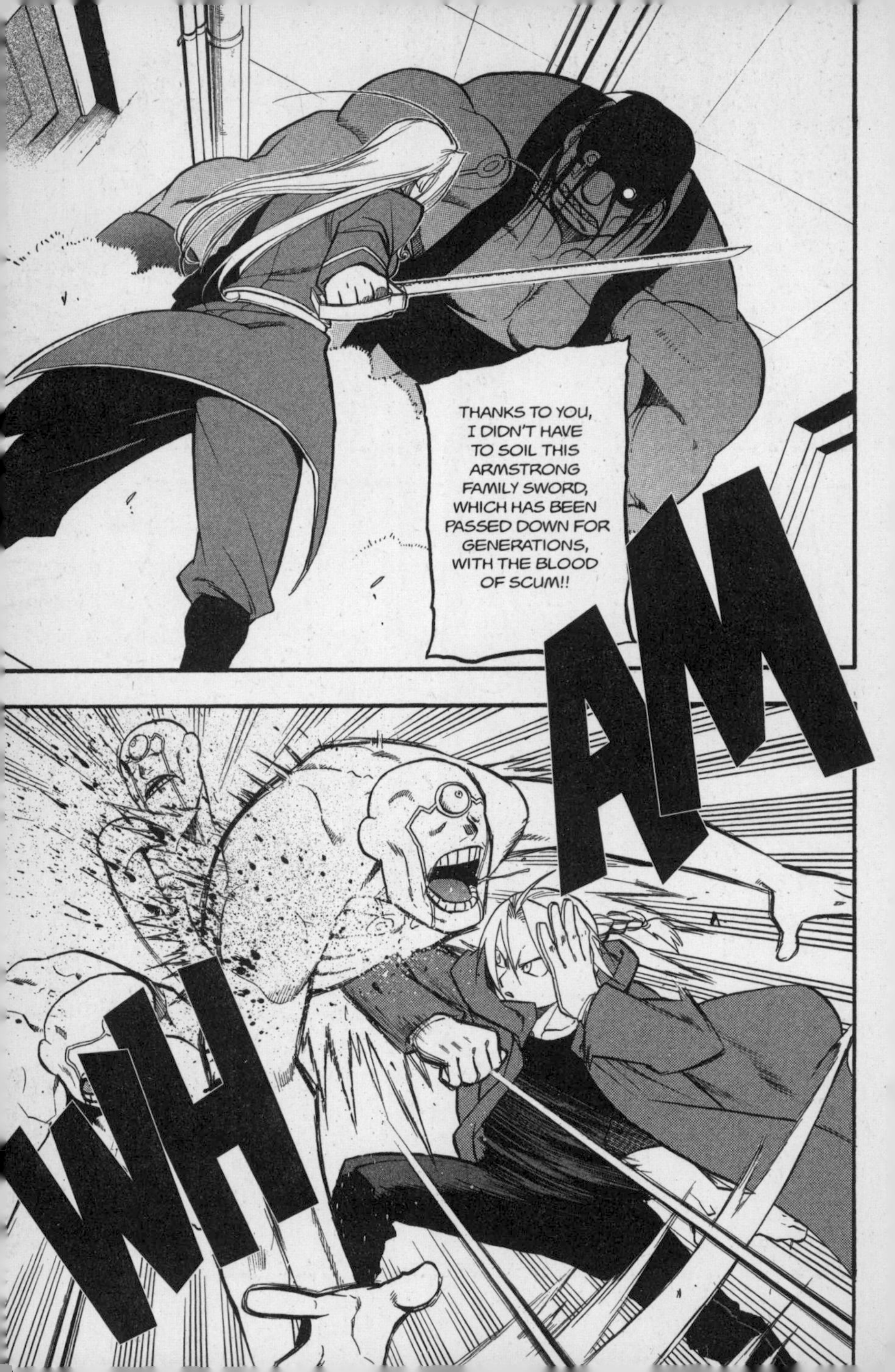
THANKS TO YOU, I DIDN'T HAVE TO SOIL THIS ARMSTRONG FAMILY SWORD, WHICH HAS BEEN PASSED DOWN FOR GENERATIONS, WITH THE BLOOD OF SCUM!!
WH
AM

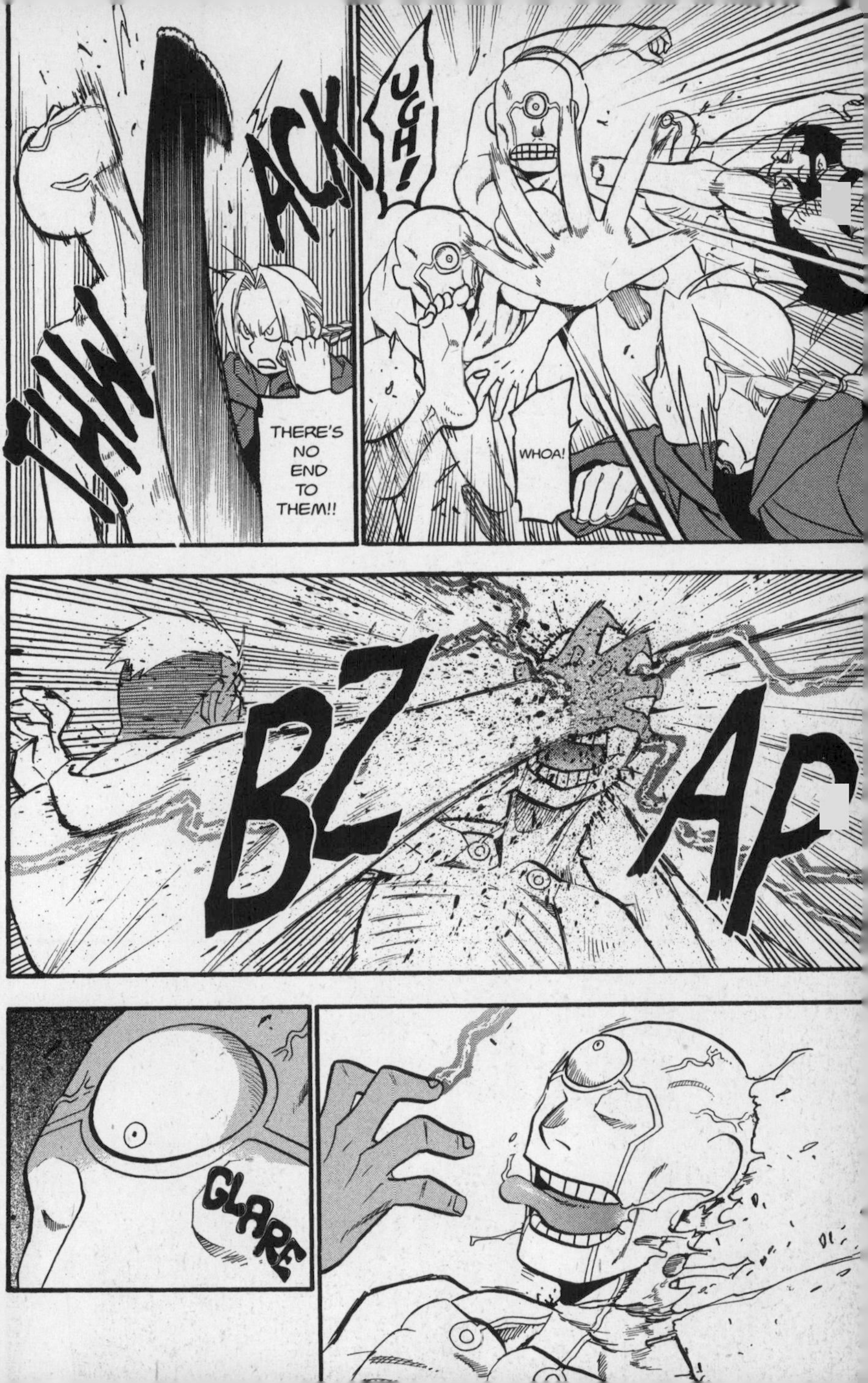
UGH!
WHOA!
THWACK
THERE'S NO END TO THEM!!
BZAP
GLARE

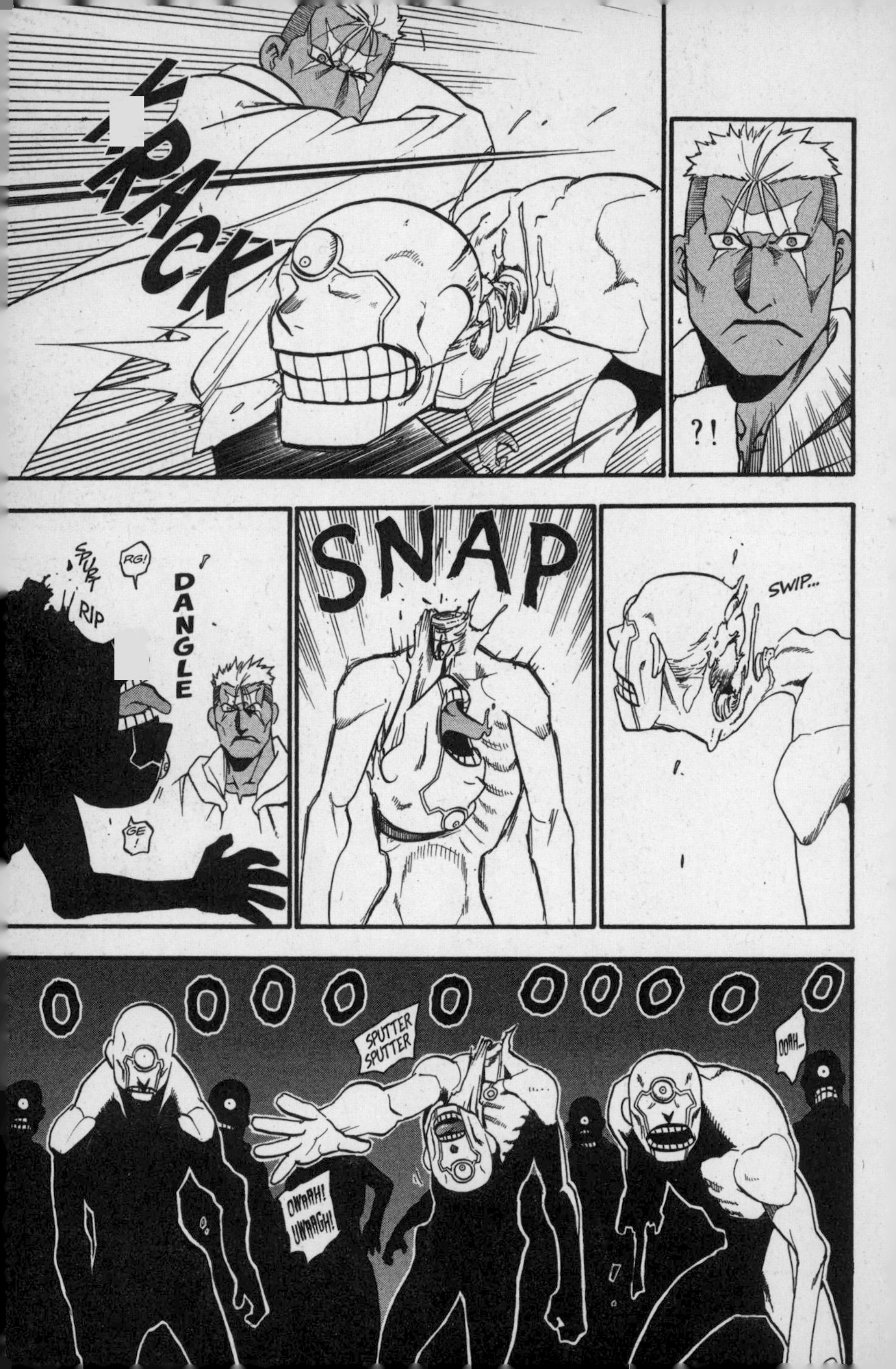
?!
RACK
SWIP...
SNAP
RG!
DANGLE
RIP
GE!
OOOOOOOOOOOOO
OOAH...
SPUTTER SPUTTER
OWAAH! UWAAGH!

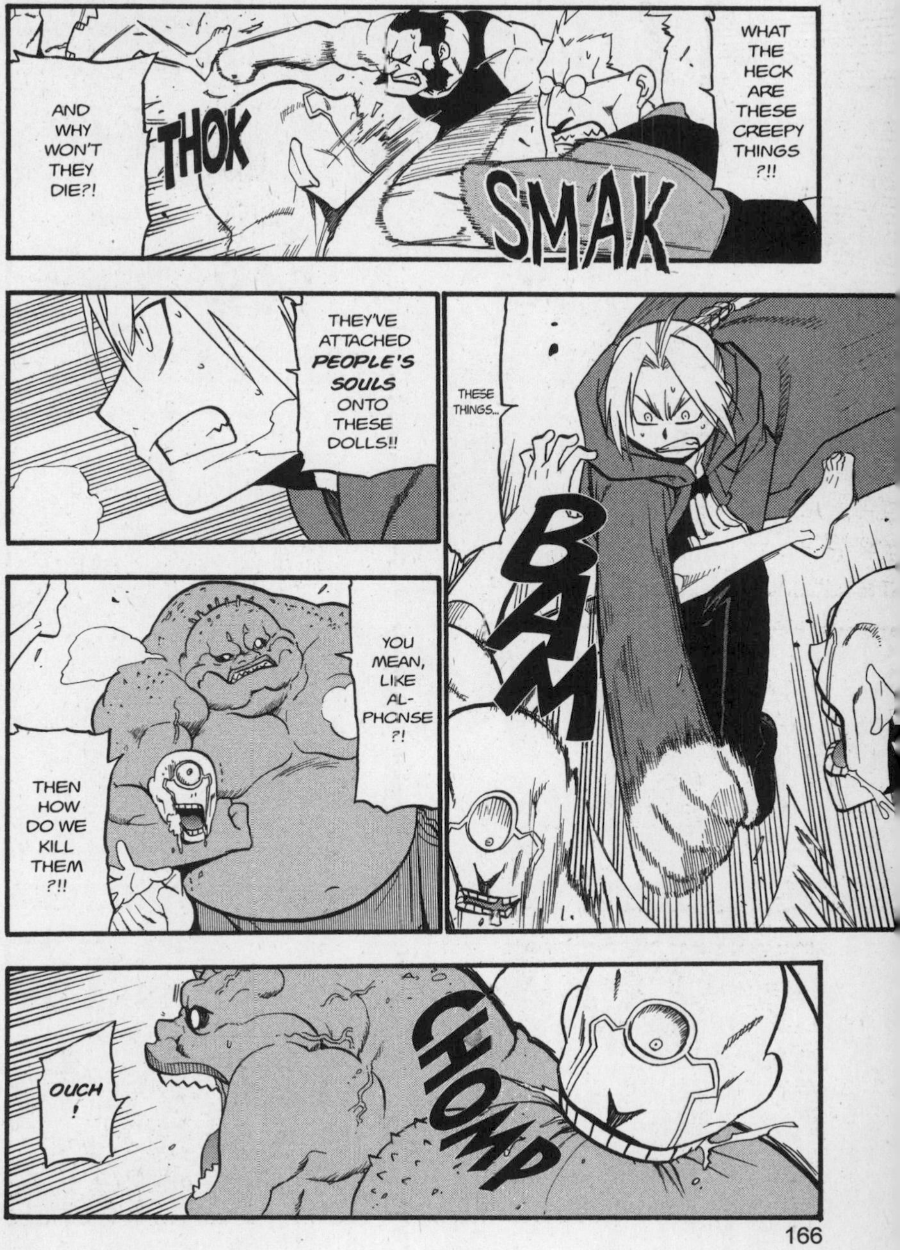

WHAT THE HECK ARE THESE CREEPY THINGS ?!!
SMAK
THOK
AND WHY WON'T THEY DIE?!
THESE THINGS...
BAM
THEY'VE ATTACHED ***PEOPLE'S SOULS*** ONTO THESE DOLLS!!
YOU MEAN, LIKE AL-PHONSE ?!
THEN HOW DO WE KILL THEM ?!!
CHOMP
OUCH !

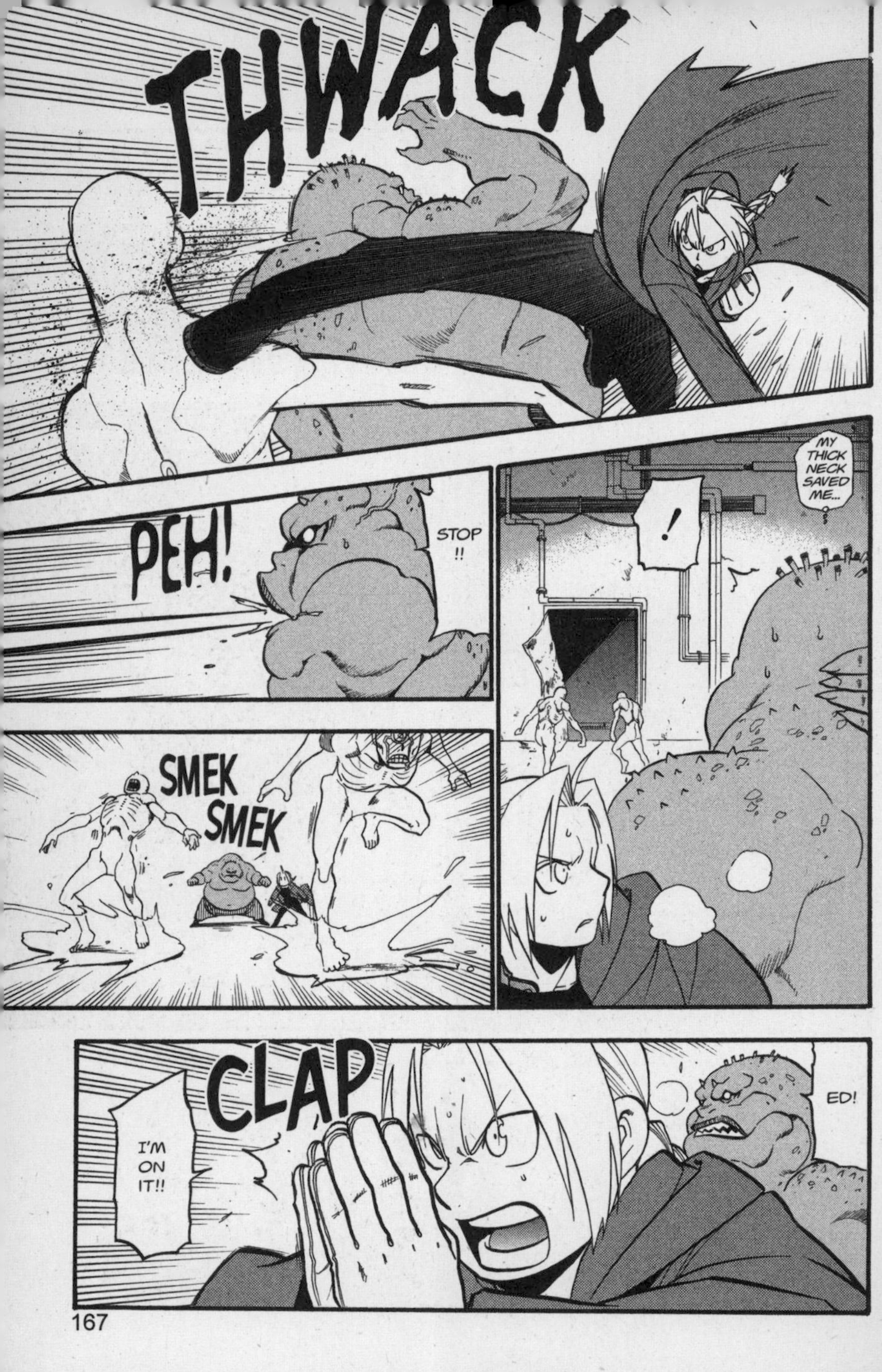
THWACK
MY THICK NECK SAVED ME...
!
STOP !!
PEH!
SMEK SMEK
ED!
CLAP
I'M ON IT!!

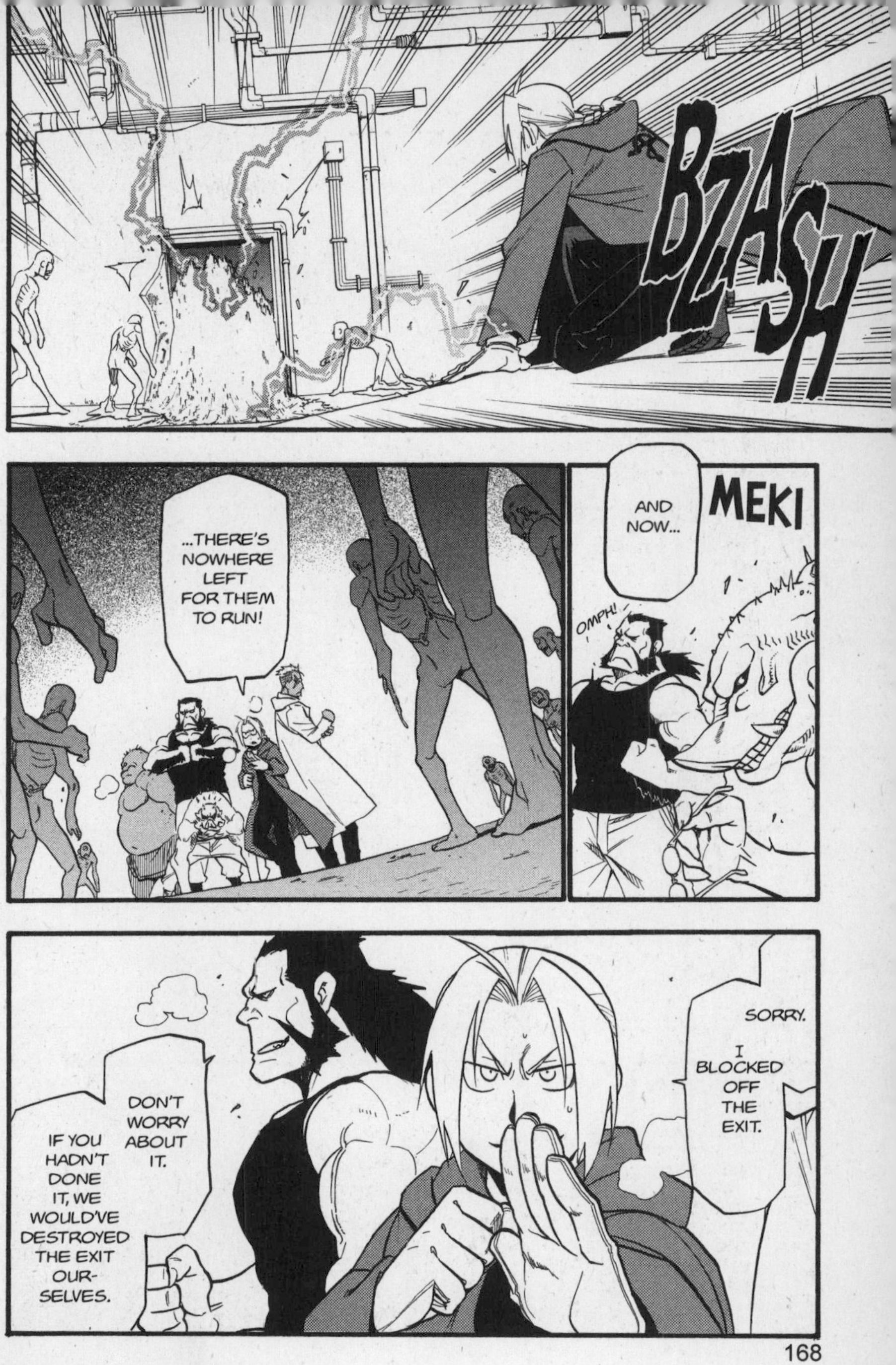
BZASH
AND NOW...
MEKI
OMPH!
...THERE'S NOWHERE LEFT FOR THEM TO RUN!
SORRY.
I BLOCKED OFF THE EXIT.
DON'T WORRY ABOUT IT.
IF YOU HADN'T DONE IT, WE WOULD'VE DESTROYED THE EXIT OUR-SELVES.

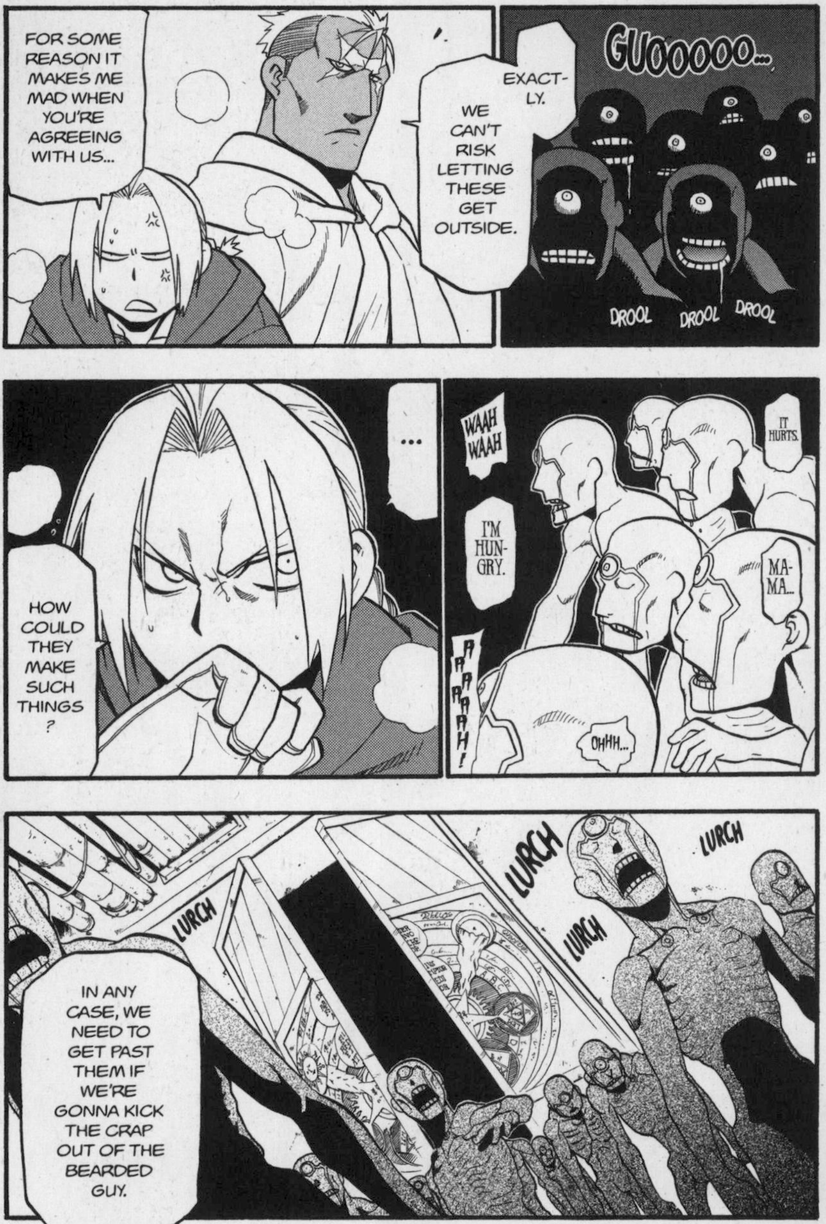
GUOOOOO...
DROOL DROOL DROOL
EXACT-LY.
WE CAN'T RISK LETTING THESE GET OUTSIDE.
FOR SOME REASON IT MAKES ME MAD WHEN YOU'RE AGREEING WITH US...
IT HURTS.
WAAH WAAH
MA-MA...
I'M HUN-GRY.
AAAAAAH!
OHHH...
...
HOW COULD THEY MAKE SUCH THINGS?
LURCH
LURCH
LURCH
LURCH
IN ANY CASE, WE NEED TO GET PAST THEM IF WE'RE GONNA KICK THE CRAP OUT OF THE BEARDED GUY.

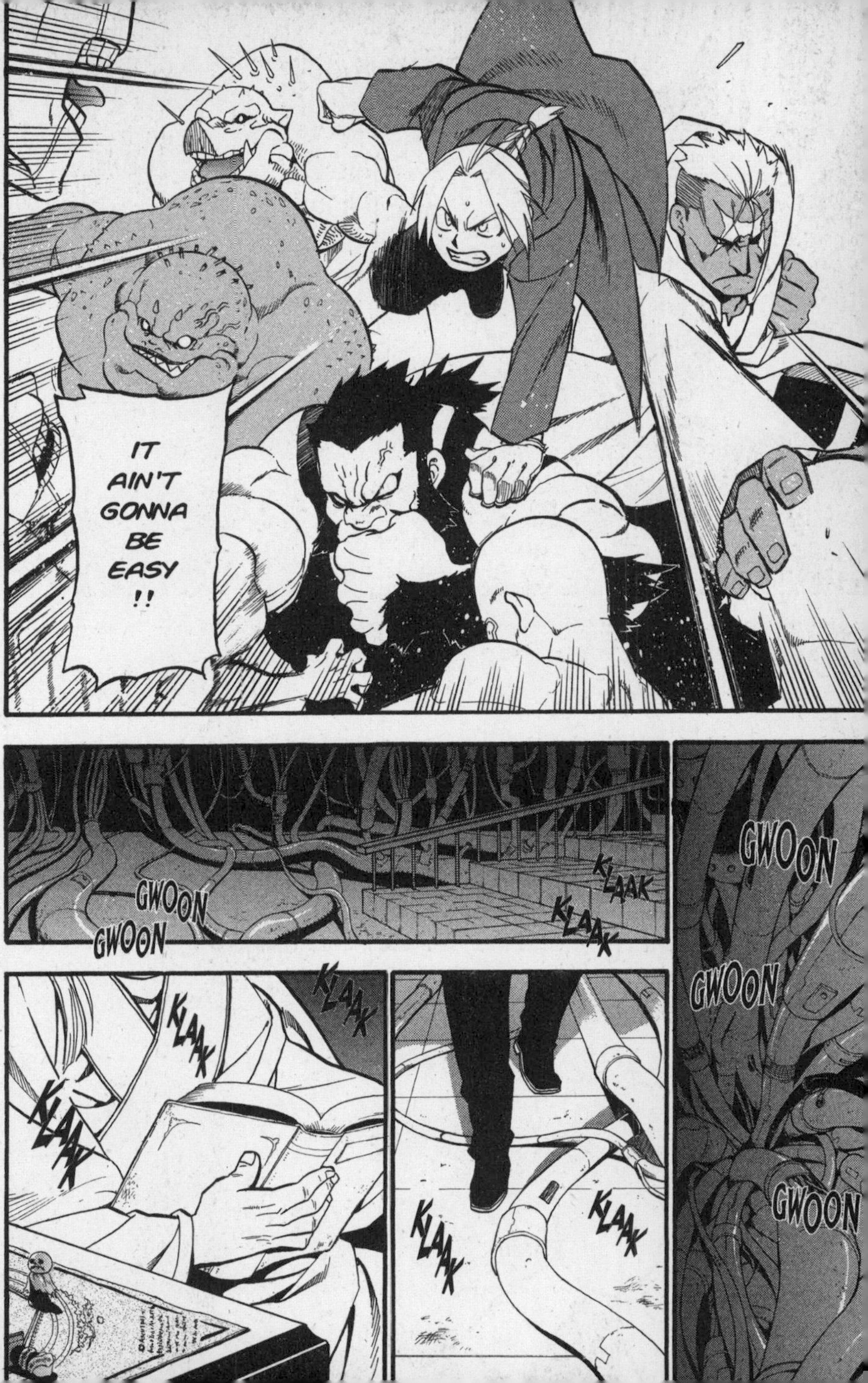
IT AIN'T GONNA BE EASY!!
GWOON
GWOON
GWOON
GWOON
GWOON
KLAAK
KLAAK
KLAAK
KLAAK
KLAAK
KLAAK
KLAAK

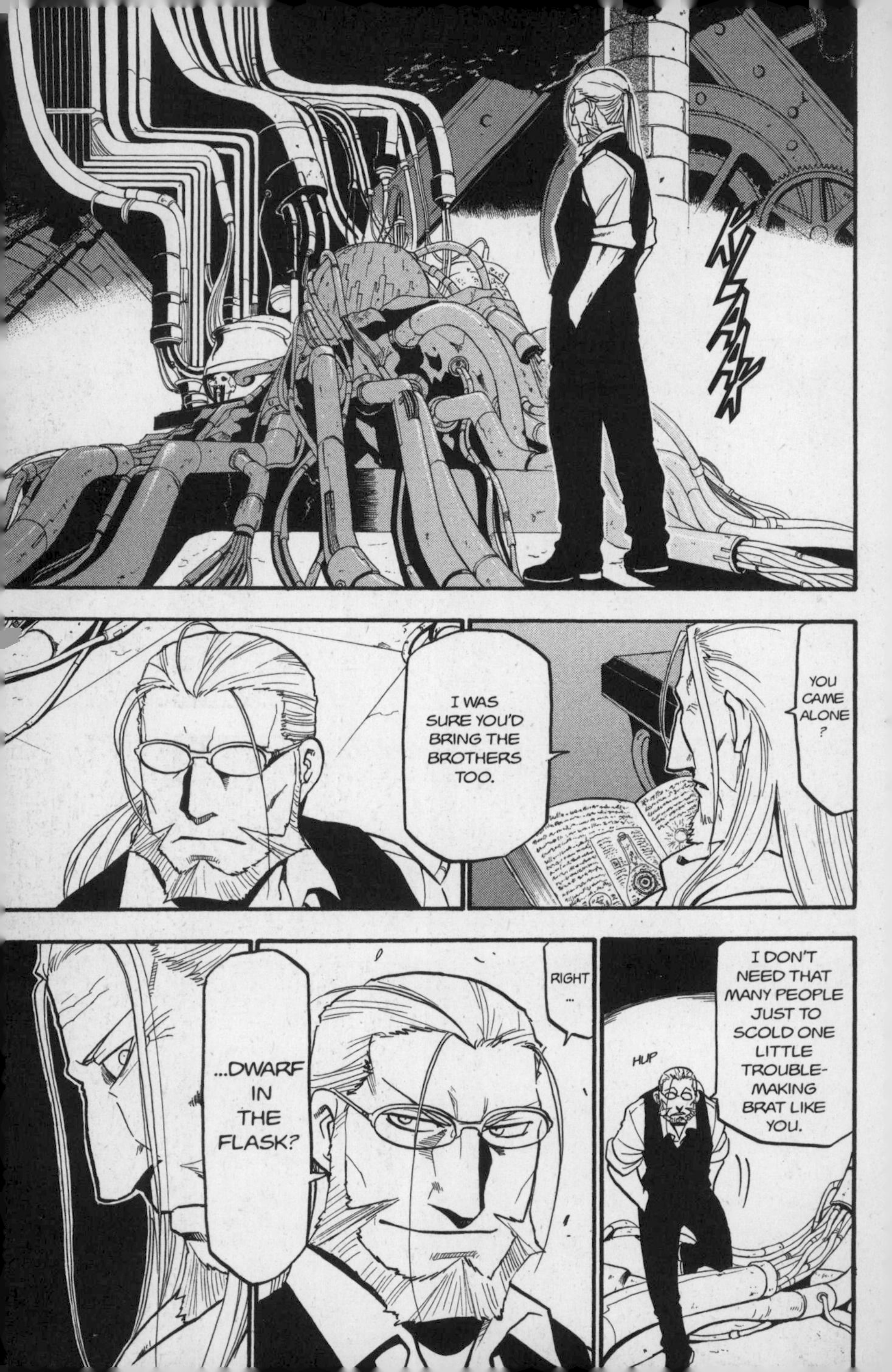
YOU CAME ALONE?
I WAS SURE YOU'D BRING THE BROTHERS TOO.
I DON'T NEED THAT MANY PEOPLE JUST TO SCOLD ONE LITTLE TROUBLE-MAKING BRAT LIKE YOU.
HUP
RIGHT...
...DWARF IN THE FLASK?

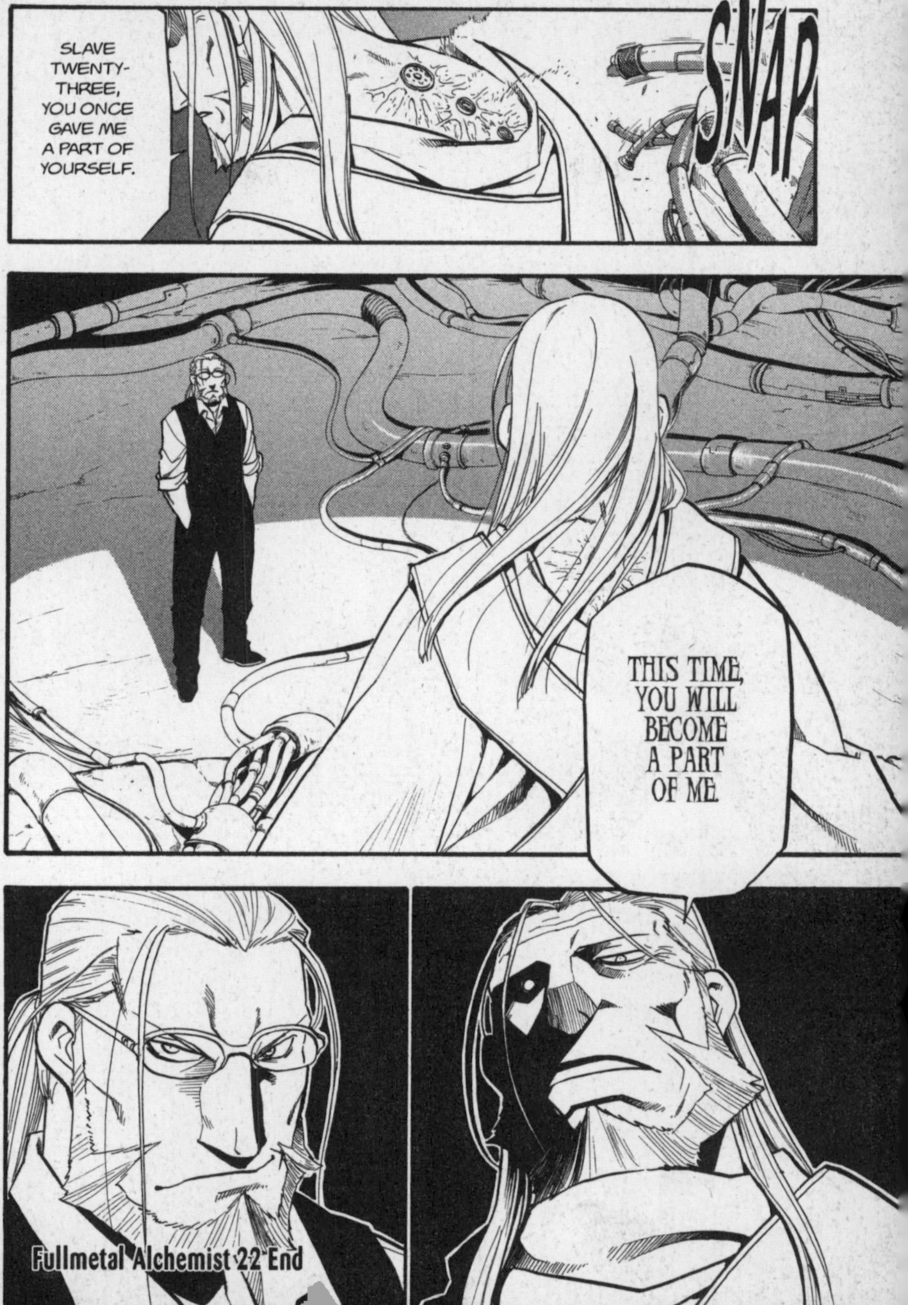
SNAP
SLAVE TWENTY-THREE, YOU ONCE GAVE ME A PART OF YOURSELF.
THIS TIME, YOU WILL BECOME A PART OF ME.
Fullmetal Alchemist 22 End

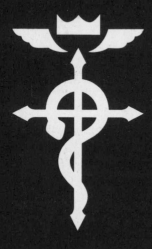

FULLMETAL
ALCHEMIST

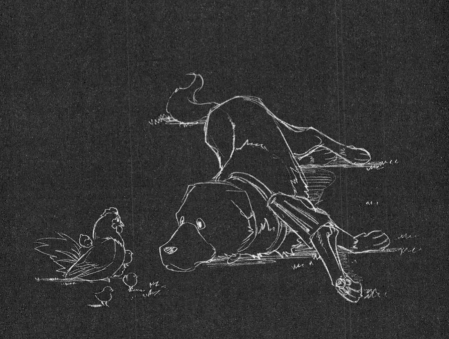

EXTRAS

From Chapter 91

HANG ON, MR. HEINKEL!!
DRAG DRAG
DON'T GIVE UP!!
WHY DO YOU INSIST ON HELPING ME WHEN YOUR OWN BODY IS FALLING APART?
BE-CAUSE YOU'RE A CAT!!!
OH, REAL-LY?

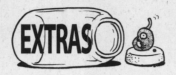

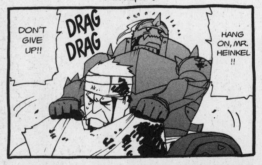

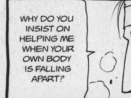

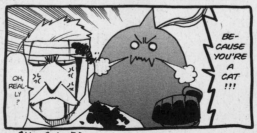

↑ Homo Sapiens Felinus

ROACH MOTEL

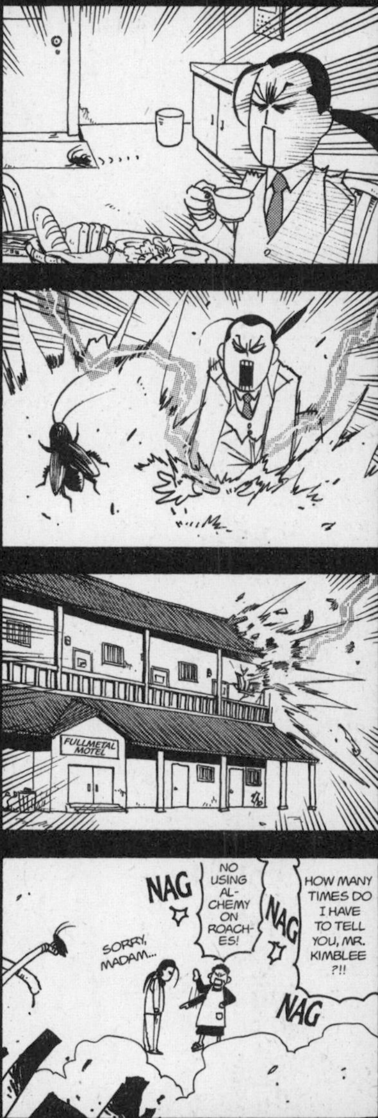
FULLMETAL MOTEL
HOW MANY TIMES DO I HAVE TO TELL YOU, MR. KIMBLEE?!!
NAG
NO USING ALCHEMY ON ROACHES!
NAG
SORRY, MADAM...
NAG

FORTUNES

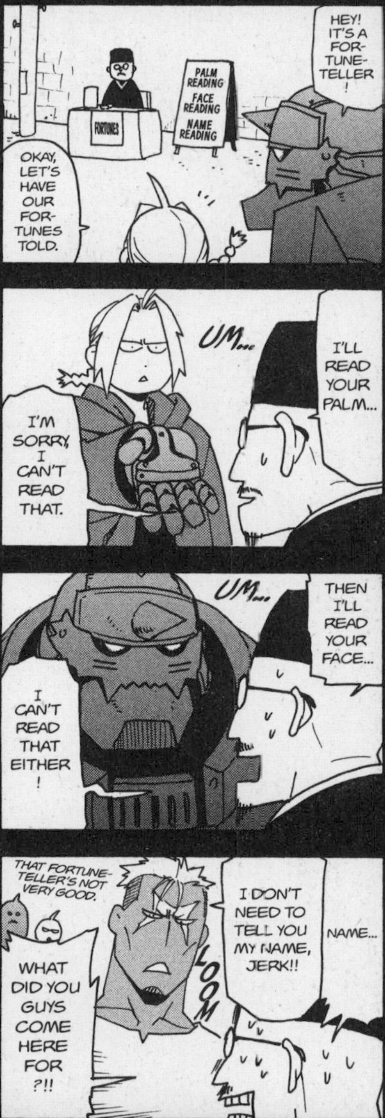
HEY! IT'S A FORTUNE-TELLER!
PALM READING
FACE READING
NAME READING
FORTUNES
OKAY, LET'S HAVE OUR FORTUNES TOLD.
I'LL READ YOUR PALM...
UM...
I'M SORRY, I CAN'T READ THAT.
THEN I'LL READ YOUR FACE...
UM...
I CAN'T READ THAT EITHER!
NAME...
I DON'T NEED TO TELL YOU MY NAME, JERK!!
LOOM
THAT FORTUNE-TELLER'S NOT VERY GOOD.
WHAT DID YOU GUYS COME HERE FOR?!!

THE DANGERS OF OVEREATING

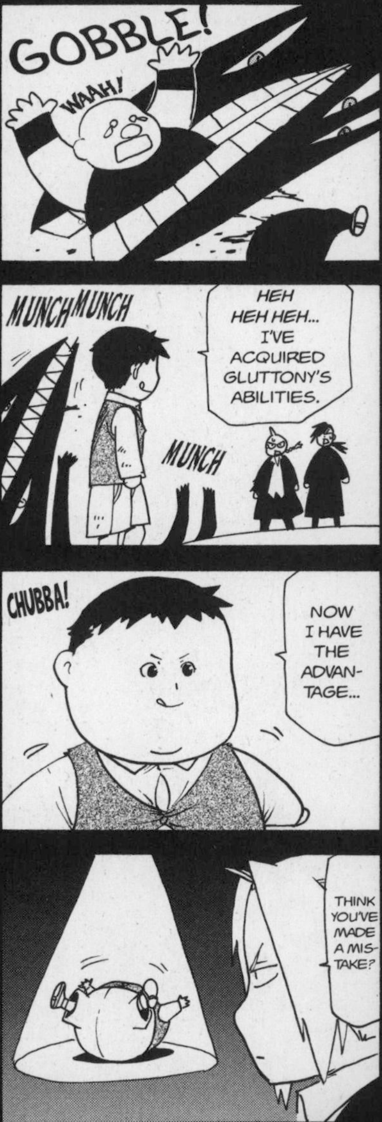
GOBBLE!
WAAH!
HEH HEH HEH... I'VE ACQUIRED GLUTTONY'S ABILITIES.
MUNCHMUNCH
MUNCH
NOW I HAVE THE ADVAN-TAGE...
CHUBBA!
THINK YOU'VE MADE A MIS-TAKE?

FULLMETAL SCIENCE KIDS!

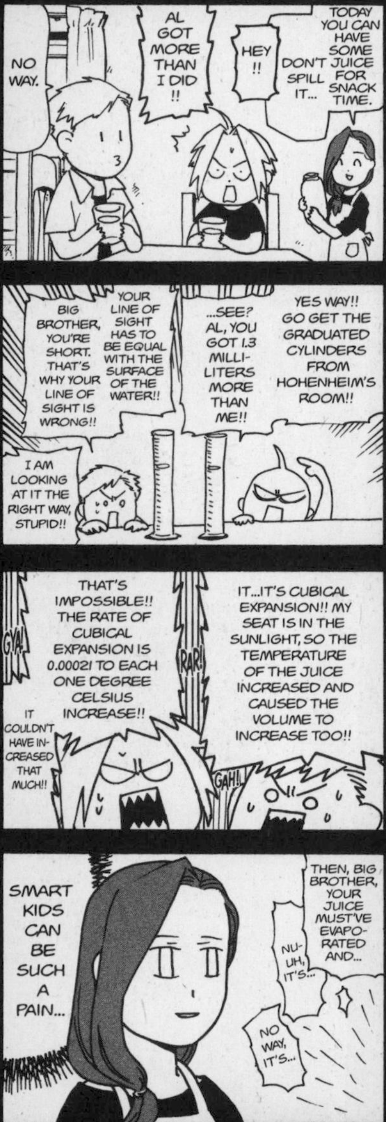
TODAY YOU CAN HAVE SOME JUICE FOR SNACK TIME.
DON'T SPILL IT...
HEY!!
AL GOT MORE THAN I DID!!
NO WAY.
YES WAY!! GO GET THE GRADUATED CYLINDERS FROM HOHENHEIM'S ROOM!!
...SEE? AL, YOU GOT 1.3 MILLI-LITERS MORE THAN ME!!
YOUR LINE OF SIGHT HAS TO BE EQUAL WITH THE SURFACE OF THE WATER!!
BIG BROTHER, YOU'RE SHORT. THAT'S WHY YOUR LINE OF SIGHT IS WRONG!!
I AM LOOKING AT IT THE RIGHT WAY, STUPID!!
IT...IT'S CUBICAL EXPANSION!! MY SEAT IS IN THE SUNLIGHT, SO THE TEMPERATURE OF THE JUICE INCREASED AND CAUSED THE VOLUME TO INCREASE TOO!!
RAR!!
THAT'S IMPOSSIBLE!! THE RATE OF CUBICAL EXPANSION IS 0.00021 TO EACH ONE DEGREE CELSIUS INCREASE!!
GYA!
GAH!!
IT COULDN'T HAVE IN-CREASED THAT MUCH!!
THEN, BIG BROTHER, YOUR JUICE MUST'VE EVAPO-RATED AND...
NU-UH, IT'S...
NO WAY, IT'S...
SMART KIDS CAN BE SUCH A PAIN...

THE ROACH'S REVENGE

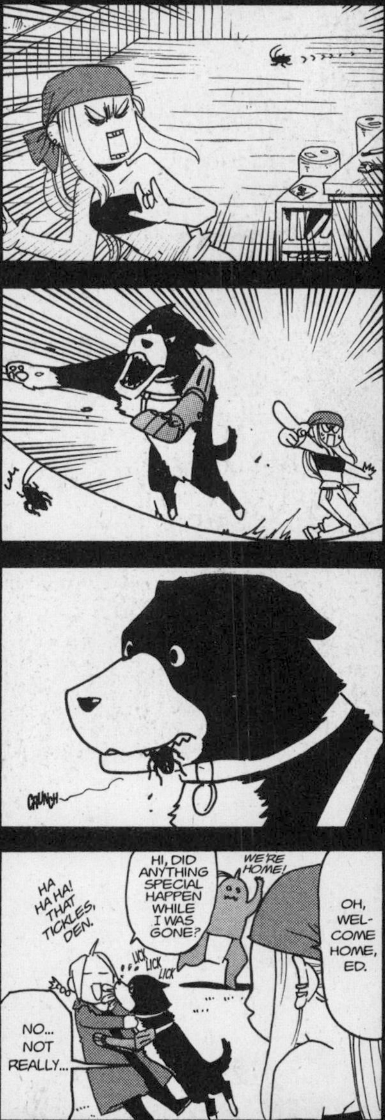
CRUNCH~
WE'RE HOME!
OH, WELCOME HOME, ED.
HI, DID ANYTHING SPECIAL HAPPEN WHILE I WAS GONE?
HA HA HA! THAT TICKLES, DEN.
LICK LICK LICK
NO... NOT REALLY...

CAMPAIGN PROMISES

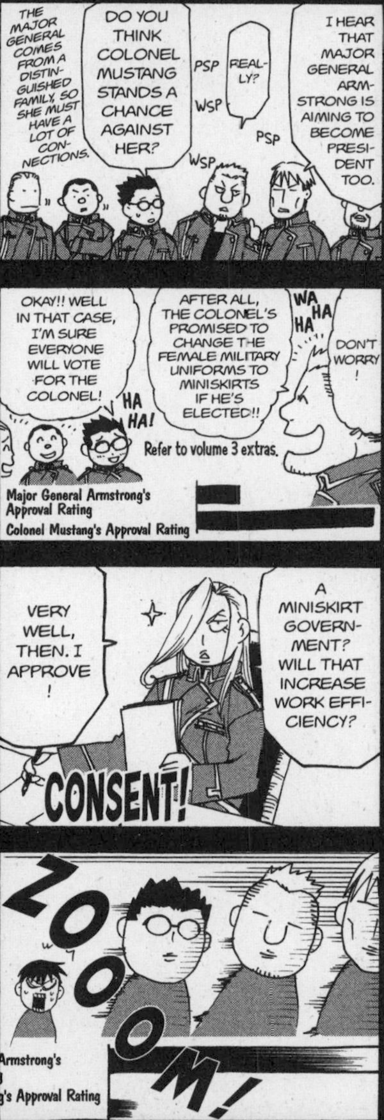
I HEAR THAT MAJOR GENERAL ARMSTRONG IS AIMING TO BECOME PRESIDENT TOO.
PSP
REALLY?
PSP
WSP
WSP
DO YOU THINK COLONEL MUSTANG STANDS A CHANCE AGAINST HER?
THE MAJOR GENERAL COMES FROM A DISTINGUISHED FAMILY, SO SHE MUST HAVE A LOT OF CONNECTIONS.
DON'T WORRY!
WA HA HA
AFTER ALL, THE COLONEL'S PROMISED TO CHANGE THE FEMALE MILITARY UNIFORMS TO MINISKIRTS IF HE'S ELECTED!!
OKAY!! WELL IN THAT CASE, I'M SURE EVERYONE WILL VOTE FOR THE COLONEL!
HA HA!
Refer to volume 3 extras.
Major General Armstrong's Approval Rating
Colonel Mustang's Approval Rating
A MINISKIRT GOVERNMENT? WILL THAT INCREASE WORK EFFICIENCY?
VERY WELL, THEN. I APPROVE!
CONSENT!
ZOOOOOM!

FULLMETAL ALCHEMIST 22

SPECIAL THANKS to:

Jun Tohko
Noriko Tsubota
Kori Sakano
Masashi Mizutani
Haruhi Nakamura
Manatsu Sakura
Mr. Coupon
Kazufumi Kaneko
Kei Takanamazu

My Editor, Yuichi Shimomura

AND YOU!!

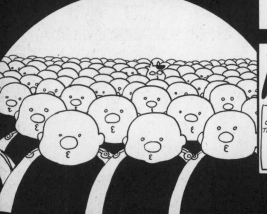

Fullmetal Is Coming to the Wii

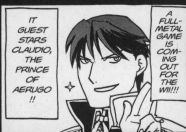

A FULL-METAL GAME IS COMING OUT FOR THE WII!!!
IT GUEST STARS CLAUDIO, THE PRINCE OF AERUGO!!
SQUEAL!
YOUR MAJESTY!
HE'S SO COOL!
LOOK THIS WAY, PLEASE!
LORD CLAUDIO!
SWOOOOOOON
EEEK!
KYAAA!
I WANNA MARRY HIM!!
SQUEAL!
SQUEAL!
LOOK THIS WAY, PLEASE!
SWOON SWOON
HE'S SO HANDSOME! KYAAA!
ALSO, WHEN PLAYING AS THE COLONEL, YOU CAN SPONTANEOUSLY COMBUST!!
FO—OM
OKAY, THAT'S A LIE.

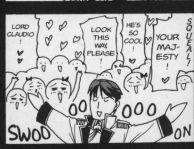

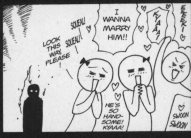

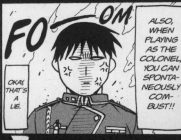

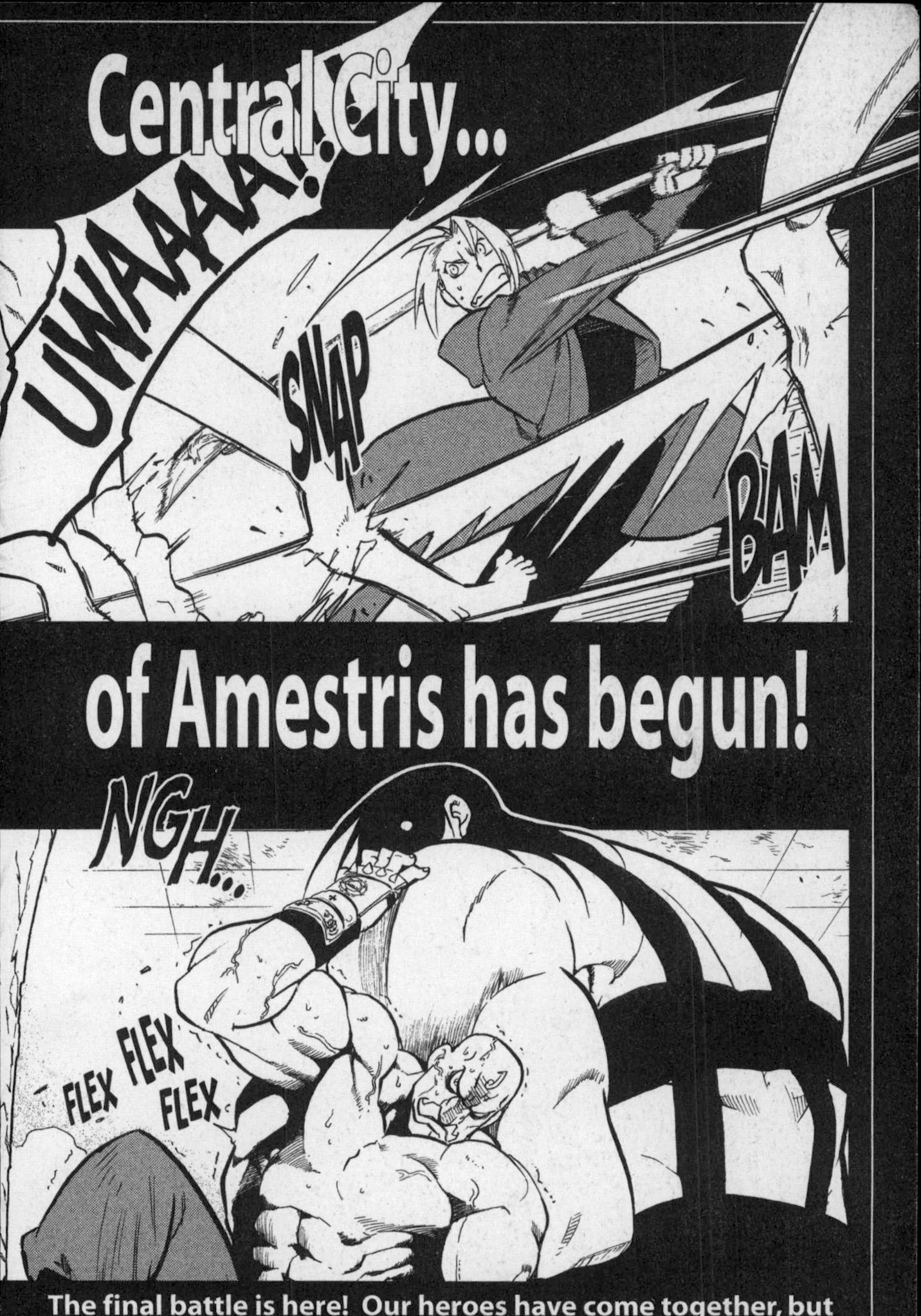
Central City...
UWAAAA!!
SNAP
BAM
of Amestris has begun!
NGH...
FLEX FLEX
FLEX
FLEX

The final battle is here! Our heroes have come together, but the forces of evil are many and strong. Who will survive the carnage? What is the price of learning the truth?!

Deep Beneath

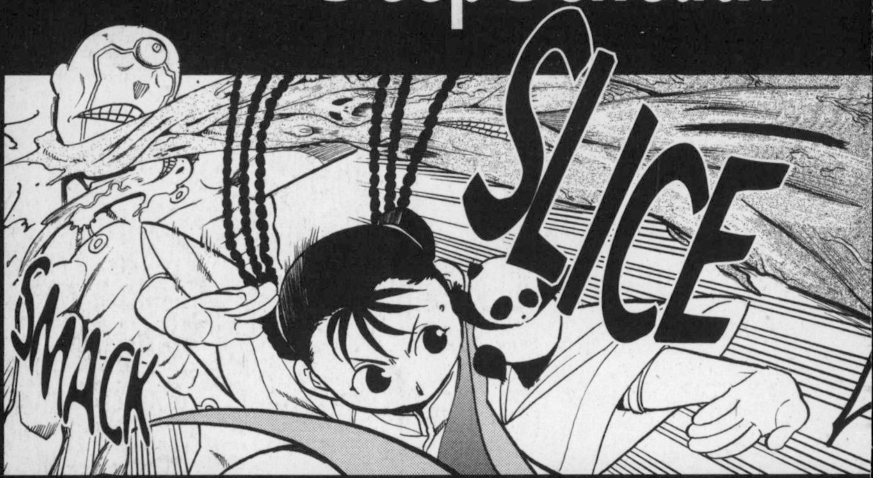
SLICE
SMACK

...the battle for the fate

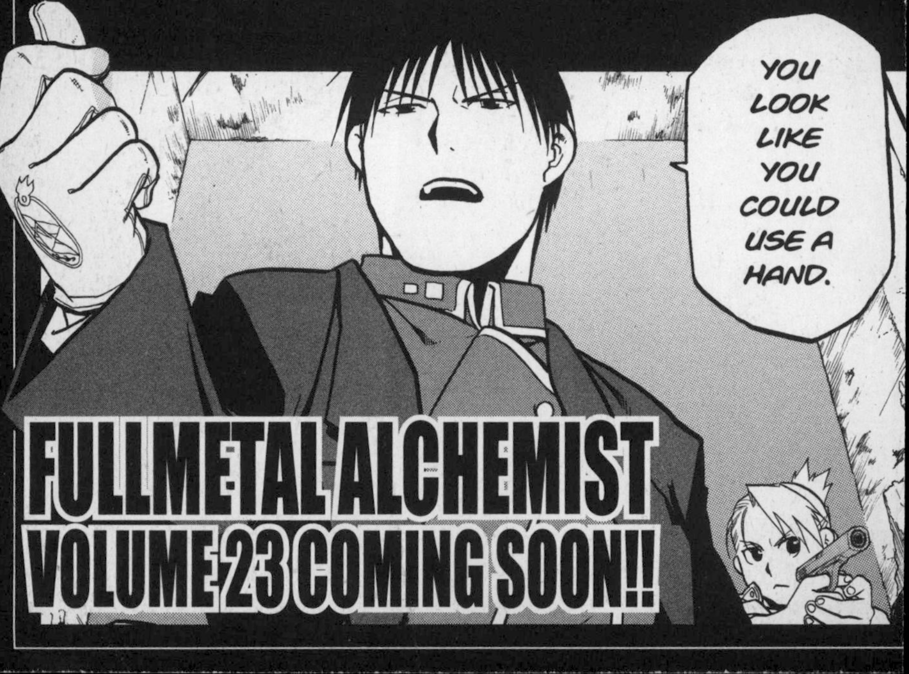
YOU LOOK LIKE YOU COULD USE A HAND.
FULLMETAL ALCHEMIST
VOLUME 23 COMING SOON!!

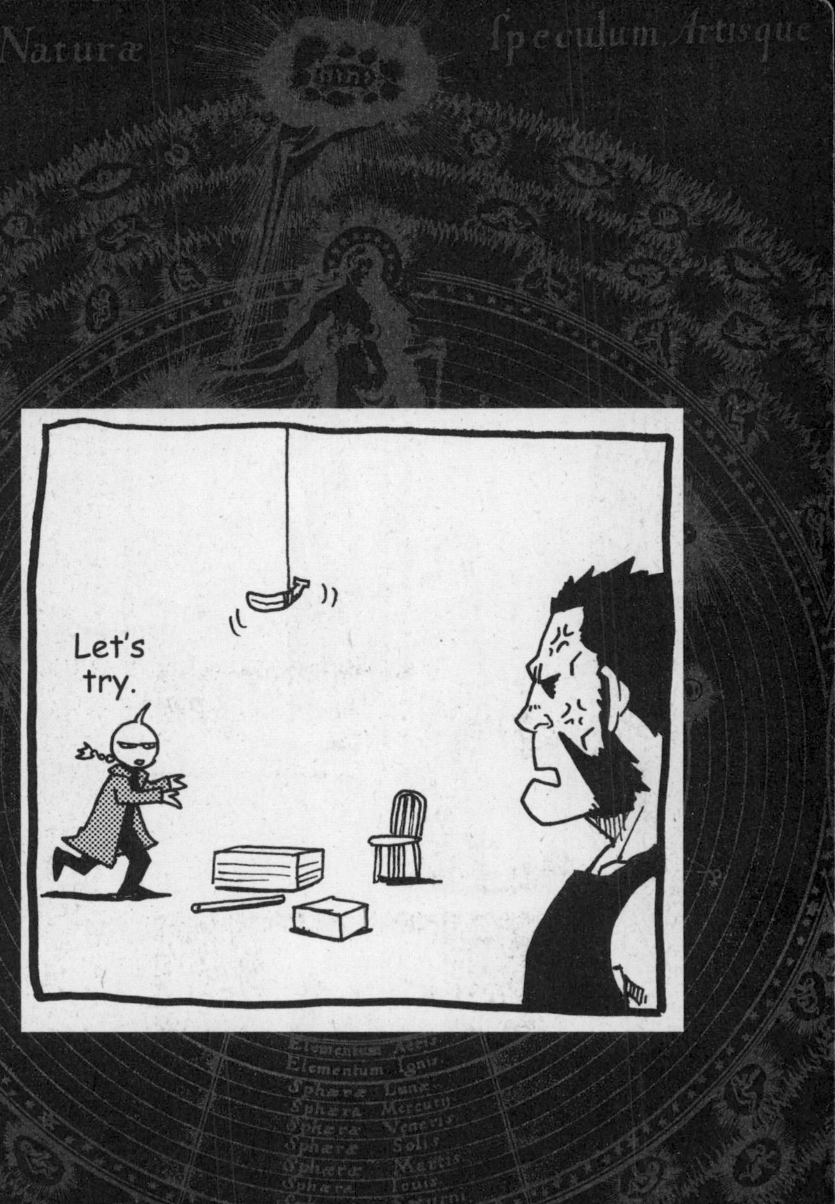
Naturæ
Speculum Artisque
Let's try.
Elementum Ignis
Sphæra Lunæ
Sphæra Mercurii
Sphæra Veneris
Sphæra Solis
Sphæra Martis
Sphæra Iovis

ZO
ZO
ZO
ZO
How useful!!
GULP...

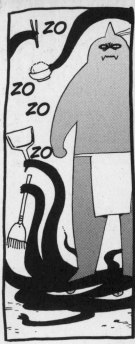

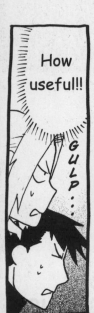

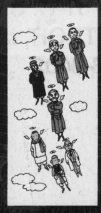

LOVE ♥ MANGA?

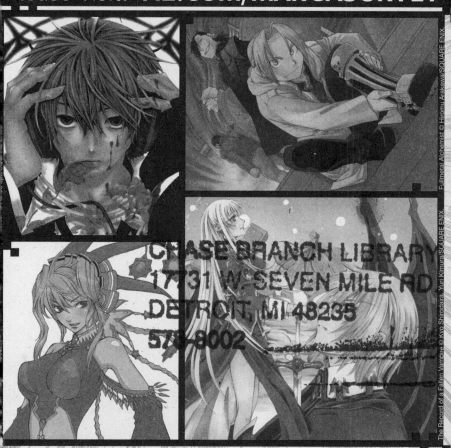